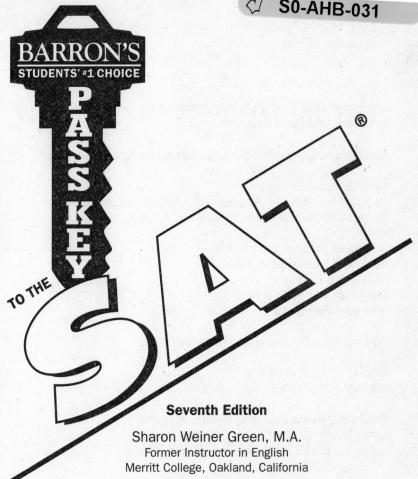

BARRON'S
STUDENTS' #1 CHOICE

PASS KEY
TO THE
SAT®

Seventh Edition

Sharon Weiner Green, M.A.
Former Instructor in English
Merritt College, Oakland, California

Ira K. Wolf, Ph.D.
President, PowerPrep, Inc.
Former High School Teacher, College Professor,
and University Director of Teacher Preparation

BARRON'S EDUCATIONAL SERIES, INC.

© Copyright 2008, 2006, 2005, 2001, 1998, 1994
by Barron's Educational Series, Inc.

Adapted from *Barron's SAT,* © 2008 by Barron's Educational Series, Inc.

All inquiries should be addressed to:
Barron's Educational Series, Inc.
250 Wireless Boulevard
Hauppauge, New York 11788
www.barronseduc.com

Library of Congress Control Number: 2008023620

ISBN-13: 978-0-7641-3806-5
ISBN-10: 0-7641-3806-5

Library of Congress Cataloging-in-Publication Data
Green, Sharon, 1939–
   Pass key to the SAT / Sharon Weiner Green,—7th ed.
      p. cm.
   Rev. ed. of: Barron's pass key to the SAT. 6th ed. c2006.
   Includes index.
   ISBN-13: 978-0-7641-3806-5
   ISBN-10: 0-7641-3806-5
   1. SAT (Educational test)—Study guides.   2. Universities and
colleges—United States—Entrance examinations—Study guides.
I. Wolf, Ira K.   II. Green, Sharon, 1939– Barron's pass key to the SAT.
III. Title.

   LB2353.56.B765 2008
   378.1'662—dc22   2008023620

Contents

Preface

You have in your hands *Barron's Pass Key to the SAT*, the compact version of Barron's classic *SAT* review book. Small enough to toss in your backpack, portable enough to read on the bus, this short course in SAT preparation provides you with the basic tips and strategies you need to cope with the SAT.

If you feel unready for the SAT, if you don't quite know what to expect on it, *Pass Key* may be just the eye-opener you need.

It offers you dozens of specific tips that will help you attack every type of SAT question, and provides you with practice exercises.

It offers you the exclusive SAT High Frequency Word List, your best chance to acquaint yourself with the actual words that computer analysis shows occur again and again on recently published SATs.

It not only gives you all of the math facts and formulas you need to know, it provides more than a dozen special tactics (all illustrated with sample problems) to show you how to answer every type of SAT math question.

It thoroughly covers the writing skills section of the SAT, providing you with useful tips for dealing with the multiple-choice questions, as well as showing you how to tackle writing a 25-minute essay.

Best of all, it offers you the chance to take not one, but two complete practice SAT exams that correspond to the SAT in content, format, and level of difficulty. Each test has an answer key and complete solutions and explanations.

Read the tips. Go over the strategies. Do the practice exercises. *Then* take the practice SATs and see how you score. Study the answer explanations, especially those for questions you were unsure of or answered incorrectly. You'll come out feeling far more secure about what it will be like to take the SAT.

SAT Format   Total Time: 4 Hours and 5 Minutes

Section 1:	**Essay**	
Time—25 minutes		

Section 2:	**Mathematics—**	20 Standard Multiple-Choice
	20 Questions	
Time—25 minutes		

Section 3:	**Critical Reading—**	8 Sentence Completion
	24 Questions	4 Reading Comprehension
		(2 short passages)
		12 Reading Comprehension
		(1 long passage)
Time—25 minutes		

Break—*10 minutes*

Section 4:	**Writing Skills—**	11 Improving Sentences
	35 Questions	18 Identifying Sentence Errors
		6 Improving Paragraphs
Time—25 minutes		

Section 5:	**Experimental**	This section could be
		Critical Reading, Mathematics,
		or Writing Skills
Time—25 minutes		

Section 6:	**Mathematics—**	8 Standard Multiple-Choice
	18 Questions	10 Student-Produced
		(Grid-in)
Time—25 minutes		

Break—*10 minutes*

Section 7:	**Critical Reading—**	5 Sentence Completion
	24 Questions	4 Reading Comprehension
		(2 paired short passages)
		15 Reading Comprehension
		(2 long passages)
Time—25 minutes		

Section 8:	Mathematics— 16 Questions	16 Standard Multiple-Choice
Time—20 minutes		

Section 9:	Critical Reading— 19 Questions	6 Sentence Completion 13 Reading Comprehension (2 paired long passages)
Time—20 minutes		

Section 10:	Writing Skills— 14 Questions	14 Improving Sentences
Time—10 minutes		

<u>Note</u>: The "experimental" section can be an extra 25-minute critical reading, mathematics, or writing skills section. This section, which permits the test-makers to try out new questions, does not count in your score; but because there is no way to know which section is the experimental one, you must do your best on every section.

Section 1 is *always* the essay. Sections 2–7, which are each 25-minutes long, can come *in any order*. In particular, the experimenal section is <u>not necessarily</u> Section 5—it can be any of Sections 2–7. Sections 8 and 9 are *always* a 20-minute mathematics section and a 20-minute critical reading section—*in either order*. Section 10 is always the 10-minute writing skills section.

*The above format is used in both model tests in this book, except that the model tests don't have an experimental section. Therefore, the model tests take 25 minutes less than an actual SAT.

SAT Test Dates

Test Dates	Registration Deadlines	
	Regular	Late
2008 October 4 November 1 December 6	September 9 September 26 November 5	September 16 October 10 November 18
2009 January 24 March 14 May 2 June 6	December 26 February 10 March 31 May 5	January 6 February 24 April 9 May 15

Acknowledgments

The authors gratefully acknowledge the following copyright holders for permission to reprint material used in reading passages:

Pages 51–53: From *Sculpture/Inuit*, ©1971. Reprinted with permission of the Canadian Arts Council and James Houston.

Pages 59–61: From "Renaissance to Modern Tapestries in the Metropolitan Museum of Art" in the *Metropolitan Museum Bulletin*, Spring 1987 by Edith Appleton Standen, ©1987. Reprinted with permission of the Metropolitan Museum of Art.

Pages 64–66: From *The Greenpeace Book of Dolphins*, John May, editor ©1990. Reprinted with permission of Greenpeace.

Pages 236–238: From *Bury My Heart at Wounded Knee: An Indian History of the American West* by Dee Brown ©1970 by Dee Brown. Reprinted with permission of Henry Holt & Co., LLC.

Pages 266–267: From *Black Boy* by Richard Wright. Copyright ©1937, 1942, 1944, 1945 by Richard Wright. Renewed 1973 by Ellen Wright. Reprinted by permission of HarperCollins, Inc.

Pages 269–270: From *King Solomon's Ring* by Konrad Z. Lorenz, ©1952 Harper & Row. Reprinted with permission of HarperCollins Publishers, Inc.

Pages 284–285: From "Let's Say You Wrote Badly This Morning" in *The Writing Habit* by David Huddle, ©1989, 1994 University Press of New England.

Pages 286–287: From "My Two One-Eyed Coaches" by George Garrett, ©1987. Reprinted with permission of *The Virginia Quarterly Review*, Spring 1987, Vol. 63, No. 2.

Pages 373–375: From *Athabasca* by Alistair MacLean. Copyright ©1980 by Alistair MacLean. Reprinted by permission of Doubleday, a division of Random House, Inc.

Pages 376–378: From *The Uses of Enchantment* by Bruno Bettelheim. Copyright ©1975, 1976 by Bruno Bettelheim. Reprinted with permission of Alfred A. Knopf.

Pages 391–392: From *Native Stranger: A Black American's Journey into the Heart of Africa* by Eddy L. Harris, ©1992. Reprinted by permission of Simon & Schuster.

Pages 392–394: From *Turning Japanese* by David Mura, ©1991 by David Mura. Reprinted by permission of Grove/Atlantic, Inc.

1   About the SAT

COMMONLY ASKED QUESTIONS ABOUT THE SAT

What Is the SAT?

The SAT is a standardized exam that most high school students take before applying for college. Generally, students take the SAT for the first time as high school juniors. If they do very well, they are through. If they want to try to boost their scores, they can take the test a second or even a third time.

The SAT tests you in three areas: reading, writing, and mathematical reasoning. As a result, each time you take the test you get three separate scores: a critical reading score, a writing score, and a math score. Each of these scores will fall somewhere between 200 and 800. For all three tests, the median score is 500, meaning that about 50 percent of all students score below 500 and about 50 percent above 500. In talking about their results, students often add the three scores (the sums range from 600 to 2400, with a median of about 1500) and say, "John got a 1560," or "Mary got a 2000."

What Types of Questions Are on the Critical Reading Sections?

There are two types of questions on the critical reading sections: sentence completions, and reading comprehension questions. All are multiple-choice questions, with five answer choices. The sentence completion questions ask you to fill in the blanks. You have to find the word or phrase that best completes the sentence's meaning. The reading comprehension questions test your ability to understand what you read—both content and technique. Each critical reading section will include one or two long reading passages followed by from six to thirteen reading comprehension questions. Two sections will also include short reading passages of about 100 words, each followed by two questions. The questions ask about the passage's main idea or specific details, the author's attitude to the subject, the author's logic and techniques, the implications of the discussion, or the meaning of specific words. Some passages are paired: you will be asked to answer two or three questions that compare the viewpoints of two passages on the same subject.

For strategies, tips, and practice on critical reading questions, turn to Chapter 3.

What Types of Questions Are on the Writing Skills Sections?

There are three types of multiple-choice questions on the writing skills sections: improving sentences, identifying sentence errors, and improving paragraphs. As in the critical reading sections, these questions give you five answer choices.

Question Type	Your Task
Improving Sentences	Select the wording that will produce the most effective sentence.
Identifying Errors	Spot the underlined word or phrase that is grammatically incorrect.
Improving Paragraphs	Revise a flawed student essay to create a clear, readable second draft.

In addition, one writing skills section gives you the opportunity for a practical demonstration of your skill as a writer: it has you write an actual essay on a topic you have never seen before, allowing you only 25 minutes to do so.

For strategies, tips, and practice on writing skills questions and on writing essays under time pressure, turn to Chapter 5.

What Types of Questions Are on the Math Sections?

There are two types of questions on the math sections: the five-choice multiple-choice type, and student-produced response questions, also known as grid-ins. The standard multiple-choice questions are like the questions you're used to seeing in your math textbooks and on math tests in school. The student-produced response questions are similar in content to the standard multiple-choice questions. They differ only in the fact that no answer choices are given: you must figure out your answer and enter it on a grid.

For strategies, tips, and practice for the math questions, as well as information about the use of calculators on the test, turn to Chapter 6.

How Is the SAT Scored?

First, the machine that grades your SAT will calculate your *raw score* for each part of the test (critical reading, writing, and mathematics). On the SAT, every question is worth exactly the same amount: 1 point. A correct answer to a critical reading question for which you may have to read a whole paragraph is worth no more than a correct response to a sentence completion question that you can answer in a few seconds. You get no more credit for a correct answer to the hardest math question than you do for the easiest.

- For each question that you answer correctly, you earn 1 raw score point.
- For each multiple-choice question that you answer incorrectly, you lose $\frac{1}{4}$ point.
- Questions that you leave out have no effect on your score.

Here's how it works:

$$\text{\# Right} - \frac{\text{\# Wrong}}{4} = \text{Raw Score}$$

There are 67 critical reading questions on the SAT. If you answer 44 correctly, get 11 wrong, and leave out 12, what will your critical reading raw score be?

$$44 - \frac{11}{4} = 41\frac{1}{4}, \text{ or a rounded raw score of 41}$$

If you answer 44 correctly, get 0 wrong, and leave out 23, what will your raw score be?

44!

Does this mean you should skip every question that puzzles you and answer only questions that you are *sure* of getting right? No. On average, you will break even by guessing wildly on questions that you don't know how to do or haven't even read, and you will come out ahead by guessing any time that you can eliminate one or more of the choices.

Once the machine calculates your raw scores in critical reading, writing, and math, it then converts them to scaled scores between 200 (the lowest possible grade) and 800 (the highest possible grade), with a median score of 500. Those scaled scores are what you'll see on your score report online.

How many questions do you have to answer correctly to earn a scaled score of 500 or better? Not as many as you might think! Look at an actual SAT score conversion table on the College Board web site or in *The Official SAT Study Guide for the New SAT*. You'll see some thing like this:

Critical Reading Conversion Table
(Maximum Raw Score, 67 Points)

Raw Score	Scaled Score Range
35	500–560
34	500–560
33	490–550
32	480–540

On each part of the test, if you earn a raw score of *half* the number of points possible, you will wind up with a scaled score of 500 or more. That means that you do *not* have to answer all, or even most, of the questions on the test to come up with a good score. In fact, unless you are in the top 5 percent of all students, and think that you might score over 700 on one of the parts, you shouldn't even attempt to finish that part. Working slowly and carefully will undoubtedly earn you higher scores.

How Important Is the SAT?

In addition to your application form, the essays you write, and the letters of recommendation that your teachers and guidance counselor write, colleges receive two important pieces of numerical data. One is your high school transcript, which shows the grades you have earned in all your courses in 3½-*years*. The other is your SAT scores, which show how well you performed in 3¾ *hours* one Saturday morning. Which is more important? Your transcript, by far. However, your scores on the SAT definitely do count, and it is precisely because you want your SAT scores to be as high as possible that you purchased this book. If you use this book wisely, you will not be disappointed.

How Can This Book Help You Score High on the SAT?

This book is packed full with review materials, practice exercises, and test-taking strategies. Use them: They'll prepare you to do well on the SAT. The vocabulary list will help boost your word power. Chapter 5 will give you practical advice on essay-writing, advice that will help you not only on the SAT but also on every other essay test you have to take. Chapter 6 will pinpoint the important math facts and formulas you need to know and show you how to handle each type of math question. The dozens of testing tips and strategies will teach you how to make the most of what you learn.

After going through this review and taking the practice tests at the end of the book, you will know exactly what to expect on the SAT. You will be ready to face the test with confidence, knowing you have done your best to prepare yourself.

2 Tips and Strategies for the SAT

The easiest way to answer a question correctly is to know the answer. If you know what all the words mean in a sentence completion question and you understand the relationship between the sentence's elements, you won't have any trouble choosing the right answer. If you know exactly how to solve a mathematics question and you don't make any mistakes in arithmetic, you won't have any trouble choosing the right answer. But you won't always be absolutely sure of the right answer. Here are some suggestions that may help you. (You'll find specific strategies and tips for each type of question in later chapters of the book.)

GUESSING

More controversy surrounds the issue of guessing than any other aspect of the SAT. If you run out of time and still have 10 questions to go, should you guess? If you do, on average you will get two right and miss the other eight. Is that good or bad? Neither. For the two that you get right, your raw score will increase by two points; for the eight that you miss, your raw score will decrease by $8 \times \frac{1}{4} = 2$ points. The most likely scenario is that your raw score (and hence your scaled score) will not change. So whether or not you guess randomly is a personal decision.

There is no decision to make, however, if you can eliminate some of the choices—now *you must guess*. Suppose that the five answer choices to a particular math question are

(A) –2 (B) –1 (C) 0 (D) 1 (E) 2

and that although you have no idea how to solve it, you know that the answer must be positive. Eliminate (A), (B), and (C) and guess (D) or (E). Similarly, if you can eliminate three of the choices in a sentence completion, but you have no idea which of the other two choices is correct because they contain words that you never heard of, *you must guess.*

The reason for this is simple. When you guess between two choices, you have a 50-50 chance of being right. If you had 10 such questions on the test, on average you would get half right and half wrong. For the five correct answers your raw score would increase by five points; for the five incorrect answers your raw score would decrease by $5 \times \frac{1}{4} = 1\frac{1}{4}$ points. This would result in a raw score gain of $3\frac{3}{4}$ points. That doesn't sound like much. However, that raw score gain of $3\frac{3}{4}$ points would raise your scaled score by about 30 or 40 points. You simply cannot afford not to guess.

If you can only eliminate one or two choices, the results are not as dramatic, but *it still pays to guess.*

TIMING

You have only a limited amount of time in which to complete each section of the test, and you don't want to waste any of it. So here are three suggestions.

1. Memorize the directions for each type of question. They appear in the practice tests, later in this book. They present the same information that you will find on the SAT. However, the time you spend reading directions at the actual test is test time. If you don't have to read the directions, you have that much more time to answer the questions.

2. By the time you get to the actual test, you should have a fair idea of how much time to spend on each question. If a question is taking too long, leave it and go on to the next question. This is no time to try to show the world that you can stick to a job no matter how long it takes. All the machine that grades the test

will notice is that you didn't have any correct answers after question 17.

3. In every group of questions (except for reading comprehension and improving paragraph sets), the questions proceed from easy to medium to difficult. It makes no sense to miss a few easy questions by going too fast, just so you have time to work on some difficult questions at the end, which you may miss anyway. Almost all students taking the SAT make the mistake of trying to answer too many questions. On all sections, it is better to go slower and not finish than to go faster, get to the end, but make some careless mistakes on some easy questions along the way. Unless you expect to score over 700 on one of the parts of the test, if you are answering all the questions in that part, you are probably going too fast. *You will increase your score by slowing down and answering fewer questions.*

HOW TO USE THIS BOOK

To help you make the best use of your time before the SAT, we have created two possible study plans to follow. Select the plan that best reflects your situation, and feel free to modify it as necessary.

7-Day Study Plan

With only seven days to go before the SAT, your best bet is to concentrate on working through our practice tests. Use the following pattern:

Day 1

Get a general overview of what to expect by reading the general test-taking strategies in Chapter 2, the pointers on critical reading questions in Chapter 3, and the tips on writing skills multiple-choice questions in Chapter 5. Quickly scan the pointers on essay-writing in Chapter 5 as well. Look over the mathematics tips in Chapter 6, in particular the list of mathematical formulas. Pay particular attention to the formulas you already know: This is not the time to try to master something new.

Day 2

Take Practice Exam 1 under simulated test conditions. Complete the exam in one sitting. Use a clock or timer. Allow precisely 25 minutes each for sections 1 through 6, and 20 minutes each for sections 7 and 8, and 10 minutes total for section 9. After each section, give yourself a five-minute break. When you have finished the exam, check your answers against the answer key.

Day 3

Go through the answer explanations for Practice Exam 1, concentrating on the explanations to any questions you answered incorrectly. Refer to the tips in Chapters 3, 5, and 6 as necessary.

Day 4

Based on your performance on Practice Exam 1, decide which area of study you most need to review. Turn to that chapter, reread the introduction and specific tips, and work through the practice exercises that follow. Review your answers.

Day 5

In Chapter 5, reread the general introduction to essay-writing and practice outlining short essays. Write a 25-minute essay based on one of these outlines. Check your practice essay for grammatical errors.

Day 6

Take Practice Exam 2 under simulated test conditions, following the directions given for Day 2. Once again, when you have finished the exam, check your answers against the answer key.

Day 7

Go through the answer explanations for Practice Exam 2, concentrating on the explanations to any questions you answered incorrectly.

30-Day Study Plan

With a full month to go before the SAT, you have plenty of time to review the tips on critical reading, writing, and mathematical reasoning in Chapters 3, 5, and 6 to increase your familiarity with frequently tested vocabulary terms, and to work your way through our practice tests. Use the following pattern:

Day 1

Get a general overview of what to expect by reading the general test-taking strategies in Chapter 2. Pay particular attention to the tips on guessing and timing.

Day 2

Take Practice Exam 1 under simulated test conditions. Complete the exam in one sitting. Use a clock or timer. Allow precisely 25 minutes each for sections 1 through 6, 20 minutes each for sections 7 and 8, and 10 minutes total for section 9. After each section, give yourself a five-minute break. When you have finished the exam, check your answers against the answer key.

Day 3

Go through the answer explanations for Practice Exam 1, concentrating on the explanations to any questions you answered incorrectly.

Day 4

Study the first 30 words on the High-Frequency Word List in Chapter 4. Pay special attention to the words that are unfamiliar to you.

Day 5

Read the introduction to the mathematical reasoning sections in Chapter 6, including the guidelines for using a calculator. Review the list of important formulas and key facts, refreshing your memory of concepts you have covered in school.

Day 6

Study the second group of 30 words on the High-Frequency Word List in Chapter 4. Again, pay special attention to the words that are unfamiliar to you.

Day 7

Read the general introduction to the critical reading sections in Chapter 3. Then study the specific tips on answering sentence completion questions and do Practice Exercise A. Check your answers.

Day 8

Study the third group of 30 words on the High-Frequency Word List in Chapter 4.

Day 9

In Chapter 6, read Mathematical Reasoning Tips 1–5 on working with diagrams. Then review Tips 6–9 on how to improve your speed and accuracy in answering these questions.

Day 10

In Chapter 6, do the Practice Exercises following Tip 9 and review your answers.

Day 11

Study the fourth group of 30 words on the High-Frequency Word List in Chapter 4.

Day 12

In Chapter 3, do Sentence Completion Practice Exercises B and C. Check your answers.

Day 13

Study the fifth group of 30 words on the High-Frequency Word List in Chapter 4.

Day 14

In Chapter 5, read the general introduction to essay-writing and practice outlining short essays.

Day 15

In Chapter 5, write a draft essay based on one of your outlines. Check your practice essay for grammatical errors.

Day 16

In Chapter 6, read Mathematical Reasoning Tips 10–14 on answering multiple-choice questions. Then do the Practice Exercises following Tip 14 and review your answers.

Day 17

Study the sixth group of 30 words on the High-Frequency Word List in Chapter 4.

Day 18

In Chapter 5, read the general introduction to the writing skills section. Then study the specific tips on answering error identification questions and do Practice Exercise A. Check your answers.

Day 19

Study the seventh group of 30 words on the High-Frequency Word List in Chapter 4.

Day 20

In Chapter 5, study the specific tips on answering sentence improvement and paragraph improvement questions. Then do Practice Exercises B and C. Check you answers.

Day 21

Study the eighth group of 30 words on the High-Frequency Word List in Chapter 4.

Day 22

In Chapter 5, write a second draft essay based on one of your outlines. Check your practice essay for grammatical errors.

Day 23

In Chapter 6, study Mathematical Reasoning Tips 15–16 on handling grid-in questions. Then do the Practice Exercises following Tip 16 and review your answers.

Day 24

In Chapter 3, study the specific tips on handling reading comprehension questions and do Practice Exercises A, B, and C. Check your answers.

Day 25

Study the ninth group of 30 words on the High-Frequency Word List in Chapter 4.

Day 26

In Chapter 5, write a final draft essay based on one of your outlines. Check your practice essay for grammatical errors.

Day 27

Study the tenth and final group of words on the High-Frequency Word List in Chapter 4.

Day 28

Take Practice Exam 2 under simulated test conditions. Complete the exam in one sitting. Use a clock or timer. Allow precisely 25 minutes each for sections 1 through 6, 20 minutes each for sections 7 and 8, and 10 minutes total for section 9. After each section, give yourself a five-minute break. When you have finished the exam, check your answers against the answer key.

Day 29

Go through the answer explanations for Practice Exam 2, concentrating on the explanations to any questions you answered incorrectly. Refer to the tips in Chapters 3, 5, and 6 as necessary. In Chapter 6, once again review the list of important formulas and key facts, this time concentrating on those concepts that gave you difficulty when you took your practice exams.

Day 30

Follow the instructions in Chapter 2, Before the Test. Do not study. Just relax, knowing you have done a good job preparing yourself to take the SAT.

BEFORE THE TEST

1. Set out your test kit the night before. You will need your admission ticket, a photo ID (a driver's license or a non-driver picture ID, a passport, or a school ID), your calculator, four or five sharp No. 2 pencils (with erasers), plus a map or directions showing how to get to the test center.

2. Get a good night's sleep so you are well rested and alert.

3. Wear comfortable clothes. Dress in layers. Bring a sweater in case the room is cold.

4. Bring an accurate watch—not one that beeps—in case the room has no clock.

5. Don't be late. Allow plenty of time for getting to the test site. You want to be in your seat, relaxed, before the test begins.

DURING THE TEST

1. Do not waste any time reading the directions or looking at the sample problems at the beginning of every section. You already know all of the rules for answering each question type that appears on the SAT. They will not change.

2. First answer all the easy questions; then tackle the hard ones if you have time.

3. Pace yourself. Don't work so fast that you start making careless errors. On the other hand, don't get bogged down on any one question.

4. Play the percentages: Guess whenever you can eliminate one or more of the answers.

5. Make educated guesses, not random ones. Don't mark down answers when you haven't even looked at the questions.

6. Watch out for eye-catchers, answer choices that are designed to tempt you into guessing wrong.

7. Change answers only if you have a reason for doing so; don't change them on a last-minute hunch or whim.

8. Check your assumptions. Make sure you are answering the question asked and not the one you *thought* was going to be asked.

9. Remember that you are allowed to write in the test booklet. Use it to do your math computations and to draw diagrams. Underline key words in sentence completion questions and reading passages. Cross out any answer choices you are *sure* are wrong. Circle questions you want to return to.

10. Be careful not to make any stray marks on your answer sheet. The test is graded by a machine, and a machine cannot tell the difference between an accidental mark and a filled-in answer.

11. Check frequently to make sure you are answering the questions in the right spots.

12. Remember that you don't have to answer every question to do well.

3 The Critical Reading Sections: Strategies, Tips, and Practice

In this chapter you'll learn how best to handle the two types of critical reading questions on the SAT—sentence completions and reading comprehension—using strategies and tips that have helped thousands of SAT-takers before you. You'll also find practice exercises for both question types. After doing the exercises, you'll feel confident taking the exam because you'll be familiar with the types of questions on it.

General Tips for Answering Critical Reading Questions

1. When you are answering the critical reading questions, remember that the test is looking for the best answer, the most likely answer. This is not the time to try to show how clever you can be by imagining exotic situations that would justify different answers. If you can imagine a weird situation that would make one of the sentence completions correct—Forget it! This test is scored by a machine, which has absolutely no imagination or sense of humor; an imaginative answer is a wrong answer. Stick to the most likely answer.

2. Remember also that the sentence completion sections begin with easy questions and get harder as they go along. Likewise, sprinkled throughout the reading comprehension sections are easy "vocabulary-in-context" questions. If you get bogged down

answering time-consuming questions and forget about the time, you may never get to the easy questions up ahead.

3. Consider secondary meanings of words. If none of the answer choices seem right to you, take another look. A word may have more than one meaning.

THE SENTENCE COMPLETION QUESTION

The sentence completion questions ask you to choose the best way to complete a sentence from which one or two words have been omitted. These questions test a combination of reading comprehension skills and vocabulary. The sentences cover a wide variety of topics, but this is not a test of your general knowledge. You may feel more comfortable if you are familiar with the topic the sentence is discussing, but you should be able to handle any of the sentences using what you know about how the English language works.

Tips to Help You Cope

1. Before you look at the choices, read the sentence and think of a word that makes sense. The word you think of may not be the exact word that appears in the answer choices, but it will probably be similar in meaning to the right answer.

2. Look at all the possible answers before you make your final choice. You are looking for the word that *best* fits the meaning of the sentence as a whole. Test each answer choice, substituting it for the missing word. That way you can satisfy yourself that you have come up with the answer that best fits.

3. In double-blank sentences, test one blank at a time, not two. First read through the entire sentence.

Quickly decide which blank you want to work on. Then insert the appropriate word from each answer pair in that blank. Ask yourself whether this particular word makes sense in this blank. If a word makes *no* sense in the sentence, you can eliminate that answer pair.

4. Use your knowledge of word parts and context clues to get at the meanings of unfamiliar words. If a word used by the author is unfamiliar, or if an answer choice is unknown to you, look at its context in the sentence to see whether the context provides a clue to the meaning of the word. Often authors will use an unfamiliar word and then immediately define it within the same sentence. Similarly, look for familiar word parts—prefixes, suffixes, and roots—in unfamiliar words.

5. Watch out for negative words and prefixes and words signaling frequency or duration. Only a small change makes these two sentences very different in meaning:

> They were not lovers.
> They were not often lovers.

6. Watch out for words that have more than one meaning. Before you rule out an answer choice, consider whether the word has any secondary meanings. *Partial,* for example, means *incomplete*, as in "a partial list of contributors." It can also mean *biased*, as in "too partial to be fair to both sides," or *having a liking for* something, as in "I am highly partial to chocolate."

7. Look for words or phrases that indicate a contrast between one idea and another—words like *although, however, despite,* or *but.* In such cases an antonym or near-antonym for another word in the sentence should provide the correct answer.

8. Look for words or phrases that indicate support for

an idea—words like *in the same way, in addition,* and *also.* In such cases, a synonym or near-synonym for another word in the sentence may provide the correct answer.

9. Look for words or phrases that indicate that one thing causes another—words like *because, since, therefore,* or *thus.*

10. In eliminating answer choices, check words for positive or negative connotations. Ask yourself whether the sentence calls for a positive or negative word.

Examples to Get You Started

EXAMPLE 1

Think of a word that makes sense.

See how the first tip works with the following sentence.

The psychologist set up the experiment to test the rat's ----; he wished to see how well the rat adjusted to the changing conditions it had to face.

Even before you look at the answer choices, you can figure out what the answer *should* be.

A psychologist is trying to test some particular quality or characteristic of a rat. What quality? How do you get the answer?

Look at the sentence's second clause, the part following the semicolon. This clause is being used to define or clarify what the psychologist is trying to test. He is trying to see how well the rat *adjusts.* What words does this suggest to you? *Flexibility,* possibly, or *adaptability.* Either of these words could complete the sentence's thought.

Here are the five answer choices given.

(A) reflexes   (B) communicability   (C) stamina
(D) sociability   (E) adaptability

The best answer clearly is (E) adaptability.

EXAMPLE 2

Look at all the possible answers.

When you're racing the clock, you feel like marking down the first correct-sounding answer you come across. *Don't.* You may be going too fast.

Because the enemy had a reputation for engaging in sneak attacks, we were ---- on the alert.

(A) frequently   (B) furtively   (C) evidently   (D) constantly
(E) occasionally.

A hasty reader might be content with choice (A), *frequently*, but *frequently* is not the best fit. The best answer is choice (D), *constantly*, because "frequent" periods of alertness would not be enough to provide the necessary protection against sneak attacks that could occur at any time. "Constant" vigilance is called for: the troops would have to be always on the alert.

EXAMPLE 3

Test one blank at a time, not two.

Use the process of elimination to help you narrow things down.

The author portrays research psychologists not as disruptive ---- in the field of psychotherapy, but as effective ---- working ultimately toward the same ends as the psychotherapists.

(A) proponents..opponents
(B) antagonists..pundits
(C) interlocutors..surrogates
(D) meddlers..usurpers
(E) intruders..collaborators

Turn to the second part of the sentence. The research psychologists are portrayed as effective *blanks* working ultimately toward the same ends as the psychotherapists. The key phrase here is "working ultimately toward the same ends." Thus, the research psychologists are in effect collaborating with the psychotherapists to achieve a common goal. This immediately suggests that the correct answer is choice (E). Test the first word of that answer pair in the first blank. The adjective "disruptive" suggests that the first missing word is negative in tone. *Intruders* (people who rudely or inappropriately barge in) is definitely a negative term. Choice (E) continues to look good.

Reread the sentence with both words in place, making sure both words make sense. "The author portrays research psychologists not as disruptive intruders in the field of psychotherapy, but as effective collaborators working ultimately toward the same ends as the psychotherapists." Both words make perfect sense. The correct answer is choice (E).

EXAMPLE 4

Use your knowledge of word parts.

After a tragedy, many people claim to have had a ---- of disaster.

(A) taste   (B) dislike   (C) presentiment   (D) context
(E) verdict

Take the unfamiliar word *presentiment.* Break it down into parts. A *sentiment* is a *feeling* (the root *sens* means *feel*). *Pre-* means *before.* A *presentiment* is something you *feel before* it happens, a foreboding. Your best answer is choice (C).

EXAMPLE 5

Watch out for negative words.

For example, watch out for *not:* it's easy to overlook, but it's a key word.

Madison was not ---- person and thus made few public addresses; but those he made were memorable, filled with noble phrases.

(A) a reticent   (B) a stately   (C) an inspiring
(D) an introspective   (E) a communicative

What would happen if you overlooked *not* in this question? Probably you'd wind up choosing (A):

Madison was a *reticent* (quiet; reserved) man. *For this reason* he made few public addresses.

Unfortunately, you'd have gotten things backwards. The sentence isn't telling you what Madison was like. It's telling you what he was *not* like. And he was not a *communicative* person; he didn't express himself freely. However, when he did get around to expressing himself, he had valuable things to say.

EXAMPLE 6

Be on the lookout for words with secondary meanings.

The political climate today is extremely _____: no one can predict what the electorate will do next.

(A) malevolent   (B) pertinent   (C) claustrophobic
(D) lethargic   (E) volatile

If you have seen the word *volatile* only in the context of science class ("Acetone is an extremely *volatile* liquid: it evaporates instantly"), you may not realize it can be used to describe moods as well as chemicals. A volatile political climate is a changeable, unstable one. The correct answer is choice (E).

EXAMPLE 7

Look for words that signal a contrast.

We expected him to be jubilant over his victory, but he was ---- instead.

(A) triumphant   (B) adult   (C) morose   (D) talkative
(E) culpable

But suggests that the winner's expected reaction contrasts with his actual one. Instead of being "jubilant" (extremely joyful), he is sad. The correct answer is choice (C), *morose.*

EXAMPLE 8

Look for words that indicate similarities.

During the Middle Ages, plague and other ---- decimated the populations of entire towns.

(A) pestilences   (B)   immunizations   (C) proclivities
(D) indispositions   (E) demises

The presence of *and* linking two items in a series indicates that the missing word may be a synonym or near-synonym for the other linked word. In this case, *pestilences* are, like the plague, deadly epidemic diseases: the medieval Black Plague was one type of pestilence. The correct answer is choice (A).

Note, by the way, that the missing word, like *plague*, must be a word with *extremely* negative associations. Therefore, you can eliminate any word with positive or neutral ones. You can even eliminate words with *mildly* negative connotations. *Immunization* (a process giving the ability to resist a disease) has a positive effect: you may dislike your flu shot, but you prefer it to coming down with the flu. You can eliminate choice (B). *Proclivities* (natural tendencies), in themselves, are neutral (you can have a proclivity for neatness, as well as proclivity for violence); they are not by definition inevitably negative. Therefore, you can eliminate choice (C). Similarly, while *indispositions* (slight illnesses; minor unwillingness) are negative, they are only mildly so. You can eliminate choice (D). Choice (E), *demises* (deaths) also fails to work in this context. Thus, you are left with the correct answer, choice (A).

EXAMPLE 9

Look for words that signal cause and effect.

Tarantulas apparently have little sense of ----, for a hungry one will ignore a loudly chirping cricket placed in its cage unless the cricket happens to get in its way.

(A) touch   (B) time   (C) hearing
(D) self-preservation   (E) temperature

For sets up a relationship of cause and effect. Why does the tarantula ignore the loudly chirping cricket? Because, it seems, the tarantula does not hear the cricket's chirps. Apparently, it has little sense of hearing. The correct answer is choice (C).

EXAMPLE 10

Checks words for positive or negative connotations.

Although she enjoyed great renown as a movie star in the 1940s, Gloria Stuart experienced her greatest ---- when she was featured in *Titanic* in 1997.

(A) reprieve   (B) disclosure   (C) celebrity   (D) setback
(E) incentive

The phrase "experienced her greatest ----" indicates that something highly positive happened to Stuart when she returned to the motion picture industry. Therefore, you know that only positive words (such as *success, triumph,* or *renown*) make sense in the blank, and you can eliminate any answers with negative words. Thus, you can immediately eliminate choice (D), *setback.* In addition, you can eliminate any words that make *no* sense whatsoever. Specifically, you can eliminate choice (B), *disclosure.* It makes no sense to talk about experiencing a disclosure.

Look at the first part of the sentence. Though Stuart won fame in the 1940s, she enjoyed even more fame in the 1990s. In other words, she enjoyed her greatest *celebrity.* The correct answer is choice (C).

Practice Exercises   Answers given on page 33.

Each of the following sentences contains one or two blanks; these blanks indicate that a word or set of words has been left out. Below the sentence are five words or phrases, lettered A through E. Select the word or set of words that best completes the sentence.

Example:

Fame is ----; today's rising star is all too soon tomorrow's washed-up has-been.

(A) rewarding   (B) gradual   (C) essential
(D) spontaneous   (E) transitory

Exercise A

1. The selection committee for the exhibit was amazed to see such fine work done by a mere ----.

   (A) connoisseur   (B) artist   (C) amateur   (D) entrepreneur
   (E) exhibitionist

2. The teacher suspected cheating as soon as he noticed the pupil's ---- glances at his classmate's paper.

   (A) futile   (B) sporadic   (C) furtive   (D) cold
   (E) inconsequential

3. Known for his commitment to numerous worthy causes, the philan-thropist deserved ---- for his ----.

   (A) recognition..folly
   (B) blame..hypocrisy
   (C) reward..modesty
   (D) admonishment..wastefulness
   (E) credit..altruism

4. Miss Watson termed Huck's behavior --- because in her opinion nothing could excuse his deliberate disregard of her commands.

   (A) devious   (B) intolerant   (C) irrevocable
   (D) indefensible   (E) boisterous

5. Either the surfing at Maui is ----, or I went there on an off day.

(A) consistent   (B) thrilling   (C) invigorating
(D) overrated   (E) scenic

6. Your ---- remarks spoil the effect of your speech; try not to stray from your subject.

(A) innocuous   (B) digressive   (C) derogatory
(D) persistent   (E) enigmatic

7. The fundraising ball turned out to be a ---- : it started late, attracted too few dancers, and lost almost a million dollars.

(A) debacle   (B) blockbuster   (C) deluge
(D) gala   (E) milestone

8. She was pleased by the accolades she received; like everyone else, she enjoyed being ----.

(A) entertained   (B) praised   (C) playful
(D) vindicated   (E) charitable

9. The stereotypical image of masculinity assumes that weeping is ---- "unmanly" behavior, and not simply a human reaction that may be ---- by either sex.

(A) inexplicably..repented
(B) excessively..discerned
(C) essentially..defined
(D) inherently..adopted
(E) intentionally..exaggerated

10. The tapeworm is an example of ---- organism, one that lives within or on another creature, deriving some or all of its nutriment from its host.

(A) a hospitable   (B) an exemplary   (C) a parasitic
(D) an autonomous   (E) a protozoan

11. There was a hint of carelessness about her appearance, as though the cut of her blouse or the fit of her slacks was a matter of ---- to her.

(A) satisfaction   (B) aesthetics   (C) indifference
(D) significance   (E) controversy

12. Many educators argue that a ---- grouping of students would improve instruction because it would limit the range of student abilities in the classroom.

(A) heterogeneous   (B) systematic   (C) homogeneous
(D) sporadic   (E) fragmentary

13. The younger members of the company resented the domineering and ---- manner of the office manager.

(A) urbane   (B) prudent   (C) convivial
(D) imperious   (E) objective

14. Bluebeard was noted for his ---- jealousy, a jealousy so extreme that it passed all reasonable bounds.

(A) transitory   (B) rhetorical   (C) stringent
(D) callous   (E) inordinate

15. I regret that my remarks seemed ----; I never intended to belittle you.

(A) inadequate   (B) justified   (C) unassailable
(D) disparaging   (E) shortsighted

Exercise B

1. A ---- glance pays ---- attention to details.

(A) furtive..meticulous   (B) cursory..little   (C) cryptic..close
(D) keen..scanty   (E) fleeting..vigilant

2. With its elaborately carved, convoluted lines, furniture of the Baroque period was highly ---- .

(A) functional   (B) primitive   (C) linear
(D) spare   (E) ornate

3. His excessive pride in his accomplishments was ---- : he had accomplished little if anything at all.

(A) unjustified   (B) innocuous   (C) systematic
(D) rational   (E) critical

4. A ---- relationship links the rhinoceros and the oxpecker (or rhinoceros bird), for the two are mutually dependent.

(A) monolithic   (B) superficial   (C) symbiotic
(D) debilitating   (E) stereotypical

5. When we saw black smoke billowing from the wing of the plane, we were certain that disaster was ----.

(A) unlikely   (B) opportune   (C) imminent
(D) undeserved   (E) averted

6. I can vouch for his honesty; I have always found him ---- and carefully observant of the truth.

(A) arbitrary   (B) plausible   (C) volatile
(D) veracious   (E) innocuous

7. This well-documented history is of importance because it carefully ---- the ---- accomplishments of Native American artists who are all too little known to the public at large.

   (A) recognizes..negligible
   (B) overlooks..purported
   (C) scrutinizes..illusory
   (D) distorts..noteworthy
   (E) substantiates..considerable

8. Perhaps because he feels ---- by an excess of parental restrictions and rules, at adolescence the repressed child may break out dramatically.

   (A) nurtured   (B) appeased   (C) confined
     (D) fascinated   (E) liberated

9. Sue felt that Jack's ---- in the face of the compelling evidence which she had presented was an example of his ---- mind.

   (A) truculence..unbiased
   (B) skepticism..open
   (C) incredulity..closed
   (D) acquiescence..keen
   (E) reluctance..impartial

10. As a girl, Emily Dickinson was ---- but also ---- : extraordinarily intense about her poetry yet exceptionally inhibited socially.

    (A) zealous..gregarious
    (B) ardent..repressed
    (C) prudent..reserved
    (D) rash..intrusive
    (E) impulsive..dedicated

11. The good night's sleep had ---- effect on the weary climber, who woke refreshed and eager to resume the ascent.

    (A) an innocuous   (B) a tonic   (C) a minor
      (D) an enervating   (E) a detrimental

12. She is an interesting ----, an infinitely shy person who, in apparent contradiction, possesses an enormously intuitive ---- for understanding people.

    (A) aberration..disdain
    (B) caricature..talent
    (C) specimen..loathing
    (D) phenomenon..disinclination
    (E) paradox..gift

13. The coach's harsh rebuke deeply wounded the star quarterback, who had never been ---- like that before.

    (A) summoned   (B) reprimanded   (C) stimulated
    (D) placated   (E) ignored

14. Because he was ----, he shunned human society.

    (A) a misanthrope   (B) an oligarch   (C) an anomaly
    (D) a stereotype   (E) a nonentity

15. Ernest Hemingway's prose is generally esteemed for its ---- ; as one critic puts it, Hemingway "cuts out unneeded words."

    (A) sensitivity   (B) economy   (C) gusto
    (D) breadth   (E) intricacy

Exercise C

1. Crows are extremely ---- : their harsh cries easily drown out the songs of neighboring birds.

    (A) fickle   (B) swarthy   (C) raucous
    (D) cordial   (E) versatile

2. The critic maintained that the current revival was the most fatuous and ---- production of the entire theatrical season.

    (A) gripping   (B) inane   (C) prophetic
    (D) memorable   (E) salubrious

3. Jean Georges was famous for his ---- cuisine, which brought together ingredients from many cooking traditions—Thai, Chinese, French— and combined them in innovative ways.

    (A) aesthetic   (B) clandestine   (C) homogeneous
    (D) eclectic   (E) conventional

4. Believing that all children possess a certain natural intelligence, the headmaster exhorted the teachers to discover and ---- each student's ---- talents.

   (A) suppress..unrecognized
   (B) develop..intrinsic
   (C) redirect..specious
   (D) belittle..dormant
   (E) cultivate..gratuitous

5. The ---- of such utopian notions is reflected by the quick disintegration of the idealistic community at Brooke Farm.

   (A) timeliness   (B) creativity   (C) impracticability
   (D) effervescence   (E) vindication

6. We were amazed that a man who had been heretofore the most ---- of public speakers could, in a single speech, electrify an audience and bring them cheering to their feet.

   (A) enthralling   (B) accomplished   (C) pedestrian
   (D) auspicious   (E) masterful

7. Despite the mixture's ---- nature, we found that by lowering its temperature in the laboratory we could dramatically reduce its tendency to vaporize.

   (A) resilient   (B) volatile   (C) homogeneous
   (D) insipid   (E) acerbic

8. Her novel published to universal acclaim, her literary gifts acknowledged by the chief figures of the Harlem Renaissance, her reputation as yet ----by envious slights, Hurston clearly was at the ----of her career.

   (A) undamaged..ebb   (B) untarnished..zenith
   (C) untainted..extremity   (D) blackened..mercy
   (E) unmarred..brink

9. Fitness experts claim that jogging is ----; once you begin to jog regularly, you may be unable to stop, because you are sure to love it more and more all the time.

   (A) exhausting   (B) illusive   (C) addictive
   (D) exotic   (E) overrated

10. Although newscasters often use the terms Chicano and Latino ----, students of Hispanic-American culture are profoundly aware of the ---- the two.

(A) interchangeably..dissimilarities between
(B) indifferently..equivalence of
(C) deprecatingly..controversies about
(D) unerringly..significance of
(E) confidently..origins of

11. She maintained that the proposed legislation was ---- because it simply established an affirmative action task force without making any appropriate provision to fund such a force.

(A) inevitable   (B) inadequate   (C) prudent
    (D) necessary   (E) beneficial

12. The faculty senate warned that, if its recommendations were to go unheeded, the differences between the administration and the teaching staff would be ---- and eventually rendered irreconcilable.

(A) rectified   (B) exacerbated   (C) imponderable
    (D) eradicated   (E) alienated

13. Paradoxically, Helen, who had been a strict mother to her children, proved ---- mistress to her cats.

(A) a harsh   (B) an indolent   (C) an ambivalent
    (D) a cautious   (E) a lenient

14. The supervisor's evaluation was ---- , for she noted the employee's strong points and limitations without overly emphasizing either.

(A) equitable   (B) laudatory   (C) practicable
    (D) slanted   (E) dogmatic

15. She has sufficient tact to ---- the ordinary crises of diplomatic life; however, even her diplomacy is insufficient to enable her to ---- the current emergency.

(A) negotiate..comprehend
(B) survive..exaggerate
(C) handle..weather
(D) ignore..transform
(E) aggravate..resolve

Answer Key

Exercise A

1. **C**	5. **D**	9. **D**	13. **D**
2. **C**	6. **B**	10. **C**	14. **E**
3. **E**	7. **A**	11. **C**	15. **D**
4. **D**	8. **B**	12. **C**	

Exercise B

1. **B**	5. **C**	9. **C**	13. **B**
2. **E**	6. **D**	10. **B**	14. **A**
3. **A**	7. **E**	11. **B**	15. **B**
4. **C**	8. **C**	12. **E**	

Exercise C

1. **C**	5. **C**	9. **C**	13. **E**
2. **B**	6. **C**	10. **A**	14. **A**
3. **D**	7. **B**	11. **B**	15. **C**
4. **B**	8. **B**	12. **B**	

Answer Explanations

Exercise A

1. **C** The key word here is *amazed*. It would not amaze a selection committee for an artist to submit fine work for their consideration. However, it might well amaze the committee to have an *amateur*, nonprofessional person do so.

2. **C** What sort of glances would make a teacher suspect a pupil was cheating? *Furtive* (sneaky; secretive) glances would.

3. **E** What did the philanthropist deserve for his commitment to worthy causes? He deserved *credit* for his *altruism* (unselfish concern for others).

4. **D** Behavior that nothing could excuse by definition is *indefensible* (unpardonable; inexcusable).

5. **D** The sentence implies that surfing at Maui is usually thought to be good. The speaker was disappointed when he went surfing there. Two possibilities exist: either the surfing that day was atypically poor ("I went there on an off day") or surfing at Maui is basically *overrated* (too highly valued). Note how the "either … or" structure sets up a contrast between the two clauses.

6. **B** The second half of the sentence advises the writer to try not to stray from his or her subject. In other words, the writer is advised to avoid making *digressive* (off-target, wandering) remarks.

7. **A** A fundraising event that lost almost a million dollars clearly would deserve to be described as a *debacle* (disaster; total failure).

8. **B** Accolades are expressions of approval. The young lady receiving these accolades enjoys being *praised*.

9. **D** A stereotype is an oversimplified, conventional image. According to the stereotype, "boys don't cry." The stereotype assumes that crying is *inherently* (by its very nature) not manly. It rejects the notion that crying is simply a human reaction that either sex may *adopt* (take on).

10. **C** By definition, an organism that lives within or on another creature, getting its nourishment from its host, is *parasitic*.

11. **C** Someone who did not care about her appearance would consider the look of her clothing a matter of *indifference* (little or no concern).

12. **C** A *homogeneous* (uniform in composition; essentially alike) class grouping by definition would limit the range of student abilities in the classroom.

13. **D** Subordinates would be likely to resent a domineering and *imperious* (overbearing; dictatorial) superior.

14. **E** Something so extreme that it passes all reasonable bounds is by definition *inordinate* (excessive).

15. **D** The key word here is *belittle*. Although the speaker did not intend to belittle anyone, his remarks seemed *disparaging* (disrespectful; belittling).

Exercise B

1. **B** A *cursory* (superficial; passing) glance by definition pays *little* attention to details.

2. **E** By definition, elaborately carved furniture is *ornate* (elaborately ornamental; showy),

3. **A** Someone who has accomplished little or nothing does not deserve to take pride in his accomplishments; his pride is *unjustified* (unwarranted; baseless).

4. **C** Symbiosis is an interdependent, often mutually beneficial relationship between groups or species. Such a mutually dependent relationship is described as *symbiotic.*

5. **C** The appearance of the black smoke signals the passengers that disaster is *imminent* (about to occur at any moment).

6. **D** Someone observant of the truth is by definition *veracious* (truthful; honest).

7. **E** Why is this history important? It is important because it carefully *substantiates* (supports; bears out; confirms) the *considerable* (substantial; significant) accomplishments of the Indian artists. Note the positive tone of the sentence as a whole. In the second blank, the word describing the accomplishments of the Indian artists must be positive as well.

8. **C** An excess of restrictions and rules most likely would make someone feel *confined* (restricted).

9. **C** *Incredulity* (disbelief) when faced with compelling (convincing; strongly persuasive) evidence might well be a sign of a *closed* mind, a mind not open to new arguments and ideas.

10. **B** Note the parallel structure in this sentence. Both halves of the sentence contrast two descriptions of the poet. The second half states she was "extraordinarily intense about her poetry," yet she was "inhibited socially." Similarly, the first half states she was *ardent* (passionate; enthusiastic), but also *repressed* (emotionally subdued) in dealing with people.

11. **B** By definition, *a tonic* effect is physically or mentally invigorating; it refreshes you.

12. **E** The key word here is *contradiction*. An infinitely shy person, uncomfortable around people, who nevertheless had a strong *gift* or talent for understanding people, would be appear to be a *paradox* or contradiction.

13. **B** The key word here is *rebuke* (scolding; censure). The coach has rebuked the quarterback. In other words, the coach has *reprimanded* (scolded) him.

14. **A** Someone who shuns human society is by definition a *misanthrope* (one who hates mankind).

15. **B** A writer who cuts out unneeded words is an economical writer, one who uses the minimum of words needed for effectiveness. Critics praise Hemingway's lean prose style for its *economy* (conciseness).

Exercise C

1. **C** Harsh cries that drown out other sounds are by definition *raucous* (grating; strident; hoarse).

2. **B** The key word here is *fatuous* (idiotic; silly). A fatuous theatrical production is by definition *inane* (silly; absurd).

3. **D** Something *eclectic* is made up of elements drawn from distinctly different sources. Coming from Thai, Chinese, and French cooking traditions, Jean Georges' cuisine (style of cooking) is decidedly *eclectic*.

4. **B** The key concept here is the notion that children possess "a certain natural intelligence." This intelligence exists in every child: it belongs to the child by the child's very nature. It is the teacher's task to discover and *develop* such inborn, *intrinsic* talents.

5. **C** The idealistic community at Brooke Farm quickly disintegrated (fell apart). The rapid break-up of the community suggests the *impracticability* of such utopian notions, which are incapable of being put into practice with the means available.

6. **C** Why were people amazed that this speaker could electrify an audience? They were amazed because his previous speeches had been nothing to cheer about. In fact, up to then he had been the most *pedestrian* (uninspired; unexciting) of speakers.

7. **B** Something *volatile* by definition tends to vaporize or evaporate readily.

8. **B** A writer whose work was universally acclaimed or applauded and whose reputation was not yet *tarnished* or stained would be at the *zenith* or high point of her career.

9. **C** Addiction is the state of being psychologically or physically enslaved to a habit or practice. If, once you begin to jog regularly, you are unable to break the habit, then you may describe jogging as *addictive*.

10. **A** People who are aware of the *dissimilarities* (differences) between the terms Chicano and Latino would not use these terms *interchangeably* (as if one term could be used in place of the other, with no difference in meaning).

11. **B** Legislation that established a task force without providing any money to fund that force would clearly be *inadequate*.

12. **B** The warning indicates that the differences between the administration and the teaching staff will become so much worse that they will become irreconcilable (impossible to reconcile or bring into harmony). In other words, the differences will become *exacerbated* (aggravated; inflamed; worsened).

13. **E** The word *paradoxically* signals a contrast between the children's strict mother and the cat's *lenient* (indulgent; easy-going) owner.

14. **A** In noting both the employee's strong points and limitations in an evenhanded manner, the supervisor is being fair or *equitable*.

15. **C** Although she has enough diplomacy or tact to *handle* (deal with) ordinary crises, she does not have enough to *weather* (survive; get through) an extraordinary emergency.

THE READING COMPREHENSION QUESTION

SAT reading comprehension questions test your ability to understand what you read—both content and technique. Each critical reading section will include one or two long reading passages of different length, followed by six to thirteen questions. Two of the three critical reading sections will also include two short reading passages (each about 100 words long), followed by four questions. The third critical reading section on the SAT will consist of a pair of passages with some questions on one passage, some on the other, and some comparing the two.

The questions that come after each passage are not arranged in order of difficulty. They are arranged to suit the way the passage's content is organized. (A question based on information found at the beginning of the passage will come before a question based on information at the passage's end.) If you are stumped by a tough reading question, do not skip the other questions on that passage. A tough question may be just one question away from an easy one.

Tips to Help You Cope

1. Save the reading comprehension questions for last. On the SAT, you get the same points for answering a "quick and easy" question correctly as you do for answering a time-consuming one. Reading questions take time. Answer the less time-consuming questions first.

2. When you have a choice, tackle a passage with a familiar subject before one with an unfamiliar one. It is hard to concentrate when you read about something wholly unfamiliar to you. Give yourself a break. When there are several passages in a section, first tackle the one that most interests you or that deals with a topic that you know well.

3. In tackling the reading passages, be flexible in your approach. Students often ask whether it is better to read the passage first or the questions first. The

answer is, there is no one true way. It depends on the passage, and *it depends on you.*

The Questions First Approach

Read the italicized introduction and the opening sentence of the passage, and then head straight for the questions. As you read a question, be on the lookout for key words, either in the question itself or among the answer choices. Then run your eye down the passage, looking for those key words or their synonyms. When you locate your key word, read that sentence and a couple of sentences around it and see whether you can confidently answer the question based on just that small portion of the passage. If you can't, be flexible: skim the entire passage and choose your answer.

The Passage First Approach

Read the entire passage quickly but with understanding and then turn to the questions. You do not have to remember *everything* in the passage; you just need to get a general sense of the points that are being made. Again, be flexible: if you are having trouble reading a passage, turn to the questions before you finish the passage. The wording of the questions may help you understand what the passage is talking about. You can test both approaches as you work through the reading comprehension practice exercises at the end of this chapter. Try some passages tackling the questions one at a time, each time reading the question first before turning to the passage to find the correct answer. Try others reading through the entire passage before you answer the questions. See which approach works better for you.

4. Read as rapidly as you can with understanding, but do not force yourself. Do not worry about the time element. If you worry about not finishing the test, you will begin to take short cuts and miss the correct answer in your haste.

5. Make use of the italicized introductions to acquaint yourself with the text. As you read the italicized introductory material and tackle the passage's opening sentences, try to anticipate what the passage will be about. You'll be in a better position to understand what you read.

6. As you continue reading, try to remember in which part of the passage the author makes major points. In that way, when you start looking for the phrase or sentence which will justify your choice of answer, you will be able to save time by going to that section of the passage immediately rather than having to reread the entire section.

7. When you tackle the questions, go back to the passage to verify your choice of answer. Do not rely on your memory alone.

8. Watch out for words or phrases in the question that can alert you to the kind of question being asked. Questions asking for information stated in the passage:

> *the author asserts*
> *the author mentions all of the following EXCEPT*
> *according to the passage*
> *according to the author*

Questions asking you to draw a conclusion:

> *it can be inferred*
> *would most likely*
> *is best described*
> *it can be argued*
> *suggests that*
> *the author implies*
> *the author probably considers*
> *would probably*

Questions asking about the main idea of the passage:

> *which of the following titles*
> *main/central/primary purpose*
> *main point of the passage*

chiefly concerned with
passage as a whole
primary emphasis
Questions asking about contextual meaning:
as used in the passage
what the author means in saying
in context, the word/phrase
in the context of the passage

9. When asked to find the main idea, be sure to check the opening and summary sentences of each paragraph. Authors typically provide readers with a sentence that expresses a paragraph's main idea succinctly. Although such topic sentences may appear anywhere in the paragraph, readers customarily look for them in the opening or closing sentences.

10. When asked to choose a title, watch out for choices that are too specific or too broad. A paragraph is a group of sentences revolving around a central theme. An appropriate title for a paragraph, therefore, must include this central theme. It should be neither too broad nor too narrow in its scope; it should be specific and yet comprehensive enough to include all the essentials. A good title for a passage of two or more paragraphs should include the thoughts of ALL the paragraphs.

11. When asked to make inferences, take as your answer what the passage logically suggests, not what it states directly. Look for clues in the passage; then choose as your answer a statement which is a logical development of the information the author has provided.

12. When asked to determine the questions of attitude, mood, or tone, look for words that convey emotion, express values, or paint pictures. These images and descriptive phrases get the author's feelings across.

13. Use the line numbers in the questions to be sure you've gone back to the correct spot in the passage.

Fortunately, the lines are numbered in the passages, and the questions often refer you to specific lines in the passage by number. It takes less time to locate a line number than to spot a word or phrase.

14. Try to answer all the questions on a particular passage. Don't let yourself get bogged down on any one question. Skip the one that's got you stumped, but make a point of coming back to it later, after you've answered one or two more questions on the passage. Often, working through other questions on the same passage will provide you with information you can use to answer questions that stumped you the first time around.

15. When asked to give the meaning of an unfamiliar word, look for nearby context clues. Words in the immediate vicinity of the word you are trying to define will often give you a sense of the meaning of the unfamiliar word.

16. When dealing with double passages, tackle them one at a time. After reading the lines in italics introducing both passages, read Passage 1; then jump straight to the questions, and answer all those based on Passage 1. Next read Passage 2; then answer all the questions based on Passage 2. Finally, tackle the two or three questions that refer to both passages. Go back to both passages as needed.

Practice Exercises   Answers given on page 69.

> Each passage below precedes questions based on its content.
> Answer all questions following a passage based on what that
> passage <u>states</u> directly or <u>implies</u>.

Exercise A

Each of the following passages comes from a novel or
short story collection that has provided reading passages on prior
SATs. Use this exercise to acquaint yourself with the sort of fiction
you will confront on the test and to practice answering critical reading questions based on literature.

The following passage is taken from Great Expectations *by Charles
Dickens. In it, the hero, Pip, recollects a dismal period in his youth
during which he for a time lost hope of ever bettering his fortunes.*

It is a most miserable thing to feel ashamed of home.
There may be black ingratitude in the thing, and the punishment may be retributive and well deserved; but, that it is a
Line miserable thing, I can testify. Home had never been a very
(5) pleasant place to me, because of my sister's temper. But Joe
had sanctified it and I believed in it. I had believed in the best
parlor as a most elegant salon; I had believed in the front
door as a mysterious portal of the Temple of State whose
solemn opening was attended with a sacrifice of roast fowls;
(10) I had believed in the kitchen as a chaste though not magnificent
apartment; I had believed in the forge as the glowing road to
manhood. Now, it was all coarse and common, and I would not
have had Miss Havisham and Estella see it on any account.
Once, it had seemed to me that when I should at last roll
(15) up my shirt sleeves and go into the forge, Joe's 'prentice, I

should be distinguished and happy. Now the reality was in my hold, I only felt that I was dusty with the dust of small coal, and that I had a weight upon my daily remembrance to which the anvil was a feather. There have been occasions in

(20) my later life (I suppose as in most lives) when I have felt for a time as if a thick curtain had fallen on all its interest and romance, to shut me out from any thing save dull endurance any more. Never has that curtain dropped so heavy and blank, as when my way in life lay stretched out straight

(25) before me through the newly-entered road of apprenticeship to Joe.

I remember that at a later period of my "time," I used to stand about the churchyard on Sunday evenings, when night was falling, comparing my own perspective with the windy

(30) marsh view, and making out some likeness between them by thinking how flat and low both were, and how on both there came an unknown way and a dark mist and then the sea. I was quite as dejected on the first working-day of my apprenticeship as in that after time; but I am glad to know that I

(35) never breathed a murmur to Joe while my indentures lasted. It is about the only thing I *am* glad to know of myself in that connection.

For, though it includes what I proceed to add, all the merit of what I proceed to add was Joe's. It was not because

(40) I was faithful, but because Joe was faithful, that I never ran away and went for a soldier or a sailor. It was not because I had a strong sense of the virtue of industry, but because Joe had a strong sense of the virtue of industry, that I worked with tolerable zeal against the grain. It is not possible to know

(45) how far the influence of any amiable honesthearted duty-going man flies out into the world; but it is very possible to know how it has touched one's self in going by, and I know right well that any good that intermixed itself with my apprenticeship came of plain contented Joe, and not of restless

(50) aspiring discontented me.

1. The passage as a whole is best described as

   (A) an analysis of the reasons behind a change in attitude
   (B) an account of a young man's reflections on his emotional state
   (C) a description of a young man's awakening to the harsh conditions
       of working class life
   (D) a defense of a young man's longings for romance and glamour
   (E) a criticism of young people's ingratitude to their elders

2. It may be inferred from the passage that the young man has been
   apprenticed to a

   (A) cook
   (B) forger
   (C) coal miner
   (D) blacksmith
   (E) grave digger

3. In the passage, Joe is portrayed most specifically as

   (A) distinguished
   (B) virtuous
   (C) independent
   (D) homely
   (E) coarse

4. The passage suggests that the narrator's increasing discontent with
   his home during his apprenticeship was caused by

   (A) a new awareness on his part of how his home would appear to
       others
   (B) the increasing heaviness of the labor involved
   (C) the unwillingness of Joe to curb his sister's temper
   (D) the narrator's lack of an industrious character
   (E) a combination of simple ingratitude and sinfulness

5. According to the passage, the narrator gives himself a measure of
   credit for

   (A) working diligently despite his unhappiness
   (B) abandoning his hope of a military career
   (C) keeping his menial position secret from Miss Havisham
   (D) concealing his despondency from Joe
   (E) surrendering his childish beliefs

The following passage is excerpted from the short story "Clay" in Dubliners *by James Joyce. In this passage, tiny, unmarried Maria oversees tea for the washerwomen, all the while thinking of the treat in store for her: a night off.*

The matron had given her leave to go out as soon as the women's tea was over and Maria looked forward to her evening out. The kitchen was spick and span: the cook said *Line* you could see yourself in the big copper boilers. The fire was *(5)* nice and bright and on one of the side-tables were four very big barmbracks. These barmbracks seemed uncut; but if you went closer you would see that they had been cut into long thick even slices and were ready to be handed round at tea. Maria had cut them herself.

(10)   Maria was a very, very small person indeed but she had a very long nose and a very long chin. She talked a little through her nose, always soothingly: "Yes, my dear," and "No, my dear." She was always sent for when the women quarrelled over their tubs and always succeeded in making *(15)* peace. One day the matron had said to her:

"Maria, you are a veritable peace-maker!"

And the sub-matron and two of the Board ladies had heard the compliment. And Ginger Mooney was always saying what she wouldn't do to the dummy who had charge *(20)* of the irons if it wasn't for Maria. Everyone was so fond of Maria.

When the cook told her everything was ready, she went into the women's room and began to pull the big bell. In a few minutes the women began to come in by twos and *(25)* threes, wiping their steaming hands in their petticoats and pulling down the sleeves of their blouses over their red steaming arms. They settled down before their huge mugs which the cook and the dummy filled up with hot tea, already mixed with milk and sugar in huge tin cans. Maria super- *(30)* intended the distribution of the barmbrack and saw that every

woman got her four slices. There was a great deal of laughing
and joking during the meal. Lizzie Fleming said Maria was
sure to get the ring and, though Fleming had said that for so
many Hallow Eves, Maria had to laugh and say she didn't
(35) want any ring or man either; and when she laughed her grey-
green eyes sparkled with disappointed shyness and the tip of
her nose nearly met the tip of her chin. Then Ginger Mooney
lifted her mug of tea and proposed Maria's health while all
the other women clattered with their mugs on the table, and
(40) said she was sorry she hadn't a sup of porter to drink it in.
And Maria laughed again till the tip of her nose nearly met
the tip of her chin and till her minute body nearly shook itself
asunder because she knew that Mooney meant well though,
of course, she had the notions of a common woman.

6. The author's primary purpose in the second paragraph is to

   (A) introduce the character of a spinster
   (B) describe working conditions in a public institution
   (C) compare two women of different social classes
   (D) illustrate the value of peace-makers in society
   (E) create suspense about Maria's fate

7. The language of the passage most resembles the language of

   (A) a mystery novel
   (B) an epic
   (C) a fairy tale
   (D) institutional board reports
   (E) a sermon

8. It can be inferred from the passage that Maria would most likely view
the matron as which of the following?

   (A) A political figurehead
   (B) An inept administrator
   (C) A demanding taskmaster
   (D) An intimate friend
   (E) A benevolent superior

9. We may infer from the care with which Maria has cut the barmbracks (lines 6–8) that

(A) she fears the matron
(B) she is in a hurry to leave
(C) she expects the Board members for tea
(D) it is a dangerous task
(E) she takes pride in her work

10. It can be inferred from the passage that all the following are characteristic of Maria EXCEPT

(A) a deferential nature
(B) eagerness for compliments
(C) respect for authority
(D) dreams of matrimony
(E) reluctance to compromise

The following passage is taken from Jane Austen's novel Mansfield Park. *This excerpt presents Sir Thomas Bertram, owner of Mansfield Park, who has just joined the members of his family.*

     Sir Thomas was indeed the life of the party, who at his suggestion now seated themselves round the fire. He had the best right to be the talker; and the delight of his sensations in
Line being again in his own house, in the center of his family,
(5) after such a separation, made him communicative and chatty in a very unusual degree; and he was ready to answer every question of his two sons almost before it was put. All the little particulars of his proceedings and events, his arrivals and departures, were most promptly delivered, as he sat by Lady
(10) Bertram and looked with heartfelt satisfaction at the faces around him—interrupting himself more than once, however, to remark on his good fortune in finding them all at home—coming unexpectedly as he did—all collected together exactly as he could have wished, but dared not depend on.
(15)   By not one of the circle was he listened to with such unbroken unalloyed enjoyment as by his wife, whose feelings were so warmed by his sudden arrival, as to place her nearer

agitation than she had been for the last twenty years. She
had been almost fluttered for a few minutes, and still
(20) remained so sensibly animated as to put away her work,
move Pug from her side, and give all her attention and all the
rest of her sofa to her husband. She had no anxieties for anybody to cloud *her* pleasure; her own time had been irre-
proachably spent during his absence; she had done a great
(25) deal of carpet work and made many yards of fringe; and she
would have answered as freely for the good conduct and
useful pursuits of all the young people as for her own. It was
so agreeable to her to see him again, and hear him talk, to
have her ear amused and her whole comprehension filled by
(30) his narratives, that she began particularly to feel how dread-
fully she must have missed him, and how impossible it
would have been for her to bear a lengthened absence.

Mrs. Norris was by no means to be compared in happiness to her sister. Not that she was incommoded by many
(35) fears of Sir Thomas's disapprobation when the present state
of his house should be known, for her judgment had been so
blinded, that she could hardly be said to show any sign of
alarm; but she was vexed by the manner of his return. It had
left her nothing to do. Instead of being sent for out of the
(40) room, and seeing him first, and having to spread the happy
news through the house, Sir Thomas, with a very reasonable
dependence perhaps on the nerves of his wife and children,
had sought no confidant but the butler, and had been following him almost instantaneously into the drawing-room. Mrs.
(45) Norris felt herself defrauded of an office on which she had
always depended, whether his arrival or his death were to be
the thing unfolded; and was now trying to be in a bustle without having any thing to bustle about. Would Sir Thomas have
consented to eat, she might have gone to the housekeeper
(50) with troublesome directions; but Sir Thomas resolutely
declined all dinner; he would take nothing, nothing till tea
came—he would rather wait for tea. Still Mrs. Norris was at

intervals urging something different; and in the most interesting moment of his passage to England, when the alarm of a
(55) French privateer was at the height, she burst through his
recital with the proposal of soup. "Sure, my dear Sir Thomas,
a basin of soup would be a much better thing for you than
tea. Do have a basin of soup."

Sir Thomas could not be provoked. "Still the same anxi-
(60) ety for everybody's comfort, my dear Mrs. Norris," was his
answer. "But indeed I would rather have nothing but tea."

11. We can infer from the opening paragraph that Sir Thomas is
customarily

(A) unwelcome at home
(B) tardy in business affairs
(C) dissatisfied with life
(D) more restrained in speech
(E) lacking in family feeling

12. The passage suggests that Sir Thomas's sudden arrival

(A) was motivated by concern for his wife
(B) came as no surprise to Lady Bertram
(C) was timed by him to coincide with a family reunion
(D) was expected by the servants
(E) was received with mixed emotions

13. Which of the following titles best describes the passage?

(A) An Unexpected Return
(B) The Conversation of the Upper Class
(C) Mrs. Norris's Grievance
(D) A Romantic Reunion
(E) An Account of a Voyage Abroad

14. The author's tone in her description of Lady Bertram's sensations
(lines 15–32) is

(A) markedly scornful
(B) mildly bitter
(C) gently ironic
(D) manifestly indifferent
(E) warmly sympathetic

15. By stressing that Lady Bertram "had no anxieties for anybody to cloud *her* pleasure" (lines 22–23), the author primarily intends to imply that

(A) Lady Bertram was hardhearted in ignoring the sufferings of others
(B) it was unusual for Lady Bertram to be so unconcerned
(C) others in the company had reason to be anxious
(D) Sir Thomas expected his wife to be pleased to see him
(E) Lady Bertram lived only for pleasure

16. Sir Thomas's attitude toward Mrs. Norris can best be described as one of

(A) sharp irritation
(B) patient forbearance
(C) solemn disapproval
(D) unreasoned alarm
(E) unmixed delight

17. The office of which Mrs. Norris feels herself defrauded is most likely that of

(A) butler
(B) housekeeper
(C) wife
(D) world traveler
(E) message-bearer

Exercise B

The best Eskimo carvings of all ages seem to
possess a powerful ability to reach across the great
barriers of language and time and communicate
Line directly with us. The more we look at these carvings,
(5)   the more life we perceive hidden within them. We
discover subtle living forms of the animal, human,
and mystical world. These arctic carvings are not
the cold sculptures of a frozen world. Instead, they
reveal to us the passionate feelings of a vital people
(10) well aware of all the joys, terrors, tranquility, and
wildness of life around them.

Eskimo carvers are people moved by dreams. In
spite of all their new contacts with the outsiders, they
are still concerned with their own kind of mystical
(15) imagery. The most skillful carvers possess a bold
confidence, a direct approach to their art that has a
freedom unsullied by any kind of formalized training.
Eskimo carvers have strong, skilled hands, used to
forcing hard materials with their simple tools. Their
(20) hunting life and the northern environment invigorates
them. Bad weather often imposes a special kind of
leisure, giving them time in which to perfect their
carvings.

They are among the last of the hunting societies
(25) that have retained some part of the keen sense of
observation that we have so long forgotten. The
carvers are also butchers of meat, and therefore
masters in the understanding of animal anatomy.
Flesh and bones and sheaths of muscle seem to move
(30) in their works. They show us how to drive the
caribou, how to hold a child, how to walk cautiously
on thin ice. Through their eyes we understand the
dangerous power of a polar bear. In the very best
of Eskimo art we see vibrant animal and human
(35) forms that stand quietly or tensely, strongly radiating
a sense of life. We can see, and even feel with our
hands, the cold sleekness of seals, the hulking weight
of walrus, the icy swiftness of trout, the flowing
rhythm in a flight of geese. In their art we catch
(40) brief glimpses of a people who have long possessed
a very different approach to the whole question of
life and death.

In Eskimo art there is much evidence of humor
which the carvers have in abundance. Some of the
(45) carvings are caricatures of themselves, of ourselves,
and of situations, or records of ancient legends. Their
laughter may be subtle, or broad and Chaucerian.

Perhaps no one can accurately define the right
way or wrong way to create a carving. Each carver
(50) must follow his own way, in his own time. Technique in itself is meaningless unless it serves to
express content. According to the Eskimo, the best
carvings possess a sense of movement that seems
to come from within the material itself, a feeling
(55) of tension, a living excitement.

1. The author is primarily concerned with

(A) showing how Eskimo carvings achieve their effects
(B) describing how Eskimo artists resist the influence of outsiders
(C) discussing the significant characteristics of Eskimo art
(D) explaining how Eskimo carvers use their strength to manipulate
   hard materials
(E) interpreting the symbolism of Eskimo art

2. The author's attitude toward Eskimo art is one of

(A) condescension
(B) awe
(C) admiration
(D) regret
(E) bewilderment

3. With which of the following statements would the author most likely
agree?

(A) Formal training may often destroy an artist's originality.
(B) Artists should learn their craft by studying the work of experts.
(C) The content of a work of art is insignificant.
(D) Caricatures have no place in serious art.
(E) Eskimo art is interesting more as an expression of a life view than
   as a serious art form.

4. The author gives examples of the subjects of Eskimo carvings primarily to

(A) show that they have no relevance to modern life
(B) indicate the artist's lack of imagination
(C) imply that other artists have imitated them
(D) prove that the artists' limited experience of life has been a handi-
   cap
(E) suggest the quality and variety of the work

5. According to the passage, Eskimo carvings have all the following
EXCEPT

(A) wit
(B) subtlety
(C) emotional depth
(D) stylistic uniformity
(E) anatomical accuracy

        Charlotte Stanhope was at this time about thirty-
    five years old; and, whatever may have been her
    faults, she had none of those which belong to old
Line young ladies. She neither dressed young, nor talked
(5)   young, nor indeed looked young. She appeared to
    be perfectly content with her time of life, and in no
    way affected the graces of youth. She was a fine
    young woman; and had she been a man, would have
    been a fine young man. All that was done in the
(10) house, and was not done by servants, was done by
    her. She gave the orders, paid the bills, hired and
    dismissed the domestics, made the tea, carved the
    meat, and managed everything in the Stanhope
    household. She, and she alone, could ever induce her
(15) father to look into the state of his worldly concerns.
    She, and she alone, could in any degree control the
    absurdities of her sister. She, and she alone, prevented
    the whole family from falling into utter disrepute and
    beggary. It was by her advice that they now found
(20) themselves very unpleasantly situated in Barchester.
        So far, the character of Charlotte Stanhope is not
    unprepossessing. But it remains to be said, that the
    influence which she had in her family, though it had
    been used to a certain extent for their worldly well-
(25) being, had not been used to their real benefit, as it
    might have been. She had aided her father in his
    indifference to his professional duties, counselling
    him that his livings were as much his individual

property as the estates of his elder brother were the
(30) property of that worthy peer. She had for years past
stifled every little rising wish for a return to England
which the reverend doctor had from time to time
expressed. She had encouraged her mother in her
idleness in order that she herself might be mistress
(35) and manager of the Stanhope household. She had
encouraged and fostered the follies of her sister,
though she was always willing, and often able, to
protect her from their probable result. She had done
her best, and had thoroughly succeeded in spoiling
(40) her brother, and turning him loose upon the world
an idle man without a profession, and without a
shilling that he could call his own.

Miss Stanhope was a clever woman, able to talk
on most subjects, and quite indifferent as to what
(45) the subject was. She prided herself on her freedom
from English prejudice, and she might have added,
from feminine delicacy. On religion she was a pure
freethinker, and with much want of true affection,
delighted to throw out her own views before the
(50) troubled mind of her father. To have shaken what
remained of his Church of England faith would have
gratified her much; but the idea of his abandoning
his preferment in the church had never once presented
itself to her mind. How could he indeed, when
(55) he had no income from any other source?

6. The passage as a whole is best characterized as

   (A) a description of the members of a family
   (B) a portrait of a young woman's moral and intellectual temperament
   (C) an illustration of the evils of egotism
   (D) an analysis of family dynamics in aristocratic society
   (E) a contrast between a virtuous daughter and her disreputable family

7. The tone of the passage is best described as

(A) self-righteous and moralistic
(B) satirical and candid
(C) sympathetic and sentimental
(D) bitter and disillusioned
(E) indifferent and unfeeling

8. On the basis of the passage, which of the following statements about Dr. Stanhope can most logically be made?

(A) He is even more indolent than his wife.
(B) He resents having surrendered his authority to his daughter.
(C) He feels remorse for his professional misconduct.
(D) He has little left of his initial religious beliefs.
(E) He has disinherited his son without a shilling.

9. It can be inferred from the passage that Charlotte's mother (lines 33–35) is which of the following?

I.   An affectionate wife and mother
II. A model of the domestic arts
III. A woman of unassertive character

(A) I only
(B) II only
(C) III only
(D) I and III only
(E) II and III only

10. The passage suggests that Charlotte possesses all of the following characteristics EXCEPT

(A) an inappropriate flirtatiousness
(B) a lack of reverence
(C) a materialistic nature
(D) a managing disposition
(E) a touch of coarseness

The following passage on the nature of the surface of the earth is taken from a basic geology text.

Of the 197 million square miles making up the surface of the globe, 71 percent is covered by interconnecting bodies of marine water; the Pacific Ocean
Line alone covers half the earth and averages near 14,000
(5) feet in depth. The *continents*—Eurasia, Africa, North America, South America, Australia, and Antarctica —are the portions of the *continental masses* rising above sea level. The submerged borders of the continental masses are the *continental shelves*, beyond
(10) which lie the deep-sea basins.

The oceans attain their greatest depths not in their central parts, but in certain elongated furrows, or long narrow troughs, called *deeps*. These profound troughs have a peripheral arrangement,
(15) notably around the borders of the Pacific and Indian oceans. The position of the deeps near the continental masses suggests that the deeps, like the highest mountains, are of recent origin, since otherwise they would have been filled with waste from the
(20) lands. This suggestion is strengthened by the fact that the deeps are frequently the sites of world-shaking earthquakes. For example, the "tidal wave" that in April, 1946, caused widespread destruction along Pacific coasts resulted from a strong earth-
(25) quake on the floor of the Aleutian Deep.

The topography of the ocean floors is none too well known, since in great areas the available soundings are hundreds or even thousands of miles apart. However, the floor of the Atlantic is becoming fairly
(30) well known as a result of special surveys since 1920. A broad, well-defined ridge—the mid-Atlantic ridge—runs north and south between Africa and the

two Americas, and numerous other major irregular-
ities diversify the Atlantic floor. Closely spaced
(35) soundings show that many parts of the oceanic floors
are as rugged as mountainous regions of the continents. Use of the recently perfected method of echo
sounding is rapidly enlarging our knowledge of
submarine topography. During World War II great
(40) strides were made in mapping submarine surfaces,
particularly in many parts of the vast Pacific basin.
     The continents stand on the average 2870 feet—
slightly more than half a mile—above sea level.
North America averages 2300 feet; Europe averages
(45) only 1150 feet; and Asia, the highest of the larger
continental subdivisions, averages 3200 feet. The
highest point on the globe, Mount Everest in the
Himalayas, is 29,000 feet above the sea; and as the
greatest known depth in the sea is over 35,000 feet,
(50) the maximum *relief* (that is, the difference in altitude
between the lowest and highest points) exceeds
64,000 feet, or exceeds 12 miles. The continental
masses and the deep-sea basins are relief features
of the first order; the deeps, ridges, and volcanic
(55) cones that diversify the sea floor, as well as the
plains, plateaus, and mountains of the continents,
are relief features of the second order. The lands
are unendingly subject to a complex of activities
summarized in the term *erosion*, which first sculp-
(60) tures them in great detail and then tends to reduce
them ultimately to sealevel. The modeling of the
landscape by weather, running water, and other
agents is apparent to the keenly observant eye and
causes thinking people to speculate on what must
(65) be the final result of the ceaseless wearing down
of the lands. Long before there was a science of
geology, Shakespeare wrote "the revolution of the
times makes mountains level."

11. It can be inferred from lines 1–4 that the largest ocean is the

    (A) Atlantic
    (B) Pacific
    (C) Indian
    (D) Aleutian Deep
    (E) Arctic

12. According to lines 15–17, the peripheral furrows or *deeps* are found

    (A) only in the Pacific and Indian oceans
    (B) near earthquakes
    (C) near the shore
    (D) in the center of the ocean
    (E) to be 14,000 feet in depth in the Pacific

13. The passage indicates that the continental masses

    (A) comprise 29 percent of the earth's surface
    (B) consist of six continents
    (C) rise above sea level
    (D) are partially underwater
    (E) are relief features of the second order

14. The "revolution of the times" as used in the final sentence means

    (A) the passage of years
    (B) the current rebellion
    (C) the science of geology
    (D) the action of the ocean floor
    (E) the overthrow of natural forces

15. From this passage, it can be inferred that earthquakes

    (A) occur only in the peripheral furrows
    (B) occur more frequently in newly formed land or sea formations
    (C) are a prime cause of soil erosion
    (D) will ultimately "make mountains level"
    (E) are caused by the weight of water pressing on the earth's surface

The following passage is taken from the introduction to the catalog of a major exhibition of Flemish tapestries.

Tapestries are made on looms. Their distinctive
weave is basically simple: the colored weft threads

interface regularly with the monochrome warps, as
Line   in darning or plain cloth, but as they do so, they form
(5)   a design by reversing their direction when a change
of color is needed. The wefts are beaten down to
cover the warps completely. The result is a design
or picture that is the fabric itself, not one laid upon
a ground like an embroidery, a print, or brocading.
(10)   The back and front of a tapestry show the same
design. The weaver always follows a preexisting
model, generally a drawing or painting, known as the
cartoon, which in most cases he reproduces as exactly
as he can. Long training is needed to become a pro-
(15)   fessional tapestry weaver. It can take as much as a
year to produce a yard of very finely woven tapestry.
Tapestry-woven fabrics have been made from
China to Peru and from very early times to the present day, but large wall hangings in this technique,
(20)   mainly of wool, are typically Northern European.
Few examples predating the late fourteenth century
have survived, but from about 1400 tapestries were
an essential part of aristocratic life. The prince or
great nobleman sent his plate and his tapestries
(25)   ahead of him to furnish his castles before his arrival
as he traveled through his domains; both had the
same function, to display his wealth and social
position. It has frequently been suggested that
tapestries helped to heat stone-walled rooms, but
(30)   this is a modern idea; comfort was of minor importance in the Middle Ages. Tapestries were portable
grandeur, instant splendor, taking the place, north
of the Alps, of painted frescoes further south. They
were hung without gaps between them, covering
(35)   entire walls and often doors as well. Only very occasionally were they made as individual works of art
such as altar frontals. They were usually commissioned

or bought as sets, or "chambers," and constituted
the most important furnishings of any grand room,
(40) except for the display of plate, throughout the Middle
Ages and the sixteenth century. Later, woven silks,
ornamental wood carving, stucco decoration, and
painted leather gradually replaced tapestry as
expensive wall coverings, until at last wallpaper was
(45) introduced in the late eighteenth century and
eventually swept away almost everything else.
　　　By the end of the eighteenth century, the "tapestry-
room" [a room with every available wall surface
covered with wall hangings] was no longer fashion-
(50) able: paper had replaced wall coverings of wool and
silk. Tapestries, of course, were still made, but in
the nineteenth century they often seem to have been
produced mainly as individual works of art that
astonish by their resemblance to oil paintings, tours
(55) de force woven with a remarkably large number
of wefts per inch. In England during the second
half of the century, William Morris attempted to
reverse this trend and to bring tapestry weaving
back to its true principles, those he considered to
(60) have governed it in the Middle Ages. He imitated
medieval tapestries in both style and technique,
using few warps to the inch, but he did not make
sets; the original function for which tapestry is so
admirably suited—completely covering the walls
(65) of a room and providing sumptuous surroundings
for a life of pomp and splendor—could not be
revived. Morris's example has been followed, though
with less imitation of medieval style, by many
weavers of the present century, whose coarsely
(70) woven cloths hang like single pictures and can be
admired as examples of contemporary art.

16. Tapestry weaving may be characterized as which of the following?

    I. Time-consuming
    II. Spontaneous in concept
    III. Faithful to an original

    (A) I only
    (B) III only
    (C) I and II only
    (D) I and III only
    (E) II and III only

17. The word "distinctive" in line 1 means

    (A) characteristic
    (B) stylish
    (C) discriminatory
    (D) eminent
    (E) articulate

18. Renaissance nobles carried tapestries with them to demonstrate their

    (A) piety
    (B) consequence
    (C) aesthetic judgment
    (D) need for privacy
    (E) dislike for cold

19. In contrast to nineteenth century tapestries, contemporary tapestries

    (A) are displayed in sets of panels
    (B) echo medieval themes
    (C) faithfully copy oil paintings
    (D) have a less fine weave
    (E) indicate the owner's social position

20. The primary purpose of the passage is to

    (A) explain the process of tapestry making
    (B) contrast Eastern and Western schools of tapestry
    (C) analyze the reasons for the decline in popularity of tapestries
    (D) provide a historical perspective on tapestry making
    (E) advocate a return to a more colorful way of life

Exercise C

The questions that follow the two passages in this section relate to the content of both, and to their relationship. The correct response may be stated outright in the passages or merely suggested.

Questions 1–13 are based on the following passages.

The following passages are excerpted from popular articles on dolphins, the first dating from the 1960s, the second written in 1990.

Passage 1

Most of the intelligent land animals have prehensile, grasping organs for exploring their environment—hands in human beings and their anthropoid relatives, the sensitive
Line inquiring trunk in the elephant. One of the surprising things
(5) about the dolphin is that his superior brain is unaccompanied by any type of manipulative organ. He has, however, a remarkable range-finding ability involving some sort of echo-sounding. Perhaps this acute sense—far more accurate than any that human ingenuity has been able to devise artificially
(10) —brings him greater knowledge of his watery surroundings than might at first seem possible. Human beings think of intelligence as geared to things. The hand and the tool are to us the unconscious symbols of our intellectual attainment. It is difficult for us to visualize another kind of lonely, almost
(15) disembodied intelligence floating in the wavering green fairy-land of the sea—an intelligence possibly near or comparable to our own but without hands to build, to transmit knowledge by writing, or to alter by one hairsbreadth the planet's surface. Yet at the same time there are indications that this is a
(20) warm, friendly, and eager intelligence quite capable of coming to the assistance of injured companions and striving to

rescue them from drowning. Dolphins left the land when
mammalian brains were still small and primitive. Without the
stimulus provided by agile exploring fingers, these great sea
(25) mammals have yet taken a divergent road toward intelligence
of a high order. Hidden in their sleek bodies is an impressively elaborated instrument, the reason for whose appearance is a complete enigma. It is as though both the human
being and the dolphin were each part of some great eye
(30) which yearned to look both outward on eternity and inward
to the sea's heart—that fertile entity like the mind in its
swarming and grotesque life.

Passage 2

Nothing about dolphins has been more widely or pas-
sionately discussed over the centuries than their supposed
(35) intelligence and communicative abilities. In fact, a persistent
dogma holds that dolphins are among the most intelligent of
animals and that they communicate with one another in complex ways. Implicit in this argument is the belief that dolphin
cultures are at least as ancient and rich as our own. To sup-
(40) port the claim of high intelligence amongst dolphins, proponents note that they have large brains, live in societies
marked as much by co-operative as by competitive interactions and rapidly learn the artificial tasks given to them in
captivity. Indeed, dolphins are clearly capable of learning
(45) through observation and have good memories. People who
spend time with captive dolphins are invariably impressed by
their sense of humor, playfulness, quick comprehension of
body language, command of situations, mental agility, and
emotional resilience. Individual dolphins have distinctive per-
(50) sonalities and trainers often speak of being trained by their
subjects, rather than the other way round.

The extremely varied repertoires of sounds made by
dolphins are often invoked as *prima facie* evidence of

advanced communication abilities. In addition, some "scien-
(55) tific" experiments done by John Lilly and his associates
during the 1950s and 1960s were claimed to show that dolphins communicate not only with one another but also with
humans, mimicking human speech and reaching out across
the boundaries that divide us.

(60)   These conclusions about dolphin intelligence and communication have not withstood critical scrutiny. While they
have fueled romantic speculation, their net impact has been
to mislead. Rather than allowing dolphins to be discovered
and appreciated for what they are, Lilly's vision has forced us
(65) to measure these animals' value according to how close they
come to equalling or exceeding our own intelligence, virtue,
and spiritual development.

          The issues of dolphin intelligence and communication
have been inseparable in most people's minds, and the pre-
(70) sumed existence of one has been taken as proof of the other,
a classic case of begging the question. Not surprisingly then,
most experiments to evaluate dolphin intelligence have
measured the animals' capacity for cognitive processing as
exhibited in their understanding of the rudiments of
(75) language.

          From the early work of researchers like Dwight Batteau
and Jarvis Bastian through the more recent work of Louis
Herman and associates, dolphins have been asked to accept
simple information, in the form of acoustic or visual symbols
(80) representing verbs and nouns, and then to act on the information following a set of commands from the experimenter.

          The widely publicized results have been somewhat dis-
appointing. Although they have demonstrated that dolphins
do have the primary skills necessary to support understand-
(85) ing and use of a language, they have not distinguished the
dolphins from other animals in this respect. For example,
some seals, animals we do not normally cite as members of
the intellectual or communicative elite, have been found to
have the same basic capabilities.

(90)   What, then, do the results of experiments to date mean?
Either we have not devised adequate tests to permit us to
detect, measure, and rank intelligence as a measure of a
given species' ability to communicate, or we must acknowledge that the characteristics that we regard as rudimentary
(95) evidence of intelligence are held more commonly by many
"lower" animals than we previously thought.

1. According to Passage 1, which of the following statements about dolphins is true?

   (A) They have always been water-dwelling creatures.
   (B) They at one time possessed prehensile organs.
   (C) They lived on land in prehistoric times.
   (D) Their brains are no longer mammalian in nature.
   (E) They developed brains to compensate for the lack of a prehensile
       organ.

2. The author of Passage 1 suggests that human failure to understand
   the intelligence of the dolphin is due to

   (A) the inadequacy of human range-finding equipment
   (B) a lack of knowledge about the sea
   (C) the want of a common language
   (D) the primitive origins of the human brain
   (E) the human inclination to judge other life by our own

3. In Passage 1, the author's primary purpose is apparently to

   (A) examine the dolphin's potential for surpassing humankind
   (B) question the need for prehensile organs in human development
   (C) refute the theory that dolphins are unable to alter their physical
       environment
   (D) reassess the nature and extent of dolphin intelligence
   (E) indicate the superiority of human intelligence over that of the
       dolphin

4. The word "acute" in line 8 means

   (A) excruciating
   (B) severe
   (C) keen
   (D) sudden and intense
   (E) brief in duration

5. The "impressively elaborated instrument" referred to in lines 26–27 is best interpreted to mean which of the following?

   (A) A concealed manipulative organ
   (B) An artificial range-finding device
   (C) A complex, intelligent brain
   (D) The dolphin's hidden eye
   (E) An apparatus for producing musical sounds

6. According to the author's simile in line 31, the human mind and the heart of the sea are alike in that both

   (A) teem with exotic forms of life
   (B) argue in support of intelligence
   (C) are necessary to the evolution of dolphins
   (D) are directed outward
   (E) share a penchant for the grotesque

7. Which of the following best characterizes the tone of Passage 1?

   (A) Restrained skepticism
   (B) Pedantic assertion
   (C) Wondering admiration
   (D) Amused condescension
   (E) Ironic speculation

8. The author of Passage 2 puts quotation marks around the word *scientific* in lines 54–55 to indicate he

   (A) is faithfully reproducing Lilly's own words
   (B) intends to define the word later in the passage
   (C) believes the reader is unfamiliar with the word as used by Lilly
   (D) advocates adhering to the scientific method in all experiments
   (E) has some doubts as to how scientific those experiments were

9. The author of Passage 2 maintains that the writings of Lilly and his associates have

   (A) overstated the extent of dolphin intelligence
   (B) been inadequately scrutinized by critics
   (C) measured the worth of the dolphin family
   (D) underrated dolphins as intelligent beings
   (E) established criteria for evaluating dolphin intelligence

10. By calling the argument summarized in lines 68–70 a classic case of begging the question, the author of Passage 2 indicates he views it with

(A) trepidation
(B) optimism
(C) detachment
(D) skepticism
(E) credulity

11. Which of the following would most undercut the studies on which the author bases his conclusion in lines 90–96?

(A) Evidence proving dolphin linguistic abilities to be far superior to those of other mammals
(B) An article recording attempts by seals and walruses to communicate with human beings
(C) The reorganization of current intelligence tests by species and level of difficulty
(D) A reassessment of the definition of the term "lower animals"
(E) The establishment of a project to develop new tests to detect intelligence in animals

12. The author of Passage 2 would find Passage 1

(A) typical of the attitudes of Lilly and his associates
(B) remarkable for the perspective it offers
(C) indicative of the richness of dolphin culture
(D) supportive of his fundamental point of view
(E) intriguing for its far-reaching conclusions

13. Compared to Passage 2, Passage 1 is

(A) more figurative
(B) less obscure
(C) more objective
(D) more current
(E) less speculative

Answer Key

Exercise A

1. **B**	6. **A**	11. **D**	16. **B**
2. **D**	7. **C**	12. **E**	17. **E**
3. **B**	8. **E**	13. **A**	
4. **A**	9. **E**	14. **C**	
5. **D**	10. **E**	15. **C**	

Exercise B

1. **C**	6. **B**	11. **B**	16. **D**
2. **C**	7. **B**	12. **C**	17. **A**
3. **A**	8. **D**	13. **D**	18. **B**
4. **E**	9. **C**	14. **A**	19. **D**
5. **D**	10. **A**	15. **B**	20. **D**

Exercise C

1. **C**	5. **C**	9. **A**	13. **A**
2. **E**	6. **A**	10. **D**	
3. **D**	7. **C**	11. **A**	
4. **C**	8. **E**	12. **A**	

Answer Explanations

Exercise A

1. **B** The opening lines indicate that the narrator is *reflecting on his feelings*. Throughout the passage he uses words like "miserable," "ashamed," and "discontented" to describe his emotional state. Choice A is incorrect. The narrator does not analyze or dissect a change in attitude; he describes an ongoing attitude.

Choice C is incorrect. The passage gives an example of emotional self-awareness, not of political consciousness.

Choice D is incorrect. The narrator condemns rather than defends the longings that brought him discontentment.

Choice E is incorrect. The narrator criticizes himself, not young people in general.

2. **D** The references to the forge (line 11) and the anvil (line 19) support Choice D. None of the other choices are suggested by the passage.

3. **B** Note the adjectives used to describe Joe: "faithful," "industrious," "kind." These are virtues, and Joe is fundamentally *virtuous*.

Choice A is incorrect. Joe is plain and hardworking, not eminent and distinguished.

Choice C is incorrect. The passage portrays not Joe but the narrator as desiring to be independent.

Choice D is incorrect. It is unsupported by the passage.

Choice E is incorrect. The narrator thinks his life is coarse; he thinks Joe is virtuous.

4. **A** Choice A is supported by lines 12 and 13 in which the narrator states he "would not have had Miss Havisham and Estella see (his home) on any account."

Choices B and C are incorrect. Nothing in the passage suggests either might be the case.

Choice D is incorrect. Though the narrator may not show himself as hard-working, nothing in the passage suggests laziness led to his discontent.

Choice E is incorrect. Nothing in the passage suggests sinfulness has prompted his discontent. In addition, although ingratitude may play a part in his discontent, shame at his background plays a far greater part.

5. **D** In lines 34 and 35, the narrator manages to say something good about his youthful self: "I am glad to know I never breathed a murmur to Joe." He gives himself credit for *concealing his despondency*.

Choices A and B are incorrect. The narrator gives Joe all the credit for his having worked industriously and for his not having run away to become a soldier.

Choices C and E are incorrect. They are unsupported by the passage.

6. **A** Throughout the second paragraph, the author pays particular attention to Maria's appearance, her behavior, her effect on others. If she had been *introduced* previously in the text, there would be no need to present these details about her at this point in the passage.

7. **C** The descriptions of the bright and shiny kitchen where you "could see yourself in the big copper boilers" and of tiny, witch-like Maria with her long nose and long chin belong to the realm of *fairy tales*.

8. **E** The passage mentions the matron twice: once, in the opening line, where she gives Maria permission to leave work early; once, in lines 15 and 16, where she pays Maria a compliment. Given this context, we can logically infer that Maria views the matron positively, finding her a *benevolent* or kindly *supervisor*.
Choices A, B, and C are incorrect. Nothing in the passage suggests Maria has a negative view of the matron.
Choice D is incorrect. Given Maria's relatively menial position, it is unlikely she and the matron would be close or intimate friends.

9. **E** To slice loaves so neatly and invisibly takes a great deal of care. The author specifically states that Maria has cut the loaves. Not only that, he emphasizes the importance of her having done so by placing this statement at the end of the paragraph (a key position). As the subsequent paragraphs point up, Maria is hungry for compliments. Just as she takes pride in her peacemaking, she takes pride in her ability to slice barmbracks evenly.

10. **E** Maria helps others to compromise or become reconciled; she herself is not necessarily unwilling to compromise.
The passage suggests that Choice A is characteristic of Maria. She speaks soothingly and respectfully. Therefore, Choice A is incorrect.
The passage suggests that Choice B is characteristic of Maria. Maria's response to Ginger Mooney's toast shows her enjoyment of being noticed in this way. Therefore, Choice B is incorrect.
The passage suggests that Choice C is characteristic of Maria. Maria's obedience to the cook and to the matron shows her respect for authority. Therefore, Choice C is incorrect.
The passage suggests that Choice D is characteristic of Maria. Maria's disappointed shyness and her forced laughter about a wedding ring and husband show that she has wistful dreams of marriage. Therefore, Choice D is incorrect.

11. **D** By stating that his joy at his return "made him communicative and chatty in a very unusual degree" (lines 5 and 6), the opening paragraph implies that Sir Thomas is usually *more restrained in speech*. Choice D is correct.

    Choice A is incorrect. Nothing in the passage suggests he is usually unwelcome in his own home.

    Choices B and C are incorrect. Neither is supported by the opening paragraph.

    Choice E is incorrect. Sir Thomas's delight at finding his family together "exactly as he could have wished" indicates he does not lack family feeling.

    Remember, when asked to make inferences, base your answers on what the passage implies, not what it states directly.

12. **E** The opening sentence of the second paragraph states that none of the members of his family listened to him with such "unbroken unalloyed enjoyment" as his wife did. Her enjoyment was complete and unmixed with other emotions. This suggests that others in the group face Sir Thomas's arrival not with complete pleasure but *with mixed emotions*.

    Choice A is incorrect. It is unsupported by the passage.

    Choice B is incorrect. Lady Bertram's fluttered or discomposed state on his arrival indicates her surprise.

    Choice C is incorrect. Lines 12 and 13 indicate that Sir Thomas did not expect to find his whole family at home. Therefore, he had not timed his arrival to coincide with a reunion.

    Choice D is incorrect. Sir Thomas has had to seek out the butler and confide the news of his arrival to him (lines 41–43). Therefore, the servants had not expected his arrival.

13. **A** The phrases "coming unexpectedly as he did" (line 13) and "his sudden arrival" (line 17) support the idea that Sir Thomas has returned unexpectedly. Note that these key phrases are found in the closing sentence of the first paragraph and in the opening sentence of the second paragraph. Sir Thomas's unexpected return is central to the passage.

    Choice B is incorrect. Although the persons talking belong to the upper classes, as a title "The Conversation of the Upper Class" is too vague.

    Choice C is incorrect. Mrs. Norris's complaint or grievance (the subject of the third paragraph) is too narrow in scope to be an appropriate title for the passage as a whole.

Choice D is incorrect. Although Lady Bertram is quite pleased to have her husband home again, their reunion is placid rather than emotional or romantic.

Choice E is incorrect. Although Sir Thomas gives an account of his voyage in the first paragraph, the passage places its emphasis on the reactions of his family to his surprising return.

Remember, when asked to choose a title, watch out for choices that are too specific or too broad.

14. **C** Examine Lady Bertram's behavior carefully. She is not agitated (though she is "nearer agitation than she had been for the last twenty years"). She is so moved by her husband's return that she actually moves her lap dog from the sofa and makes room for her husband. Clearly, the author is making fun of Lady Bertram's idio-syncratic behavior, describing her quirky reactions in a lightly mocking, *gently ironic* way.

15. **C** The author italicizes the word *her* for emphasis. Lady Bertram had no worries to take away from her pleasure at Sir Thomas's return. However, she is unusual in this. The author's emphasis on her happiness *serves to suggest that others in the group have reason to be less happy about Sir Thomas's arrival.*

16. **B** Refusing to be provoked by Mrs. Norris's interruptions, Sir Thomas demonstrates *patient forbearance* or restraint.

Choice A is incorrect. Line 59 states that Sir Thomas "could not be provoked." Therefore, he showed no irritation.

Choice C is incorrect. Sir Thomas remarks courteously on Mrs. Norris's anxiety for everybody's comfort (lines 59 and 60). This implies that he in general approves rather than disapproves of her concern.

Choice D is incorrect. It is unsupported by the passage.

Choice E is incorrect. Given Mrs. Norris's interruptions of his story, it is unlikely Sir Thomas would view her with *unmixed delight.*

17. **E** Mrs. Norris has looked forward to spreading the news of Sir Thomas's return (or of his death!). The office she has lost is that of herald or *message-bearer*.

Choice A is incorrect. Mrs. Norris wishes to give orders to the butler, not to be the butler.

Choice B is incorrect for much the same reason.

Choice C is incorrect. Mrs. Norris is the sister of Sir Thomas's wife; the passage does not indicate that she has any desire to be his wife.

Choice D is incorrect. Mrs. Norris wishes to give news of the traveler, not to be the traveler.

Exercise B

1. **C** Each paragraph discusses some important feature or *significant characteristic* of Eskimo art (its mystical quality, realistic understanding of anatomy, humor, etc.).

2. **C** The author's use of such terms as "powerful ability" (line 2), "masters in the understanding of animal anatomy" (line 28), and "living excitement" (line 55) indicates an *admiration* for the art.

3. **A** The author's comment in lines 16 and 17 that Eskimo art "has a freedom unsullied (unstained or undefiled) by any kind of formalized training" suggests that he would agree that formal training might defile or *destroy an artist's originality* and freedom of expression.

4. **E** Each example the author provides describes a type of Eskimo sculpture (man driving a caribou, woman holding a child, geese flying, polar bear charging) and gives the reader a sense of its *quality and variety*.

5. **D** Use the process of elimination to answer this question.
   Choice A is incorrect. Line 43 states "there is much evidence of humor" in Eskimo art.
   Choice B is incorrect. Humor in Eskimo carvings "may be subtle" (line 47).
   Choice C is incorrect. Eskimo carvings reveal "the passionate feelings of a vital people" (line 9); they possess *emotional depth*.
   Choice E is incorrect. Eskimo sculptors are "masters in the understanding of animal anatomy" (line 28). Their works are characterized by *anatomical accuracy*.
   Only Choice D is left. It is the correct answer. If "no one can accurately define the right way or wrong way to create a carving" (lines 48 and 49), clearly Eskimo carving lacks *stylistic uniformity*.

6. **B** The passage as a whole is a portrait of Charlotte Stanhope's moral and intellectual temperament or character. The opening sentence

of each paragraph describes some aspect of her behavior or character which the paragraph then goes on to develop.

Remember, when asked to find the main idea, be sure to check the opening and summary sentences of each paragraph.

Choice A is incorrect. While the various members of the family are described, they are described only in relationship to Charlotte.

Choice C is incorrect. Although Charlotte may well be selfish or egotistical, she does do some good for others. The passage does not illustrate the evils of egotism.

Choice D is incorrect. The passage analyzes Charlotte; it discusses the members of her family only in relationship to her.

Choice E is incorrect. While Charlotte has her virtues, the passage stresses her faults. While her family may not be described as admirable, nothing suggests that they are disreputable (not well-esteemed or well-regarded).

7. **B** The author presents Charlotte *candidly* and openly: her faults are not concealed. The author also presents her *satirically*: her weaknesses and those of her family are mocked or made fun of. If you find the characters in a passage foolish or pompous, the author may well be writing satirically.

Choice A is incorrect. While the author is concerned with Charlotte's moral character, he is not *moralistic* or *self-righteous*; he is describing her character, not preaching a sermon against her.

Choice C is incorrect. The author is unsympathetic to Charlotte's faults and he is not *sentimental* or emotionally excessive about her.

Choice D is incorrect. *Bitterness* is too strong a term to describe the author's tone. He has no reason to be bitter.

Choice E is incorrect. While the author's tone is not highly emotional, it is better to describe it as satiric than as *unfeeling*.

8. **D** Lines 50 and 51 mention the troubled mind of Dr. Stanhope, and state that Charlotte would have enjoyed shaking "*what remained* of his Church of England faith." The phrase "what remained" implies that little is left of Dr. Stanhope's original religious faith.

Choice A is incorrect. There is no comparison made between the two elder Stanhopes. Both are *indolent* (lazy).

Choice B is incorrect. Since only Charlotte could persuade her father to look after his affairs (lines 14 and 15), he apparently was willing to let her manage matters for him and willingly surrendered his authority.

Choice C is incorrect. There is no evidence in the passage that Dr. Stanhope feels regret or remorse.

Choice E is incorrect. While Charlotte's brother is described as moneyless (lines 41 and 42), there is no evidence in the passage that Dr. Stanhope has disinherited him.

9. **C** There is no evidence in the passage that Charlotte's mother is an affectionate wife and mother; similarly, there is no evidence that she is excellent in the "domestic arts" (making tea; managing the household—the very tasks assumed by Charlotte).

Statements I and II are incorrect. Only Statement III is correct. The sole mention of Charlotte's mother (lines 33–35) states that she was encouraged in her idleness by Charlotte. She lacks the willpower to resist Charlotte's encouragements. Thus, she shows herself to be a woman of unassertive, pliable character.

10. **A** The first paragraph emphasizes that Charlotte "in no way affected the graces of youth." Her manner is that of an assured mistress of a household, not a flirt.

Choice B is incorrect. Charlotte is a free-thinker (one who denies established beliefs) and thus lacks reverence or respect for religion.

Choice C is incorrect. Charlotte is concerned with her family's worldly well-being and makes her father attend to his material concerns. Thus, she has a materialistic nature.

Choice D is incorrect. Charlotte manages everything and everybody.

Choice E is incorrect. Charlotte's coarseness (vulgarity; crudeness) is implied in the reference to her "freedom...from feminine delicacy" (lines 45–47).

11. **B** We are told that 71 percent of the earth is covered by water and that the Pacific Ocean covers half the earth. The Pacific is obviously the largest ocean.

12. **C** The peripheral furrows or *deeps* are discussed in lines 13–25. We are told that these deeps are near the continental masses, and, therefore, near the shore.

13. **D** The last sentence of the first paragraph discusses the submerged or *underwater* portions of the continental masses.

Key Words: masses, percent, sea level, submerged, relief.

14. **A** Terms such as "unendingly," "ultimately," and "ceaseless" indicate that the mountains are made level over an enormous *passage of years*.

15. **B** The passage states that the *deeps*, the site of frequent earth-quakes, are of recent origin: they were formed comparatively recently. This suggests that newly formed land and sea forma-tions may have a greater frequency of earthquake occurrence than older, more stable formations.

Remember, when asked to make inferences, base your answers on what the passage implies, not what it states directly.

16. **D** Tapestry weaving is time-consuming, taking "as much as a year to produce a yard." In addition, it is faithful to the original ("The weaver always follows a preexisting model.") It is not, however, spontaneous in concept.

17. **A** The author mentions tapestry's distinctive or *characteristic* weave as something that distinguishes tapestry-woven materials from other fabrics (prints, brocades, etc.).

18. **B** By using tapestries "to display his wealth and social position," the nobleman is using them to demonstrate his *consequence* or importance.

19. **D** In comparison to the tightly-woven tapestries of the nineteenth century, present day wall-hangings are described as "coarsely woven cloths." Thus, they *have a less fine weave* than their prede-cessors.

20. **D** The passage explains the process of tapestry making and men-tions that large wall-hangings are Western rather than Eastern in origin. Choices A and B do not reflect the passage's primary pur-pose. This purpose is to *provide an historical perspective on tapestry making*.

Exercise C

1. **C** Passage 1 states: "Dolphins left the land when mammalian brains were still small and primitive" (lines 22 and 23). This indicates that dolphins were once *land* animals, mammals like ourselves, whose evolutionary development took them back into the sea.

2. **E** The passage indicates that human beings think of intelligence in terms of our own ability to manipulate our environment—our abil-ity to build and do all sorts of things with our hands. Since dol-phins have no hands, we have trouble appreciating their high level of intelligence because of our *inclination to judge other life by our own*.

3. **D** Passage 1 attempts to *reassess the nature and extent of dolphin intelligence*, first giving reasons why human beings may have trouble appreciating how intelligent dolphins really are and then, in the concluding sentence, reflecting how dolphin intelligence (that looks "inward to the sea's heart") may complement human intelligence (that looks "outward on eternity").

4. **C** The dolphin's acute echo-sounding sense is a sharp, *keen* sense that enables the dolphin to sound or measure the ocean depths by using echoes.

5. **C** The entire passage has concentrated on the dolphin's brain, so it is safe to assume that this is what is meant by "impressively elaborated instrument." The items listed in the other answer choices have not been mentioned. Note that Choice B, an artificial range-finding device, is incorrect because the dolphin's range-finding ability is entirely natural, not artificial.

6. **A** The sea's heart is like the human mind in that it swarms or *teems* (abounds) with grotesque or *exotic forms of life*.

7. **C** The author's tone is distinctly *admiring*. The passage speaks of the dolphins' "remarkable range-finding ability," mentions their care for each other, and repeatedly praises dolphin intelligence.

8. **E** The quotation marks here indicate that the word in quotes is being used in a special sense (often an ironic one). In this case, as the next paragraph makes abundantly clear, the author is critical of both the results and the influence of Lilly's experiments. He *has some doubts as to how scientific those experiments were*.

9. **A** According to the author of Passage 2, by claiming that "dolphins communicate not only with one another but also with humans, mimicking human speech and reaching out across the boundaries that divide us" (lines 56–59), Lilly and his associates have *overstated* their case, misrepresenting *the extent of dolphin intelligence*. Choice B is incorrect. In stating that Lilly's conclusions have not withstood (stood up against) critical scrutiny, the author indicates that they *have* been critically scrutinized to an appropriate degree.

10. **D** "Begging the question" refers to assuming the truth of the very point whose truth or falsehood you're trying to establish. The author of Passage 2 considers the reasoning in this argument flawed; he views it with doubt or *skepticism*.

11. **A** Proof that dolphins are *far superior in linguistic capability* to seals and other mammals clearly would contradict the results of the studies the author cites and would thus *undercut* or weaken their impact.

12. **A** In its glorification of dolphin intelligence as something that equals or possibly exceeds human intelligence, the author of Passage 2 would find Passage 1 *typical of the attitudes of Lilly and his associates*.

13. **A** Passage 1 is filled with images. The sea is a "wavering green fairyland." The dolphin's brain is an "impressively elaborated instrument." Mammals take "a divergent road." The passage concludes with an elaborate simile. It is clearly *more figurative* than Passage 2.

    Choice B is incorrect. With its enigmatic references to some "impressively elaborated instrument" and to a "great eye" staring at eternity, Passage 1 is far more *obscure* than Passage 2.

    Choice C is incorrect. Passage 1 is heavily slanted in favor of the superiority of dolphin intelligence. It is not *more objective* or impartial than Passage 2, which attempts to give a short survey of research on dolphin intelligence, summing up current experiments and providing historical background.

    Choice D is incorrect. The italicized introduction indicates that Passage 2 was written almost thirty years after Passage 1. By definition, it presents a more *current*, up-to-date view of the topic. *Always pay attention to information contained in the introductions to the reading passages.*

    Choice E is incorrect. Passage 1's conclusion is sheer conjecture or *speculation*.

4 Building Your Vocabulary

Recognizing the meaning of words is essential to comprehending what you read. The more you stumble over unfamiliar words in a text, the more you have to take time out to look up words in your dictionary, the more likely you are to wind up losing track of what the author has to say.

To succeed in college, you must develop a college-level vocabulary. The time you put in now learning vocabulary-building techniques for the SAT will pay off later, and not just on the day of the test. In this chapter you will find a fundamental tool that will help you build your vocabulary: Barron's SAT High-Frequency Word List.

No matter how little time you have before you take the SAT, you can familiarize yourself with the sort of vocabulary you will be facing on the test. Look over the words on our SAT High-Frequency Word List: each of these words, ranging from everyday words such as *abstract* and *relevant* to less commonly known ones such as *abstruse* and *surreptitious*, has appeared (as answer choices or as question words) from five to twenty times on SATs published in the past two decades.

Not only will looking over the SAT High-Frequency Word List reassure you that you *do* know some SAT-type words, but also it may well help you on the actual day of the test. These words have turned up on recent tests; some of them may turn up on the test you take.

For those of you who intend to work your way through the *entire* SAT High-Frequency Word List and feel the need for a plan, we recommend that you follow the procedures described below in order to use the list most profitably:

1. Divide the list into groups of twenty words.
2. Allot a definite time each day for the study of a group.
3. Devote at least one hour to each group.
4. First go through the group looking at the short, simple-looking words (6 letters at most). Mark those you don't know. In studying, pay particular attention to them.
5. Go through the group again looking at the longer words. Pay particular attention to words with more than one meaning and familiar-looking words which have unusual definitions that come as a surprise to you. Study these secondary definitions.
6. List unusual words on index cards that you can shuffle and review from time to time. (Study no more than 5 cards at a time.)
7. Use the illustrative sentences as models and make up new sentences of your own.
8. In making up new sentences, use familiar examples and be concrete: the junior high school band tuning up sounds *discordant*, the wicked queen in "Snow White" is *malicious.*

For each word, the following is provided:

1. The word (printed in heavy type).
2. Its part of speech (abbreviated).
3. A brief definition.
4. A sentence illustrating the word's use.
5. Whenever appropriate, related words are provided, together with their parts of speech.

The word list is arranged in strict alphabetical order.

SAT HIGH-FREQUENCY WORD LIST

abridge V. condense or shorten. Because the publishers felt the public wanted a shorter version of *War and Peace*, they proceeded to *abridge* the novel.

abstemious ADJ. sparing in eating and drinking; temperate. Concerned whether her vegetarian son's *abstemious* diet provided him with sufficient protein, the worried mother begged him to eat more.

abstract ADJ. theoretical; not concrete; nonrepresentational. To him, hunger was an *abstract* concept; he had never missed a meal.

abstruse ADJ. obscure; profound; difficult to understand. She read *abstruse* works in philosophy.

accessible ADJ. easy to approach; obtainable. We asked our guide whether the ruins were *accessible* on foot.

acclaim V. applaud; announce with great approval. The NBC sportscasters *acclaimed* every American victory in the Olympics and decried every American defeat. also N.

acknowledge V. recognize; admit. Although I *acknowledge* that the Beatles' tunes sound pretty dated today, I still prefer them to the "gangsta rap" songs my brothers play.

adulation N. flattery; admiration. The rock star thrived on the *adulation* of his groupies and yes men. adulate, V.

adversary N. opponent. The young wrestler struggled to defeat his *adversary*.

adversity N. misfortune; distress. In *Up from Slavery*, young Booker T. Washington shows courage and perseverance in his struggles with *adversity*.

advocate V. urge; plead for. The abolitionists *advocated* freedom for the slaves. also N.

aesthetic ADJ. artistic; dealing with or capable of appreciation of the beautiful. The beauty of Tiffany's stained glass appealed to Alice's *aesthetic* sense. aesthete, N.

affable ADJ. easily approachable; warmly friendly. Accustomed to cold, aloof supervisors, Nicholas was amazed at how *affable* his new employer was.

affirmation N. positive assertion; confirmation; solemn pledge by one who refuses to take an oath. Despite Tom's *affirmations* of innocence, Aunt Polly still suspected he had eaten the pie.

alleviate V. relieve. This should *alleviate* the pain; if it does not, we shall have to use stronger drugs.

aloof ADJ. apart; reserved. Shy by nature, she remained *aloof* while all the rest conversed.

altruistic ADJ. unselfishly generous; concerned for others. In providing tutorial assistance and college scholarships for hundreds of economically disadvantaged youths, Eugene Lang performed a truly *altruistic* deed. altruism, N.

ambiguous ADJ. unclear or doubtful in meaning. His *ambiguous* instructions misled us; we did not know which road to take. ambiguity, N.

ambivalence N. the state of having contradictory or conflicting emotional attitudes. Torn between loving her parents one minute and hating them the next, she was confused by the *ambivalence* of her feelings. ambivalent, ADJ.

analogous ADJ. comparable. Some feminists contend that a woman's need for a man is *analogous* to a fish's need for a bicycle. analogy, N.

anarchist N. person who rebels against the established order. Only the total overthrow of all governmental regulations would satisfy the *anarchist.*

anecdote N. short account of an amusing or interesting event. Rather than make concrete proposals for welfare reform, President Reagan told *anecdotes* about poor people who became wealthy despite their impoverished backgrounds.

animosity N. active enmity; ill will. The recent killings on the West Bank have sharpened the longstanding *animosity* between the Palestinians and the Israelis.

antagonism N. hostility; active resistance. Barry showed *antagonism* toward his new stepmother by ignoring her whenever she tried talking to him. antagonistic, ADJ.

antidote N. medicine to counteract a poison or disease. When Marge's child accidentally swallowed some cleaning fluid, the poison control hotline instructed Marge how to administer the *antidote*.

antiquated ADJ. old-fashioned; obsolete. Philip had grown so accustomed to editing his papers on word processors that he thought typewriters were too *antiquated* for him to use.

apathy N. lack of caring; indifference. A firm believer in democratic government, she could not understand the *apathy* of people who never bothered to vote. apathetic, ADJ.

appease V. pacify; soothe. We have discovered that, when we try to *appease* our enemies, we encourage them to make additional demands.

apprehension N. fear. His nervous glances at the passersby on the deserted street revealed his *apprehension*.

arbitrary ADJ. unreasonable or capricious; randomly selected without any reason; based solely on one's unrestricted will or judgment. The coach claimed the team lost because the umpire made some *arbitrary* calls.

archaic ADJ. antiquated. "Methinks," "thee," and "thou" are *archaic* words that are no longer part of our normal vocabulary.

arid ADJ. dry; barren. The cactus has adapted to survive in an *arid* environment.

arrogance N. pride; haughtiness. Convinced that Emma thought she was better than anyone else in the class, Ed rebuked her for her *arrogance*.

articulate ADJ. effective; distinct. Her *articulate* presentation of the advertising campaign impressed her employers. also v.

artifact N. object made by human beings, either handmade or mass-produced. Archaeologists debated the significance of the *artifacts* discovered in the ruins of Asia Minor but came to no conclusion about the culture they represented.

artisan N. a manually skilled worker. Elderly *artisans* from Italy trained Harlem teenagers to carve the stone figures that would decorate the new wing of the cathedral.

ascendancy N. controlling influence. Leaders of religious cults maintain *ascendancy* over their followers by methods that can verge on brainwashing.

ascetic ADJ. practicing self-denial; austere. The wealthy, self-indulgent young man felt oddly drawn to the strict, *ascetic* life led by members of some monastic orders. also N.

aspire V. seek to attain; long for. Because he *aspired* to a career in professional sports, Philip enrolled in a graduate program in sports management. aspiration, N.

astute ADJ. wise; shrewd; keen. The painter was an *astute* observer, noticing every tiny detail of her model's appearance and knowing the exact importance of each one.

attribute V. ascribe; explain. I *attribute* her success in science to the encouragement she received from her parents.

augment V. increase; add to. Armies *augment* their forces by calling up reinforcements; teachers *augment* their salaries by taking odd jobs.

austere ADJ. forbiddingly stern; severely simple and unornamented. The headmaster's *austere* demeanor tended to scare off the more timid students who never visited his study willingly. The room reflected the man, *austere* and bare, like a monk's cell, with no touches of luxury to moderate its *austerity*.

authoritarian ADJ. favoring or exercising total control; nondemocratic. The people had no control over their own destiny; they were forced to obey the dictates of the *authoritarian* regime. also N.

autonomous ADJ. self-governing. This island is a colony; however, in most matters, it is *autonomous* and receives no orders from the mother country. autonomy, N.

aversion N. firm dislike. Bert had an *aversion* to yuppies; Alex had an *aversion* to punks. Their mutual *aversion* was so great that they refused to speak to one another.

belie V. contradict; give a false impression. His coarse, hard-bitten exterior *belied* his inner sensitivity.

benevolent ADJ. generous; charitable. His *benevolent* nature prevented him from refusing any beggar who accosted him. benevolence, N.

bolster V. support; reinforce. The debaters amassed file boxes full of evidence to *bolster* their arguments.

braggart N. boaster. Modest by nature, she was no *braggart*, preferring to let her accomplishments speak for themselves.

brevity N. conciseness. *Brevity* is essential when you send a telegram or cablegram; you are charged for every word.

cajole V. coax; wheedle. Diane tried to *cajole* her father into letting her drive the family car. cajolery, N.

calculated ADJ. deliberately planned; likely. Lexy's choice of clothes to wear to the debate tournament was carefully *calculated*. Her conventional suit was *calculated* to appeal to the conservative judges.

candor N. frankness; open honesty. Jack can carry *candor* too far: when he told Jill his honest opinion of her, she nearly slapped his face. candid, ADJ.

capricious ADJ. fickle; incalculable. The storm was *capricious* and changed course constantly.

censorious ADJ. critical. *Censorious* people delight in casting blame.

censure V. blame; criticize. The senator was *censured* for behavior inappropriate to a member of Congress. also N.

coercion N. use of force to get someone to obey. The inquisitors used both physical and psychological *coercion* to force Joan of Arc to deny that her visions were sent by God. coerce, V.

commemorate V. honor the memory of. The statue of the Minute Man *commemorates* the valiant soldiers who fought in the Revolutionary War.

compile V. assemble; gather; accumulate. We planned to *compile* a list of the words most frequently used on SAT examinations.

complacency N. self-satisfaction; smugness. Full of *complacency* about his latest victories, he looked smugly at the row of trophies on his mantelpiece. complacent, ADJ.

compliance N. readiness to yield; conformity in fulfilling requirements. When I give an order, I expect *compliance*, not defiance. The design for the new school had to be in *compliance* with the local building code. comply, V.

composure N. mental calmness. Even the latest work crisis failed to shake her *composure*.

comprehensive ADJ. thorough; inclusive. This book provides a *comprehensive* review of verbal and math skills for the SAT.

concede V. admit; yield. Despite all the evidence Monica had assembled, Mark refused to *concede* that she was right.

conciliatory ADJ. reconciling; soothing. She was still angry despite his *conciliatory* words. conciliate, V.

concise ADJ. brief and compact. When you define a new word, be *concise*; the shorter the definition, the easier it is to remember.

concur V. agree. Did you *concur* with the decision of the court or did you find it unfair?

condone V. overlook voluntarily; forgive. We cannot *condone* your recent criminal cooperation with the gamblers.

conflagration N. great fire. In the *conflagration* that followed the 1906 earthquake, much of San Francisco was destroyed.

confound V. confuse; puzzle. No mystery could *confound* Sherlock Holmes for long.

consensus N. general agreement. After hours of debate, the *consensus* of the group was that we should approve the executive director's proposal.

constraint N. compulsion; repression of feelings. Because he trusted his therapist completely, he discussed his feelings openly with her without feeling the least *constraint*. constrain, V.

contend V. assert earnestly; struggle; compete. Sociologist Harry Edwards *contends* that young black athletes are exploited by some college recruiters.

contentious ADJ. quarrelsome. Disagreeing violently with the referees' ruling, the coach became so *contentious* that they threw him out of the game.

contract V. compress or shrink; make a pledge; catch a disease. Warm metal expands; cold metal *contracts*.

conviction N. strongly held belief. Nothing could shake his *conviction* that she was innocent. (secondary meaning)

cordial ADJ. gracious; heartfelt. Our hosts greeted us at the airport with a *cordial* welcome and a hearty hug.

corroborate V. confirm. Unless we find a witness to *corroborate* your evidence, it will not stand up in court.

credulity N. belief on slight evidence. The witch doctor took advantage of the *credulity* of the superstitious natives. credulous, ADJ.

criterion N. standard used in judging. What *criterion* did you use when you selected this essay as the prizewinner? criteria, PL.

cryptic ADJ. mysterious; hidden; secret. Thoroughly baffled by Holmes's *cryptic* remarks, Watson wondered whether Holmes was intentionally concealing his thoughts about the crime.

cursory ADJ. casual; hastily done. Because a *cursory* examination of the ruins indicates the possibility of arson, we believe the insurance agency should undertake a more extensive investigation of the fire's cause.

curtail V. shorten; reduce. Diane told Herb that she couldn't go out with him because her dad had ordered her to *curtail* her social life.

decorum N. propriety; orderliness and good taste in manners. Even the best-mannered students have trouble behaving with *decorum* on the last day of school. decorous, ADJ.

deference N. courteous regard for another's wish. In *deference* to his desires, the employers granted him a holiday. defer, V.

degradation N. humiliation; debasement; degeneration. Some secretaries object to fetching the boss a cup of coffee because they resent the *degradation* of being made to do such lowly tasks. degrade, V.

delineate N. portray. He is a powerful storyteller, but he is weakest when he attempts to *delineate* character. delineation, N.

denounce V. condemn; criticize. The reform candidate *denounced* the corrupt city officers for having betrayed the public's trust. denunciation, N.

deplore V. regret; disapprove of. Although I *deplore* the vulgarity of your language, I defend your right to express yourself freely.

depravity N. corruption; wickedness. The *depravity* of the tyrant's behavior shocked all. deprave, V.

deprecate V. express disapproval of; protest against; belittle. A firm believer in old-fashioned courtesy, Miss Post *deprecated* the modern tendency to address new acquaintances by their first names. deprecatory, ADJ.

deride V. ridicule; make fun of. The critics *derided* his pretentious dialogue and refused to take his play seriously. derision, N.

derivative ADJ. unoriginal; derived from another source. Although her early poetry was clearly *derivative* in nature, the critics thought she had promise and eventually would find her own voice.

despondent ADJ. depressed; gloomy. To the dismay of his parents, William became seriously *despondent* after he broke up with Jan; they despaired of finding a cure for his gloom. despondency, N.

detached ADJ. emotionally removed; calm and objective; indifferent. A psychoanalyst must maintain a *detached* point of view and stay uninvolved with her patients' personal lives. detachment, N. (secondary meaning)

deterrent N. something that discourages; hindrance. Does the threat of capital punishment serve as a *deterrent* to potential killers? deter, V.

detrimental ADJ. harmful; damaging. The candidate's acceptance of major financial contributions from a well-known racist ultimately proved *detrimental* to his campaign, for he lost the backing of many of his early grassroots supporters. detriment, N.

devious ADJ. roundabout; erratic; not straightforward. The Joker's plan was so *devious* that it was only with great difficulty we could follow its shifts and dodges.

devise V. think up; invent; plan. How clever he must be to have *devised* such a devious plan! What ingenious inventions might he have *devised* if he had turned his mind to science and not to crime.

diffuse ADJ. wordy; rambling; spread out (like a gas). If you pay authors by the word, you tempt them to produce *diffuse* manuscripts rather than brief ones. diffusion, N.

digression N. wandering away from the subject. Nobody minded when Professor Renoir's lectures wandered away from their official theme; his *digressions* were always more fascinating than the topic of the day. digress, V.

diligence N. steadiness of effort; persistent hard work. Her employers were greatly impressed by her *diligence* and offered her a partnership in the firm. diligent, ADJ.

diminution N. lessening; reduction in size. Old Jack was as sharp at eighty as he had been at fifty; increasing age led to no *diminution* of his mental acuity.

discerning ADJ. mentally quick and observant; having insight. Because he was considered the most *discerning* member of the firm, he was assigned the most difficult cases. discern, V. discernment, N.

disclose V. reveal. Although competitors offered him bribes, he refused to *disclose* any information about his company's forthcoming product. disclosure, N.

discordant ADJ. not harmonious; conflicting. Nothing is quite so *discordant* as the sound of a junior high school orchestra tuning up.

discount V. disregard. Be prepared to *discount* what he has to say about his ex-wife.

discrepancy N. lack of consistency; difference. The police noticed some *discrepancies* in his description of the crime and did not believe him.

discriminating ADJ. able to see differences; prejudiced. They feared he was not sufficiently *discriminating* to judge complex works of modern art. (secondary meaning) discrimination, N.

disdain V. view with scorn or contempt. In the film *Funny Face*, the bookish heroine *disdained* fashion models for their lack of intellectual interests. also N.

disinclination N. unwillingness. Some mornings I feel a great *disinclination* to get out of bed.

dismiss V. put away from consideration; reject. Believing in John's love for her, she *dismissed* the notion that he might be unfaithful. (secondary meaning)

disparage V. belittle. Do not *disparage* anyone's contribution; these little gifts add up to large sums. disparaging, ADJ.

disparity N. difference; condition of inequality. Their *disparity* in rank made no difference at all to the prince and Cinderella.

disperse V. scatter. The police fired tear gas into the crowd to *disperse* the protesters.

disputatious ADJ. argumentative; fond of argument. People avoided discussing contemporary problems with him because of his *disputatious* manner.

disseminate V. distribute; spread; scatter (like seeds). By their use of the Internet, propagandists have been able to *disseminate* their pet doctrines to new audiences around the globe.

dissent V. disagree. In the recent Supreme Court decision, Justice O'Connor *dissented* from the majority opinion. also N.

divergent ADJ. differing; deviating. The two witnesses presented the jury with remarkably *divergent* accounts of the same episode. divergence, N.

doctrine N. teachings, in general; particular principle (religious, legal, etc.) taught. He was so committed to the *doctrines* of his faith that he was unable to evaluate them impartially.

document V. provide written evidence. She kept all the receipts from her business trip in order to *document* her expenses for the firm. also N.

dogmatic ADJ. opinionated; arbitrary; doctrinal. We tried to discourage Doug from being so *dogmatic*, but never could convince him that his opinions might be wrong.

dubious ADJ. questionable; filled with doubt. Many critics of the SAT contend the test is of *dubious* worth. Jay claimed he could get a perfect 2400 on the SAT, but Ellen was *dubious*: she knew he hadn't cracked a book in three years.

duplicity N. double-dealing; hypocrisy. When Tanya learned that Mark had been two-timing her, she was furious at his *duplicity*.

eclectic ADJ. composed of elements drawn from disparate sources. His style of interior decoration was *eclectic*: bits and pieces of furnishings from widely divergent periods, strikingly juxtaposed to create a unique decor. eclecticism, N.

egotism N. excessive self-centeredness; sense of self-importance; conceit. Pure *egotism:* "But enough of this chit-chat about you and your little problems. Let's talk about what's really important: *Me!*"

elated ADJ. overjoyed; in high spirits. Grinning from ear to ear, Bonnie Blair was clearly *elated* by her Olympic victory. elation, N.

eloquence N. expressiveness; persuasive speech. The crowds were stirred by Martin Luther King's *eloquence.* eloquent, ADJ.

elusive ADJ. evasive; baffling; hard to grasp. Trying to pin down exactly when the contractors would be done remodeling the house, Nancy was frustrated by their *elusive* replies. elude, V.

embellish V. adorn; ornament. The costume designer *embellished* the leading lady's ball gown with yards and yards of ribbon and lace.

emulate V. imitate; rival. In a brief essay, describe a person you admire, someone whose virtues you would like to *emulate.*

endorse V. approve; support. Everyone waited to see which one of the rival candidates for the city council the mayor would *endorse.* (secondary meaning) endorsement, N.

enhance V. increase; improve. You can *enhance* your chances of being admitted to the college of your choice by learning to write well; an excellent essay can *enhance* any application.

enigma N. puzzle. Despite all attempts to decipher the code, it remained an *enigma.*

enmity N. ill will; hatred. At Camp David, President Carter labored to bring an end to the *enmity* that prevented the peaceful coexistence of Egypt and Israel.

ephemeral ADJ. short-lived; fleeting. The mayfly is an *ephemeral* creature.

equivocal ADJ. ambiguous; intentionally misleading. Rejecting the candidate's *equivocal* comments on tax reform, the reporters pressed him to state clearly where he stood on the issue. equivocate, V.

erroneous ADJ. mistaken; wrong. I thought my answer was correct, but it was *erroneous.*

erudite ADJ. learned; scholarly. Though his fellow students thought him *erudite*, Paul knew he would have to study many years before he could consider himself a scholar.

esoteric ADJ. hard to understand; known only to the chosen few. *New Yorker* short stories often include *esoteric* allusions to obscure people and events: the implication is, if you are in the in-crowd, you'll get the reference; if you come from Cleveland, you won't.

eulogy N. expression of praise, often on the occasion of someone's death. Instead of delivering a spoken *eulogy* at Genny's memorial service, Jeff sang a song he had written in her honor.

euphemism N. mild expression in place of an unpleasant one. The expression "he passed away" is a *euphemism* for "he died."

exacerbate V. worsen; embitter. The latest bombing *exacerbated* England's already existing bitterness against the IRA, causing the prime minister to break off the peace talks abruptly.

exalt V. raise in rank or dignity; praise. The actor Alec Guinness was *exalted* to the rank of knighthood by the queen.

execute V. put into effect; carry out. The choreographer wanted to see how well she could *execute* a pirouette. (secondary meaning) execution, N.

exemplary ADJ. serving as a model; outstanding. At commencement the dean praised Ellen for her *exemplary* behavior as class president.

exemplify V. serve as an example of; embody. For a generation of ballet goers, Rudolf Nureyev *exemplified* the ideal of masculine grace.

exhaustive ADJ. thorough; comprehensive. We have made an *exhaustive* study of all published SAT tests and are happy to share our research with you.

exhilarating ADJ. invigorating and refreshing; cheering. Though some of the hikers found tramping through the snow tiring, Jeffrey found the walk on the cold, crisp day *exhilarating*.

exonerate V. acquit; exculpate. I am sure this letter naming the actual culprit will *exonerate* you.

expedient ADJ. suitable; practical, politic. A pragmatic politician, he was guided by what was *expedient* rather than by what was ethical. expediency, N.

expedite V. hasten. Because we are on a tight schedule, we hope you will be able to *expedite* the delivery of our order.

explicit ADJ. totally clear; definite; outspoken. Don't just hint around that you're dissatisfied; be *explicit* about what's bugging you.

exploit V. make use of, sometimes unjustly. Cesar Chavez fought attempts to *exploit* migrant farmworkers in California. exploitation, N.

extol V. praise; glorify. The president *extolled* the astronauts, calling them the pioneers of the Space Age.

extraneous ADJ. not essential; superfluous. No wonder Ted can't think straight! His mind is so cluttered up with *extraneous* trivia, he can't concentrate on the essentials.

extricate V. free; disentangle. He found that he could not *extricate* himself from the trap.

exuberance N. overflowing abundance; joyful enthusiasm; flamboyance; lavishness. I was bowled over by the *exuberance* of Annie's welcome. What an enthusiastic greeting!

facilitate V. help bring about; make less difficult. Rest and proper nourishment should *facilitate* the patient's recovery.

fallacious ADJ. false; misleading. Paradoxically, *fallacious* reasoning does not always yield erroneous results: even though your logic may be faulty, the answer you get may nevertheless be correct. fallacy, N.

fanaticism N. excessive zeal; extreme devotion to a belief or cause. When Islamic fundamentalists demanded the death of Salman Rushdie because his novel questioned their faith, world opinion condemned them for their *fanaticism*.

fastidious ADJ. difficult to please; squeamish. Bobby was such a *fastidious* eater that he would eat a sandwich only if his mother first cut off every scrap of crust.

feasible ADJ. practical. Is it *feasible* to build a new stadium for the Yankees on New York's west side? Without additional funding, the project is clearly unrealistic.

fervor N. glowing ardor. Their kiss was full of the *fervor* of first love.

flagrant ADJ. conspicuously wicked. We cannot condone such *flagrant* violations of the rules.

frivolous ADJ. lacking in seriousness; self-indulgently carefree; relatively unimportant. Though Nancy enjoyed Bill's *frivolous*, lighthearted companionship, she sometimes wondered whether he could ever be serious. frivolity, N.

frugality N. thrift; economy. In economically hard times, anyone who doesn't practice *frugality* risks bankruptcy. frugal, ADJ.

furtive ADJ. stealthy; sneaky. The boy gave a *furtive* look at his classmate's test paper.

garrulous ADJ. loquacious; wordy; talkative. My Uncle Henry can out-talk any three people I know; he is the most *garrulous* person in Cayuga County. garrulity, N.

glutton N. someone who eats too much. When Mother saw that Bobby had eaten all the cookies, she called him a little *glutton*. gluttonous, ADJ.

gratify V. please. Lori's parents were *gratified* by her outstanding performance on the SAT.

gratuitous ADJ. given freely; unwarranted; uncalled for. Quit making *gratuitous* comments about my driving; no one asked you for your opinion.

gravity N. seriousness. We could tell we were in serious trouble from the *gravity* of her expression. (secondary meaning) grave, ADJ.

gregarious ADJ. sociable. Typically, party-throwers are *gregarious;* hermits are not.

guile N. deceit; duplicity; wiliness; cunning. Iago uses considerable *guile* to trick Othello into believing that Desdemona has been unfaithful.

gullible ADJ. easily deceived. He preyed upon *gullible* people, who believed his stories of easy wealth.

hamper V. obstruct. The minority party agreed not to *hamper* the efforts of the leaders to secure a lasting peace.

hardy ADJ. sturdy; robust; able to stand inclement weather. We asked the gardening expert to recommend particularly *hardy* plants that could withstand our harsh New England winters.

haughtiness N. pride; arrogance. When she realized that Darcy believed himself too good to dance with his inferiors, Elizabeth took great offense at his *haughtiness*.

hedonist N. one who believes that pleasure is the sole aim in life. A thoroughgoing *hedonist*, he considered only his own pleasure and ignored any claims others had on his money or time.

heresy N. opinion contrary to popular belief; opinion contrary to accepted religion. Galileo's assertion that the earth moved around the sun directly contradicted the religious teachings of his day; as a result, he was tried for *heresy*. heretic, N.

hierarchy N. arrangement by rank or standing; authoritarian body divided into ranks. To be low man on the totem pole is to have an inferior place in the *hierarchy*.

homogeneous ADJ. of the same kind. Educators try to put pupils of similar abilities into the same classes because they believe that this *homogeneous* grouping is advisable. homogeneity, N.

hypocritical ADJ. pretending to be virtuous; deceiving. I resent his *hypocritical* posing as a friend for I know he is interested only in his own advancement. hypocrisy, N.

hypothetical ADJ. based on assumptions or hypotheses. Why do we have to consider *hypothetical* cases when we have actual case histories that we can examine? hypothesis, N.

idiosyncrasy N. individual trait, usually odd in nature; eccentricity. One of Richard Nixon's little *idiosyncrasies* was his liking for ketchup on cottage cheese. One of Hannibal Lecter's little *idiosyncrasies* was his liking for human flesh.

illusory ADJ. deceptive; not real. Unfortunately, the costs of running a concession stand were so high that Tom's profits proved *illusory*.

immutable ADJ. unchangeable. All things change over time; nothing is *immutable*.

impair V. injure; hurt. Drinking alcohol can *impair* your ability to drive safely; if you're going to drink, don't drive.

impeccable ADJ. faultless. The uncrowned queen of the fashion industry, Diana was acclaimed for her *impeccable* taste.

impede V. hinder; block; delay. A series of accidents *impeded* the launching of the space shuttle.

implausible ADJ. unlikely; unbelievable. Though her alibi seemed *implausible*, it turned out to be true.

implement V. put into effect; supply with tools. The mayor was unwilling to *implement* the plan until she was sure it had the governor's backing. also N.

impudence N. impertinence; insolence. Kissed on the cheek by a perfect stranger, Lady Catherine exclaimed, "Of all the nerve! Young man, I should have you horse-whipped for your *impudence*."

inadvertent ADJ. unintentional; careless or heedless. Elizabeth, I am sure your omission from the guest list was *inadvertent:* Darcy would never intentionally slight you so.

inane ADJ. silly; senseless. There's no point in what you're saying. Why are you bothering to make such *inane* remarks?

incisive ADJ. cutting; sharp. His *incisive* remarks made us see the fallacy in our plans.

incite V. arouse to action. The demagogue *incited* the mob to take action into its own hands.

inclusive ADJ. tending to include all. The comedian turned down the invitation to join the Players' Club, saying any club that would let him in was too *inclusive* for him.

incongruous ADJ. not fitting; absurd. Dave saw nothing *incongruous* about wearing sneakers with his tuxedo; he couldn't understand why his date took one look at him and started to laugh. incongruity, N.

inconsequential ADJ. insignificant; unimportant. Brushing off Ali's apologies for having broken the wine glass, Tamara said, "Don't worry about it; it's *inconsequential.*"

incorrigible ADJ. uncorrectable. Though Widow Douglass hoped to reform Huck, Miss Watson pronounced him *incorrigible* and said he would come to no good end.

indict V. charge. If the grand jury *indicts* the suspect, he will go to trial. indictment, N.

indifferent ADJ. unmoved; lacking concern. Because she felt no desire to marry, she was *indifferent* to his constant proposals.

indiscriminate ADJ. choosing at random; confused. She disapproved of her son's *indiscriminate* television viewing and decided to restrict him to educational programs.

induce V. persuade; bring about. After the quarrel, Tina said nothing could *induce* her to talk to Tony again. inducement, N.

inert ADJ. inactive; lacking power to move. "Get up, you lazybones," she cried to her husband, who lay in bed *inert.* inertia, N.

ingenious ADJ. clever; resourceful. Kit admired the *ingenious* way that her computer keyboard opened up to reveal the built-in CD-ROM. ingenuity, N.

inherent ADJ. firmly established by nature or habit. Katya's *inherent* love of justice caused her to champion anyone she considered treated unfairly by society.

innate ADJ. inborn. Mozart's parents soon recognized young Wolfgang's *innate* talent for music.

innocuous ADJ. harmless. An occasional glass of wine with dinner is relatively *innocuous* and should have no ill effect on you.

innovation N. change; introduction of something new. She loved *innovations* just because they were new. innovate, V.

insipid ADJ. lacking in flavor; dull. Flat prose and flat ginger ale are equally *insipid;* both lack sparkle.

instigate V. urge; start; provoke. Rumors of police corruption led the mayor to *instigate* an investigation into the department's activities.

insularity N. narrow-mindedness; isolation. The *insularity* of the islanders manifested itself in their suspicion of anything foreign. insular, ADJ.

integrity N. uprightness; wholeness. Lincoln, whose personal *integrity* has inspired millions, fought a civil war to maintain the *integrity* of the Republic, that these United States might remain undivided for all time.

intervene V. come between. When close friends get into a fight, be careful if you try to *intervene;* they may join forces to gang up on you.

intimidate V. frighten. I'll learn karate and then those big bullies won't be able to *intimidate* me any more.

intrepid ADJ. fearless. For her *intrepid* conduct nursing the wounded during the war, Florence Nightingale was honored by Queen Victoria.

inundate v. overwhelm; flood; submerge. This semester I am *inundated* with work: you should see the piles of paperwork flooding my desk. Until the great dam was built, the waters of the Nile used to *inundate* the river valley like clockwork every year.

invert v. turn upside down or inside out. When he *inverted* his body in a hand stand, he felt the blood rush to his head.

ironic ADJ. resulting in an unexpected and contrary manner. It is *ironic* that his success came when he least wanted it.

lament v. grieve; express sorrow. Even advocates of the war *lamented* the loss of so many lives in combat. lamentation, N.

laud v. praise. The Soviet premier *lauded* the heroic efforts of the rescue workers after the Armenian earthquake. laudable, laudatory, ADJ.

lavish ADJ. liberal; wasteful. The actor's *lavish* gifts pleased her. also v.

lethargic ADJ. drowsy; dull. The stuffy room made her *lethargic:* she felt as if she was about to nod off.

levity N. lack of seriousness; lightness. Stop giggling and wriggling around in your seats; such *levity* is improper in church.

linger v. loiter or dawdle; continue or persist. Hoping to see Juliet pass by, Romeo *lingered* outside the Capulet house for hours. Though Mother made stuffed cabbage on Monday, the smell *lingered* around the house for days.

listless ADJ. lacking in spirit or energy. We had expected him to be full of enthusiasm and were surprised by his *listless* attitude.

lofty ADJ. very high. Though Barbara Jordan's fellow students used to tease her about her *lofty* ambitions, she rose to hold one of the highest positions in the land.

malicious ADJ. hateful; spiteful. Jealous of Cinderella's beauty, her *malicious* stepsisters expressed their spite by forcing her to do menial tasks. malice, N.

marred ADJ. damaged; disfigured. She had to refinish the *marred* surface of the table. mar, V.

materialism N. preoccupation with physical comforts and things. By its nature, *materialism* is opposed to idealism, for where the *materialist* emphasizes the needs of the body, the idealist emphasizes the needs of the soul.

methodical ADJ. systematic. An accountant must be *methodical* and maintain order among his financial records.

meticulous ADJ. excessively careful; painstaking; scrupulous. Martha Stewart was a *meticulous* housekeeper, fussing about each and every detail that went into making up her perfect home.

miserly ADJ. stingy; mean. The *miserly* old man hoarded his coins not out of prudence but out of greed. miser, N.

mitigate V. appease. Nothing he did could *mitigate* her wrath; she was unforgiving.

morose ADJ. ill-humored; sullen; melancholy. Forced to take early retirement, Bill acted *morose* for months until he shook off his sullen mood and reverted to his usual cheerful self.

mundane ADJ. worldly as opposed to spiritual; everyday. Uninterested in philosophical questions, Tom talked only of *mundane* matters such as the latest basketball results.

negate V. cancel out; nullify; deny. A sudden surge of adrenalin can *negate* the effects of fatigue: there's nothing like a good shock to wake you up.

nonchalance N. indifference; lack of concern; composure. Cool, calm, and collected under fire, James Bond shows remarkable *nonchalance* in the face of danger.

notoriety N. disrepute; ill fame. To the starlet, any publicity was good publicity: if she couldn't have a good reputation, she'd settle for *notoriety*. notorious, ADJ.

novelty N. something new; newness. The computer is no longer a *novelty* around the office. novel, ADJ.

nurture v. nourish; educate; foster. The Head Start program attempts to *nurture* pre-kindergarten children so that they will do well when they enter public school. also N.

obliterate v. destroy completely. The tidal wave *obliterated* several island villages.

oblivion N. forgetfulness. Her works had fallen into a state of *oblivion;* no one bothered to read them. oblivious, ADJ.

obscure v. darken; make unclear. At times he seemed purposely to *obscure* his meaning, preferring mystery to clarity.

obstinate ADJ. stubborn. We tried to persuade him to give up smoking, but he was *obstinate* and refused to change.

ominous ADJ. threatening. These clouds are *ominous;* they suggest a severe storm is on the way.

opaque ADJ. dark; not transparent. The *opaque* window shade kept the sunlight out of the room. opacity, N.

opportunist N. individual who sacrifices principles for expediency by taking advantage of circumstances. Forget ethics! He's such an *opportunist* that he'll vote in favor of any deal that will give him a break.

optimist N. person who looks on the good side. The pessimist says the glass is half-empty; the *optimist* says it is half-full.

opulence N. extreme wealth; luxuriousness; abundance. The glitter and *opulence* of the ballroom took Cinderella's breath away. opulent, ADJ.

orator N. public speaker. The abolitionist Frederick Douglass was a brilliant *orator* whose speeches centered on the evils of slavery.

ostentatious ADJ. showy; pretentious; trying to attract attention. Trump's latest casino in Atlantic City is the most *ostentatious* gambling palace in the East; it easily outglitters its competitors. ostentation, N.

pacifist N. one opposed to force; antimilitarist. The *pacifists* urged that we reduce our military budget and recall our troops stationed overseas.

partisan ADJ. one-sided; prejudiced; committed to a party. On certain issues of conscience, she refused to take a *partisan* stand. also N.

peripheral ADJ. marginal; outer. We lived, not in central London, but in one of those *peripheral* suburbs that spring up on the outskirts of a great city.

perpetuate V. make something last; preserve from extinction. Some critics attack *The Adventures of Huckleberry Finn* because they believe Twain's book *perpetuates* a false image of Blacks in this country.

pervasive ADJ. permeating; spread throughout every part. Despite airing them for several hours, she could not rid her clothes of the *pervasive* odor of mothballs that clung to them. pervade, V.

pessimism N. belief that life is basically bad or evil; gloominess. The good news we have been receiving lately indicates that there is little reason for your *pessimism*.

phenomena N., PL. observable facts; subjects of scientific investigation. We kept careful records of the *phenomena* we noted in the course of these experiments.

philanthropist N. lover of mankind; doer of good. As he grew older, he became famous as a *philanthropist* and benefactor of the needy.

piety N. religious devotion; godliness. The nuns in the convent were noted for their *piety;* they spent their days in worship and prayer. pious, ADJ.

placate V. pacify; conciliate. The store manager tried to *placate* the angry customer.

ponderous ADJ. weighty; unwieldy. His humor lacked the light touch; his jokes were always *ponderous.*

pragmatic ADJ. practical (as opposed to idealistic); concerned with the practical worth or impact of something. This coming trip to France should provide me with a *pragmatic* test of the value of my conversational French class.

preclude v. make impossible; eliminate. The fact that the band was already booked to play in Hollywood on New Year's Eve *precluded* their accepting the New Year's Eve gig in London they were offered.

precocious ADJ. advanced in development. Listening to the grown-up way the child discussed serious topics, we couldn't help remarking how *precocious* she was. precocity, N.

predator N. creature that seizes and devours another animal; person who robs or exploits others. A wide variety of *predators*—cats, owls, hawks—catch mice for dinner. A carnivore is by definition *predatory*, for he *preys* on weaker creatures.

predecessor N. former occupant of a post. I hope I can live up to the fine example set by my late *predecessor* in this office.

presumptuous ADJ. arrogant; taking liberties. It seems *presumptuous* for one so relatively new to the field to challenge the conclusions of its leading experts. presumption, N.

pretentious ADJ. ostentatious; pompous; making unjustified claims; overly ambitious. None of the other prize winners are wearing their medals; isn't it a bit *pretentious* of you to wear yours?

prevalent ADJ. widespread; generally accepted. A radical committed to social change, Reed had no patience with the conservative views *prevalent* in the America of his day.

prodigal ADJ. wasteful; reckless with money. The *prodigal* son squandered his inheritance. also N.

profane v. violate; desecrate. Tourists are urged not to *profane* the sanctity of holy places by wearing improper garb. also ADJ.

profound ADJ. deep; not superficial; complete. Freud's remarkable insights into human behavior caused his fellow scientists to honor him as a *profound* thinker. profundity, N.

profusion N. lavish expenditure; overabundant condition. Seldom have I seen food and drink served in such *profusion* as at the wedding feast.

proliferation N. rapid growth; spread; multiplication. Times of economic hardship inevitably encourage the *proliferation* of countless get-rich-quick schemes. proliferate, v.

prolific ADJ. abundantly fruitful. She was a *prolific* writer and wrote as many as three books a year.

provincial ADJ. pertaining to a province; limited in outlook; unsophisticated. As *provincial* governor, Sir Henry administered the Queen's law in his remote corner of Canada. Caught up in local problems, out of touch with London news, he became sadly *provincial*.

proximity N. nearness. The deer sensed the hunter's *proximity* and bounded away.

prudent ADJ. cautious; careful. A miser hoards money not because he is *prudent* but because he is greedy. prudence, N.

qualified ADJ. limited; restricted. Unable to give the candidate full support, the mayor gave him only a *qualified* endorsement. (secondary meaning)

quandary N. dilemma. When both Harvard and Stanford accepted Laura, she was in a *quandary* as to which school she should attend.

ramble V. wander aimlessly (physically or mentally). Listening to the teacher *ramble*, Judy wondered whether he'd ever get to his point.

rancor N. bitterness; hatred. Thirty years after the war, she could not let go of the past but was still consumed with *rancor* against the foe.

ratify V. approve formally; verify. Before the treaty could go into effect, it had to be *ratified* by the president.

rebuttal N. refutation; response with contrary evidence. The defense lawyer confidently listened to the prosecutor sum up his case, sure that she could answer his arguments in her *rebuttal*.

recluse N. hermit; loner. Disappointed in love, Miss Emily became a *recluse*; she shut herself away in her empty mansion and refused to see another living soul. reclusive, ADJ.

recount v. narrate or tell; count over again. A born storyteller, my father loved to *recount* anecdotes about his early years in New York.

rectify v. set right; correct. You had better send a check to *rectify* your account before American Express cancels your credit card.

redundant ADJ. superfluous; excessively wordy; repetitious. Your composition is *redundant;* you can easily reduce its length. redundancy, N.

refute v. disprove. The defense called several respectable witnesses who were able to *refute* the false testimony of the prosecution's only witness.

relegate v. banish to an inferior position; delegate; assign. After Ralph dropped his second tray of drinks that week, the manager swiftly *relegated* him to a minor post cleaning up behind the bar.

remorse N. guilt; self-reproach. The murderer felt no *remorse* for his crime.

renounce v. abandon; discontinue; disown; repudiate. Joan of Arc refused to *renounce* her statements even though she knew she would be burned at the stake as a witch.

repel v. drive away; disgust. At first, the Beast's ferocious appearance *repelled* Beauty, but she came to love the tender heart hidden behind that beastly exterior.

reprehensible ADJ. deserving blame. Shocked by the viciousness of the bombing, politicians of every party uniformly condemned the terrorists' *reprehensible* deed.

reprimand v. reprove severely; rebuke. Every time Ermengarde made a mistake in class, she was afraid that Miss Minchin would *reprimand* her and tell her father how badly she was doing in school. also N.

reprove v. censure; rebuke. The principal *reproved* the students when they became unruly in the auditorium. reproof, N.

repudiate v. disown; disavow. He announced that he would *repudiate* all debts incurred by his wife.

reserve N. self-control; formal but distant manner. Although some girls were attracted by Mark's air of *reserve,* Judy was put off by it, for she felt his aloofness indicated a lack of openness. reserved, ADJ.

resigned ADJ. unresisting; patiently submissive. Bob Cratchit was too *resigned* to his downtrodden existence to protest Scrooge's bullying. resignation, N.

resolution N. determination; resolve. Nothing could shake his *resolution* that his children would get the best education possible. resolute, ADJ.

resolve N. determination; firmness of purpose. How dare you question my *resolve* to take up skydiving! Of course I haven't changed my mind!

restraint N. moderation or self-control; controlling force; restriction. Control yourself, young lady! Show some *restraint!*

reticence N. reserve; uncommunicativeness; inclination to silence. Fearing his competitors might get advance word about his plans from talkative staff members, Hughes preferred *reticence* from his employees to loquacity.

retract V. withdraw; take back. He dropped his libel suit after the newspaper finally *retracted* its statement. retraction, N.

reverent ADJ. respectful; worshipful. Though I bow my head in church and recite the prayers, sometimes I don't feel properly *reverent.* revere, V.

rhetorical ADJ. pertaining to effective communication; insincere in language. To win his audience, the speaker used every *rhetorical* trick in the book.

rigor N. severity. Many settlers could not stand the *rigors* of the harsh New England winters.

robust ADJ. vigorous; strong. After pumping iron and taking karate for six months, the little old lady was far more *robust* in health and could break a plank with her fist.

sage N. person celebrated for wisdom. Hearing tales of a mysterious Master of All Knowledge who lived in the hills of Tibet, Sandy was possessed with a burning desire to consult the legendary *sage.* also ADJ.

sanction v. approve; ratify. Nothing will convince me to *sanction* the engagement of my daughter to such a worthless young man.

satirical ADJ. mocking. The humor of cartoonist Gary Trudeau often is *satirical;* through the comments of the Doonesbury characters, Trudeau ridicules political corruption and folly.

saturate v. soak thoroughly. *Saturate* your sponge with water until it can't hold any more.

scanty ADJ. meager; insufficient. Thinking his helping of food was *scanty,* Oliver Twist asked for more.

scrupulous ADJ. conscientious; extremely thorough. Though Alfred is *scrupulous* in fulfilling his duties at work, he is less conscientious about his obligations to his family and friends.

scrutinize v. examine closely and critically. Searching for flaws, the sergeant *scrutinized* every detail of the private's uniform.

seclusion N. isolation; solitude. One moment she loved crowds; the next, she sought *seclusion.*

servile ADJ. slavishly submissive; fawning; cringing. Constantly fawning on his employer, Uriah Heep was a *servile* creature.

skeptic N. doubter; person who suspends judgment until the evidence supporting a point of view has been examined. I am a *skeptic* about the new health plan; I want some proof that it can work. skepticism, N.

sluggish ADJ. slow; lazy; lethargic. After two nights without sleep, she felt *sluggish* and incapable of exertion.

somber ADJ. gloomy; depressing. From the doctor's grim expression, I could tell he had *somber* news.

sporadic ADJ. occurring irregularly. Although you can still hear *sporadic* outbursts of laughter and singing outside, the big Halloween parade has passed; the party's over till next year.

squander v. waste. The prodigal son *squandered* the family estate.

stagnant ADJ. motionless; stale; dull. The *stagnant* water was a breeding ground for disease. stagnate, V.

static ADJ. unchanging; lacking development. Nothing had changed at home; things were *static*. stasis, N.

submissive ADJ. yielding; timid. Crushed by his authoritarian father, Will had no defiance left in him; he was totally *submissive* in the face of authority.

subordinate ADJ. occupying a lower rank; inferior; submissive. Bishop Proudie's wife expected the *subordinate* clergy to behave with great deference to her.

subside V. settle down; descend; grow quiet. The doctor assured us that the fever would eventually *subside*.

substantiate V. establish by evidence; verify; support. These endorsements from satisfied customers *substantiate* our claim that Barron's *How to Prepare for the New SAT* is the best SAT-prep book on the market.

succinct ADJ. brief; terse; compact. Don't bore your audience with excess verbiage: be *succinct*.

superficial ADJ. trivial; shallow. Since your report gave only a *superficial* analysis of the problem, I cannot give you more than a passing grade.

superfluous ADJ. excessive; overabundant; unnecessary. Please try not to include so many *superfluous* details in your report; just give me the bare facts. superfluity, N.

surpass V. exceed. Her SAT scores *surpassed* our expectations.

surreptitious ADJ. secret; furtive; sneaky; hidden. Hoping to discover where his mom had hidden the Christmas presents, Timmy took a *surreptitious* peek into the master bedroom closet.

susceptible ADJ. impressionable; easily influenced; having little resistance, as to a disease; receptive to. Said the patent medicine man to his very *susceptible* customer: "Buy this new miracle drug, and you will no longer be *susceptible* to the common cold."

sustain V. experience; support; nourish. He *sustained* such a severe injury that the doctors feared he would be unable to work to *sustain* his growing family.

sycophant N. servile flatterer; bootlicker; yes man. Fed up with the toadies and flunkies who made up his entourage, the star cried, "Get out, all of you! I'm sick of *sycophants*!" sycophancy, N.

taciturn ADJ. habitually silent; talking little. The stereotypical cowboy is a *taciturn* soul, answering lengthy questions with a "Yep" or "Nope."

temper V. moderate; restrain; tone down or toughen (steel). Not even her supervisor's grumpiness could *temper* Nancy's enthusiasm for her new job.

tentative ADJ. provisional; experimental. Your *tentative* plans sound plausible; let me know when the final details are worked out.

terse ADJ. concise; abrupt; pithy. There is a fine line between speech that is *terse* and to the point and speech that is too abrupt.

thrive V. prosper; flourish. Despite the impact of the recession on the restaurant trade, Philip's cafe *thrived*.

tranquillity N. calmness; peace. After the commotion and excitement of the city, I appreciate the *tranquillity* of these fields and forests.

transient ADJ. momentary; temporary; staying for a short time. Ann's joy at finding the perfect Christmas gift for Phil was *transient*; she still had to find presents for her cousins. Located near the airport, this hotel caters to a largely *transient* trade.

trite ADJ. hackneyed; commonplace. The *trite* and predictable situations in many television programs turn off many viewers, who, in turn, turn off their sets.

turbulence N. state of violent agitation. We were frightened by the *turbulence* of the ocean during the storm.

turmoil N. great commotion and confusion. Lydia running off with a soldier! Mother fainting at the news! The Bennet household was in *turmoil*.

undermine V. weaken; sap. The recent corruption scandals have *undermined* many people's faith in the city government. The recent torrential rains have washed away much of the cliffside; the deluge threatens to *undermine* the pillars supporting several houses at the edge of the cliff.

uniformity N. sameness; monotony. After a while, the *uniformity* of TV situation comedies becomes boring.

unwarranted ADJ. unjustified; groundless; undeserved. We could not understand Martin's *unwarranted* rudeness to his mother's guests.

usurp V. seize another's power or rank. The revolution ended when the victorious rebel general succeeded in his attempt to *usurp* the throne.

vacillate V. waver; fluctuate. Uncertain which suitor she ought to marry, the princess *vacillated*, saying now one, now the other. The boss likes his staff to be decisive. When he asks for your opinion, whatever you do, don't *vacillate*. vacillation, N.

venerate V. revere. In Tibet today, the common people still *venerate* their traditional spiritual leader, the Dalai Lama.

verbose ADJ. wordy. This article is too *verbose;* we must edit it.

vigor N. active strength. Although he was over seventy years old, Jack had the *vigor* of a man in his prime. vigorous, ADJ.

vilify V. slander. Refusing to wage a negative campaign, the candidate would not stoop to *vilifying* his opponent's reputation. vilification, N.

vindicate V. clear from blame; exonerate; justify or support. The lawyer's goal was to *vindicate* her client and prove him innocent on all charges. The critics' extremely favorable reviews *vindicate* my opinion that *The Full Monty* is a brilliant movie.

virtuoso N. highly skilled artist. The child prodigy Yehudi Menuhin grew into a *virtuoso* whose violin performances thrilled millions. virtuosity, N.

volatile ADJ. changeable; explosive; evaporating rapidly. The political climate today is extremely *volatile;* no one can predict what the electorate will do next. Ethyl chloride is an extremely *volatile* liquid; it evaporates instantly.

whimsical ADJ. capricious; fanciful. He dismissed his generous gift to his college as a sentimental fancy, an old man's *whimsical* gesture.

zealot N. fanatic; person who shows excessive zeal. Though Glenn was devout, he was no *zealot*; he never tried to force his beliefs on his friends.

5

The Writing Skills Sections: Strategies, Tips, and Practice

In this chapter you'll learn how best to tackle the three types of multiple-choice writing skills questions on the SAT—identifying sentence errors, improving sentences, and improving paragraphs—and how best to approach the timed essay-writing portion of the test. You'll find practice exercises for each question type, plus a selection of SAT-style essay topics for your practice essays. After working through this chapter, you'll be thoroughly familiar with the contents of these new sections on the SAT.

General Tips for Answering Multiple-Choice Writing Skills Questions

1. Read all the answer choices before you decide which is correct.
2. Use your ear for the language to help you decide that something is wrong. Remember, you don't have to name the error, or be able to explain why it is wrong. All you have to do is recognize that something *is* wrong. On the early, easy questions in a set, if a word or phrase sounds wrong to you, it probably is, even if you don't know why.
3. Pay particular attention to the shorter answer choices. Good prose is economical. Often the correct answer choice will be the shortest, most direct way of making a point.

4. Remember that not every sentence contains an error or needs to be improved. Ten to twenty percent of the time, the sentence is correct as it stands. Do not get so caught up in hunting for errors that you start seeing errors that aren't there.

THE IDENTIFYING SENTENCE ERRORS QUESTION

The identifying sentence errors questions ask you to spot an error in the underlined sections of a sentence. (Everything in the sentence that is *not* underlined is by definition correct.) You do not have to correct the sentence or explain what is wrong. Most sentences will have just one error. Some sentences will have none. When you can find no error in the underlined sections of the sentence, you must select choice E, <u>No error</u>, as your answer.

Tips to Help You Cope

1. First read the sentence to get a feel for its structure and sense.

2. Remember that the error, if there is one, must be in the underlined part of the sentence. You don't have to worry about making improvements that could be made in the rest of the sentence. For example, if you have a sentence in which the subject is plural and the verb is singular, you could call either one the error. But if only the verb is underlined, the error for that sentence is the verb.

3. Look first for the most common errors. Most of the sentences will have errors. If you are having trouble finding mistakes, check for some of the more common ones: subject-verb agreement, pronoun-antecedent problems, misuse of adjectives and adverbs, dangling modifiers. But look for errors only in the underlined parts of the sentence.

Examples to Get You Started

EXAMPLE 1

If one follows the <u>discipline</u> of Hatha Yoga, <u>you know</u>
　　　　　　　　　　　A　　　　　　　　　　　　　　B

the critical importance of physical purification <u>to render</u>
　　　　　　　　　　　　　　　　　　　　　　　　　　C

the body <u>fit for</u> the practice of higher meditation.
　　　　　　D

<u>No error</u>
　　E

What's wrong with the sentence above? The writer makes an abrupt, unnecessary shift in person, switching from the pronoun one ("one follows") to the pronoun you ("you know"). There are two ways to fix this sentence. You can rewrite it like this:

If you follow the discipline of Hatha Yoga, you know the critical importance of physical purification to render the body fit for the practice of higher meditation.

You can also rewrite it like this:

If one follows the discipline of Hatha Yoga, one knows the critical importance of physical purification to render the body fit for the practice of higher meditation.

However, your job is not to rewrite the sentence. Your job is simply to spot the error, and that error *must be in an underlined part*. You know the shift in person is incorrect. That means the error is Choice B.

In answering error identification questions, focus on the underlined portions of the sentence. Don't waste your time thinking of other ways to make the sentence work.

EXAMPLE 2

> In my history class I learned <u>why</u> the American colonies
> <u>   A   B</u>
> <u>opposed the British</u>, how they organized the militia, and
>   C
> <u>the work of the Continental Congress.</u> <u>No error</u>
>   D   E

The last part of this sentence probably sounds funny to you—awkward, strange, wooden. You may not know exactly what it is, but something sounds wrong here. If you followed your instincts and chose choice D as the error, you would be right. The error is a lack of parallel structure. The sentence is listing three things you learned, and they should all be in the same form. Your ear expects the pattern to be the same. Since the first two items listed are clauses, the third should be too: "In my history class I learned why the American colonies opposed the British, how they organized the militia, and how the Continental Congress worked."

EXAMPLE 3

> Marilyn and <u>I</u> ran as <u>fast</u> as we could, but we missed
>   A   B
> our train, <u>which</u> made <u>us</u> late for work. <u>No error</u>
>   C   D   E

Imagine that you have this sentence, and you can't see what is wrong with it. Start at the beginning and check each answer choice. *I* is part of the subject, so it is the right case: after all, you wouldn't say "Me ran fast." *Fast* can be an adverb, so it is being used correctly here. *Which* is a pronoun, and needs a noun for its antecedent. The only available noun is *train*, but that doesn't make sense (the train didn't make us late—*missing* the train made us late). So there is your error, choice C.

Once you have checked each answer choice, if you still can't find an error, choose choice E, "No error." A certain number of questions have no errors.

THE IMPROVING SENTENCES QUESTION

The next set of questions in this section involves spotting the form of a sentence that works best. In these improving sentences questions, you will be presented with five different versions of the same sentence; you must choose the best one.

Your challenge here is to select an effective, error-free sentence, one that clearly and concisely expresses the meaning of the original sentence. Occasionally, the original wording of the sentence is most effective. If that is the case, select the first answer choice, choice A, which simply repeats the sentence's original wording.

Tips to Help You Cope

1. If you spot an error in the underlined section, eliminate any answer that also contains that error. Remember, you still don't have to be able to explain what is wrong. You just need to pick something that sounds correct. If the error you found in the underlined section is absent from more than one of the answer choices, look over those choices again to see if they add any new errors.

2. If you don't spot the error in the underlined section, look at the answer choices to see what is changed. Sometimes it's hard to spot what's wrong with the underlined section in a sentence correction question. When that happens, turn to the answer choices. Find the changes in the answers. The changes will tell you what kind of error is being tested. When you substitute the answer choices in the original sentence, ask yourself which of these

choices makes the sentence seem clearest to you. That may well be the correct answer choice.

3. Make sure that all parts of the sentence are logically connected. Not all parts of a sentence are created equal. Some parts should be subordinated to the rest, connected with subordinating conjunctions or relative pronouns, not just added on with *and*. Overuse of *and* frequently makes sentences sound babyish. Compare "We had dinner at the Hard Rock Cafe, and we went to a concert" with "After we had dinner at the Hard Rock Cafe, we went to a concert."

4. Make sure that all parts of a sentence given in a series are similar in form. If they are not, the sentence suffers from a lack of parallel structure. The sentence "I'm taking classes in algebra, history, and how to speak French" lacks parallel structure. *Algebra* and *history* are nouns, names of subjects. The third subject should also be a noun: *conversational French*.

Examples to Get You Started

EXAMPLE 1

See whether you can spot the error in the underlined section of the sentence below.

<u>Being as I had studied for the test</u> with a tutor, I was confident.

(A) Being as I had studied for the test
(B) Being as I studied for the test
(C) Since I studied for the test
(D) Since I had studied for the test
(E) Because I studied for the test

Since you immediately recognize that *Being as* is not acceptable as a conjunction in standard written English, you can eliminate choices A and B right away. But you also know that both *Since* and *Because* are perfectly acceptable conjunctions, so you have to look more closely at choices C, D, and E. The only other changes these choices make are in the tense of the verb. Since the studying occurred before the taking of the test, the past perfect tense, *had studied*, is correct, so the answer is choice D. Even if you hadn't known that, you could have figured it out. Since *Because* and *Since* are both acceptable conjunctions, and since choices C and E both use the same verb, *studied,* in the simple past tense, those two choices must be wrong. Otherwise, they would both be right, and the SAT doesn't have questions with two right answers.

EXAMPLE 2

When you can't spot any error in the underlined section of the sentence, closely examine each of the answer choices to determine what may be wrong.

Even the play's most minor characters work together with extraordinary skill, their interplay creates a moving theatrical experience.

(A) their interplay creates a moving theatrical experience
(B) a moving theatrical experience is created by their interplay
(C) and their interplay creates a moving theatrical experience
(D) and a moving theatrical experience being the creation of their interplay
(E) with their interplay they create a moving theatrical experience

Look at the underlined section of the sentence. Nothing seems wrong with it. It could stand on its own as an independent sentence: *Their interplay creates a moving theatrical experience.* Choices B and E are similar to it, for both could stand as independent sentences. Choices C and D, however, are not independent sentences; both begin with the linking word *and.* The error needing correction here is the common comma splice, in which two sentences are carelessly linked with only a comma. Choice C corrects this error in the simplest way possible, adding the word *and* to tie these sentences together.

EXAMPLE 3

Sometimes the underlined section of a sentence may be grammatically correct but rhetorically ineffective. In such cases, your job is to find an answer that works better than the original does, one that packs more punch.

The rock star always had enthusiastic fans <u>and they loved him</u>.

(A) and they loved him
(B) and they loving him
(C) what loved him
(D) who loved him
(E) which loved him

The original version of this sentence doesn't have any grammatical errors, but it is a poor sentence because it doesn't connect its two clauses logically. The second clause ("and they loved him") is merely adding information about the fans, so it should be turned into an adjective clause, introduced by a relative pronoun. Choices D and E both seem to fit, but you know that *which* should never be used to refer to people, so choice D is obviously the correct answer.

EXAMPLE 4

In this chapter we'll analyze both types of questions, <u>suggest useful techniques for tackling them, providing some sample items for you to try</u>.

(A) suggest useful techniques for tackling them, providing some sample items for you to try
(B) suggest useful techniques for tackling them, providing some sample items which you can try
(C) suggest useful tactics for tackling them, and provide some sample items for you to try

    (D) and suggest useful techniques for tackling them by
        providing some sample items for you to try

    (E) having suggested useful techniques for tackling
        them and provided some sample items for you to try

To answer questions like this correctly, you must pay particular attention to what the sentence means. You must first decide whether *analyzing, suggesting,* and *providing* are logically equal in importance here. Since they are—all are activities that "we" will do—they should be given equal emphasis. Only choice C provides the proper parallel structure.

EXAMPLE 5

The turning point in the battle of Waterloo probably was Blucher, <u>who was arriving</u> in time to save the day.

(A) Blucher, who was arriving

(B) Blucher, in that he arrived

(C) Blucher's arrival

(D) when Blucher was arriving

(E) that Blucher had arrived

Which answer choice uses the fewest words? Choice C, *Blucher's arrival.* It also happens to be the right answer.

Choice C is both concise in style and correct in grammar. Look back at the original sentence. Strip it of its modifiers, and what is left? "The turning point . . . was Blucher." A turning point is not a person; it is a *thing.* The turning point in the battle was not Blucher, but Blucher's *action,* the thing he did. The correct answer is choice C, *Blucher's arrival.* Pay particular attention to such concise answer choices. If a concise choice sounds natural when you substitute it for the original underlined phrase, it's a reasonable guess.

THE IMPROVING PARAGRAPHS QUESTION

In the improving paragraphs questions, you will confront a flawed student essay followed by several questions. In some cases, you must select the answer choice that best rewrites and combines portions of two separate sentences. In others, you must decide where in the essay a sentence best fits. In still others, you must choose what sort of additional information would most strengthen the writer's argument. Here is an example of this type of question.

[1] Nowadays the average cost of a new home in San Francisco is over $500,000. [2] For this reason it is not surprising that people are talking about a cheaper new type of home called a Glidehouse. [3] The Glidehouse is a type of factory-built housing. [4] It was designed by a young woman architect named Michelle Kaufmann. [5] Michelle was disgusted by having to pay $600,000 for a fixer-upper. [6] So she designed a kind of a modular house with walls that glide.

Sentences 3, 4, and 5 (reproduced below) could best be written in which of the following ways?

The Glidehouse is a type of factory-built housing. It was designed by a young woman architect named Michelle Kaufmann. Michelle was disgusted by having to pay $600,000 for a fixer-upper.

(A) (Exactly as shown above)

(B) The Glidehouse typifies factory-built housing. A young woman architect named Michelle Kaufmann designed it, having been disgusted at having to pay $600,000 for a fixer-upper.

(C) The Glidehouse is a type of factory-built home, it was a young woman architect named Michelle Kaufmann who designed it because she resented having to pay $600,000 for a fixer-upper.

(D) An example of housing that has been built in a factory, the Glidehouse was the design of a young woman architect named Michelle Kaufmann whom having to pay $600,000 for a fixer-upper resented.

(E) The Glidehouse, a factory-built home, was designed

by the young architect Michelle Kaufmann, who resented having to pay $600,000 for a fixer-upper.

In the original essay, sentences 3, 4, and 5 are wordy and rely heavily on passive voice constructions. Read aloud, they sound choppy. Choice E combines these three simple sentences into a single sentence that is both coherent and grammatically correct.

Tips to Help You Cope

1. First read the passage; then read the questions. Whether you choose to skim the student essay quickly or to read it closely, you need to have a reasonable idea of what the student author is trying to say before you set out to correct this rough first draft.

2. First tackle the questions that ask you to improve individual sentences; then tackle the ones that ask you to strengthen the passage as a whole. In the sentence correction questions, you've just been weeding out ineffective sentences and selecting effective ones. Here you're doing more of the same. It generally takes less time to spot an effective sentence than it does to figure out a way to strengthen an argument or link up two paragraphs.

3. Consider whether the addition of signal words or phrases—transitions—would strengthen the passage or particular sentences within it. If the essay is trying to contrast two ideas, it might benefit from the addition of a contrast signal.

    Contrast Signals: *although, despite, however, in contrast, nevertheless, on the contrary, on the other hand.*

    If one portion of the essay is trying to support or continue a thought developed elsewhere in the passage, it might benefit from the addition of a support signal.

Support Signals: *additionally, furthermore, in addition, likewise, moreover.*

If the essay is trying to indicate that one thing causes another, it might benefit from the addition of a cause and effect signal.

Cause and Effect Signals: *accordingly, as a result of, because, consequently, hence, therefore, thus.*

Pay particular attention to answer choices that contain such signal words.

4. When you tackle the questions, *go back to the passage* to verify each answer choice. See whether your revised version of a particular sentence sounds right in its context. Ask yourself whether your choice follows naturally from the sentence before.

COMMON GRAMMAR AND USAGE ERRORS

Some errors are more common than others in this section. Here are a dozen that appear frequently on the examination. Watch out for them when you do the practice exercises and when you take the SAT.

The Run-On Sentence

Mary's party was very exciting, it lasted until 2 A.M.
It is raining today, I need a raincoat.

You may also have heard this error called a comma splice. It can be corrected by making two sentences instead of one:

Mary's party was very exciting. It lasted until 2 A.M.

or by using a semicolon in place of the comma:

Mary's party was very exciting; it lasted until 2 A.M.

or by proper compounding:

Mary's party was very exciting and lasted until 2 A.M.

You can also correct this error with proper subordination. The second example above could be corrected:

Since it is raining today, I need a raincoat.

It is raining today, so I need a raincoat.

The Sentence Fragment

Since John was talking during the entire class, making it impossible for anyone to concentrate.

This is the opposite of the first error. Instead of too much in one sentence, here you have too little. Do not be misled by the length of the fragment. It must have a main clause before it can be a complete sentence. All you have in this example is the cause. You still need a result. For example, the sentence could be corrected:

Since John was talking during the entire class, making it impossible for anyone to concentrate, the teacher made him stay after school.

Error in the Case of a Noun or Pronoun

Between you and I, this test is not really very difficult.

Case problems usually involve personal pronouns, which are in the nominative case (*I, he, she, we, they, who*) when they are used as subjects or predicate nominatives, and in the objective case (*me, him, her, us, them, whom*) when they are used as direct objects, indirect objects, and objects of prepositions. In this example, if you realize that *between* is a preposition, you know that *I* should be changed to the objective *me* because it is the object of a preposition.

Error in Subject-Verb Agreement

Harvard College, along with several other Ivy League schools, are sending students to the conference.

Phrases starting with *along with* or *as well as* or *in addition to* that are placed in between the subject and the verb do not affect the verb. The subject of this sentence is *Harvard College,* so the verb should be *is sending.*

There is three bears living in that house.

Sentences that begin with *there* almost always have the subject after the verb. The subject of this sentence is *bears,* so the verb should be *are.*

Error in Pronoun-Number Agreement

Every one of the girls on the team is trying to do their best.

Every pronoun must have a specific noun or noun substitute for an antecedent, and it must agree with that antecedent in number (singular or plural). In this example, *their* refers to *one* and must be singular:

Every one of the girls on the team is trying to do her best.

Error in the Tense or Form of a Verb

After the sun set behind the mountain, a cool breeze sprang up and brought relief from the heat.

Make sure the verbs in a sentence appear in the proper sequence of tenses, so that it is clear what happened when. Since, according to the sentence, the breeze did not appear until after the sun had finished setting, the setting belongs in the past perfect tense:

After the sun had set behind the mountain, a cool breeze sprang up and brought relief from the heat.

Error in Logical Comparison

I can go to California or Florida. I wonder which is best.

When you are comparing only two things, you should use the comparative form of the adjective, not the superlative:

I wonder which is better.

Comparisons must also be complete and logical.

The rooms on the second floor are larger than the first floor.

It would be a strange building that had rooms larger than an entire floor. Logically, this sentence should be corrected to:

The rooms on the second floor are larger than those on the first floor.

Adjective and Adverb Confusion

She did good on the test.

They felt badly about leaving their friends.

These are the two most common ways that adjectives and adverbs are misused. In the first example, when you are talking about how someone did, you want the adverb *well*, not the adjective *good:*

She did well on the test.

In the second example, after a linking verb like *feel* you want a predicate adjective to describe the subject:

They felt bad about leaving their friends.

Error in Modification and Word Order

Reaching for the book, the ladder slipped out from under him.

A participial phrase at the beginning of the sentence should describe the subject of the sentence. Since it doesn't make sense to think of a ladder reaching for a book, this participle is left dangling with nothing to modify. The sentence needs some rewriting:

When he reached for the book, the ladder slipped out from under him.

Error in Parallelism

In his book on winter sports, the author discusses ice-skating, skiing, hockey, and how to fish in an ice-covered lake.

Logically, equal and similar ideas belong in similar form. This shows that they are equal. In this sentence, the author discusses four sports, and all four should be presented the same way:

In his book on winter sports, the author discusses ice skating, skiing, hockey, and fishing in an ice-covered lake.

Error in Diction or Idiom

The affects of the storm could be seen everywhere.

Your ear for the language will help you handle these errors, especially if you are accustomed to reading standard English. These questions test you on words that are frequently misused, on levels of usage (informal versus formal), and on standard English idioms. In this example, the verb *affect,* meaning "to influence," has been confused with the noun *effect,* meaning "result."

The effects of the storm could be seen everywhere.

The exercises that follow will give you practice in answering the three types of questions you'll find on the Identifying Sentence Errors questions, Improving Sentences questions, and Improving Paragraphs questions. When you have completed each exercise, check your answers against the answer key. Then, read the answer explanations for any questions you either answered incorrectly or omitted.

Practice Exercises   Answers given on pages 144–145.

Exercise A

The sentences in this section may contain errors in grammar, usage, choice of words, or idioms. Either there is just one error in a sentence or the sentence is correct. Some words or phrases are underlined and lettered; everything else in the sentence is correct.

If an underlined word or phrase is incorrect, choose that letter; if the sentence is correct, select <u>No error</u>. Then blacken the appropriate space on your answer sheet.

Example:

The region has a climate <u>so severe that</u> plants
                    A

<u>growing there</u> rarely <u>had been</u> more than twelve
   B   C

inches <u>high.</u> <u>No error</u>
     D   E

                          Ⓐ Ⓑ ● Ⓓ Ⓔ

1. We were <u>already</u> to <u>leave</u> for the amusement park when John's car
           A   B

   <u>broke down;</u> we were <u>forced to</u> postpone our outing. <u>No error</u>
      C   D   E

2. <u>By order of</u> the Student Council, the <u>wearing of</u> slacks by <u>we girls</u> in
   A   B   C

   <u>school has been permitted.</u> <u>No error</u>
           D   E

3. Each one of the dogs in the show <u>require</u> a <u>special</u> <u>kind</u> <u>of diet.</u>
   A   B   C   D

   <u>No error</u>
    E

4. The major difficulty <u>confronting</u> the authorities <u>was</u> the reluctance
       A   B

   of the people to <u>talk</u>; they had been warned not to <u>say nothing</u> to
                     C   D

   the police. <u>No error</u>
               E

5. If I <u>were</u> you, I would never permit <u>him</u> to <u>take</u> part in such an
        A   B   C

   <u>exhausting and painful</u> activity. <u>No error</u>
             D   E

6. Stanford White, <u>who is</u> one of America's <u>most notable</u> architects,
                   A   B

   <u>have designed</u> many famous buildings, <u>among them</u> the original
         C   D

   Madison Square Garden. <u>No error</u>
                          E

7. The notion of <u>allowing</u> the <u>institution</u> of slavery <u>to continue to exist</u>
                 A   B   C

   in a democratic society had no appeal to either the violent followers

   of John Brown <u>nor</u> the peaceful disciples of Sojourner Truth. <u>No error</u>
                 D   E

8. Some students <u>prefer</u> watching filmstrips to <u>textbooks</u> because
                 A   B

   they feel <u>uncomfortable</u> with the presentation <u>of</u> information in a
             C   D

   non-oral form. <u>No error</u>
                  E

9. <u>There</u> was so much conversation <u>in back of</u> me <u>that</u> I <u>couldn't</u> hear
   A   B   C   D

   the actors on the stage. <u>No error</u>
                            E

10. This book is <u>too</u> elementary; <u>it can help</u> neither <u>you</u> nor <u>I</u>. <u>No error</u>
                 A   B   C   D   E

11. In a way we may say that we have reached the end of the Industrial
      　　　　A　　　　B　　　　　C　　　　　D

Revolution. No error
　　　　　　　E

12. Although the books are altogether on the shelf, they are not arranged
      　　　　　A　　　　　　B　　　　　　　　　C

in any kind of order. No error
　　　D　　　　　　　E

13. The reason for my prolonged absence from class was because I was
      　　　　　A　　　　　B　　　　　　　　　C　　　D

ill for three weeks. No error
　　　　　　　　　E

14. According to researchers, the weapons and work implements used by
      　　A　　　　　　　　　　　　　　　　　　　　　　　　　　　　B

Cro-Magnon hunters appear being actually quite "modern." No error
　　　　　　　　　　　　C　　　　　D　　　　　　　　　　　E

15. Since we were caught completely unawares, the affect of Ms. Rivera's
      　　　　　　　　　　　　A　　　　　　　B

remarks was startling; some were shocked, but others were angry.
　　　　　C　　　　　　　　　　　　　　　　D

No error
　E

16. The committee had intended both you and I to speak at the assembly;
      　　　　　　　　A　　　　　　B

however, only one of us will be able to talk. No error
　C　　　D　　　　　　　　　　　　　　E

17. The existence of rundown "welfare hotels" in which homeless
      　　　　　　　　　　　　　　　　　　　A

families reside at enormous cost to the taxpayer provides a shameful
　　　　B　　　　　　　　　C

commentary of America's commitment to house the poor. No error
　　　D　　　　　　　　　　　　　　　　　　　　　E

18. We have heard that the principal has decided whom the prize winners
                            A   B

will be and will announce the names in the assembly today. No error
C   D   E

19. As soon as the sun had rose over the mountains, the valley became
                  A   B   C

unbearably hot and stifling. No error
       D   E

20. They are both excellent books, but this one is best. No error
     A   B   C   D   E

21. Although the news had come as a surprise to all in the room, both
                         A   B

Jane and Oprah tried to do her work as though nothing had
                              C   D

happened. No error
            E

22. Even well-known fashion designers have difficulty staying on top
     A

from one season to another because of changeable moods and
            B   C   D

needs in the marketplace. No error
                                E

23. Arms control has been under discussion for decades with the
                         A

former Soviet Union, but solutions are still alluding the major powers.
       B   C   D

No error
E

24. Perhaps sports enthusiasts are realizing that jogging is not easy on
                                       A   B

joints and tendons, for the latest fad is being walking. No error
                    C   D   E

25. Technological advances <u>can cause</u> factual data to become obsolete
                      A
within a <u>short time</u>; <u>yet</u>, students should concentrate on
         B   C
<u>reasoning skills</u>, not facts. <u>No error</u>
       D   E

26. If anyone <u>cares</u> to <u>join me</u> in this campaign, <u>either</u> now or in the near
         A   B   C
future, <u>they</u> will be welcomed gratefully. <u>No error</u>
         D   E

27. The poems <u>with which</u> he occasionally <u>desired to regale</u> the
                   A   B
fashionable world were <u>invariably bad</u>—stereotyped, bombastic,
                           C
and even <u>ludicrous</u>. <u>No error</u>
            D   E

28. <u>Ever since</u> the <u>quality of</u> teacher education came under public
          A   B
scrutiny, suggestions for <u>upgrading</u> the profession are <u>abounding</u>.
                              C   D
<u>No error</u>
   E

29. Because the door was <u>locked and bolted</u>, the police <u>were</u> forced
                  A   B
to break into the apartment <u>through</u> the bedroom window. <u>No error</u>
         C   D   E

30. I will <u>always</u> <u>remember</u> you <u>standing</u> <u>by</u> me offering me
         A   B   C   D
encouragement. <u>No error</u>
                   E

31. With special training, capuchin monkeys can enable quadriplegics
                                                    _____
                                                           A
    as well as other handicapped individuals to become
    _____   _____
         B   C
    increasingly independent. No error
    _____   _____
              D   E

32. Contary to what had previously been reported, the conditions
    _____
       A
    governing the truce between Libya and Chad arranged by the
    _____   _____
        B   C
    United Nations has not yet been revealed. No error
                  ___   _____
                   D   E

33. Avid readers generally either admire or dislike Ernest Hemingway's
                                    _____
                                      A
    journalistic style of writing; few have no opinion of him. No error
                _____   _____   _____ _____
                     B   C   D   E

34. In 1986, the nuclear disaster at Chernobyl has aroused intense
                                              _____
                                                     A
    speculation about the long-term effects of radiation that continued
               _____   _____
                      B   C
    for the better part of a year. No error
    _____   _____
               D   E

35. Howard Hughes, who became the subject of bizarre rumors
                   _____ _____
                    A   B
    as a result of his exteme reclusiveness, was well-known as an aviator,
    _____
          C
    industrialist, and in producing motion pictures. No error
                  _____   _____
                              D   E

Exercise B

Some or all parts of the following sentences are underlined. The first answer choice, (A), simply repeats the underlined part of the sentence. The other four choices present four alternative ways to phrase the underlined part. Select the answer that produces the most effective sentence, one that is clear and exact, and blacken the appropriate space on your answer sheet. In selecting your choice, be sure that it is standard written English, and that it expresses the meaning of the original sentence.

Example:

The first biography of author Eudora Welty came out in 1998 and she was 89 years old at the time.

(A) and she was 89 years old at the time
(B) at the time when she was 89
(C) upon becoming an 89 year old
(D) when she was 89
(E) at the age of 89 years old

1. The child is neither encouraged to be critical or to examine all the evidence before forming an opinion.

    (A) neither encouraged to be critical or to examine
    (B) neither encouraged to be critical nor to examine
    (C) either encouraged to be critical or to examine
    (D) encouraged either to be critical nor to examine
    (E) not encouraged either to be critical or to examine

2. The process by which the community influence the actions of its members is known as social control.

    (A) influence the actions of its members
    (B) influences the actions of its members
    (C) had influenced the actions of its members
    (D) influences the actions of their members
    (E) will influence the actions of its members

3. Play being recognized as an important factor improving mental and physical health and thereby reducing human misery and poverty.

    (A) Play being recognized as
    (B) By recognizing play as
    (C) Their recognizing play as
    (D) Recognition of it being
    (E) Play is recognized as

4. To be sure, there would be scarcely any time left over for other things if school children would have been expected to have considered all sides of every matter, on which they hold opinions.

    (A) would have been expected to have considered
    (B) should have been expected to have considered
    (C) were expected to consider
    (D) will be expected to have considered
    (E) were expected to be considered

5. Using it wisely, leisure promotes health, efficiency and happiness.
    (A) Using it wisely
    (B) If it is used wisely
    (C) Having used it wisely
    (D) Because of its wise use
    (E) Because of usefulness

6. In giving expression to the play instincts of the human race, new vigor and effectiveness are afforded by recreation to the body and to the mind.

    (A) new vigor and effectiveness are afforded by recreation to the body and to the mind
    (B) recreation affords new vigor and effectiveness to the body and to the mind
    (C) there are afforded new vigor and effectiveness to the body and to the mind
    (D) by recreation the body and the mind are afforded new vigor and effectiveness
    (E) to the body and to the mind afford new vigor and effectiveness to themselves by recreation

7. Depending on skillful suggestion, argument is seldom used in adver-
    tising.

    (A) Depending on skillful suggestion, argument is seldom used in
         advertising.
    (B) Argument is seldom used in advertising, which depends instead
         on skillful suggestion.
    (C) Skillful suggestion is depended on by advertisers instead of
         argument.
    (D) Suggestion, which is more skillful, is used in place of argument
         by advertisers.
    (E) Instead of suggestion, depending on argument is used by
         skillful advertisers.

8. When this war is over, no nation will either be isolated in war or peace.

    (A) either be isolated in war or peace
    (B) be either isolated in war or peace
    (C) be isolated in neither war nor peace
    (D) be isolated either in war or in peace
    (E) be isolated neither in war or peace

9. Thanks to the prevailing westerly winds, dust blowing east from the
    drought-stricken plains travels halfway across the continent to fall on
    the cities of the East Coast.

    (A) blowing east from the drought-stricken plains
    (B) that, blowing east from the drought-stricken plains,
    (C) from the drought-stricken plains and blows east
    (D) that is from the drought-stricken plains blowing east
    (E) blowing east that is from the plains that are drought-stricken

10. Americans are learning that their concept of a research worker toiling
    alone in a laboratory and who discovers miraculous cures has been
    highly idealized and glamorized.

    (A) toiling alone in a laboratory and who discovers miraculous
         cures
    (B) toiling alone in a laboratory and discovers miraculous cures
    (C) toiling alone in a laboratory to discover miraculous cures
    (D) who toil alone in the laboratory and discover miraculous cures
    (E) has toiled alone hoping to discover miraculous cures

11. However many mistakes have been made in our past, the tradition of America, not only the champion of freedom but also fair play, still lives among millions who can see light and hope scarcely anywhere else.

(A) not only the champion of freedom but also fair play
(B) the champion of not only freedom but also of fair play
(C) the champion not only of freedom but also of fair play
(D) not only the champion but also freedom and fair play
(E) not the champion of freedom only, but also fair play

12. Examining the principal movements sweeping through the world, it can be seen that they are being accelerated by the war.

(A) Examining the principal movements sweeping through the world, it can be seen
(B) Having examined the principal movements sweeping through the world, it can be seen
(C) Examining the principal movements sweeping through the world can be seen
(D) Examining the principal movements sweeping through the world, we can see
(E) It can be seen examining the principal movements sweeping through the world

13. The FCC is broadening its view on what constitutes indecent programming, radio stations are taking a closer look at their broadcasters' materials.

(A) The FCC is broadening its view on what constitutes indecent programming
(B) The FCC, broadening its view on what constitutes indecent programming, has caused
(C) The FCC is broadening its view on what constitutes indecent programming, as a result
(D) Since the FCC is broadening its view on what constitutes indecent programming
(E) The FCC, having broadened its view on what constitutes indecent programming

14. As district attorney, Elizabeth Holtzman not only had the responsibility of supervising a staff of dedicated young lawyers <u>but she had the task of maintaining good relations with the police also.</u>

   (A) but she had the task of maintaining good relations with the police also

   (B) but she also had the task of maintaining good relations with the police

   (C) but also had the task of maintaining good relations with the police

   (D) but she had the task to maintain good relations with the police also

   (E) but also she had the task to maintain good relations with the police

15. Many politicians are now trying to take uncontroversial positions on issues; <u>the purpose being to allow them to appeal</u> to as wide a segment of the voting population as possible.

   (A) issues; the purpose being to allow them to appeal

   (B) issues in order to appeal

   (C) issues, the purpose is to allow them to appeal

   (D) issues and the purpose is to allow them to appeal

   (E) issues; that was allowing them to appeal

Exercise C

The passage below is the unedited draft of a student's essay. Parts of the essay need to be rewritten to make the meaning clearer and more precise. Read the essay carefully.

The essay is followed by six questions about changes that might improve all or part of the organization, development, sentence structure, use of language, appropriateness to the audience, or use of standard written English. In each case, choose the answer that most clearly and effectively expresses the student's intended meaning. Indicate your choice by blackening the corresponding space on the answer sheet.

[1] Throughout history, people have speculated about the future. [2] Will it be a utopia? they wondered. [3] Will injustice and poverty be eliminated? [4] Will people accept ethnic diversity, learning to live in peace? [5] Will the world be clean and unpolluted? [6] Or will technology aid us in creating a trap for ourselves we cannot escape, for example such as the world in 1984? [7] With the turn of the millennium just around the corner these questions are in the back of our minds.

[8] Science fiction often portrays the future as a technological Garden of Eden. [9] With interactive computers, TVs and robots at our command, we barely need to lift a finger to go to school, to work, to go shopping, and education is also easy and convenient. [10] Yet, the problems of the real twentieth century seem to point in another direction. [11] The environment, far from improving, keeps deteriorating. [12] Wars and other civil conflicts breakout regularly. [13] The world's population is growing out of control. [14] The majority of people on earth live in poverty. [15] Many of them are starving. [16] Illiteracy is a problem in most poor countries. [17] Diseases and malnourishment is very common. [18] Rich countries like the U.S.A. don't have the resources to help the "have-not" countries.

[19] Instead, think instead of all the silly inventions such as tablets you put in your toilet tank to make the water blue, or electric toothbrushes. [20] More money is spent on space and defense than on education and health care. [21] Advancements in agriculture can produce enough food to feed the whole country, yet people in the U.S. are starving.

[22] Although the USSR is gone, the nuclear threat continues from small countries like Iraq. [23] Until the world puts its priorities straight, we can't look for a bright future in the twenty-first century, despite the rosy picture painted for us by the science fiction writers.

1. In the context of paragraph 1, which of the following is the best revision of sentence 6?

   (A) Or will technology create a trap for ourselves from which we cannot escape, for example the world in *1984*?

   (B) Or will technology aid people in creating a trap for themselves that they cannot escape; for example, the world in *1984*?

   (C) Or will technology create a trap from which there is no escape, as it did in the world in *1984*?

   (D) Or will technology trap us in an inescapable world, for example, it did so in the world of *1984*?

   (E) Perhaps technology will aid people in creating a trap for themselves from which they cannot escape, just as they did it in the world of *1984*.

2. With regard to the essay as a whole, which of the following best describes the writer's intention in paragraph 1?

   (A) To announce the purpose of the essay
   (B) To compare two ideas discussed later in the essay
   (C) To take a position on the essay's main issue
   (D) To reveal the organization of the essay
   (E) To raise questions that will be answered in the essay

3. Which of the following is the best revision of the underlined segment of sentence 9 below?

   [9] With interactive computers, TVs and robots at our command, we barely need to lift a finger to go to school, to work, to go shopping, and education is also easy and convenient.

   (A) and to go shopping, while education is also easy and convenient
   (B) to go shopping, and getting an education is also easy and convenient
   (C) to go shopping as well as educating ourselves are all easy and convenient
   (D) to shop, and an easy and convenient education
   (E) to shop, and to get an easy and convenient education

4. Which of the following is the most effective way to combine sentences 14, 15, 16, and 17?

   (A) The majority of people on earth are living in poverty and are starving, with illiteracy, and disease and being malnourished are also a common problems.
   (B) Common problems for the majority of people on earth are poverty, illiteracy, diseases, malnourishment, and many are illiterate.
   (C) The majority of people on earth are poor, starving, sick, malnourished and illiterate.
   (D) Common among the poor majority on earth is poverty, starvation, disease, malnourishment, and illiteracy.
   (E) The majority of the earth's people living in poverty with starvation, disease, malnourishment and illiteracy a constant threat.

5. In the context of the sentences that precede and follow sentence 19, which of the following is the most effective revision of sentence 19?

   (A) Instead they are devoting resources on silly inventions such as tablets to make toilet tank water blue or electric toothbrushes.

   (B) Instead, they waste their resources on producing silly inventions like electric toothbrushes and tablets for bluing toilet tank water.

   (C) Think of all the silly inventions: tablets you put in your toilet tank to make the water blue and electric toothbrushes.

   (D) Instead, tablets you put in your toilet tank to make the water blue or electric toothbrushes are examples of useless products on the market today.

   (E) Instead of spending on useful things, think of all the silly inventions such as tablets you put in your toilet tank to make the water blue or electric toothbrushes.

6. Which of the following revisions would most improve the overall coherence of the essay?

   (A) Move sentence 7 to paragraph 2
   (B) Move sentence 10 to paragraph 1
   (C) Move sentence 22 to paragraph 2
   (D) Delete sentence 8
   (E) Delete sentence 23

Answer Key

Exercise A

1.	A	10.	E	19.	B	28.	D
2.	C	11.	E	20.	D	29.	E
3.	B	12.	B	21.	C	30.	C
4.	D	13.	D	22.	E	31.	E
5.	E	14.	C	23.	D	32.	D
6.	C	15.	B	24.	D	33.	D
7.	D	16.	B	25.	C	34.	A
8.	B	17.	D	26.	D	35.	D
9.	B	18.	B	27.	E		

Exercise B

1.	E	5.	B	9.	A	13.	D
2.	B	6.	B	10.	C	14.	C
3.	E	7.	B	11.	C	15.	B
4.	C	8.	D	12.	D		

Exercise C

1.	C	3.	E	5.	B
2.	E	4.	C	6.	C

Answer Explanations

Exercise A

1. **A** Error in diction. Should be *all ready*. *All ready* means the group is ready; *already* means prior to a given time, previously.

2. **C** Error in pronoun case. Should be *us*. The expression *us girls* is the object of the preposition *by*.

3. **B** Error in subject–verb agreement. Should be *requires*. Verb should agree with the subject (*each one*).

4. **D** Should be *to say anything. Not to say nothing* is a double negative.

5. **E** Sentence is correct.

6. **C** Error in subject–verb agreement. Since the subject is Stanford White (singular), change *have designed* to *has designed*.

7. **D** Error in use of correlatives. Change *nor* to *or*. The correct form of the correlative pairs *either* with *or*.

8. **B** Error in parallel structure. Change *textbooks* to *reading textbooks*. To have parallel structure, the linked sentence elements must share the same grammatical form.

9. **B** Error in diction. Change *in back of* to *behind*.

10. **D** Error in pronoun case. Should be *me*. Pronoun is the object of the verb *can help*.

11. **E** Sentence is correct.

12. **B** Error in diction. Should be *all together. All together* means in a group; *altogether* means entirely.

13. **D** Improper use of *because.* Change to *that* (*The reason . . . was that . . . .*).

14. **C** Incorrect verbal. Change the participle *being* to the infinitive *to be.*

15. **B** Error in diction. Change *affect* (a verb meaning to influence or pretend) to *effect* (a noun meaning result).

16. **B** Error in pronoun case. Should be *me.* Subjects of infinitives are in the objective case.

17. **D** Error in idiom. Change *commentary of* to *commentary on.*

18. **B** Error in pronoun case. Should be *who.* The pronoun is the predicate complement of *will be* and is in the nominative case.

19. **B** Should be *had risen.* The past participle of the verb *to rise* is *risen.*

20. **D** Error in comparison of modifiers. Should be *better.* Do not use the superlative when comparing two things.

21. **C** Error in pronoun–number agreement. Should be *their* instead of *her.* The antecedent of the pronoun is *Jane and Oprah* (plural).

22. **E** Sentence is correct.

23. **D** Error in diction. Change *alluding* (meaning to refer indirectly) to *eluding* (meaning to evade).

24. **D** Confusion of verb and gerund (verbal noun). Change *is being walking* to *is walking.*

25. **C** Error in coordination and subordination. Change *yet* to *therefore* or another similar connector to clarify the connection between the clauses.

26. **D** Error in pronoun–number agreement. Should be *he or she.* The antecedent of the pronoun is *anyone* (singular).

27. **E** Sentence is correct.

28. **D** Error in sequence of tenses. Change *are abounding* to *have abounded.* The present perfect tense talks about an action that occurs at one time, but is seen in relation to another time.

29. **E** Sentence is correct.

30. **C** Error in pronoun case. Should be *your*. The pronoun modifying a gerund (verbal noun) should be in the possessive case.

31. **E** Sentence is correct.

32. **D** Error in subject–verb agreement. Since the subject is *conditions* (plural), change *has* to *have*.

33. **D** Error in pronoun. Since the sentence speaks about Hemingway's style rather than about Hemingway, the phrase should read *of it,* not *of him.*

34. **A** Error in sequence of tenses. Change *has aroused* to *aroused.* The present perfect tense (*has aroused*) is used for indefinite time. In this sentence, the time is defined as *the better part of a year.*

35. **D** Lack of parallel structure. Change *in producing motion pictures* to *motion picture producer.*

Exercise B

1. **E** This question involves two aspects of correct English. *Neither* should be followed by *nor; either* by *or.* Choices A and D are, therefore, incorrect. The words *neither . . . nor* and *either . . . or* should be placed before the two items being discussed—*to be critical* and *to examine.* Choice E meets both requirements.

2. **B** This question tests agreement. Errors in subject–verb agreement and pronoun–number agreement are both involved. *Community* (singular) needs a singular verb, *influences.* Also, the pronoun that refers to *community* should be singular *(its).*

3. **E** Error in following conventions. This is an incomplete sentence or fragment. The sentence needs a verb to establish a principal clause. Choice E provides the verb (*is recognized*) and presents the only complete sentence in the group.

4. **C** *Would have been expected* is incorrect as a verb in a clause introduced by the conjunction *if. Had been expected* or *were expected* is preferable. *To have considered* does not follow correct sequence of tense and should be changed to *to consider.*

5. **B** Error in modification and word order. One way of correcting a dangling participle is to change the participial phrase to a clause. Choices B and D substitute clauses for the phrase. However,

Choice D changes the meaning of the sentence. Choice B is correct.

6. **B** Error in modification and word order. As it stands, the sentence contains a dangling modifier. This is corrected by making *recreation* the subject of the sentence, in the process switching from the passive to the active voice. Choice E also provides a subject for the sentence; however, the meaning of the sentence is changed in Choice E.

7. **B** Error in modification and word order. As presented, the sentence contains a dangling participle, *depending*. Choice B corrects this error. The other choices change the emphasis presented by the author.

8. **D** Error in word order. *Either . . . or* should precede the two choices offered (*in war* and *in peace*).

9. **A** Sentence is correct.

10. **C** Error in parallelism. In the underlined phrase, you will find two modifiers of *worker-toiling* and *who discovers*. The first is a participial phrase and the second a clause. This results in an error in parallel structure. Choice B also has an error in parallel structure. Choice C corrects this by eliminating one of the modifiers of *worker*. Choice D corrects the error in parallel structure but introduces an error in agreement between subject and verb—*who* (singular) and *toil* (plural). Choice E changes the tense and also the meaning of the original sentence.

11. **C** Error in parallelism. Parallel structure requires that *not only* and *but also* immediately precede the words they limit.

12. **D** Error in modification and word order. Choices A, B, and E are incorrect because of the dangling participle. Choice C is incoherent. Choice D correctly eliminates the dangling participle by introducing the subject *we*.

13. **D** Error in comma splice. The punctuation in Choices A and C creates a run-on sentence. Choices B and E are both ungrammatical. Choice D corrects the run-on sentence by changing the beginning clause into the adverb clause that starts with the subordinating conjunction *since*.

14. **C** Error in parallelism. Since the words *not only* immediately precede the verb in the first half of the sentence, the words *but also*

should immediately precede the verb in the second half. This error in parallel structure is corrected in choice C.

15. **B** Error in coordination and subordination. The punctuation in Choices A, C, D, and E creates an incomplete sentence or fragment. Choice B corrects the error by linking the elements with *in order to.*

Exercise C

1. **C** Choice A is awkward and shifts the pronoun usage in the paragraph from third to first person. Choice B is awkward and contains a semicolon error. A semicolon is used to separate two independent clauses. The material after the semicolon is a sentence fragment. Choice C is succinctly and accurately expressed. It is the best answer. Choice D contains a comma splice between *world* and *for.* A comma may not be used to join two independent clauses. Choice E is awkwardly expressed and contains the pronoun *it,* which lacks a clear referent.

2. **E** Choice A indirectly describes the purpose of paragraph 1 but does not identify the writer's main intention. Choices B, C, and D fail to describe the writer's main intention. Choice E accurately describes the writer's main intention. It is the best answer.

3. **E** Choice A is grammatically correct but cumbersome. Choice B contains an error in parallel construction. The clause that begins *and getting* is not grammatically parallel to the previous items on the list. Choice C contains a mixed construction. The first and last parts of the sentence are grammatically unrelated. Choice D contains faulty parallel structure. Choice E is correct and accurately expressed. It is the best answer.

4. **C** Choice A is wordy and awkwardly expressed. Choice B contains an error in parallel structure. The clause *and many are illiterate* is not grammatically parallel to the previous items on the list of problems. Choice C is concise and accurately expressed. It is the best answer. Choice D is concise, but it contains an error in subject–verb agreement. The subject is *poverty, starvation . . . etc.,* which requires a plural verb; the verb *is* is singular. Choice E is a sentence fragment; it has no main verb.

5. **B** Choice A contains an error in idiom. The standard phrase is *devoting to,* not *devoting on.* Choice B ties sentence 19 to the previous sentence and is accurately expressed. It is the best answer. Choice

C fails to improve the coherence of the paragraph. Choice D is unrelated to the context of the paragraph. Choice E is insufficiently related to the context of the paragraph.

6. **C** Choice A should stay put because it provides a transition between the questions in paragraph 1 and the beginning of paragraph 2. Choice B is a pivotal sentence in paragraph 2 and should not be moved. Choice C fits the topics of paragraph 2, therefore, sentence 22 should be moved to paragraph 2. Choice C is the best answer. Choice D is needed as an introductory sentence in paragraph 2. It should not be deleted. Choice E provides the essay with a meaningful conclusion and should not be deleted.

THE 25-MINUTE ESSAY

Your SAT essay will be graded by two readers, each of whom will assign it a score of 1 to 6, with 6 the highest possible score. They will be looking for clear, insightful essays, essays that progress smoothly from idea to idea, and that are free from most technical flaws. To write a well-developed essay in just 25 minutes takes preparation: you need to gear up.

Before the Test

Gearing Up for Writing a Timed Essay

Your first impulse in embarking on a timed writing assignment may be to begin writing immediately. This is understandable, given the time pressure you are feeling and the natural fear of being unable to complete your essay in the allotted time. It is, however, a big mistake. Taking the time to brainstorm and outline is the best way to ensure that you write a complete essay, with a strong thesis and clear organization. Plan to invest a portion of your allowed time in developing a thumbnail outline of your essay.

Although planning your essay is essential, you should also avoid devoting too much time to planning. Your first instinct, to start writing ASAP because time is short, is not entirely wrong. Time *is* short, and the key to successful timed essay writing is the ability to plan your essay quickly. For a 25-minute essay, you should plan to spend no more than five minutes on brainstorming and outlining. If this sounds like a daunting task, you are correct. Thinking clearly on the fly and responding well under extreme time pressure is difficult, but it is a skill that you can develop with practice.

How to Write an Essay in 25 Minutes

Minute One—Analyze

Look at the essay question or prompt. What is it asking you to do? Is it prompting you to explain the reasons for an opinion of yours? Is it prompting you to take a stand on a particular issue? If you are being asked to argue for or against something, you may have an immediate gut reaction to what you're being asked. Pay attention to how you feel. If your immediate reaction is "Of course!" or "Never!," ask yourself why you feel that way. See whether you can spot any key word or short phrase in the prompt that triggers your reaction. For example, consider the following essay prompt:

> "If we rest, we rust." This statement is certainly true; inactivity and lack of exertion over time can cause our skills to deteriorate through disuse. In fact, people who have ceased practicing an activity for a long period and who attempt to take it up again frequently are thwarted in doing so because of the decline of their skills.

Do you think that rest has a detrimental effect on us and that we must keep active to avoid losing our edge? Plan and write an essay in which you explain your position on this issue. You may use examples from history, literature, popular culture, current events, or personal experience to support your position.

What key words trigger your reaction? *Rest* and *rust*.

Minute Two—Brainstorm

Write down the key words you spotted in the prompt. Circle them. Now write down all the words and phrases that you associate with these key words. What words come to your mind, for example, when you think of *rest*?

Neutral words like *sleep, inactivity, motionlessness*?
Negative words like *idleness, laziness, indolence*?
Positive words like *relaxing, tranquil, trouble free*?

Even if you have never thought that there might be a connection between resting and rusting, you have some mental associations with these ideas. By brainstorming, or clustering, as this process is sometimes called, you get in touch with these associations, call up the wealth of ideas you already have, and forget any worries you may have had about having nothing to say.

Note, by the way, in the illustration that follows, the many other words and phrases that branch off from the key words *rest* and *rust*. When you brainstorm, your mind leads you in innumerable directions, hinting at the whole range of what you already know about the subject at hand. If you feel like it, draw lines and arrows linking the various words and phrases to your two key words. Don't worry about setting these words and phrases in any particular order. Just play with them, jotting them down and doodling around them—a sense of where you are going will emerge.

You have plenty to say. You have gut reactions to all sorts of questions. Trust yourself. Let the brainstorming process tap the knowledge and feelings that lie within you.

Minute Three—Take a Stand

After you have been brainstorming for a bit, something inside you is going to say, "Now—now I know what I'm going to write." Trust that inner sense. You know where you are going—now put it into words.

Look over your "map" or record of your mental associations and see what patterns have emerged. Just what is it that you have to say? Are you *for* the idea that if we rest, we rust? Are you *against* the idea? What you are doing is coming up with a statement of your position—words to express your initial gut reaction—a *thesis sentence* for your essay.

Thesis 1: I believe that if we rest, we rust, because inactivity and lack of exertion lead to loss of vitality and to decay.

Thesis 2: I believe that if we rest, we do not rust, because our times of rest enable us to restore our mental and physical energy and to gain perspective on our lives.

Here are two preliminary thesis sentences, one for, one against. Note how their main clauses start: *I believe that.* Cut out that preliminary song and dance. In your thesis sentence, simply take a stand:

If we rest, we do not rust: our times of rest enable us to restore our mental and physical energy and to gain perspective on our lives.

The examiners want to see whether you can express your ideas clearly. Make your point clear to them from the start.

In a sense, the test-makers give you your introduction. All you have to do is take the prompt and rephrase it, putting it into your own words. This does not take much work. Remember, your job is to prove your writing competence, not to demonstrate your literary style. You do not need to open your essay with a quotation (The philosopher Blaise Pascal warns us, "Our nature consists in motion; complete rest is death.") or with a statement designed to startle your reader ("Sleep is for sissies."). You simply need to take a stand. In doing so, however, you must exercise some caution: you must limit your thesis to something you can handle in a few hundred words.

The one problem with brainstorming is that you may wind up feeling that you have too much to say. Your job is not to write everything you possibly can about the topic. It is to write one or two pages and make a single clear point. Avoid starting with open-ended statements like "Keeping active is important" or "Everybody needs rest." These are weak thesis statements—they are too broad to help you focus on the topic and too vague to show why you hold the opinion that you have. In writing your thesis statement, limit yourself. State your point—and be ready to support it with reasons.

Minute Four—Outline

Now take a minute to organize what you are going to say in outline form. In a sense, your thesis sentence sets up everything else you have to say. If you have a clear thesis, the essay almost writes itself.

Your goal is to produce a four- or five-paragraph essay consisting of a brief introduction, two or three solid paragraphs presenting examples that support your thesis, and a conclusion that restates your thesis. This is what such an essay looks like:

Introduction

<u>Thesis Sentence:</u> State your point (often last sentence of opening paragraph).

<u>Summary of Essay:</u> Present your supporting examples (2–3 sentences).

Example Paragraph 1

<u>Topic Sentence:</u> State the main idea of this paragraph. Show how it relates to your thesis.

<u>Development of Example:</u> Provide specific facts about the first example. Show how this example supports your argument. Be as detailed as possible: cite names, places, events.

(3–5 sentences)

Example Paragraph 2

<u>Topic Sentence:</u> State the main idea of this paragraph. Show how it relates to your thesis.

(Use transition words to connect this paragraph to the previous example paragraph.)

<u>Development of Example:</u> Provide specific facts about the second example. Show how this example supports your argument. Be as detailed as possible: cite names, places, events.

(3–5 sentences)

Example Paragraph 3 (Optional)

Write this paragraph *only* if you have enough time left to wrap up your essay.

<u>Topic Sentence:</u> State the main idea of this paragraph. Show how it relates to your thesis.

(Use transition words to connect this paragraph to the previous example paragraph.)

<u>Development of Example:</u> Provide specific facts about the third example. Show how this example supports your argument. Be as detailed as possible: cite names, places, events.

(3–5 sentences)

> #### Conclusion
>
> Recap: Summarize your argument, restating your main points. (1 sentence)
>
> Expansion of Your Position: Revisit why this issue matters. Draw broader conclusions. Speculate about the implications of your thesis.

See how each of the thesis sentences just discussed sets up the essay, in each case requiring a slightly different outline.

Outline 1

I. Introduction—State your overall thesis

   If we rest, we rust: inactivity and lack of exertion get in the way of progress and lead to the loss of vitality and to decay.

II. State the point of your first supporting paragraph.

   We have to keep moving to keep up with others and to avoid falling behind. This is as true for industries as for individuals.

   Examples:

   A. United States auto industry's decline: GM vs. Honda

   B. Outmoded technology: pay phones, cassettes

III. State the point of your second supporting paragraph.

   We have to keep active to prevent our skills from going bad.

Examples:

A. Loss of memory with age

B. Muscles atrophy from disuse

IV. Conclusion—Restate your thesis

Outline 2

I. Introduction—State your thesis

If we rest, we do not rust: our times of rest enable us to restore our mental and physical energy and to gain perspective on our lives.

II. State the point of your first supporting paragraph.

We need times of rest to restore us mentally and physically.

Examples:

A. Sleep deprivation lowers IQ

B. New work hour limits for hospital residents

C. Exercise programs build in rest days

III. State the point of your second supporting paragraph.

Rest allows us to develop perspective and to set goals.

A. Caught up in rat race

B. My brother's gap year, when he decided what he wanted to do in life

IV. Conclusion—Restate your thesis

Good examples are:

- Detailed—names, dates, places, events
- Varied—personal, literary, historical, contemporary

Minutes Five to Seventeen—Write

You have 12 minutes to begin writing your essay. You have your opening, your outline, and your conclusion all in mind. Devote this time to putting down your thoughts, writing as much as you legibly can. Try to write neatly, but don't worry so much about neatness that you wind up clenching your pencil for dear life. There is no problem if you occasionally cross something out or erase.

Minute Eighteen—Perform a Reality Check

You have been writing for 12 minutes straight. Take a moment to see how far you have gotten in your outline. If you've written your introduction and have barely finished your first supporting paragraph, now's the time for you to abandon the idea of writing a five- or six-paragraph essay. Instead, whip through the second supporting paragraph and start on your conclusion. You need to allow yourself enough time both to come up with a good ending and to look over your essay before you turn it in.

Minutes Nineteen to Twenty-Two—Wrap Things Up

Finish the supporting paragraph you've been working on, and bring your essay to a close. You'll be able to fine-tune your essay in just a moment.

Minute Twenty-Three—Read and React

Expert writers often test their work by reading it aloud. In the exam room, you cannot read out loud. However, when you read your essay silently, take your time and listen with your inner ear to how it sounds. Read to get a sense of your essay's logic and of its rhythm. Does one sentence flow smoothly into the next? Would they flow more smoothly if you were to add a transition word or phrase (*therefore, however, nevertheless, in contrast, similarly*)? Do the sentences follow a logical order? Is any key idea or example missing? Does any sentence seem out of place? How would things sound if you cut out that awkward sentence or inserted that transition word?

Take a moment to act on your response to hearing your essay. If it sounded to you as if a transition word was needed, insert it. If it sounded to you as if a sentence should be cut, delete it. Trust your inner ear, but do not attempt to do too much. You know your basic outline for the essay is good. You have neither the need nor the time to attempt a total revision.

Minute Twenty-Four—Proofread

Think of yourself as an editor. You need to have an eye for errors that damage your text. Take a minute to look over your essay for problems in spelling and grammar. From your English classes, you should have an idea of particular words and grammatical constructions that have given you trouble in the past—sentence fragments, or phrases like "everybody except my teacher and I." See whether you can spot any of these words or constructions in your essay. Correct those errors that you find.

Minute Twenty-Five—Reword, Reread, Relax

Look over the vocabulary used in your essay. In your concern to get your thoughts on paper, have you limited yourself to an over-simple vocabulary? Have you used one word over and over again, never substituting a synonym? Try upgrading your vocabulary judiciously. Replace one word or phrase in the essay with a synonym—*deteriorating* in place of *going bad* in the sentence "We have to keep active to prevent our skills from going bad," for example. Substitute a somewhat more specific adjective or adverb for a vague one—*insignificant* in place of *not important, extremely* busy in place of *really* busy. Again, do not attempt to do too much. Change only one or two words. Replace them with stronger, college-level words, *words whose meanings you are sure you know*.

Now that you've looked over your essay like an editor, give yourself one final opportunity to hear your words again. Reread the composition to yourself, making sure that the changes you have made have not harmed the flow of your text.

You have just completed a basic four- or five-paragraph essay. Now it is time to regroup your forces and relax before you go on to the next section of the test. Take a deep breath. At this point, you have earned a break.

During the Test

Here are some basic guidelines that will keep you stress-free and focused during the essay section.

Tips to Help You Cope

1. Keep careful track of your time. Doing so is especially necessary on the essay section. Writing an essay on an unfamiliar subject is pressure enough. You don't need the added pressure that you'll feel if you lose track of the time and discover you have only 60 seconds left to write the two final paragraphs that are critical to your argument.

2. Pace yourself: keep to your essay-writing plan. You have only 25 minutes. Allow yourself 5 minutes for prewriting. Read the essay topic or prompt with care. If you haven't a clue where to begin, jot down words and ideas that pop into your mind when you look at the prompt (brainstorming). Generate questions about the topic until you come up with a point you want to make. If you have found outlining to be helpful, briefly outline what you plan to say. Then devote the remaining 20 minutes to writing your essay, reserving a minute or two at the end to clean up your draft.

3. Remember that you don't have to write a perfect essay to earn a high score. The readers are instructed to overlook false starts ("beginning stutters," some readers call them) and incomplete conclusions in determining your score. It's all too easy to psych yourself out about the essay-writing assignment and wind up so blocked that you can barely write a paragraph, much less a fully-developed essay. Relax. Loosen your grip on your pen. Shake out your fingers if that helps. Your job is to turn out a promising first draft in 25 minutes, not to create a finished work of prose.

4. Write as legibly as you possibly can. Neatness helps. If your printing is neater than your cursive and you can print rapidly, by all means print. Keep within the margins on the page. The easier you make the readers' job, the more well-disposed they will be toward your essay.

5. Follow traditional essay-writing conventions. Make a point of showing the readers you know the "right" way to set up an essay. Indent each new paragraph clearly. Use transitions—signal words and phrases, such as "consequently" and "for this reason"—to indicate your progress from idea to idea.

6. Don't alter your essay capriciously. Change what you have written only if you have a solid reason for doing so. If you have time to read over your paper and spot a grammatical error or a spelling mistake, by all means correct it, making sure your correction is legible. However, try to avoid making major alterations in your text. Last-minute changes can create more problems than they solve. You may run out of time and wind up with a muddle instead of a coherent argument. Or, in your haste to finish your revision, you may scribble sentences that not even a cryptologist could decipher.

Practice Exercises

1. You have five minutes. Select one of the following essay topics, and practice your brainstorming and outlining skills, listing three or four relevant examples that you would use in your eventual essay.

The greater the effort, the greater the glory. – Pierre Corneille

Assignment: Does the difficulty of a task determine its importance? Write an essay supporting, disputing, or qualifying the statement. You may use examples from history, literature, popular culture, current events, or personal experience to support your position.

Treating your adversary with respect is giving him an advantage to which he is not entitled. – Samuel Johnson

Assignment: Is respecting one's opponents not strategic? Write an essay supporting, disputing, or qualifying the statement. You may use examples from history, literature, popular culture, current events, or personal experience to support your position.

In crisis is cleverness born. – Chinese Proverb

Assignment: The statement above implies crises can benefit us by fostering creativity. Write an essay supporting, disputing, or qualifying the statement. You may use examples from history, literature, popular culture, current events, or personal experience to support your position.

Those who doubt themselves most generally err least. – Samuel Richardson

Assignment: Is self-doubt a strength as well a a weakness? Does self-confidence cause carelessness and error? Write an essay supporting, disputing, or qualifying the statement. You may use examples from history, literature, popular culture, current events, or personal experience to support your position.

2. You have 25 minutes. Write an essay based on one of the following topics.

Learning starts with failure; the first failure is the beginning of education. – John Hersey

Assignment: Can failure have a positive aspect? Is it educational to fail? Write an essay supporting, disputing, or qualifying the statement. You may use examples from history, literature, popular culture, current events, or personal experience to support your position.

Progress is not an illusion, it happens, but it is slow and invariably disappointing. – George Orwell

Assignment: Does progress invariably prove disappointing to people? Write an essay supporting, disputing, or qualifying the statement. You may use examples from history, literature, popular culture, current events, or personal experience to support your position.

We can succeed only by concert. It is not "Can any of us imagine better?" but, "Can we all do better?" – Abraham Lincoln

Assignment: Can we achieve success only through collective effort, rather than as individuals? Write an essay supporting, disputing, or qualifying the statement. You may use examples from history, literature, popular culture, current events, or personal experience to support your position.

Patience and tenacity of purpose are worth more than twice their weight of cleverness. – Thomas Henry Huxley

Assignment: Is consistent effort of greater importance than creativity in achieving success? Write an essay supporting, disputing, or qualifying the statement. You may use examples from history, literature, popular culture, current events, or personal experience to support your position.

How can one learn to know oneself? Never by introspection, rather by action. Try to do your duty, and you will know right away what you are like. – Johann Wolfgang Von Goethe

Assignment: Can we know who we are and what we are capable of only by testing ourselves? Write an essay supporting, disputing, or qualifying the statement. You may use examples from history, literature, popular culture, current events, or personal experience to support your position.

Progress may feel more like loss than gain. – Mason Cooley

Assignment: Does our comfort with what we know make it difficult to accept change, even when it is a change for the better? Write an essay supporting, disputing, or qualifying the statement. You may use examples from history, literature, popular culture, current events, or personal experience to support your position.

No bird soars too high, if he soars with his own wings. – William Blake

Assignment: Do we risk failure when we attempt to surpass the limits of our own abilities? Write an essay supporting, disputing, or qualifying the statement. You may use examples from history, literature, popular culture, current events, or personal experience to support your position.

6

The Mathematics Sections: Strategies, Tips, and Practice

The College Board considers the SAT to be "a test of general reasoning abilities." It attempts to use basic concepts of arithmetic, algebra, and geometry as a method of testing your ability to think logically. The Board is not testing whether you know how to calculate an average, find the area of a circle, use the Pythagorean theorem, or read a bar graph. *It assumes you can*. In fact, because the Board is not even interested in testing your memory, many of the formulas you will need are listed at the beginning of each math section. In other words, the College Board's objective is to use your familiarity with numbers and geometric figures as a way of testing your *logical thinking skills*.

Most of the arithmetic that you need to know for the SAT is taught in elementary school, and much of the other material is taught in middle school or junior high school. You do need to know some high school math, especially some elementary algebra and a little basic geometry, but not too much. To do well on the SAT, you must know this basic material. But that's not enough. You have to be able to use these concepts in ways that may be unfamiliar to you. That's where the test-taking tactics come in.

THE USE OF CALCULATORS ON THE SAT

There isn't a single question on any section of the SAT for which a calculator is required. In fact, on most questions a calculator is completely useless. There are several questions, however, for which a calculator *could* be used; and since calculators are permitted, you should definitely bring one with you when you take the SAT.

165

If you forget to bring a calculator to the actual test, you will not be able to use one, since none will be provided and you will not be allowed to share one with a friend. For the same reason, be sure that you have new batteries in your calculator or that you bring a spare, because if your calculator fails during the test, you will have to finish without one.

What Calculator Should You Use?

Almost any four-function, scientific, or graphing calculator is acceptable. Since you don't "need" a calculator at all, you don't "need" any particular type. There is absolutely no advantage to having a graphing calculator; but we do recommend at least a scientific calculator, since it is occasionally useful to have parentheses keys, ( ); a reciprocal key, $\frac{1}{x}$; and an exponent key, y^x or ^. All scientific calculators have these features.

When Should Calculators Be Used?

If you have strong math skills and are a good test-taker, you will probably use your calculator infrequently, if at all.

On the other hand, if you are less confident about your mathematical ability or your test-taking skills, you will probably find your calculator a useful tool.

Throughout this book, the icon will be placed next to a problem where the use of a calculator is recommended. As you will see, this judgment is very subjective. Sometimes a question can be answered in a few seconds, with no calculations whatsoever, if you see the best approach. In that case, the use of a calculator is not recommended. If you don't see the easy way, however, and have to do some arithmetic, you may prefer to use a calculator.

Let's look at a few sample questions on which some students would use calculators a lot, others a little, and still others not at all.

Example 1.

If $16 \times 25 \times 36 = (4a)^2$, what is the value of a?

(A) 6   (B) 15   (C) 30   (D) 36   (E) 60

(i)   **Heavy calculator use:** WITH A CALCULATOR multiply:
$16 \times 25 \times 36 = 14{,}400$. Observe that $(4a)^2 = 16a^2$, and so
$16a^2 = 14{,}400$. WITH A CALCULATOR divide:

$$a^2 = 14{,}400 \div 16 = 900.$$

Finally, WITH A CALCULATOR take the square root:
$a = \sqrt{900} = 30$. The answer is **C**.

(ii)   **Light calculator use:** Immediately notice that you can
"cancel" the 16 on the left-hand side with the 4^2 on the right-
hand side. WITH A CALCULATOR multiply: $25 \times 36 = 900$, and
WITH A CALCULATOR take the square root of 900: $\sqrt{900} = 30$.

(iii) **No calculator use:** "Cancel" the 16 and the 4^2. Notice
that $25 = 5^2$ and $36 = 6^2$, so $a^2 = 5^2 \times 6^2 = 30^2$, and $a = 30$.

Example 2 (Grid-in).

If the length of a diagonal of a rectangle is 13, and if one of the
sides is 5, what is the perimeter?

Whether you intend to use your calculator a lot, a little, or not at
all, the first thing to do is to draw a diagram.

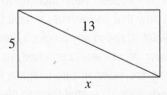

(i)   **Heavy calculator use:** By the Pythagorean theorem,
$x^2 + 5^2 = 13^2$. Observe that $5^2 = 25$, and WITH A CALCULATOR
evaluate: $13^2 = 169$. Then WITH A CALCULATOR subtract:
$169 - 25 = 144$, so $x^2 = 144$. Hit the square-root key on your
CALCULATOR to get $x = 12$. Finally, WITH A CALCULATOR add to find
the perimeter: $5 + 12 + 5 + 12 = \mathbf{34}$.

(ii) **Light calculator use:** The steps are the same as in (i) except that *some of the calculations* are done mentally: taking the square root of 144 and adding at the end.

(iii) **No calculator use:** *All calculations* are done mentally. Better yet, *no calculations are done at all,* because you immediately see that each half of the rectangle is a 5-12-13 right triangle, and you add the sides mentally.

MEMORIZE IMPORTANT FACTS AND DIRECTIONS

On the first page of every mathematics section of the SAT, you will see the following mathematical facts (see page 169), though in a slightly different arrangement:

The College Board's official guide to the SAT offers the following tip:

The test doesn't require you to memorize formulas. Commonly used formulas are provided in the test booklet at the beginning of each mathematical section.

If you interpret this to mean "Don't bother memorizing the formulas provided," this is terrible advice. It may be reassuring to know that, if you should forget a basic geometry fact, you can look it up in the box headed "Reference Information," but you should decide right now that you will never have to do that. During the test, you don't want to spend any precious time looking up facts that you can learn now. All of these "commonly used formulas" and other important facts are listed in this chapter. As you learn and review these facts, you should commit them to memory. Also in this chapter you will learn the instructions for the two types of mathematics questions on the SAT. *They will not change.* They will be exactly the same on the test you take.

Reference Information

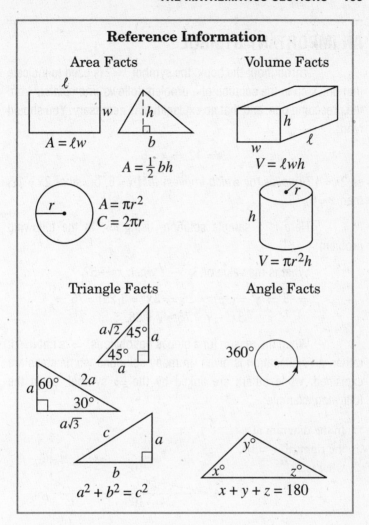

Area Facts

$A = \ell w$

$A = \frac{1}{2} bh$

$A = \pi r^2$
$C = 2\pi r$

Volume Facts

$V = \ell wh$

$V = \pi r^2 h$

Triangle Facts

$a\sqrt{2}$ 45° a 45° a

a 60° $2a$ 30° $a\sqrt{3}$

c a b
$a^2 + b^2 = c^2$

Angle Facts

360°

$y°$ $x°$ $z°$
$x + y + z = 180$

Helpful Hint

As you prepare for this test, memorize the directions for each section. *When you take the SAT, do not waste even one second reading directions.*

AN IMPORTANT SYMBOL

Throughout the book, the symbol "$\Rightarrow$" is used to indicate that one step in the solution of a problem follows *immediately* from the preceding one, and that no explanation is necessary. You should read:

$$2x = 12 \Rightarrow x = 6$$

as $2x = 12$ *implies* (or *which implies*) *that* $x = 6$, or, *since* $2x = 12$, then $x = 6$.

Here is a sample solution, using $\Rightarrow$, to the following problem:

What is the value of $3x^2 - 7$ when $x = -5$?

$$x = -5 \Rightarrow x^2 = (-5)^2 = 25 \Rightarrow 3x^2 = 3(25) = 75 \Rightarrow$$
$$3x^2 - 7 = 75 - 7 = \mathbf{68}.$$

When the reason for a step is not obvious, $\Rightarrow$ is not used: rather, an explanation is given. In many solutions, some steps are explained, while others are linked by the $\Rightarrow$ symbol, as in the following example:

In the diagram at the right, if $w = 10$, what is z?

- $w + x + y = 180$.
- Since $\triangle ABC$ is isosceles, $x = y$.
- Therefore, $w + 2y = 180 \Rightarrow 10 + 2y = 180 \Rightarrow$
  $2y = 170 \Rightarrow y = 85$.
- Finally, since $y + z = 180$, $85 + z = 180 \Rightarrow z = \mathbf{95}$.

IMPORTANT DEFINITIONS, FACTS, FORMULAS, AND STRATEGIES

1. **Sum:** the result of an addition: 8 is the sum of 6 and 2

2. **Difference:** the result of a subtraction: 4 is the difference of 6 and 2

3. **Product:** the result of a multiplication: 12 is the product of 6 and 2

4. **Quotient:** the result of a division: 3 is the quotient of 6 and 2

5. **Remainder:** when 15 is divided by 6, the quotient is 2 and the remainder is 3: $15 = 6 \times 2 + 3$

6. **Integers:** $\{\ldots, -3, -2, -1, 0, 1, 2, 3, \ldots\}$

7. **Factor** or **Divisor:** any integer that leaves no remainder (i.e., a remainder of 0) when it is divided into another integer: 1, 2, 5, 10 are the factors (or divisors) of 10

8. **Multiple:** the product of one integer by a second integer:

   $-14, -7, 0, 7, 14, 21, 28, \ldots$ are multiples of 7

   ($-14 = -2 \times 7$, $0 = 0 \times 7$, $7 = 1 \times 7$, $14 = 2 \times 7$, and so on)

9. **Even integers:** the multiples of 2: $\{\ldots, -4, -2, 0, 2, 4, \ldots\}$

10. **Odd integers:** the non-multiples of 2: $\{\ldots, -3, -1, 1, 3, 5, \ldots\}$

11. **Consecutive integers:** two or more integers, written in sequence, each of which is 1 more than the preceding one. For example:

    $7, 8, 9 \qquad -2, -1, 0, 1, 2 \qquad n, n + 1, n + 2$

12. **Prime number:** a positive integer that has exactly two divisors. The first few primes are 2, 3, 5, 7, 11, 13, 17. (*not* 1)

13. **Exponent:** a number written as a superscript: the 3 in 7^3. On the SAT, the only exponents you need to know about are positive integers: $2^n = 2 \times 2 \times 2 \times \ldots \times 2$, where 2 appears as a factor n times.

14. **Laws of Exponents:**

   For any numbers b and c and positive integers m and n:

   (i) $b^m b^n = b^{m+n}$ (ii) $\dfrac{b^m}{b^n} = b^{m-n}$ (iii) $(b^m)^n = b^{mn}$

   (iv) $b^m c^m = (bc)^m$

15. **Square root of a positive number:** if a is positive, $\sqrt{a}$ is the only positive number whose square is a: $\left(\sqrt{a}\right)^2 = \sqrt{a} \times \sqrt{a} = a$

16. The product and the quotient of two positive numbers or two negative numbers are positive; the product and the quotient of a positive number and a negative number are negative.

17. • The product of an *even* number of negative factors is positive.
   • The product of an *odd* number of negative factors is negative.

18. For any positive numbers a and b:

   $$\sqrt{ab} = \sqrt{a} \times \sqrt{b} \quad \text{and} \quad \sqrt{\dfrac{a}{b}} = \dfrac{\sqrt{a}}{\sqrt{b}}$$

19. For any real numbers a, b, and c:

   • $a(b + c) = ab + ac$ • $a(b - c) = ab - ac$

   and, if $a \neq 0$,

   • $\dfrac{b+c}{a} = \dfrac{b}{a} + \dfrac{c}{a}$ • $\dfrac{b-c}{a} = \dfrac{b}{a} - \dfrac{c}{a}$

20. To compare two fractions, use your calculator to convert them to decimals.

21. To multiply two fractions, multiply their numerators and multiply their denominators:

   $$\dfrac{3}{5} \times \dfrac{4}{7} = \dfrac{3 \times 4}{5 \times 7} = \dfrac{12}{35}$$

22. To divide any number by a fraction, multiply that number by the reciprocal of the fraction.

   $$\dfrac{3}{5} \div \dfrac{2}{3} = \dfrac{3}{5} \times \dfrac{3}{2} = \dfrac{9}{10}$$

23. To add or subtract fractions with the same denominator, add or subtract the numerators and keep the denominator:

$$\frac{4}{9} + \frac{1}{9} = \frac{5}{9} \quad \text{and} \quad \frac{4}{9} - \frac{1}{9} = \frac{3}{9} = \frac{1}{3}$$

24. To add or subtract fractions with different denominators, first rewrite the fractions as equivalent fractions with the same denominator:

$$\frac{1}{6} + \frac{3}{4} = \frac{2}{12} + \frac{9}{12} = \frac{11}{12}$$

25. **Percent:** a fraction whose denominator is 100:

$$15\% = \frac{15}{100} = .15$$

26. The *percent increase* of a quantity is

$$\frac{\text{actual increase}}{\text{original amount}} \times 100\%.$$

The *percent decrease* of a quantity is

$$\frac{\text{actual decrease}}{\text{original amount}} \times 100\%.$$

27. **Ratio:** a fraction that compares two quantities that are measured in the same units. The ratio *2 to 3* can be written $\frac{2}{3}$ or 2:3.

28. In any ratio problem, write the letter *x* after each number and use some given information to solve for *x*.

29. **Proportion:** an equation that states that two ratios (fractions) are equal. Solve proportions by cross-multiplying: if $\frac{a}{b} = \frac{c}{d}$, then $ad = bc$.

30. **Average of a set of *n* numbers:** the sum of those numbers divided by *n*:

$$\text{average} = \frac{\text{sum of the } n \text{ numbers}}{n} \quad \text{or simply}$$

$$A = \frac{\text{sum}}{n}$$

31. If you know the average, A, of a set of n numbers, multiply A by n to get their sum: sum = nA.

32. To multiply two binomials, use the FOIL method: multiply each term in the first parentheses by each term in the second parentheses and simplify by combining terms, if possible.

$$(2x - 7)(3x + 2) = (2x)(3x) + (2x)(2) + (-7)(3x) + (-7)(2) =$$
First terms   Outer terms   Inner terms   Last terms

$$6x^2 + 4x - 21x - 14 = 6x^2 - 17x - 14$$

33. The three most important binomial products on the SAT are these:
    - $(x - y)(x + y) = x^2 - y^2$
    - $(x - y)^2 = (x - y)(x - y) = x^2 - 2xy + y^2$
    - $(x + y)^2 = (x + y)(x + y) = x^2 + 2xy + y^2$

34. All distance problems involve one of three variations of the same formula:

$$\text{distance} = \text{rate} \times \text{time} \qquad \text{rate} = \frac{\text{distance}}{\text{time}}$$

$$\text{time} = \frac{\text{distance}}{\text{rate}}$$

35.

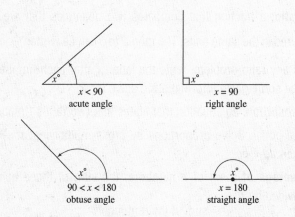

$x < 90$
acute angle

$x = 90$
right angle

$90 < x < 180$
obtuse angle

$x = 180$
straight angle

36. If two or more angles form a straight angle, the sum of their measures is 180°.

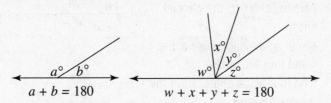

$a + b = 180$ $w + x + y + z = 180$

37. The sum of all the measures of all the angles around a point is 360°.

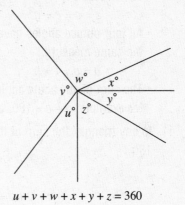

$u + v + w + x + y + z = 360$

38.

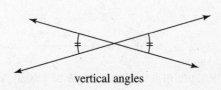

vertical angles

39. Vertical angles have equal measures.

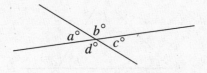

$a = c$ and $b = d.$

40. If a pair of parallel lines is cut by a transversal that is *not* perpendicular to the parallel lines:

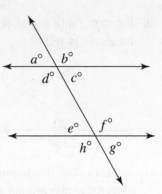

- Four of the angles are acute, and four are obtuse.
- All four acute angles have the same measure:

    $a = c = e = g$.

- All four obtuse angles have the same measure:

    $b = d = f = h$.

- The sum of any acute angle and any obtuse angle is 180°: for example, $d + e = 180$, $c + f = 180$, $b + g = 180$, ...

41. In any triangle, the sum of the measures of the three angles is 180°.

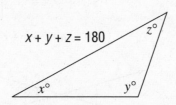

42. The measure of an exterior angle of a triangle is equal to the sum of the measures of the two opposite interior angles.

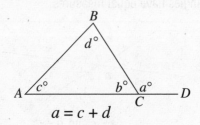

43. In any triangle:
    - the longest side is opposite the largest angle;
    - the shortest side is opposite the smallest angle;
    - sides with the same length are opposite angles with the same measure.

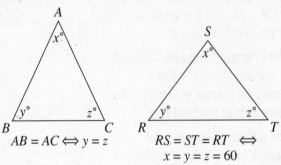

$$AB = AC \Longleftrightarrow y = z \qquad RS = ST = RT \Longleftrightarrow x = y = z = 60$$

44. In any right triangle, the sum of the measures of the two acute angles is 90°.

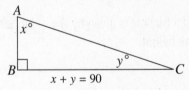

$$x + y = 90$$

45.

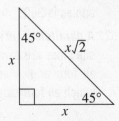

Pythagorean theorem: In a right triangle, if a and b are the lengths of the legs and c is the length of the hypotenuse, then $a^2 + b^2 = c^2$.

46. In a 45-45-90 right triangle, if the length of each leg is x, then the length of the hypotenuse is $x\sqrt{2}$.

47. In a 30-60-90 right triangle, if the length of the shorter leg is x, then the length of the longer leg is $x\sqrt{3}$, and the length of the hypotenuse is $2x$.

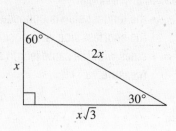

48. **The Triangle Inequality:** The sum of the lengths of any two sides of a triangle is greater than the length of the third side.

    The difference between the lengths of any two sides of a triangle is less than the length of the third side.

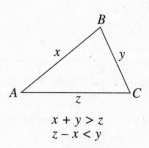

$$x + y > z$$
$$z - x < y$$

49. The area of a triangle is given by $A = \dfrac{1}{2} bh$, where b is the base and h is the height.

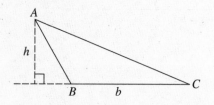
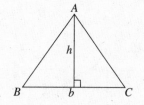

50. If A represents the area of an equilateral triangle with side s, then $A = \dfrac{s^2\sqrt{3}}{4}$.

51. In any quadrilateral, the sum of the measures of the four angles is 360°.

52. A ***parallelogram*** is a quadrilateral in which both pairs of opposite sides are parallel. A ***rectangle*** is a parallelogram in which all four angles are right angles. A ***square*** is a rectangle in which all four sides have the same length.

53. In any parallelogram:

- Opposite sides are congruent: $AB = CD$ and $AD = BC$.
- Opposite angles are congruent: $a = c$ and $b = d$.
- The sum of the measures of any two consecutive angles is 180°: $a + b = 180$, $b + c = 180$, and so on.
- The two diagonals bisect each other: $AE = EC$ and $BE = ED$.

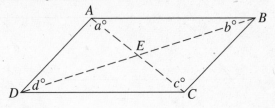

54. In any rectangle:

- The measure of each angle is 90°.
- The diagonals have the same length: $AC = BD$.

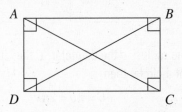

55. In any square:

- All four sides have the same length.
- Each diagonal divides the square into two 45-45-90 right triangles.
- The diagonals are perpendicular to each other: $AC \perp BD$.

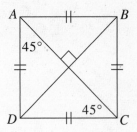

56. Formulas for perimeter and area:

- For a parallelogram: $A = bh$ and $P = 2(a + b)$.
- For a rectangle: $A = \ell w$ and $P = 2(\ell + w)$.
- For a square: $A = s^2$ or $A = \dfrac{1}{2}d^2$ and $P = 4s$.

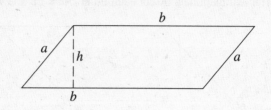

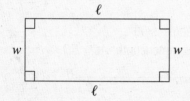 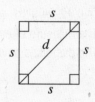

57. Let r be the radius, d the diameter, C the circumference, and A the area of a circle, then

$$d = 2r \qquad\qquad C = \pi d = 2\pi r \qquad\qquad A = \pi r^2$$

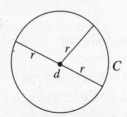

58. The formula for the volume of a rectangular solid is $V = \ell wh$, where ℓ, w, and h represent the length, width, and height, respectively.

In a cube, all the edges are equal. Therefore, if e is the edge, the formula for the volume is $V = e^3$.

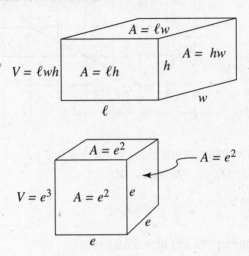

59. The formula for the surface area of a rectangular solid is $A = 2(\ell w + \ell h + wh)$. The formula for the surface area of a cube is $A = 6e^2$.

60. The formula for the volume, V, of a cylinder is $V = \pi r^2 h$, where r represents the radius of the circular top and h represents the height.

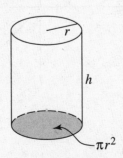

61. The distance, d, between two points, $A(x_1, y_1)$ and $B(x_2, y_2)$, can be calculated using the distance formula:

    $d = \sqrt{(x_2 - x_1)^2 + (y_2 - y_1)^2}$.

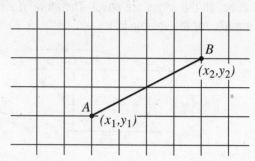

62. The formula for the slope of the line that passes through the points (x_1, y_1) and (x_2, y_2) is:

    $\text{slope} = \dfrac{y_2 - y_1}{x_2 - x_1}$

63. • The slope of any horizontal line is 0.
    • The slope of any line that goes up as you move from left to right is positive.
    • The slope of any line that goes down as you move from left to right is negative.

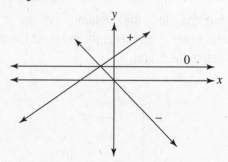

64. **The Counting Principle:** If two jobs need to be completed and there are m ways to do the first job and n ways to do the second job, then there are $m \times n$ ways to do one job followed by the other. This principle can be extended to any number of jobs.

65. If E is any event, the **probability** that E will occur is given by

$$P(E) = \frac{\text{number of favorable outcomes}}{\text{total number of possible outcomes}},$$

assuming that all of the possible outcomes are equally likely.

66.–69. Let E be an event, and let $P(E)$ be the probability that it will occur.

66. If E is *impossible,* then $P(E) = 0$.

67. If it is *certain* that E will occur, then $P(E) = 1$.

68. In all other cases, $0 < P(E) < 1$.

69. The probability that event E will *not* occur is $1 - P(E)$.

70. If an experiment is done 2 (or more) times, the probability that first one event will occur, and then a second event will occur, is the product of the probabilities.

GENERAL MATH STRATEGIES

Later in this chapter, you will learn tactics that will help you with the two specific types of math questions on the SAT. In this section you will learn several important strategies that can be used on either type of question. Mastering these tactics will improve your performance on all mathematics tests.

TACTIC 1. Draw a Diagram.

On any geometry question for which a figure is not provided, draw one (as accurately as possible) in your test booklet.

Let's consider some examples.

Example 1.

What is the area of a rectangle whose length is twice its width and whose perimeter is equal to that of a square whose area is 1?

Solution. Don't even think of answering this question until you have drawn a square and a rectangle and labeled each of them: each side of the square is 1; and if the width of the rectangle is w, its length is $2w$.

Now, write the required equation and solve it:

$$6w = 4 \Rightarrow w = \frac{4}{6} = \frac{2}{3} \Rightarrow 2w = \frac{4}{3}$$

The area of the rectangle = $lw = \left(\frac{4}{3}\right)\left(\frac{2}{3}\right) = \frac{8}{9}$.

Drawings should not be limited, however, to geometry questions; there are many other questions on which drawings will help.

Example 2.

A jar contains 10 red marbles and 30 green ones. How many red marbles must be added to the jar so that 60% of the marbles will be red?

Solution. Draw a diagram and label it. From the diagram it is clear that there are now $40 + x$ marbles in the jar, of which $10 + x$ are red. Since we want the fraction of red marbles to be

x	Red
30	Green
10	Red

$60\%\left(=\dfrac{3}{5}\right)$, we have $\dfrac{10+x}{40+x} = \dfrac{3}{5}$.

Cross-multiplying, we get:

$$50 + 5x = 120 + 3x \Rightarrow 2x = 70 \Rightarrow x = \mathbf{35}.$$

Of course, you could have set up the equation and solved it without the diagram, but the drawing makes the solution easier and you are less likely to make a careless mistake.

TACTIC 2. If a Diagram Is Drawn to Scale, Trust It, and Use Your Eyes.

Remember that every diagram that appears on the SAT has been drawn as accurately as possible *unless* you see "<u>Note</u>: Figure not drawn to scale" written below it.

For figures that are drawn to scale: line segments that appear to be the same length *are* the same length; if an angle clearly looks obtuse, it *is* obtuse; and if one angle appears larger than another, you may assume that it *is* larger.

Example 3.

In the figure at the right, what is the sum of the measures of all of the marked angles?

(A) 360°   (B) 540°
(C) 720°   (D) 900°
(E) 1080°

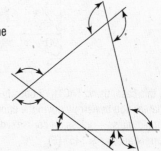

Solution. Make your best estimate of each angle, and add up the values. The five choices are so far apart that, even if you're off by 15° or more on some of the angles, you'll get the right answer. The sum of the estimates shown is 690°, so the correct answer *must* be 720° **(C)**.

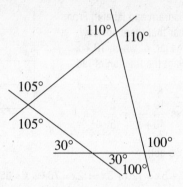

Example 4.

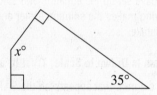

In the figure above, what is the value of *x*?

(A) 55   (B) 95   (C) 125   (D) 135   (E) 145

Solution. Since the diagram is drawn to scale, trust it. Look at *x*: it appears to be *about* 90 + 50 = 140.

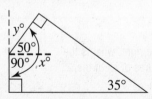

In this case, using TACTIC 2 does not get you the exact answer. It only enables you to narrow down the choices to (D) or (E). At this point you should guess—unless, of course, you know the correct solution. The correct answer is 145° **(E)**.

TACTIC 3. If a Diagram Is *Not* drawn to Scale, Redraw It to Scale, and Then Use Your Eyes.

For figures that have not been drawn to scale, you can make *no* assumptions. Lines that look parallel may not be; an angle that appears to be obtuse may, in fact, be acute; two line segments may have the same length even though one looks twice as long as the other.

Example 5.

In $\triangle ACB$, what is the value of x?

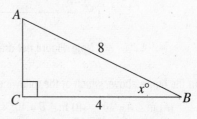

Note: Figure not drawn to scale

(A) 75   (B) 60   (C) 45   (D) 30   (E) 15

Solution. In what way is this figure not drawn to scale? $AB = 8$ and $BC = 4$, but in the figure $\overline{AB}$ is *not* twice as long as $\overline{BC}$. Redraw the triangle so that $\overline{AB}$ *is* twice as long as $\overline{BC}$. Now, just look: x is about **60 (B)**.

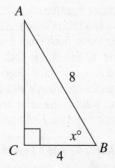

In fact, x is exactly 60. If the hypotenuse of a right triangle is twice the length of one of the legs, you have a 30-60-90 triangle, and the angle formed by the hypotenuse and that leg is 60°.

Example 6.

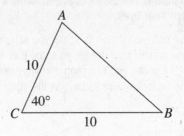

Note: Figure not drawn to scale

In the figure above, which of the following *must* be true?

(A) m∠A = 40°   (B) m∠B = 40°   (C) AB = 10
(D) AB > 10   (E) AB < 10

Solution. In the given diagram, $\overline{AB}$ is longer than $\overline{AC}$, which is 10, but *we cannot trust the diagram*. Actually, there are two things wrong: ∠C is labeled 40°, but looks much more like 60° or 70°, and $\overline{AC}$ and $\overline{BC}$ are each labeled 10, but $\overline{BC}$ is drawn much longer. Use TACTIC 3. Redraw the triangle with a 40° angle and two sides of the same length. Now, it's clear that AB < 10. Choose **E**.

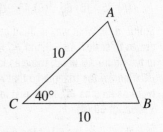

TACTIC 4. Add a Line to a Diagram.
Occasionally, after staring at a diagram, you still have no idea how to solve the problem to which it applies. It looks as though there isn't enough given information. When this happens, it often helps to draw another line in the diagram.

Example 7.

In the figure at the right, *Q* is a point on the circle whose center is *O* and whose radius is *r*, and *OPQR* is a rectangle. What is the length of diagonal $\overline{PR}$?

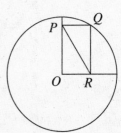

(A) r (B) r^2 (C) $\dfrac{r^2}{\pi}$ (D) $\dfrac{r\sqrt{2}}{\pi}$

(E) It cannot be determined from the information given.

Solution. If, after staring at the diagram and thinking about rectangles, circles, and the Pythagorean theorem, you're still lost, don't give up. Ask yourself, "Can I add another line to this diagram?" As soon as you think to draw in $\overline{OQ}$, the other diagonal, the problem becomes easy: the two diagonals are equal, and, since $\overline{OQ}$ is a radius, it is equal to r **(A)**.

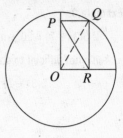

TACTIC 5. Subtract to Find Shaded Regions.

Whenever part of a figure is white and part is shaded, the straightforward way to find the area of the shaded portion is to find the area of the entire figure and then subtract from it the area of the white region. Of course, if you are asked for the area of the white region, you can, instead, subtract the shaded area from the total area. Occasionally, you may see an easy way to calculate the shaded area directly, but usually you should subtract.

Example 8.

In the figure below, $ABCD$ is a rectangle, and $\overset{\frown}{BE}$ and $\overset{\frown}{CF}$ are arcs of circles centered at A and D. What is the area of the shaded region?

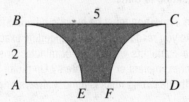

(A) $10 - \pi$ (B) $2(5 - \pi)$ (C) $2(5 - 2\pi)$
(D) $6 + 2\pi$ (E) $5(2 - \pi)$

Solution. The entire region is a 2×5 rectangle whose area is 10. Since each white region is a quarter-circle of radius 2, the combined area of these regions is that of a semicircle of radius 2:

$$\frac{1}{2}\pi(2)^2 = 2\pi.$$

Therefore, the area of the shaded region is $10 - 2\pi =$ **2(5 − π) (B)**.

TACTIC 6. Don't Do More Than You Have To.

Look for shortcuts. Since a problem can often be solved in more than one way, you should always look for the easiest method. Consider the following example.

Example 9.

If $5(3x - 7) = 20$, what is $3x - 8$?

It's not difficult to solve for x:

$$5(3x - 7) = 20 \Rightarrow 15x - 35 = 20 \Rightarrow 15x = 55 \Rightarrow$$

$$x = \frac{55}{15} = \frac{11}{3}$$

But it's too much work. Besides, once you find that $x = \frac{11}{3}$, you

still have to multiply to get $3x$: $3\left(\frac{11}{3}\right) = 11$, and then subtract

to get $3x - 8$: $11 - 8 = \mathbf{3}$.

Solution. The key is to recognize that you don't need x. Finding $3x - 7$ is easy (just divide the original equation by 5), and $3x - 8$ is just 1 less:

$$5(3x - 7) = 20 \Rightarrow 3x - 7 = 4 \Rightarrow 3x - 8 = \mathbf{3}.$$

TACTIC 7. Pay Attention to Units.

Often the answer to a question must be in units different from those used in the given data. As you read the question, <u>underline</u> exactly what you are being asked. Do the examiners want hours or minutes or seconds, dollars or cents, feet or inches, meters or centimeters? On multiple-choice questions an answer with the wrong units is almost always one of the choices.

Example 10.

At a speed of 48 miles per hour, how many minutes will be required to drive 32 miles?

(A) $\frac{2}{3}$ (B) $\frac{3}{2}$ (C) 40   (D) 45   (E) 2400

Solution. This is a relatively easy question. Just be attentive. Since

$\dfrac{32 \text{ miles}}{48 \text{ miles per hour}} = \dfrac{2}{3}$ hours. Choice A is $\dfrac{2}{3}$; but that is *not* the

correct answer because you are asked how many *minutes* will be required.

(Did you underline the word "minutes" in the question?) The correct

answer is $\dfrac{2}{3}$ hour = $\dfrac{2}{3}$ (60 minutes) = **40 minutes (C)**.

TACTIC 8. Systematically Make Lists.

When a question asks "how many," often the best strategy is to make a list of all the possibilities. It is important that you make the list in a *systematic* fashion so that you don't inadvertently leave something out. Often, shortly after starting the list, you can see a pattern developing and can figure out how many more entries there will be without writing them all down.

Example 11.

The product of three positive integers is 300. If one of them is 5, what is the least possible value of the sum of the other two?

Solution. Since one of the integers is 5, the product of the other two is 60 ($5 \times 60 = 300$). Systematically, list all possible pairs, (a, b), of positive integers whose product is 60, and check their sums. First, let $a = 1$, then 2, and so on.

a	b	$a + b$
1	60	61
2	30	32
3	20	23
4	15	19
5	12	17
6	10	16

The answer is **16**.

Example 12.

A palindrome is a number, such as 93539, that reads the same forward and backward. How many palindromes are there between 100 and 1000?

Solution. First, write down the numbers in the 100's that end in 1:

101, 111, 121, 131, 141, 151, 161, 171, 181, 191

Now write the numbers beginning and ending in 2:

202, 212, 222, 232, 242, 252, 262, 272, 282, 292

By now you should see the pattern: there are 10 palindromes beginning with 1, and 10 beginning with 2, and there will be 10 beginning with 3, 4, ..., 9 for a total of $9 \times 10 = $ **90** palindromes.

TACTIC 9. Handle Strange Symbols Properly.

On almost all SATs a few questions use symbols, such as: ⊕, □, ☺, ✠, and ✤, that you have never before seen in a mathematics problem. How can you answer such a question? Don't panic! It's easy; you are always told exactly what the symbol means! All you have to do is follow the directions carefully.

Example 13.

If $a \ ☺ \ b = \dfrac{a+b}{a-b}$, what is the value of 25 ☺ 15?

Solution. The definition of " ☺ " tells us that, whenever two numbers surround a "happy face," we are to form a fraction in which the numerator is the sum of the numbers and the denominator is their difference. Here, 25 ☺ 15 is the fraction whose numerator is 25 + 15 = 40 and whose denominator is 25 − 15 = 10: $\dfrac{40}{10} = \mathbf{4}$.

Sometimes the same symbol is used in two (or even three) questions. In these cases, the first question is easy and involves only numbers; the second is a bit harder and usually contains variables.

<u>Examples 14–15</u> refer to the following definition.

For any real numbers x and y: $x \ \Diamond \ y = xy - x - y$.

Example 14.

What is the value of $(3 \ \Diamond \ 4) \ \Diamond \ 5$?

(A) −2   (B) 6   (C) 12   (D) 15   (E) 25

Example 15.

For what positive value of a does $a \ \Diamond \ a = a$?

(A) 1   (B) 2   (C) 3   (D) 6   (E) 9

Solution 14. $3 \ \Diamond \ 4 = (3)(4) - (3) - (4) = 12 - 3 - 4 = 5$.
So $(3 \ \Diamond \ 4) \ \Diamond \ 5 = 5 \ \Diamond \ 5 = (5)(5) - 5 - 5 = 25 - 5 - 5 = \mathbf{15 \ (D)}$.

Solution 15. $a \ \Diamond \ a = a \Rightarrow (a)(a) - a - a = a \Rightarrow a^2 - 2a = a \Rightarrow$
$a^2 - 3a = 0 \Rightarrow a(a - 3) = 0 \Rightarrow a = 0$ or $a = 3$. Since a must be positive, $a = \mathbf{3 \ (C)}$.

Example 16.

For any real numbers c and d, $c \boxplus d = c^d + d^c$. What is the value of $1 \boxplus (2 \boxplus 3)$?

Solution. Remember the correct order of operations: always do first what's in the parentheses.

$$2 \boxplus 3 = 2^3 + 3^2 = 8 + 9 = 17$$
$$\text{and}$$
$$1 \boxplus 17 = 1^{17} + 17^1 = 1 + 17 = 18.$$

Grid-in **18**.

Practice Exercises   Answers given on pages 195–199.

Multiple-Choice Questions

1. In the figure at the right, if the radius of circle O is 10, what is the length of diagonal AC of rectangle $OABC$?

    (A) $\sqrt{2}$ (B) $\sqrt{10}$ (C) $5\sqrt{2}$

    (D) 10   (E) $10\sqrt{2}$

2. In the figure below, $ABCD$ is a square and AED is an equilateral triangle. If $AB = 2$, what is the area of the shaded region?

    (A) $\sqrt{3}$ (B) 2   (C) 3   (D) $4 - 2\sqrt{3}$ (E) $4 - \sqrt{3}$

3. If $5x + 13 = 31$, what is the value of $\sqrt{5x + 31}$?

    (A) $\sqrt{13}$ (B) $\sqrt{\dfrac{173}{5}}$ (C) 7   (D) 13   (E) 169

4. At Nat's Nuts a $2\dfrac{1}{4}$-pound bag of pistachio nuts costs $6.00.

    At this rate, what is the cost, in cents, of a bag weighing 9 ounces?

    (A) 1.5   (B) 24   (C) 150   (D) 1350   (E) 2400

5. In the figure at the right, three circles of radius 1 are tangent to one another. What is the area of the shaded region between the circles?

    (A) $\dfrac{\pi}{2} - \sqrt{3}$ (B) 1.5   (C) $\pi - \sqrt{3}$

    (D) $\sqrt{3} - \dfrac{\pi}{2}$ (E) $2 - \dfrac{\pi}{2}$

Questions 6–8 refer to the following definition.

For any real numbers x and y: $x \star y = x^2 - y^2$.

6. What is the value of $3 \star 5$?

   (A) −16   (B) 4   (C) 9   (D) 16   (E) 34

7. Which of the following is equivalent to $(a \star 1) \star 1$?

   (A) a (B) a^2 (C) $a^2 = 2$ (D) $a^4 - 2a^2$ (E) $a^4 - 2a^2 - 2$

8. Which of the following expressions is equal to $(a + b) \star (a - b)$?

   (A) $2a^2$ (B) $2a^2 + 2b^2$ (C) $2a^2 - 2b^2$ (D) $-4ab$ (E) $4ab$

Grid-in Questions

9. In writing all of the integers from 1 to 300, how many times is the digit 1 used?

10. If $a + 2b = 14$ and $5a + 4b = 16$, what is the average (arithmetic mean) of a and b?

11. A bag contains 4 marbles, 1 of each color: red, blue, yellow, and green. The marbles are removed at random, 1 at a time. If the first marble is red, what is the probability that the yellow marble is removed before the blue marble?

12. The area of circle *O* in the figure below is 12. What is the area of the shaded sector?

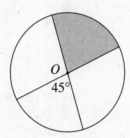

45°

Note: Figure not drawn to scale

Answer Key

1. **D**	3. **C**	5. **D**	7. **D**
2. **E**	4. **C**	6. **A**	8. **E**

9.

10.

or 2.5

11.

or 1/2 or .5

12.

or 3/2 or 1.5

Answer Explanations

1. D Even if you can't solve this problem, don't omit it. Use TACTIC 2: trust the diagram. $\overline{AC}$ is clearly longer than $\overline{OC}$, and very close to radius $\overline{OE}$.

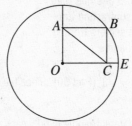

Therefore, $\overline{AC}$ must be about 10. Either by inspection or with your calculator, check the choices. They are approximately as follows:

(A) $\sqrt{2} \approx 1.4$; (B) $\sqrt{10} \approx 3.1$; (C) $5\sqrt{2} \approx 7$;

(D) 10; (E) $10\sqrt{2} \approx 14$. The answer must be **10**.

The answer *is* **10. The two diagonals are equal, and diagonal $\overline{OB}$ is a radius.

2. E Use TACTIC 5: subtract to find the shaded area. The area of square $ABCD$ is 4. By Fact 50, the area of $\triangle AED$ is

$$\frac{2^2\sqrt{3}}{4} = \frac{4\sqrt{3}}{4} = \sqrt{3}.$$ So the area of the shaded region

is $4 - \sqrt{3}$.

3. C Use TACTIC 6: don't do more than you have to. In particular, don't solve for x. Here

$$5x + 13 = 31 \Rightarrow 5x = 18 \Rightarrow 5x + 31 = 18 + 31 = 49$$
$$\sqrt{5x + 31} = \sqrt{49} = 7.$$

4. C This is a relatively simple ratio, but use TACTIC 7 and make sure you get the units right. You need to know that there are 100 cents in a dollar and 16 ounces in a pound.

$$\frac{\text{price}}{\text{weight}} : \frac{6 \text{ dollars}}{2.25 \text{ pounds}} = \frac{600 \text{ cents}}{36 \text{ ounces}} = \frac{x \text{ cents}}{9 \text{ ounces}}$$

Now cross-multiply and solve: $36x = 5400 \Rightarrow x = \mathbf{150}$.

5. **D**　Use TACTIC 4 and add some
lines: connect the centers of the
three circles to form an equilateral triangle whose sides are 2.
Now use TACTIC 5 and find the
shaded area by subtracting the
area of the three sectors from
the area of the triangle,

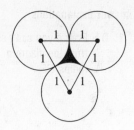

which is $\dfrac{2^2\sqrt{3}}{4} = \sqrt{3}$ (Fact 50). Since the measure of each

angle in an equilateral triangle is 60°, each sector is $\dfrac{60}{360} = \dfrac{1}{6}$

of a circle of radius 1. Together the three sectors form $\dfrac{1}{2}$ of such

a circle, so their total area is $\dfrac{1}{2}\pi(1)^2 = \dfrac{\pi}{2}$. Finally, subtract: the

area of the shaded region is $\boldsymbol{\sqrt{3} - \dfrac{\pi}{2}}$.

6. **A**　$3 \star 5 = 3^2 - 5^2 = 9 - 25 = \boldsymbol{-16}$.

7. **D**　$(a \star 1) \star 1 = (a^2 - 1) \star 1 = (a^2 - 1)^2 - 1^2 =$
$(a^4 - 2a^2 + 1) - 1 = \boldsymbol{a^4 - 2a^2}$.

8. **E**　$(a + b) \star (a - b) = (a^2 + 2ab + b^2) - (a^2 - 2ab + b^2) = \boldsymbol{4ab}$.

9. **(160)**　Use TACTIC 8. Systematically list the numbers that contain
the digit 1, writing as many as you need to see the pattern.
Between 1 and 99 the digit 1 is used 10 times as the units digit
(1, 11, 21, …, 91) and 10 times as the tens digit (10, 11, 12, …,
19) for a total of 20 times. From 200 to 299, there are 20 more
times (the same 20 but preceded by 2). Finally, from 100 to 199
there are 20 more plus 100 numbers where the digit 1 is used in
the hundreds place. The total is 20 + 20 + 20 + 100 = **160**.

10. $\left(\dfrac{5}{2}\text{ or } 2.5\right)$　Use TACTIC 6: don't do more than is necessary. You

don't need to solve this system of equations; you don't need to
know the values of a and b, only their average. Adding the two
equations gives

$$6a + 6b = 30 \Rightarrow a + b = 5 \Rightarrow \frac{a+b}{2} = \frac{5}{2} \text{ or } \boldsymbol{2.5}.$$

11. $\left(\dfrac{3}{6}\text{ or }\dfrac{1}{2}\text{ or }.5\right)$ Use TACTIC 8. Systematically list all of the orders in which the marbles could be drawn. With 4 colors, there would ordinarily have been 24 orders, but since the first marble drawn was red, there are only 6 arrangements for the other 3 colors: BYG, BGY, YGB, YBG, GYB, GBY. In 3 of these 6 the yellow comes before the blue, and in the other 3 the blue comes before the yellow. Therefore, the probability that the yellow marble will be removed before the blue marble is $\dfrac{3}{6}$ or $\dfrac{1}{2}$ or **.5**.

12. $\left(\dfrac{12}{8}\text{ or }\dfrac{3}{2}\text{ or }1.5\right)$ The shaded sector is $\dfrac{45}{360} = \dfrac{1}{8}$ of the circle, so its area is $\dfrac{1}{8}$ of 12: $\dfrac{12}{8}$ or $\dfrac{3}{2}$ or **1.5**.

If you didn't see that, use TACTIC 3 and redraw the figure to scale by making the angle as close as possible to 45°. It is now clear that the sector is $\dfrac{1}{8}$ of the circle (or very close to it).

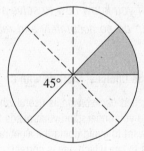

THE MULTIPLE-CHOICE QUESTION

Each math section on the SAT contains multiple-choice questions. On the first page of each section, you will see the following directions:

In this section *solve each problem,* using any available space on the page for scratchwork. *Then* decide which is the best of the choices given and fill in the corresponding oval on the answer sheet. (Emphasis added.)

The directions are very simple. Basically, they tell you to ignore, at first, the fact that these are multiple-choice questions. Just *solve each problem,* and *then* look at the five choices to see which one is best. As you will learn in this section of Chapter 6, however, that is not always the best strategy.

In this section you will learn important strategies you need to help you answer multiple-choice questions on the SAT. However, as invaluable as these tactics are, use them only when you need them. *If you know how to solve a problem and are confident that you can do so accurately and reasonably quickly, JUST DO IT!*

TACTIC 10. Test the Choices, Starting with C.

TACTIC 10, often called *backsolving,* is useful when you are asked to solve for an unknown and you understand what needs to be done to answer the question, but you want to avoid doing the algebra. The idea is simple: test the various choices to see which one is correct.

NOTE: On the SAT the answers to virtually all numerical multiple-choice questions are listed in either increasing or decreasing order. Consequently, C is the middle value; and in applying TACTIC 10, *you should always start with C.* For example, assume that choices A, B, C, D, and E are given in increasing order. Try C. If it works, you've found the answer. If C doesn't work, you should now know whether you need to test a larger number or a smaller one, and that information permits you to eliminate two more choices. If C is too small, you need a larger number, so A and B are out; if C is too large, you can eliminate D and E, which are even larger.

Examples 17 and 18 illustrate the proper use of TACTIC 10.

Example 17.

If the average (arithmetic mean) of 2, 7, and x is 12, what is the value of x?

(A) 9   (B) 12   (C) 21   (D) 27   (E) 36

Solution. Use TACTIC 10. Test choice C: $x = 21$.

- Is the average of 2, 7, and 21 equal to 12?

- No: $\dfrac{2+7+21}{3} = \dfrac{30}{3} = 10$, which is *too small.*

- Eliminate C; also, since, for the average to be 12, x must be *greater* than 21, eliminate A and B.

- Try choice D: $x = 27$. Is the average of 2, 7, and 27 equal to 12?

- Yes: $\dfrac{2+7+27}{3} = \dfrac{36}{3} = 12$. The answer is **D**.

Every problem that can be solved using TACTIC 10 can be solved directly, usually in less time. Therefore, we stress: *if you are confident that you can solve a problem quickly and accurately, just do so.*

Example 18.

If the sum of five consecutive odd integers is 735, what is the largest of these integers?

(A) 155   (B) 151   (C) 145   (D) 143   (E) 141

 Solution. Use TACTIC 10. Test choice C: 145.

- If 145 is the largest of the five integers, the integers are 145, 143, 141, 139, and 137. Quickly add them on your calculator. The sum is 705.
- Since 705 is too small, eliminate C, D, and E.
- If you noticed that the amount by which 705 is too small is 30, you should realize that each of the five numbers needs to be increased by 6; therefore, the largest is **151 (B)**.
- If you didn't notice, just try 151, and see that it works.

This solution is easy, and it avoids having to set up and solve the required equation:

$$n + (n + 2) + (n + 4) + (n + 6) + (n + 8) = 735.$$

TACTIC 11. Replace Variables with Numbers.

Mastery of TACTIC 11 is critical for anyone developing good test-taking skills. This tactic can be used whenever the five choices involve the variables in the question. There are three steps:

1. Replace each letter with an easy-to-use number.

2. Solve the problem using those numbers.

3. Evaluate each of the five choices with the numbers you picked to see which choice is equal to the answer you obtained.

Examples 19 and 20 illustrate the proper use of TACTIC 11.

Example 19.

If a is equal to b multiplied by c, which of the following is equal to b divided by c?

(A) $\dfrac{a}{bc}$ (B) $\dfrac{ab}{c}$ (C) $\dfrac{a}{c}$ (D) $\dfrac{a}{c^2}$ (E) $\dfrac{a}{bc^2}$

Solution.

- Pick three easy-to-use numbers that satisfy $a = bc$: for example, $a = 6$, $b = 2$, $c = 3$.

- Solve the problem with these numbers: $b \div c = \dfrac{b}{c} = \dfrac{2}{3}$.

- Check each of the five choices to see which one is equal to $\dfrac{2}{3}$:

- (A) $\dfrac{a}{bc} = \dfrac{6}{(2)(3)} = 1$: NO.   (B) $\dfrac{ab}{c} = \dfrac{(6)(2)}{(3)} = 4$: NO.

  (C) $\dfrac{a}{c} = \dfrac{6}{3} = 2$: NO.   (D) $\dfrac{a}{c^2} = \dfrac{6}{3^2} = \dfrac{6}{9} = \dfrac{2}{3}$: YES!

  Still check (E): $\dfrac{a}{bc^2} = \dfrac{6}{2(3^2)} = \dfrac{6}{18} = \dfrac{1}{3}$: NO.

- The answer is **D**.

Example 20.

If the sum of four consecutive odd integers is s, then, in terms of s, what is the greatest of these integers?

(A) $\dfrac{s-12}{4}$ (B) $\dfrac{s-6}{4}$ (C) $\dfrac{s+6}{4}$ (D) $\dfrac{s+12}{4}$ (E) $\dfrac{s+16}{4}$

Solution.

- Pick four easy-to-use consecutive odd integers: say, 1, 3, 5, 7. Then s, their sum, is 16.
- Solve the problem with these numbers: the greatest of these integers is 7.
- When $s = 16$, the five choices are $\dfrac{s-12}{4} = \dfrac{4}{4}$, $\dfrac{s-6}{4} = \dfrac{10}{4}$,

$\dfrac{s+6}{4} = \dfrac{22}{4}$, $\dfrac{\boldsymbol{s+12}}{\boldsymbol{4}} = \dfrac{28}{4}$, $\dfrac{s+16}{4} = \dfrac{32}{4}$.

- Only $\dfrac{28}{4}$, choice **D**, is equal to 7.

Of course, Examples 21 and 22 can be solved without using TACTIC 11 *if your algebra skills are good.*

The important point is that, if you are uncomfortable with the correct algebraic solution, you don't have to omit these questions. You can use TACTIC 11 and *always* get the right answer.

Example 21 is somewhat different. You are asked to reason through a word problem involving only variables. Most students find problems like these mind-boggling. Here, the use of TACTIC 11 is essential.

Helpful Hint

Replace the letters with numbers that are easy to use, not necessarily ones that make sense. *It is perfectly OK to ignore reality.* A school can have five students, apples can cost $10 each, trains can go 5 miles per hour or 1000 miles per hour—it doesn't matter.

Example 21.

If a school cafeteria needs c cans of soup each week for each student, and if there are s students in the school, for how many weeks will x cans of soup last?

(A) $\dfrac{cx}{s}$ (B) $\dfrac{xs}{c}$ (C) $\dfrac{s}{cx}$ (D) $\dfrac{x}{cs}$ (E) csx

Solution.

- Replace c, s, and x with three easy-to-use numbers. If a school cafeteria needs 2 cans of soup each week for each student, and if there are 5 students in the school, for how many weeks will 20 cans of soup last?
- Since the cafeteria needs $2 \times 5 = 10$ cans of soup per week, 20 cans will last for 2 weeks.
- Which of the choices equals 2 when $c = 2$, $s = 5$, and $x = 20$?
- The five choices become: $\dfrac{cx}{s} = 8$, $\dfrac{xs}{c} = 50$, $\dfrac{s}{cx} = \dfrac{1}{8}$, $\dfrac{x}{cs} = 2$, $csx = 200$.

The answer is **D**.

TACTIC 12. Choose an Appropriate Number.

TACTIC 12 is similar to TACTIC 11 in that we pick convenient numbers. However, here no variable is given in the problem. TACTIC 12 is especially useful in problems involving fractions, ratios, and percents.

Helpful Hint

In problems involving fractions, the best number to use is the least common denominator of all the fractions. In problems involving percents, the easiest number to use is 100.

Example 22.

At Central High School each student studies exactly one foreign language. Three-fifths of the students take Spanish, and one-fourth of the remaining students take Italian. If all of the others take French, what <u>percent</u> of the students take French?

(A) 10   (B) 15   (C) 20   (D) 25   (E) 30

Solution. The least common denominator of $\frac{3}{5}$ and $\frac{1}{4}$ is 20, so assume that there are 20 students at Central High. (Remember that the numbers you choose don't have to be realistic.) Then the number of students taking Spanish is $12\left(\frac{3}{5} \text{ of } 20\right)$. Of the remaining 8 students, $2\left(\frac{1}{4} \text{ of } 8\right)$ take Italian. The other 6 take French. Finally, 6 is **30%** of 20. The answer is **E**.

Example 23.

From 1994 to 1995 the sales of a book decreased by 80%. If the sales in 1996 were the same as in 1994, by what percent did they increase from 1995 to 1996?

(A) 80%   (B) 100%   (C) 120%   (D) 400%   (E) 500%

Solution. Use TACTIC 12, and assume that 100 copies were sold in 1994 (and 1996). Sales dropped by 80 (80% of 100) to 20 in 1995 and then increased by 80, from 20 back to 100, in 1996. The percent increase was

$$\frac{\text{actual increase}}{\text{original amount}} \times 100\% = \frac{80}{20} \times 100\% = \textbf{400\% (D)}.$$

TACTIC 13. Add Equations.

When a question involves two equations, either add them or subtract them. If there are three or more equations, add them.

Helpful Hint

Very often, answering a question does *not* require you to solve the equations. Remember TACTIC 6: *Do not do any more than is necessary.*

Example 24.

If $3x + 5y = 14$ and $x - y = 6$, what is the average of x and y?

(A) 0   (B) 2.5   (C) 3   (D) 3.5   (E) 5

Solution. Add the equations:

$$\begin{array}{r} 3x + 5y = 14 \\ +\ \ x - y = \ 6 \\ \hline 4x + 4y = 20 \end{array}$$

Divide each side by 4: $x + y = 5$

The average of x and y is their sum divided by 2:

$$\frac{x+y}{2} = \frac{5}{2} = 2.5$$

The answer is **B**.

Example 25.

If $a - b = 1$, $b - c = 2$, and $c - a = d$, what is the value of d?

(A) –3   (B) –1   (C) 1   (D) 3

(E) It cannot be determined from the information given.

Solution. Add the three equations:

$$a - b = 1$$
$$b - c = 2$$
$$+ \, c - a = d$$
$$\overline{\, 0 = 3 + d \Rightarrow d = -3}$$

The answer is **A**.

TACTIC 14. Eliminate Absurd Choices, and Guess.

When you have no idea how to solve a problem, eliminate all the absurd choices and *guess* from among the remaining ones.

Example 26.

The average of 5, 10, 15, and x is 20. What is x?

(A) 0   (B) 20   (C) 25   (D) 45   (E) 50

Solution. If the average of four numbers is 20, and three of them are less than 20, the other one must be greater than 20. Eliminate A and B and guess. If you further realize that, since 5 and 10 are *a lot* less than 20, x will probably be *a lot* more than 20, you can eliminate C, as well. Then guess either D or E.

Example 27.

If 25% of 220 equals 5.5% of w, what is w?

(A) 10   (B) 55   (C) 100   (D) 110   (E) 1000

Solution. Since 5.5% of w equals 25% of 220, which is surely greater than 5.5% of 220, w must be *greater* than 220. Eliminate A, B, C, and D. The answer *must* be **E**!

Practice Exercises   Answers given on pages 208–209.

1. Judy is now twice as old as Adam but 6 years ago she was 5 times as old as he was. How old is Judy now?

   (A) 10   (B) 16   (C) 20   (D) 24   (E) 32

2. If $a < b$ and c is the sum of a and b, which of the following is the positive difference between a and b?

   (A) $2a - c$ (B) $2b - c$ (C) $c - 2b$
   (D) $c - a + b$ (E) $c - a - b$

3. If w widgets cost c cents, how many widgets can you get for d dollars?

   (A) $\dfrac{100dw}{c}$ (B) $\dfrac{dw}{100c}$ (C) $100cdw$ (D) $\dfrac{dw}{c}$ (E) cdw

4. If 120% of a is equal to 80% of b, which of the following is equal to $a + b$?

   (A) $1.5a$ (B) $2a$ (C) $2.5a$ (D) $3a$ (E) $5a$

5. In the figure at the right, $WXYZ$ is a square whose sides are 12. AB, CD, EF, and GH are each 8, and are the diameters of the four semicircles. What is the area of the shaded region?

   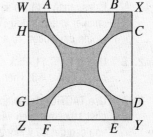

   (A) $144 - 128\pi$ (B) $144 - 64\pi$
   (C) $144 - 32\pi$ (D) $144 - 16\pi$
   (E) 16π

6. What is a divided by $a\%$ of a?

   (A) $\dfrac{a}{100}$ (B) $\dfrac{100}{a}$ (C) $\dfrac{a^2}{100}$ (D) $\dfrac{100}{a^2}$ (E) $100a$

7. On a certain Russian-American committee, $\dfrac{2}{3}$ of the members are men, and $\dfrac{3}{8}$ of the men are Americans. If $\dfrac{3}{5}$ of the committee members are Russian, what fraction of the members are American women?

   (A) $\dfrac{3}{20}$ (B) $\dfrac{11}{60}$ (C) $\dfrac{1}{4}$ (D) $\dfrac{2}{5}$ (E) $\dfrac{5}{12}$

8. Nadia will be x years old y years from now. How old was she z years ago?

(A) $x + y + z$ (B) $x + y - z$ (C) $x - y - z$
(D) $y - x - z$ (E) $z - y - x$

9. If $12a + 3b = 1$ and $7b - 2a = 9$, what is the average (arithmetic mean) of a and b?

(A) 0.1   (B) 0.5   (C) 1   (D) 2.5   (E) 5

10. If $x\%$ of y is 10, what is y?

(A) $\dfrac{10}{x}$ (B) $\dfrac{100}{x}$ (C) $\dfrac{1000}{x}$ (D) $\dfrac{x}{100}$ (E) $\dfrac{x}{10}$

Answer Key

1. **B**	3. **A**	5. **C**	7. **A**	9. **B**
2. **B**	4. **C**	6. **B**	8. **C**	10. **C**

1. B   Use TACTIC 10: backsolve, starting with C. If Judy is now 20, Adam is 10; 6 years ago, they would have been 14 and 4, which is less than 5 times as much. Eliminate C, D, and E, and try a smaller value. If Judy is now **16**, Adam is 8; 6 years ago, they would have been 10 and 2. That's it; 10 is 5 times 2.

2. B   Use TACTIC 11. Pick simple values for a, b, and c. Let $a = 1$, $b = 2$, and $c = 3$. Then $b - a = 1$. Only $2b - c$ is equal to 1.

3. A   Use TACTIC 11: replaces variables with numbers. If 2 widgets cost 10 cents, then widgets cost 5 cents each; and for 3 dollars, you can get 60 widgets. Which of the choices equals 60 when $w = 2$, $c = 10$, and $d = 3$?

Only $\dfrac{100dw}{c}$.

4. C   Use TACTIC 12: choose appropriate numbers. Since 120% of 80 = 80% of 120, let $a = 80$ and $b = 120$. Then $a + b = 200$, and $200 \div 80 = $ **2.5**.

5. C   If you don't know how to solve this, you must use TACTIC 14: eliminate the absurd choices and guess. Which choices are absurd? Certainly, A and B, both of which are negative. Also, since choice D is about 94, which is much more than half the area of the square, it is much too large. Guess between C (about 43) and E (about 50). If you remember that the way to find shaded areas is to subtract, guess C: **$144 - 32\pi$**.

6. **B**   Use TACTICS 11 and 12: replace a by a number, and use 100 since the problem involves percents.

$$100 \div (100\% \text{ of } 100) = 100 \div 100 = 1.$$

Test each choice; which one equals 1 when $a = 100$? Both A and

B are equal to $\dfrac{100}{100}$, which is 1, but you can eliminate C, D,

and E. Now test A and B with another value for a, such as 50:

$$50 \div (50\% \text{ of } 50) = 50 \div (25) = 2.$$

Now, only choice B, $\dfrac{\mathbf{100}}{\boldsymbol{a}}$, works: $\dfrac{100}{50} = 2$.

7. **A**   Use TACTIC 12: choose appropriate numbers. The LCM of all the denominators is 120, so assume that the committee has 120

members. Then there are $\dfrac{2}{3} \times 120 = 80$ men and 40 women.

Of the 80 men, $30\left(\dfrac{3}{8} \times 80\right)$ are American. Since there are

$72\left(\dfrac{3}{5} \times 120\right)$ Russians, there are $120 - 72 = 48$ Americans,

of whom 30 are men, so the other 18 are women. Finally, the

fraction of American women is $\dfrac{18}{120} = \dfrac{\mathbf{3}}{\mathbf{20}}$.

8. **C**   Use TACTIC 11: replace x, y, and z with easy-to-use numbers.

Assume Nadia will be 10 in 2 years. How old was she 3 years ago? If she will be 10 in 2 years, she is 8 now and 3 years ago was 5. Which of the choices equals 5 when $x = 10$, $y = 2$, and $z = 3$? Only $\boldsymbol{x - y - z}$.

9. **B**   Use TACTIC 13: The sum of the two equations is

$$10a + 10b = 10 \Rightarrow a + b = 1 \Rightarrow \dfrac{a+b}{2} = \dfrac{1}{2} \text{ or } \mathbf{0.5}.$$

10. **C**   Use TACTICS 11 and 12. Since 100% of 10 is 10, let $x = 100$ and $y = 10$. When $x = 100$, choices C and E are each 10. Eliminate A, B, and D, and try some other numbers: 50% of 20 is 10. Of C

and E, only $\dfrac{\mathbf{1000}}{\boldsymbol{x}} = 20$ when $x = 50$.

THE GRID-IN QUESTION

On the SAT, one 25-minute section contains 10 questions for which no choices are given. These are the grid-in problems, which represent the type of question with which you are most familiar—you solve a problem and then write the answer on your answer sheet. The only difference is that, on the SAT, you must enter the answer on a special grid that can be read by a computer.

Your answer sheet will have 10 blank grids, one for each question. Each one will look like the grid on the left below. After solving a problem, the first step is to write the answer in the four boxes at the top of the grid. You then blacken the appropriate oval under each box. For example, if your answer to a question is 2450, you write 2450 at the top of the grid, one digit in each box, and then in each column blacken the oval that contains the number you wrote at the top of the column. This is not difficult; but there are some special rules concerning grid-in questions, so let's go over them before you practice gridding in some numbers.

1. The only symbols that appear in the grid are the digits 0 to 9, a decimal point, and a slash (/), used to write fractions. Keep in mind that, since there is no negative sign, ***the answer to every grid-in question is a positive number or zero***.

2. You will receive credit for a correct answer no matter where you grid it. For example, the answer 17 could be gridded in any of three positions:

Neverthelesss, we suggest that you consistently ***write all your answers*** the way numbers are usually displayed—***to the right, with blank spaces at the left***.

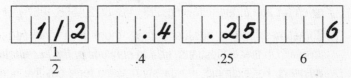

$\frac{1}{2}$ .4   .25   6

3. ***Never round off your answers***. If a decimal answer will fit in the grid and you round it off, your answer will be marked wrong. For example, if the answer is .148 and you correctly round it off to the nearest hundredth and enter .15, you will receive *no credit*. If a decimal answer will not fit in the grid, enter a decimal point in the first column, followed by the first three digits. For example, if your answer is 0.454545..., enter it as .454. You would receive credit if you rounded it to .455, but don't. You might occasionally make a mistake in rounding, whereas you'll *never* make a mistake if you just copy the first three digits. *Note:* If the correct answer has more than two decimal digits, *you must use all four columns of the grid*. You will receive *no credit* for .4 or .5 or .45. (These answers are not accurate enough.)

4. ***Never write a 0 before the decimal point***. The first column of the grid doesn't even have a 0 in it. If the correct answer is 0.3333..., you must grid it as .333. You can't grid 0.33, and 0.3 is not accurate enough.

5. ***Be aware that you can never enter a mixed number***. If your answer is $2\frac{1}{2}$, you *cannot* leave a space and enter your

   answer as 2 1/2, and if you enter $\boxed{2\,|\,1\,/\,2}$, it will be read as $\frac{21}{2}$ and marked wrong. You must enter $2\frac{1}{2}$ as the

   improper fraction $\frac{5}{2}$ or as the decimal 2.5.

6. Since full credit is given for any equivalent answer, use these guidelines to ***enter your answer in the simplest way***. If your answer is $\frac{6}{9}$, you should enter 6/9. (However, credit would be given for any of the following: 2/3, 4/6, 8/12, .666, .667.)

7. Sometimes grid-in questions have more than one correct answer. On these questions, ***grid in only one of the acceptable answers***. For example, if a question asked for a positive number less than 100 that was divisible by both 5 and 7, you could enter *either* 35 *or* 70, but not both. Similarly, if a question asked for a number between $\frac{3}{7}$ and $\frac{5}{9}$, you could enter any

   one of hundreds of possibilities: fractions such as $\frac{1}{2}$ and $\frac{4}{9}$ or *any* decimal between .429 and .554—.43 or .499 or .52, for example.

8. ***Keep in mind that there is no penalty for a wrong answer to a grid-in question***. Therefore, you might as well guess, even if you have no idea what to do. As you will see shortly, there are some strategies for making intelligent guesses.

9. Be sure to ***grid every answer very carefully***. The computer does not read what you have written in the boxes; it reads only the answer in the grid. If the correct answer to a question is 100 and you write 100 in the boxes, but accidentally grid in 200, you get *no* credit.

10. If you know that the answer to a question is 100, can you just grid it in and not bother writing it on top? Yes, you will get full credit, and so some SAT guides recommend that you don't waste time writing the answer. This is terrible advice. Instead, **write each answer in the boxes**. It takes less than 2 seconds per answer to do this, and it definitely cuts down on careless errors in gridding. More important, if you go back to check your work, it is much easier to read what's in the boxes on top than what's in the grid.

Testing Tactics

TACTIC 15. Backsolve.

If you think of a grid-in problem as a multiple-choice question in which the choices accidentally got erased, you can still use TACTIC 10: test the choices. You just have to make up the choices as you go.

Example 28.

If the average (arithmetic mean) of 2, 7, and x is 12, what is the value of x?

Solution. You could start with 10; but if you immediately realize that the average of 2, 7, and 10 is less than 10 (so it can't be 12), you'll try a bigger number, say 20. The average of 2, 7, and 20 is

$$\frac{2 + 7 + 20}{3} = \frac{29}{3} = 9\frac{2}{3},$$

which is too small. Try $x = 30$:

$$\frac{2 + 7 + 30}{3} = \frac{39}{3} = 13,$$

just a bit too big. Since 12 is closer to 13 than it is to $9\frac{2}{3}$, your next choice should be closer to 30 than 20, surely more than 25. Your third try might well be **27**, which works.

Example 29.

For every positive number $x \neq 20$: $\boxed{x} = 20 + x$ and $\textcircled{x} = 20 - x$.

If $\dfrac{\boxed{x}}{\textcircled{x}} = 4$, what is the value of x?

Solution. In order for $20 - x$ to be positive, x has to be less than 20.

Try $x = 15$: $\dfrac{20+15}{20-15} = \dfrac{35}{5} = 7$. That's too big.

Try $x = 10$: $\dfrac{20+10}{20-10} = \dfrac{30}{10} = 3$. That's too small.

Try $x = 12$: $\dfrac{20+12}{20-12} = \dfrac{32}{8} = \mathbf{4}$. That's it.

TACTIC 16. Choose an Appropriate Number.

This is exactly the same as TACTIC 12. The most appropriate numbers to choose are 100 for percent problems, the LCD (least common denominator) for fraction problems, and the LCM (least common multiple) of the coefficients for problems involving equations. Each of the problems discussed under TACTIC 12 could have been a grid-in, because we didn't even look at the choices until we had the correct answer.

Example 30.

During an Election Day sale, the price of every television set in a store was reduced by $33\frac{1}{3}$%. By what percent must these sale prices be raised so that the TVs now sell for their original prices? (Do not grid the % sign.)

Solution. Since this problem involves percents, you should think about using 100. But the fraction $\frac{1}{3}$ is also involved, so 300 is an even better choice. Assume the original price was \$300. Since $33\frac{1}{3}$% of $300 = \frac{1}{3}$ of $300 = 100$, the sale price was \$200. To restore the price to \$300, it must now be raised by \$100. The percent increase is

$$\frac{\text{actual increase}}{\text{original amount}} \times 100\% = \frac{100}{200} \times 100\% = \mathbf{50\%}.$$

Practice Exercises   Answers given on pages 217–219.

> Directions: Enter your response to these problems on the grids on page 216.

1. For what number $b > 0$ is it true that b divided by b% of b equals b?

2. Patty has 150 coins, each of which is a dime or a quarter. If she has $27.90, how many quarters does she have?

3. A fair coin is flipped repeatedly. Each time it lands "heads," Ali gets a point, and whenever it lands "tails," Jason gets a point. The game continues until someone gets 5 points. If the score is now 4 to 3 in Ali's favor, and the probability that Ali will win the game is k times the probability that Jason will win the game, what is the value of k?

4. At a certain university, $\frac{1}{4}$ of the applicants failed to meet minimum standards and were rejected immediately. Of those who met the standards, $\frac{2}{5}$ were accepted. If 1200 applicants were accepted, how many applied?

5. More than half of the members of the Key Club are girls. If $\frac{4}{7}$ of the girls and $\frac{7}{11}$ of the boys in the Key Club attended the April meeting, what is the smallest number of members the club could have?

6. Jessica copied a column of numbers and added them. The only mistake she made was that she copied one number as 5095 instead of 5.95. If the sum she got was 8545.05, what should the answer have been?

7. Jerry spent $105 for a tool kit and a box of nails. If the tool kit cost $100 more than the nails, how many boxes of nails could be purchased for the price of the tool kit?

8. Ken is now 3 times as old as his younger sister, but in 7 years he will be only twice as old as she will be then. How old is Ken now?

9. The value of an investment increased 50% in 1992 and again in 1993. In each of 1994 and 1995 the value of the investment decreased by 50%. At the end of 1995 the value of the investment was how many times the value at the beginning of 1992?

10. How many integers between 1 and 1000 are the product of two consecutive integers?

1.

2.

3.

4.

5.

6.

7.

8.

9.

10.

Answer Key

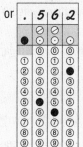

1. **10**
2. **86**
3. **3**
4. **4000**
5. **25**
6. **3456**
7. **41**
8. **21**
9. **9/16** or **.562**
10. **31**

Answer Explanations

1. (10) $b \div (b\% \text{ of } b) = b \div \left(\dfrac{b}{100} \times b \right) =$

$b \div \left(\dfrac{b^2}{100} \right) = b \times \dfrac{100}{b^2} = \dfrac{100}{b}.$

Since this value is to equal b, you have

$$\dfrac{100}{b} = b \Rightarrow b^2 = 100 \Rightarrow b = \mathbf{10}.$$

2. (86)   Use TACTIC 15: backsolve. Pick an easy starting value, say $q = 100$. If this gives a value greater than \$27.90, decrease q; if it gives a value less than \$27.90, increase q.

Number of Quarters	Number of Dimes	Value
100	50	\$25.00 + \$5.00 = \$30.00
80	70	\$20.00 + \$7.00 = \$27.00
85	65	\$21.25 + \$6.50 = \$27.75
86	64	\$21.50 + \$6.40 = \$27.90

3. (3)   Jason can win only if the next two flips are both tails. The probability of that happening is $\frac{1}{2} \times \frac{1}{2} = \frac{1}{4}$. Therefore, the probability that Ali wins is $1 - \frac{1}{4} = \frac{3}{4}$.

Since $\frac{3}{4} = 3\left(\frac{1}{4}\right)$, $k = \mathbf{3}$.

4. (4000)   Use TACTIC 16: choose an appropriate number. The LCD of $\frac{1}{4}$ and $\frac{2}{5}$ is 20, so *assume* that there were 20 applicants. Then $\frac{1}{4}(20) = 5$ failed to meet the minimum standards. Of the remaining 15 applicants, $\frac{2}{5}$, or 6, were accepted, so 6 of every 20 applicants were accepted. Set up a proportion:

$$\frac{6}{20} = \frac{1200}{x} \Rightarrow 6x = 24{,}000 \Rightarrow x = \mathbf{4000}.$$

5. (25)   Since $\frac{4}{7}$ of the girls attended the meeting, the number of girls in the club must be a multiple of 7: 7, 14, 21, ... Similarly, the number of boys in the club must be a multiple of 11: 11, 22, ... Since there are at least 11 boys and there are more girls than boys, there must be at least 14 girls. The smallest possible total is $14 + 11 = \mathbf{25}$.

6. (3456)   To get the correct sum, subtract the number Jessica added in error and add the number she left out:
$8545.05 - 5095 + 5.95 = \mathbf{3456}$.

7. (41)   The first thing to do is to calculate the prices of the tool kit and the nails. *Be careful*—they are *not* $100 and $5. You can get the answer algebraically or by trial and error. If you let x = cost of the nails, then $100 + x$ = cost of the tool kit, and

$$x + (100 + x) = 105 \Rightarrow 2x + 100 = 105 \Rightarrow$$
$$2x = 5 \Rightarrow x = 2.5.$$

Then the nails cost $2.50, and the tool kit $102.50. Finally, $102.50 \div 2.50 = \mathbf{41}$.

8. (21)   Use TACTIC 16. Pick a value for the sister's age—say, 2. Then Ken is 6. In 7 years, sister and brother will be 9 and 13, respectively. No good; 13 is less than twice 9. Try a bigger number—5. Then Ken is 15, and in 7 years the two will be 12 and 22. That's closer, but still too small. Try 7. Then Ken is **21**, and in 7 years his sister and he will be 14 and 28. That's it!

9. $\left(.562 \text{ or } \dfrac{9}{16}\right)$ Use TACTIC 16. Pick an easy-to-use starting value—$100, say. Then the value of the investment at the end of each of the 4 years 1992, 1993, 1994, 1995 was $150, $225, $112.50, $56.25, so the final value was .5625 times the initial value. Note that some initial values would lead to an answer more easily expressed as a fraction. For example, if you start with $16, the yearly values would be $24, $36, $18, and $9, and the answer would be $\dfrac{9}{16}$.

10. (31)   Use TACTIC 8. List the integers systematically: 1×2, 2×3, ... , 24×25, ... You don't have to multiply and list the products ($2, 6, 12, ... , 600, ...$); you just have to know when to stop. The largest product less than 1000 is $31 \times 32 = 992$, so there are **31** numbers.

SUMMARY OF IMPORTANT TIPS AND TACTICS

1. Whenever you know how to answer a question directly, just do it. The tactics given in this chapter should be used only when you need them.

2. Memorize all the formulas you need to know. Even though some of them are printed on the first page of each math section, during the test you do not want to waste any time referring back to that reference material.

3. Be sure to bring a calculator, but use it only when you need it. Don't use it for simple arithmetic that you can easily do in your head.

4. Remember that no problem requires lengthy or difficult computations. If you find yourself doing a lot of arithmetic, stop and reread the question. You are probably not answering the question asked.

5. Answer every question you attempt. Even if you can't solve it, you can almost always eliminate two or more choices. Often you know that an answer must be negative, but two or three of the choices are positive, or an answer must be even, and some of the choices are odd.

6. Unless a diagram is labeled "<u>Note</u>: Figure not drawn to scale," it is perfectly accurate, and you can trust it in making an estimate.

7. When a diagram has not been provided, draw one, especially on any geometry problem.

8. If a diagram has been provided, feel free to label it, mark it up in any way, including adding line segments, if necessary.

9. Answer any question for which you can estimate the answer, even if you are not sure you are correct.

10. Don't panic when you see a strange symbol in a question, It will always be defined. Getting the correct answer just involves following the directions given in the definition.

11. When a question involves two equations, either add them or subtract them. If there are three or more, just add them.

12. Never make unwarranted assumptions. Do not assume numbers are positive or integers. If a question refers to two numbers, do not assume that they have to be different. If you know a figure has four sides, do not assume that it is a rectangle.

13. Be sure to work in consistent units. If the width and length of a rectangle are 8 inches and 2 feet, respectively, either convert the 2 feet to 24 inches or the 8 inches to two-thirds of a foot before calculating the area or perimeter.

Standard Multiple-Choice Questions

1. Whenever you answer a question by backsolving, start with Choice C.

2. When you replace variables with numbers, choose easy-to-use numbers, whether or not they are realistic.

3. Choose appropriate numbers. The best number to use in percent problems is 100. In problems involving fractions, the best number to use is the least common denominator.

4. When you have no idea how to solve a problem, eliminate all of the absurd choices and guess.

Student-Produced Response (Grid-in) Questions

1. Write your answer in the four spaces at the top of the grid, and *carefully* grid in your answer below. No credit is given for a correct answer if it has been gridded improperly.

2. Remember that the answer to a grid-in question can never be negative.

3. You can never grid in a mixed number—you must convert it to an improper fraction or a decimal.

4. If a fraction can fit in the four spaces of the grid, enter it. If not, use your calculator to convert it to a decimal (by dividing) and enter a decimal point followed by the first three decimal digits.

5. When gridding a decimal, do not write a 0 before the decimal point.

6. If a question has more than one possible answer, only grid in one of them.

7. There is no penalty for wrong answers on grid-in questions, so you should grid in anything that seems reasonable, rather than leave out a question.

7 Practice SAT Exams

You are now about to take a major step in preparing yourself to handle an actual SAT. Before you are two practice tests patterned after the released SAT practice exam. Up to now, you've concentrated on specific areas and on general testing techniques. You've mastered testing tips and worked on practice exercises. Now you have a chance to test yourself before you walk in that test center door.

These practice tests resemble the SAT in format, in difficulty, and in content. When you take one, take it as if it *were* the actual SAT.

Build Your Stamina

Don't start and stop and take time out for a soda or for a phone call. To do well on the SAT, you have to focus on the test, the test, and nothing but the test for hours at a time. Most high school students have never had to sit through a four-hour examination before they take their first SAT. To survive such a long exam takes stamina, and, as marathon runners know, the only way to build stamina is to put in the necessary time.

Refine Your Skills

You know how to maximize your score by tackling easy questions first and by eliminating wrong answers whenever you can. Put these skills into practice. If you find yourself spending too much time on any one question, skip it and move on. Remember to check frequently to make sure you are answering the questions in the right spots. This is a great chance for you to get these skills down pat.

Take a Deep Breath—and Smile!

It's hard to stay calm when those around you are tense, and you're bound to run into some pretty tense people when you take the SAT. So you may experience a slight case of "exam nerves" on the big day. Don't worry about it.

1. Being keyed up for an examination isn't always bad: you may outdo yourself because you are so worked up.

2. Total panic is unlikely to set in: you know too much.

3. You know you can handle a 3¾-hour test.

4. You know you can handle the sorts of questions you'll find on the SAT.

5. You know you can omit several questions and still score high. Answer only 50–60% of the questions correctly and you'll still get an average or better than average score (and dozens of solid, well-known colleges are out there right now, looking for serious students with just that kind of score). Answer more than that correctly and you should wind up with a superior score.

Make Your Practice Pay—Approximate the Test

1. Complete an entire Practice Exam at one sitting.

2. Use a clock or timer.

3. Allow precisely 25 minutes each for sections 1 through 7, 20 minutes each for sections 8 and 9, and 10 minutes for section 10. (If you have time left over, review your answers in that section.)

4. After sections 3 and 7, give yourself a ten-minute break.

5. Allow no talking in the test room.

6. Work rapidly without wasting time.

ANSWER SHEETS—TEST 1

Section 1

To write your essay, use the front and back of one sheet of standard-ruled loose-leaf paper.

If any section has more answer spaces than questions, leave the extra spaces blank.

Section 2

1 Ⓐ Ⓑ Ⓒ Ⓓ Ⓔ   10 Ⓐ Ⓑ Ⓒ Ⓓ Ⓔ   19 Ⓐ Ⓑ Ⓒ Ⓓ Ⓔ
2 Ⓐ Ⓑ Ⓒ Ⓓ Ⓔ   11 Ⓐ Ⓑ Ⓒ Ⓓ Ⓔ   20 Ⓐ Ⓑ Ⓒ Ⓓ Ⓔ
3 Ⓐ Ⓑ Ⓒ Ⓓ Ⓔ   12 Ⓐ Ⓑ Ⓒ Ⓓ Ⓔ   21 Ⓐ Ⓑ Ⓒ Ⓓ Ⓔ
4 Ⓐ Ⓑ Ⓒ Ⓓ Ⓔ   13 Ⓐ Ⓑ Ⓒ Ⓓ Ⓔ   22 Ⓐ Ⓑ Ⓒ Ⓓ Ⓔ
5 Ⓐ Ⓑ Ⓒ Ⓓ Ⓔ   14 Ⓐ Ⓑ Ⓒ Ⓓ Ⓔ   23 Ⓐ Ⓑ Ⓒ Ⓓ Ⓔ
6 Ⓐ Ⓑ Ⓒ Ⓓ Ⓔ   15 Ⓐ Ⓑ Ⓒ Ⓓ Ⓔ   24 Ⓐ Ⓑ Ⓒ Ⓓ Ⓔ
7 Ⓐ Ⓑ Ⓒ Ⓓ Ⓔ   16 Ⓐ Ⓑ Ⓒ Ⓓ Ⓔ   25 Ⓐ Ⓑ Ⓒ Ⓓ Ⓔ
8 Ⓐ Ⓑ Ⓒ Ⓓ Ⓔ   17 Ⓐ Ⓑ Ⓒ Ⓓ Ⓔ
9 Ⓐ Ⓑ Ⓒ Ⓓ Ⓔ   18 Ⓐ Ⓑ Ⓒ Ⓓ Ⓔ

Section 3

1 Ⓐ Ⓑ Ⓒ Ⓓ Ⓔ   10 Ⓐ Ⓑ Ⓒ Ⓓ Ⓔ   19 Ⓐ Ⓑ Ⓒ Ⓓ Ⓔ
2 Ⓐ Ⓑ Ⓒ Ⓓ Ⓔ   11 Ⓐ Ⓑ Ⓒ Ⓓ Ⓔ   20 Ⓐ Ⓑ Ⓒ Ⓓ Ⓔ
3 Ⓐ Ⓑ Ⓒ Ⓓ Ⓔ   12 Ⓐ Ⓑ Ⓒ Ⓓ Ⓔ   21 Ⓐ Ⓑ Ⓒ Ⓓ Ⓔ
4 Ⓐ Ⓑ Ⓒ Ⓓ Ⓔ   13 Ⓐ Ⓑ Ⓒ Ⓓ Ⓔ   22 Ⓐ Ⓑ Ⓒ Ⓓ Ⓔ
5 Ⓐ Ⓑ Ⓒ Ⓓ Ⓔ   14 Ⓐ Ⓑ Ⓒ Ⓓ Ⓔ   23 Ⓐ Ⓑ Ⓒ Ⓓ Ⓔ
6 Ⓐ Ⓑ Ⓒ Ⓓ Ⓔ   15 Ⓐ Ⓑ Ⓒ Ⓓ Ⓔ   24 Ⓐ Ⓑ Ⓒ Ⓓ Ⓔ
7 Ⓐ Ⓑ Ⓒ Ⓓ Ⓔ   16 Ⓐ Ⓑ Ⓒ Ⓓ Ⓔ   25 Ⓐ Ⓑ Ⓒ Ⓓ Ⓔ
8 Ⓐ Ⓑ Ⓒ Ⓓ Ⓔ   17 Ⓐ Ⓑ Ⓒ Ⓓ Ⓔ
9 Ⓐ Ⓑ Ⓒ Ⓓ Ⓔ   18 Ⓐ Ⓑ Ⓒ Ⓓ Ⓔ

ANSWER SHEETS—TEST 1

Section 4

1 Ⓐ Ⓑ Ⓒ Ⓓ Ⓔ   13 Ⓐ Ⓑ Ⓒ Ⓓ Ⓔ   25 Ⓐ Ⓑ Ⓒ Ⓓ Ⓔ
2 Ⓐ Ⓑ Ⓒ Ⓓ Ⓔ   14 Ⓐ Ⓑ Ⓒ Ⓓ Ⓔ   26 Ⓐ Ⓑ Ⓒ Ⓓ Ⓔ
3 Ⓐ Ⓑ Ⓒ Ⓓ Ⓔ   15 Ⓐ Ⓑ Ⓒ Ⓓ Ⓔ   27 Ⓐ Ⓑ Ⓒ Ⓓ Ⓔ
4 Ⓐ Ⓑ Ⓒ Ⓓ Ⓔ   16 Ⓐ Ⓑ Ⓒ Ⓓ Ⓔ   28 Ⓐ Ⓑ Ⓒ Ⓓ Ⓔ
5 Ⓐ Ⓑ Ⓒ Ⓓ Ⓔ   17 Ⓐ Ⓑ Ⓒ Ⓓ Ⓔ   29 Ⓐ Ⓑ Ⓒ Ⓓ Ⓔ
6 Ⓐ Ⓑ Ⓒ Ⓓ Ⓔ   18 Ⓐ Ⓑ Ⓒ Ⓓ Ⓔ   30 Ⓐ Ⓑ Ⓒ Ⓓ Ⓔ
7 Ⓐ Ⓑ Ⓒ Ⓓ Ⓔ   19 Ⓐ Ⓑ Ⓒ Ⓓ Ⓔ   31 Ⓐ Ⓑ Ⓒ Ⓓ Ⓔ
8 Ⓐ Ⓑ Ⓒ Ⓓ Ⓔ   20 Ⓐ Ⓑ Ⓒ Ⓓ Ⓔ   32 Ⓐ Ⓑ Ⓒ Ⓓ Ⓔ
9 Ⓐ Ⓑ Ⓒ Ⓓ Ⓔ   21 Ⓐ Ⓑ Ⓒ Ⓓ Ⓔ   33 Ⓐ Ⓑ Ⓒ Ⓓ Ⓔ
10 Ⓐ Ⓑ Ⓒ Ⓓ Ⓔ   22 Ⓐ Ⓑ Ⓒ Ⓓ Ⓔ   34 Ⓐ Ⓑ Ⓒ Ⓓ Ⓔ
11 Ⓐ Ⓑ Ⓒ Ⓓ Ⓔ   23 Ⓐ Ⓑ Ⓒ Ⓓ Ⓔ   35 Ⓐ Ⓑ Ⓒ Ⓓ Ⓔ
12 Ⓐ Ⓑ Ⓒ Ⓓ Ⓔ   24 Ⓐ Ⓑ Ⓒ Ⓓ Ⓔ

Section 6

1 Ⓐ Ⓑ Ⓒ Ⓓ Ⓔ   4 Ⓐ Ⓑ Ⓒ Ⓓ Ⓔ   7 Ⓐ Ⓑ Ⓒ Ⓓ Ⓔ
2 Ⓐ Ⓑ Ⓒ Ⓓ Ⓔ   5 Ⓐ Ⓑ Ⓒ Ⓓ Ⓔ   8 Ⓐ Ⓑ Ⓒ Ⓓ Ⓔ
3 Ⓐ Ⓑ Ⓒ Ⓓ Ⓔ   6 Ⓐ Ⓑ Ⓒ Ⓓ Ⓔ

ANSWER SHEETS—TEST 1

Section 6 (continued)

9

10

11

12

13

14

15

16

ANSWER SHEETS—TEST 1

Section 6 (continued)

17

18

Section 7

1 Ⓐ Ⓑ Ⓒ Ⓓ Ⓔ   10 Ⓐ Ⓑ Ⓒ Ⓓ Ⓔ   19 Ⓐ Ⓑ Ⓒ Ⓓ Ⓔ
2 Ⓐ Ⓑ Ⓒ Ⓓ Ⓔ   11 Ⓐ Ⓑ Ⓒ Ⓓ Ⓔ   20 Ⓐ Ⓑ Ⓒ Ⓓ Ⓔ
3 Ⓐ Ⓑ Ⓒ Ⓓ Ⓔ   12 Ⓐ Ⓑ Ⓒ Ⓓ Ⓔ   21 Ⓐ Ⓑ Ⓒ Ⓓ Ⓔ
4 Ⓐ Ⓑ Ⓒ Ⓓ Ⓔ   13 Ⓐ Ⓑ Ⓒ Ⓓ Ⓔ   22 Ⓐ Ⓑ Ⓒ Ⓓ Ⓔ
5 Ⓐ Ⓑ Ⓒ Ⓓ Ⓔ   14 Ⓐ Ⓑ Ⓒ Ⓓ Ⓔ   23 Ⓐ Ⓑ Ⓒ Ⓓ Ⓔ
6 Ⓐ Ⓑ Ⓒ Ⓓ Ⓔ   15 Ⓐ Ⓑ Ⓒ Ⓓ Ⓔ   24 Ⓐ Ⓑ Ⓒ Ⓓ Ⓔ
7 Ⓐ Ⓑ Ⓒ Ⓓ Ⓔ   16 Ⓐ Ⓑ Ⓒ Ⓓ Ⓔ   25 Ⓐ Ⓑ Ⓒ Ⓓ Ⓔ
8 Ⓐ Ⓑ Ⓒ Ⓓ Ⓔ   17 Ⓐ Ⓑ Ⓒ Ⓓ Ⓔ
9 Ⓐ Ⓑ Ⓒ Ⓓ Ⓔ   18 Ⓐ Ⓑ Ⓒ Ⓓ Ⓔ

ANSWER SHEETS—TEST 1

Section 8

1 Ⓐ Ⓑ Ⓒ Ⓓ Ⓔ   10 Ⓐ Ⓑ Ⓒ Ⓓ Ⓔ   19 Ⓐ Ⓑ Ⓒ Ⓓ Ⓔ
2 Ⓐ Ⓑ Ⓒ Ⓓ Ⓔ   11 Ⓐ Ⓑ Ⓒ Ⓓ Ⓔ   20 Ⓐ Ⓑ Ⓒ Ⓓ Ⓔ
3 Ⓐ Ⓑ Ⓒ Ⓓ Ⓔ   12 Ⓐ Ⓑ Ⓒ Ⓓ Ⓔ   21 Ⓐ Ⓑ Ⓒ Ⓓ Ⓔ
4 Ⓐ Ⓑ Ⓒ Ⓓ Ⓔ   13 Ⓐ Ⓑ Ⓒ Ⓓ Ⓔ   22 Ⓐ Ⓑ Ⓒ Ⓓ Ⓔ
5 Ⓐ Ⓑ Ⓒ Ⓓ Ⓔ   14 Ⓐ Ⓑ Ⓒ Ⓓ Ⓔ   23 Ⓐ Ⓑ Ⓒ Ⓓ Ⓔ
6 Ⓐ Ⓑ Ⓒ Ⓓ Ⓔ   15 Ⓐ Ⓑ Ⓒ Ⓓ Ⓔ   24 Ⓐ Ⓑ Ⓒ Ⓓ Ⓔ
7 Ⓐ Ⓑ Ⓒ Ⓓ Ⓔ   16 Ⓐ Ⓑ Ⓒ Ⓓ Ⓔ   25 Ⓐ Ⓑ Ⓒ Ⓓ Ⓔ
8 Ⓐ Ⓑ Ⓒ Ⓓ Ⓔ   17 Ⓐ Ⓑ Ⓒ Ⓓ Ⓔ
9 Ⓐ Ⓑ Ⓒ Ⓓ Ⓔ   18 Ⓐ Ⓑ Ⓒ Ⓓ Ⓔ

Section 9

1 Ⓐ Ⓑ Ⓒ Ⓓ Ⓔ   8 Ⓐ Ⓑ Ⓒ Ⓓ Ⓔ   15 Ⓐ Ⓑ Ⓒ Ⓓ Ⓔ
2 Ⓐ Ⓑ Ⓒ Ⓓ Ⓔ   9 Ⓐ Ⓑ Ⓒ Ⓓ Ⓔ   16 Ⓐ Ⓑ Ⓒ Ⓓ Ⓔ
3 Ⓐ Ⓑ Ⓒ Ⓓ Ⓔ   10 Ⓐ Ⓑ Ⓒ Ⓓ Ⓔ   17 Ⓐ Ⓑ Ⓒ Ⓓ Ⓔ
4 Ⓐ Ⓑ Ⓒ Ⓓ Ⓔ   11 Ⓐ Ⓑ Ⓒ Ⓓ Ⓔ   18 Ⓐ Ⓑ Ⓒ Ⓓ Ⓔ
5 Ⓐ Ⓑ Ⓒ Ⓓ Ⓔ   12 Ⓐ Ⓑ Ⓒ Ⓓ Ⓔ   19 Ⓐ Ⓑ Ⓒ Ⓓ Ⓔ
6 Ⓐ Ⓑ Ⓒ Ⓓ Ⓔ   13 Ⓐ Ⓑ Ⓒ Ⓓ Ⓔ   20 Ⓐ Ⓑ Ⓒ Ⓓ Ⓔ
7 Ⓐ Ⓑ Ⓒ Ⓓ Ⓔ   14 Ⓐ Ⓑ Ⓒ Ⓓ Ⓔ

Section 10

1 Ⓐ Ⓑ Ⓒ Ⓓ Ⓔ   6 Ⓐ Ⓑ Ⓒ Ⓓ Ⓔ   11 Ⓐ Ⓑ Ⓒ Ⓓ Ⓔ
2 Ⓐ Ⓑ Ⓒ Ⓓ Ⓔ   7 Ⓐ Ⓑ Ⓒ Ⓓ Ⓔ   12 Ⓐ Ⓑ Ⓒ Ⓓ Ⓔ
3 Ⓐ Ⓑ Ⓒ Ⓓ Ⓔ   8 Ⓐ Ⓑ Ⓒ Ⓓ Ⓔ   13 Ⓐ Ⓑ Ⓒ Ⓓ Ⓔ
4 Ⓐ Ⓑ Ⓒ Ⓓ Ⓔ   9 Ⓐ Ⓑ Ⓒ Ⓓ Ⓔ   14 Ⓐ Ⓑ Ⓒ Ⓓ Ⓔ
5 Ⓐ Ⓑ Ⓒ Ⓓ Ⓔ   10 Ⓐ Ⓑ Ⓒ Ⓓ Ⓔ   15 Ⓐ Ⓑ Ⓒ Ⓓ Ⓔ

PRACTICE TEST 1
SECTION 1

ESSAY
Time allowed: 25 Minutes

Turn to your answer sheet and write your essay on the lined portion of the page. To receive credit, you must write your essay in the area provided.

Write on the assigned topic below. If you write on any other topic, your essay will be given a score of zero.

Write or print legibly: your readers will be unfamiliar with your handwriting, and you want them to be able to read what you write.

The excerpt appearing below makes a point about a particular topic. Read the passage carefully, and think about the assignment that follows.

Since the invention of television, the medium has had its ups and downs. At first, television watching was a communal affair; the first television set owners in a neighborhood would proudly invite the neighbors in to view the marvelous box. In time, however, television came to have an isolating effect on viewers; as the painter Andy Warhol once said, "When I got my first television set, I stopped caring so much about having close relationships."

ASSIGNMENT: What are your thoughts on the idea that television has turned out to isolate people instead of bringing them together? Compose an essay in which you express your views on this topic. Your essay may support, refute, or qualify the views expressed in the excerpt. What you write, however, must be relevant to the topic under discussion. Additionally, you must support your viewpoint, explaining your reasoning and providing examples based on your studies and/or experience.

PRACTICE TEST 1
SECTION 2

24 Questions—25 Minutes

Select the best answer to each of the following questions; then blacken the appropriate space on your answer sheet.

Each of the following sentences contains one or two blanks; each blank indicates that a word or set of words has been left out. Below the sentence are five words or phrases, lettered A through E. Select the word or set of words that best completes the sentence.

Example:

Fame is ----; today's rising star is all too soon tomorrow's washed-up has-been.

(A) rewarding   (B) gradual   (C) essential
    (D) spontaneous   (E) transitory

---

1. Because of their frequent disarray, confusion, and loss of memory, those hit by lightning while alone are sometimes ---- victims of assault.

   (A) mistaken for
   (B) attracted to
   (C) unaware of
   (D) avoided by
   (E) useful to

2. Having published more than three hundred books in less than fifty years, science fiction writer Isaac Asimov may well be the most ---- author of our day.

(A) fastidious
(B) insecure
(C) outmoded
(D) prolific
(E) indigenous

3. Because his time was limited, Weng decided to read the ---- novel *War and Peace* in ---- edition.

(A) wordy..an unedited
(B) lengthy..an abridged
(C) famous..a modern
(D) romantic..an autographed
(E) popular..a complete

4. In giving a speech, the speaker's goal is to communicate ideas clearly and ----, so that the audience will be in no ---- about the meaning of the speech.

(A) effectively..haste
(B) indirectly..distress
(C) vigorously..discomfort
(D) unambiguously..confusion
(E) tactfully..suspense

5. Although gregarious by nature, Lisa became quiet and ---- after she was unexpectedly laid off from work.

(A) autonomous   (B) susceptible   (C) assertive
  (D) withdrawn   (E) composed

6. The increasingly popular leader of America's second largest tribe, Cherokee Chief Wilma Mankiller, has ---- the myth that only males can be leaders in American Indian government.

(A) shattered   (B) perpetuated   (C) exaggerated
  (D) confirmed   (E) venerated

7. The commission of inquiry censured the senator for his ---- expenditure of public funds, which they found to be ----.

(A) flagrant..cursory
(B) improper..vindicated
(C) lavish..unjustifiable
(D) judicious..blameworthy
(E) arbitrary..critical

8. Despite their ---- of Twain's *Huckleberry Finn* for its stereotyped portrait of the slave Jim, even the novel's ---- agreed that it is a masterpiece of American prose.

   (A) admiration..critics
   (B) denunciation..supporters
   (C) criticism..detractors
   (D) defense..censors
   (E) praise..advocates

Read each of the passages below, and then answer the questions that follow the passage. The correct response may be stated outright or merely suggested in the passage.

Questions 9 and 10 are based on the following passage.

Consider the humble jellyfish. Headless, spineless, without a heart or brain, it has such a simple exterior that it seems the most primitive of creatures. Unlike its sessile
Line (attached to a surface, as an oyster is attached to its shell)
(5) relatives whose stalks cling to seaweed or tropical coral reefs, the free-swimming jellyfish, or medusa, drifts along the ocean shore, propelling itself by pulsing, muscular contractions of its bell-shaped body. Yet beneath the simple surface of this aimlessly drifting, supposedly primitive crea-
(10) ture is an unusually sophisticated set of genes, as recent studies of the invertebrate animal phylum Cnidaria (pronounced nih-DARE-ee-uh) reveal.

9. Which assertion about jellyfish is supported by the passage?

   (A) They move at a rapid rate.
   (B) They are cowardly.
   (C) They lack mobility.
   (D) They have a certain degree of intelligence.
   (E) They are unexpectedly complex.

10. The last sentence of the passage serves primarily to

- (A) explain the origin of a term
- (B) contradict an assumption
- (C) provide an example
- (D) cite a well-known fact
- (E) describe a process

Questions 11 and 12 are based on the following passage.

The passage below is excerpted from Somerset Maugham's The Moon and Sixpence, *first published in 1919.*

The faculty for myth is innate in the human race. It seizes with avidity upon any incidents, surprising or mysterious, in the career of those who have at all distinguished
Line themselves from their fellows, and invents a legend. It is
(5) the protest of romance against the commonplace of life.
The incidents of the legend become the hero's surest passport to immortality. The ironic philosopher reflects with a
smile that Sir Walter Raleigh is more safely enshrined in
the memory of mankind because he set his cloak for the
(10) Virgin Queen to walk on than because he carried the
English name to undiscovered countries.

11. As used in the passage, the word "faculty" (line 1) most nearly means

- (A) capacity
- (B) distinction
- (C) authority
- (D) teaching staff
- (E) branch of learning

12. In lines 6–11, the author mentions Sir Walter Raleigh primarily to

- (A) demonstrate the importance of Raleigh's voyages of discovery
- (B) mock Raleigh's behavior in casting down his cloak to protect the queen's feet from the mud
- (C) illustrate how legendary events outshine historical achievements in the public's mind
- (D) distinguish between Raleigh the courtier and Raleigh the seafarer
- (E) remind us that historical figures may act in idiosyncratic ways

Questions 13–24 are based on the following passage.

The passage below is excerpted from the introduction to Bury My Heart at Wounded Knee, *written in 1970 by the Native American historian Dee Brown.*

Since the exploratory journey of Lewis and Clark to the Pacific Coast early in the nineteenth century, the number of published accounts describing the "opening" of the
Line   American West has risen into the thousands. The greatest
(5)   concentration of recorded experience and observation came out of the thirty-year span between 1860 and 1890—the period covered by this book. It was an incredible era of violence, greed, audacity, sentimentality, undirected exuberance, and an almost reverential attitude toward the ideal of
(10)   personal freedom for those who already had it.

During that time the culture and civilization of the American Indian was destroyed, and out of that time came virtually all the great myths of the American West—tales of fur traders, mountain men, steamboat pilots, goldseekers,
(15)   gamblers, gunmen, cavalrymen, cowboys, harlots, missionaries, schoolmarms, and homesteaders. Only occasionally was the voice of the Indian heard, and then more often than not it was recorded by the pen of a white man. The Indian was the dark menace of the myths, and even if he had
(20)   known how to write in English, where would he have found a printer or a publisher?

Yet they are not all lost, those Indian voices of the past. A few authentic accounts of American western history were recorded by Indians either in pictographs or in translated
(25)   English, and some managed to get published in obscure journals, pamphlets, or books of small circulation. In the late nineteenth century, when the white man's curiosity about Indian survivors of the wars reached a high point, enterprising newspaper reporters frequently interviewed
(30)   warriors and chiefs and gave them an opportunity to

express their opinions on what was happening in the West. The quality of these interviews varied greatly, depending upon the abilities of the interpreters, or upon the inclination of the Indians to speak freely. Some feared reprisals for

(35) telling the truth, while others delighted in hoaxing reporters with tall tales and shaggy-dog stories. Contemporary newspaper statements by Indians must therefore be read with skepticism, although some of them are masterpieces of irony and others burn with outbursts of poetic fury.

(40)   Among the richest sources of first-person statements by Indians are the records of treaty councils and other formal meetings with civilian and military representatives of the United States government. Isaac Pitman's new stenographic system was coming into vogue in the second half

(45) of the nineteenth century, and when Indians spoke in council a recording clerk sat beside the official interpreter.

       Even when the meetings were in remote parts of the West, someone usually was available to write down the speeches, and because of the slowness of the translation

(50) process, much of what was said could be recorded in longhand. Interpreters quite often were half-bloods who knew spoken languages but seldom could read or write. Like most oral peoples they and the Indians depended upon imagery to express their thoughts, so that the English

(55) translations were filled with graphic similes and metaphors of the natural world. If an eloquent Indian had a poor interpreter, his words might be transformed to flat prose, but a good interpreter could make a poor speaker sound poetic.

       Most Indian leaders spoke freely and candidly in coun-

(60) cils with white officials, and as they became more sophisticated in such matters during the 1870s and 1880s, they demanded the right to choose their own interpreters and recorders. In this latter period, all members of the tribes were free to speak, and some of the older men chose such

(65) opportunities to recount events they had witnessed in the past, or sum up the histories of their peoples. Although the Indians who lived through this doom period of their civilization have vanished from the earth, millions of their words are preserved in official records. Many of the more impor-
(70) tant council proceedings were published in government documents and reports.

Out of all these sources of almost forgotten oral history, I have tried to fashion a narrative of the conquest of the American West as the victims experienced it, using their
(75) own words whenever possible. Americans who have always looked westward when reading about this period should read this book facing eastward.

This is not a cheerful book, but history has a way of intruding upon the present, and perhaps those who read it
(80) will have a clearer understanding of what the American Indian is, by knowing what he was. They may learn something about their own relationship to the earth from a people who were true conservationists. The Indians knew that life was equated with the earth and its resources, that
(85) America was a paradise, and they could not comprehend why the intruders from the East were determined to destroy all that was Indian as well as America itself.

13. The author finds the period of 1860–1890 noteworthy because
   - (A) the journals of the Lewis and Clark expedition were made public during this time
   - (B) in that period the bulk of original accounts of the "winning of the West" were produced
   - (C) during these years American Indians made great strides in regaining their lands
   - (D) only a very few documents dating from this period are still extant
   - (E) people still believed in personal freedom as an ideal

14. The author most likely uses quotation marks around the word "opening" (line 3) because

    (A) the West was closed rather than opened during this period of time

    (B) the American West actually was opened for settlement much earlier in the century

    (C) from a Native American perspective it is an inaccurate term

    (D) he is citing an authoritative source

    (E) he has employed the word in its figurative sense

15. A main concern of the author in this passage is to

    (A) denounce the white man for his untrustworthiness and savagery

    (B) evaluate the effectiveness of the military treaty councils

    (C) argue for the improved treatment of Indians today

    (D) suggest that Indian narratives of the conquest of the West are similar to white accounts

    (E) introduce the background of the original source materials for his text

16. The word "concentration" in line 5 means

    (A) memory

    (B) attention

    (C) diligence

    (D) imprisonment

    (E) accumulation

17. In describing the ideal of freedom revered by the pioneers as "personal freedom for those who already had it" (line 10), the author is being

    (A) enthusiastic

    (B) ironic

    (C) prosaic

    (D) redundant

    (E) lyrical

18. According to the passage, nineteenth-century newspaper accounts of interviews with Indians may contain inaccuracies for which of the following reasons?

   I. Lack of skill on the part of the translators

  II. The tendency of the reporters to overstate what they were told by the Indians

  III. The Indians' misgivings about possible retaliations

    (A) I only

    (B) III only

    (C) I and II only

    (D) I and III only

    (E) I, II, and III

19. The author's tone in describing the Indian survivors can best be described as

    (A) skeptical

    (B) detached

    (C) elegiac

    (D) obsequious

    (E) impatient

20. The author is most impressed by which aspect of the English translations of Indian speeches?

    (A) Their vividness of imagery

    (B) Their lack of frankness

    (C) The inefficiency of the process

    (D) Their absence of sophistication

    (E) Their brevity of expression

21. The word "flat" in line 57 means

    (A) smooth

    (B) level

    (C) pedestrian

    (D) horizontal

    (E) unequivocal

22. In treaty councils before 1870, most Indians did not ask for their own interpreters and recorders because

    (A) they could not afford to hire people to take down their words
    (B) the white officials provided these services as a matter of course
    (C) they were unaware that they had the option to demand such services
    (D) they preferred speaking for themselves without the help of translators
    (E) they were reluctant to have their words recorded for posterity

23. The author most likely suggests that Americans should read this book facing eastward (lines 75–77)

    (A) in an inappropriate attempt at levity
    (B) out of respect for Western superstitions
    (C) in order to read by natural light
    (D) because the Indians came from the East
    (E) to identify with the Indians' viewpoint

24. The phrase "equated with" in line 84 means

    (A) reduced to an average with
    (B) necessarily tied to
    (C) numerically equal to
    (D) fulfilled by
    (E) differentiated by

YOU MAY GO BACK AND REVIEW THIS SECTION IN THE
REMAINING TIME, BUT DO NOT WORK IN ANY OTHER
SECTION UNTIL TOLD TO DO SO. **S T O P**

PRACTICE TEST 1
SECTION 3

20 Questions—25 Minutes

For each problem in this section determine which of the five choices is correct and blacken the corresponding choice on your answer sheet. You may use any blank space on the page for your work.

Notes:
- You may use a calculator whenever you think it will be helpful.
- Only real numbers are used. No question or answer on this test involves a complex or imaginary number.
- Use the diagrams provided to help you solve the problems. Unless you see the words "Note: Figure not drawn to scale" under a diagram, it has been drawn as accurately as possible. Unless it is stated that a figure is three-dimensional, you may assume it lies in a plane.
- For any function, f, the domain, unless specifically restricted, is the set of all real numbers for which $f(x)$ is also a real number.

Reference Information

Area Facts

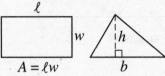

$A = \ell w$

$A = \frac{1}{2} bh$

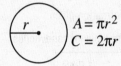

$A = \pi r^2$
$C = 2\pi r$

Volume Facts

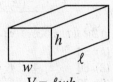

$V = \ell w h$

$V = \pi r^2 h$

Triangle Facts

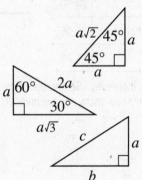

$a^2 + b^2 = c^2$

Angle Facts

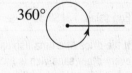

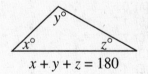

$x + y + z = 180$

---

1. Every Sunday Greg jogs 3 miles. For the rest of the week, each day he jogs 1 mile more than the preceding day. How many miles does Greg jog in 2 weeks?

(A) 42
(B) 63
(C) 84
(D) 98
(E) 117

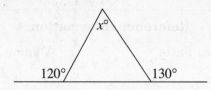

2. In the figure above, what is the value of x?

(A) 50
(B) 60
(C) 70
(D) 110
(E) It cannot be determined from the information given.

3. The following table lists the prices of eight types of sandwiches:

Sandwich	Price	Sandwich	Price
Roast beef	$5.25	Tuna fish	$4.25
Corned beef	$5.00	Salami	$4.50
BLT	$4.00	Grilled cheese	$3.95
Egg salad	$3.50	Club	$5.75

If the price of a tuna fish sandwich is increased 75¢ and the price of every other sandwich is increased 50¢, how many sandwiches will be more expensive than the tuna fish?

(A) 0
(B) 1
(C) 2
(D) 3
(E) 4

4. When a gymnast competes at the Olympics, each of six judges awards a score between 0 and 10. The highest and lowest scores are discarded, and the gymnast's final mark is the average (arithmetic mean) of the remaining scores. What would be a gymnast's mark if the judges' scores were 9.6, 9.4, 9.5, 9.7, 9.2, and 9.6?

(A) 9.5
(B) 9.525
(C) 9.55
(D) 9.575
(E) 9.6

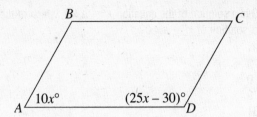

5. In parallelogram *ABCD* above, what is the value of *x*?

(A) 2
(B) 4
(C) 6
(D) 20
(E) 60

6. Three lines are drawn in a plane. Which of the following CANNOT be the total number of points of intersection?

(A) 0
(B) 1
(C) 2
(D) 3
(E) They all could.

7. If $a - b = 10$, and $a^2 - b^2 = 20$, what is the value of *b*?

(A) −6
(B) −4
(C) 4
(D) 6
(E) It cannot be determined from the information given.

8. A dealer in rare metals owns 1000 ounces of silver. If every year she sells half of the silver she owns and doesn't acquire any more, which of the following is an expression for the number of ounces of silver she will own *t* years from now where *t* is a positive integer?

(A) $\dfrac{1000}{2t}$

(B) $1000 \times 2t$

(C) 1000×2^{-t}

(D) $\dfrac{1000}{2^{-t}}$

(E) 1000×2^{t}

9. If $x = 9$ is a solution of the equation $x^2 - a = 0$, which of the following is a solution of $x^4 - a = 0$?

(A) −81
(B) −3
(C)   0
(D)   9
(E) 81

10. The following table shows the hourly wages earned by the 16 employees of a small company and the number of employees who earn each wage.

Wages per Hour	Number of Employees
$6	3
8	5
10	4
13	4

What is the average (arithmetic mean) of the median and the mode of this set of data?

(A) 4.5
(B)   8
(C) 8.5
(D)   9
(E) 9.5

11. The degree measure of each of the three angles of a triangle is an integer. Which of the following CANNOT be the ratio of their measures?

(A) 2:3:4
(B) 3:4:5
(C) 4:5:6
(D) 5:6:7
(E) 6:7:8

12. If $3x + 2y = 11$ and $2x + 3y = 17$, what is the average (arithmetic mean) of x and y?

(A) 2.5
(B) 2.8
(C) 5.6
(D) 5.8
(E) 14

Questions 13 and 14 refer to the following definition.

W	X
Y	Z

is a *number square* if $W + Z = X + Y$
and $2W = 3X$.

13. If

3	X
Y	7

is a *number square*, what is the value of Y?

(A) 0
(B) 2
(C) 4
(D) 6
(E) 8

14. If

W	X
Y	W

is a *number square*, $Y =$

(A) $\dfrac{3}{4} W$

(B) W

(C) $\dfrac{4}{3} W$

(D) $3W$

(E) $4W$

15. When the price of gold went up, a jeweler raised the prices on certain rings by 60%. On one ring, however, the price was accidentally reduced by 60%. By what percent must the incorrect price be increased to reflect the proper new price?

(A) 60%
(B) 120%
(C) 300%
(D) 400%
(E) It depends on the original price of the ring.

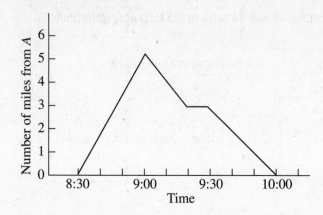

16. John rode his bicycle 5 miles along a straight road from A to B and back. The graph above shows how far he was from A at any given time. Not counting the time he stopped, what was John's average speed, in miles per hour, for the round trip?

(A) $6\dfrac{2}{3}$

(B) $7\dfrac{1}{2}$

(C) $8\dfrac{4}{7}$

(D) 10

(E) It cannot be determined from the graph.

17. Let A, B, and C be three points in a plane such that $AB:BC = 3:5$. Which of the following can be the ratio $AB:AC$?

   I. 1:2
  II. 1:3
 III. 3:8

(A) I only
(B) II only
(C) III only
(D) I and III only
(E) I, II, and III

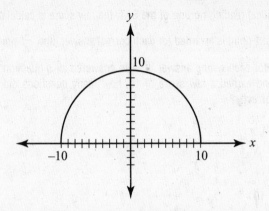

18. The semicircle above is the graph of the function

    $f(x) = \sqrt{100 - x^2}$. If $g(x)$ is defined by

    $g(x) = f(3x) + 3$, what is $g(2)$?

    (A) $\sqrt{19} + 3$

    (B) $\sqrt{96} + 3$
    (C) 5
    (D) 9
    (E) 11

19. A right circular cylinder has a radius of 8 and a height of π^2. If a cube
    has the same volume as the cylinder, what is the length of an edge of
    the cube?

    (A) $4\sqrt{\pi}$

    (B) $8\sqrt{\pi}$

    (C) $4\pi\sqrt{\pi}$
    (D) 4π
    (E) 8π

20. On the critical reading portion of the SAT, the raw score is calculated as follows: 1 point is awarded for each correct answer, and $\frac{1}{4}$ point is deducted for each wrong answer. If Ellen answered all q questions on the test and earned a raw score of 10, how many questions did she answer correctly?

(A) $q - 10$

(B) $\frac{q}{5}$

(C) $\frac{q}{5} - 10$

(D) $\frac{q - 10}{5}$

(E) $8 + \frac{q}{5}$

PRACTICE TEST 1
SECTION 4

35 Questions—25 Minutes

Select the best answer to each of the following questions; then blacken the appropriate space on your answer sheet.

Some or all parts of the following sentences are underlined. The first answer choice, (A), simply repeats the underlined part of the sentence. The other four choices present four alternative ways to phrase the underlined part. Select the answer that produces the most effective sentence, one that is clear and exact, and blacken the appropriate space on your answer sheet. In selecting your choice, be sure that it is standard written English, and that it expresses the meaning of the original sentence.

Example:

The first biography of author Eudora Welty came out in 1998 and she was 89 years old at the time.

(A) and she was 89 years old at the time
(B) at the time when she was 89
(C) upon becoming an 89 year old
(D) when she was 89
(E) at the age of 89 years old

1. Because he spoke out against Hitler's policies was why Dietrich <u>Bonhoeffer, a Lutheran pastor in Nazi Germany, was arrested and eventually hanged by the Gestapo.</u>

   (A) Because he spoke out against Hitler's policies was why Dietrich Bonhoeffer, a Lutheran pastor in Nazi Germany, was arrested and eventually hanged by the Gestapo.
   (B) Dietrich Bonhoeffer, a Lutheran pastor in Nazi Germany, was arrested and eventually hanged by the Gestapo because he spoke out against Hitler's policies.
   (C) Because he spoke out against Hitler's policies, Dietrich Bonhoeffer, a Lutheran pastor in Nazi Germany, was arrested and eventually hung by the Gestapo.
   (D) Dietrich Bonhoeffer, a Lutheran pastor in Nazi Germany, being arrested and eventually hung because he spoke out against Hitler's policies.
   (E) A Lutheran pastor in Nazi Germany, Dietrich Bonhoeffer, spoke out against Hitler's policies so that he arrested and eventually hung.

2. The difference between Liebniz and Schopenhauer is that <u>the former is optimistic; the latter, pessimistic.</u>

   (A) the former is optimistic; the latter, pessimistic
   (B) the former is optimistic, the latter, pessimistic
   (C) while the former is optimistic; the latter, pessimistic
   (D) the former one is optimistic; the latter one is a pessimistic
   (E) the former is optimistic; the latter being pessimistic

3. Most students like to read <u>these kind of books</u> during their spare time.

   (A) these kind of books
   (B) these kind of book
   (C) this kind of book
   (D) this kinds of books
   (E) those kind of books

4. John was imminently qualified for the position because he had studied computer programming and how to operate an IBM machine.

   (A) imminently qualified for the position because he had studied
       computer programming and how to operate an IBM machine
   (B) imminently qualified for the position since studying computer
       programming and the operation of an IBM machine
   (C) eminently qualified for the position because he had studied
       computer programming and how to operate an IBM machine
   (D) eminently qualified for the position because he had studied
       computer programming and the operation of an IBM machine
   (E) eminently qualified for the position because he has studied
       computer programming and how to operate an IBM machine

5. The idea of inoculating people with smallpox to protect them from
   later attacks was introduced into Europe by Mary Wortley Montagu,
   who learned of it in Asia.

   (A) Mary Wortley Montagu, who learned of it in Asia
   (B) Mary Wortley Montagu, who learned of them in Asia
   (C) Mary Wortley Montagu, who learned it of those in Asia
   (D) Mary Wortley Montagu, learning of it in Asia
   (E) Mary Wortley Montagu, because she learned of it in Asia

6. In general, the fate of Latin American or East Asian countries will
   affect America more than it does Britain or France.

   (A) will affect America more than it does
   (B) will effect America more than it does
   (C) will affect America more than they do
   (D) will effect America more than they do
   (E) will affect America more than they would

7. While campaigning for President, Dole nearly exhausted his funds
   and must raise money so that he could pay for last-minute television
   commercials.

   (A) exhausted his funds and must raise money so that he could pay
   (B) would exhaust his funds to raise money so that he could pay
   (C) exhausted his funds and had to raise money so that he can pay
   (D) exhausted his funds and had to raise money so that he could pay
   (E) exhausted his funds and must raise money so that he can pay

8. Athletic coaches stress <u>not only eating nutritious meals but also to get</u> adequate sleep.

   (A) not only eating nutritious meals but also to get
   (B) to not only eat nutritious meals but also getting
   (C) not only to eat nutritious meals but also getting
   (D) not only the eating of nutritious meals but also getting
   (E) not only eating nutritious meals but also getting

9. The goal of the remedial program was <u>that it enables</u> the students to master the basic skills they need to succeed in regular coursework.

   (A) that it enables
   (B) by enabling
   (C) to enable
   (D) where students are enabled
   (E) where it enables

10. Having revised her dissertation with some care, <u>that her thesis advisor rejected the changes distressed her greatly.</u>

    (A) that her thesis advisor rejected the changes distressed her greatly
    (B) she found her thesis advisor's rejection of the changes greatly distressing
    (C) her thesis advisor's rejection of the changes was a great distress
    (D) she was greatly distressed about her thesis advisor rejecting the changes
    (E) her distress at her thesis advisor's rejection of the changes was great

11. Running an insurance agency left Charles Ives little time for composition, yet he <u>nevertheless developed a unique musical idiom.</u>

    (A) nevertheless developed a unique musical idiom
    (B) nevertheless developed a very unique musical idiom
    (C) therefore developed a uniquely musical idiom
    (D) nevertheless developed his musical idiom uniquely
    (E) however developed a very unique and idiomatic music

The sentences in this section may contain errors in grammar, usage, choice of words, or idioms. Either there is just one error in a sentence or the sentence is correct. Some words or phrases are underlined and lettered; everything else in the sentence is correct.

If an underlined word or phrase is incorrect, choose that letter; if the sentence is correct, select No error. Then blacken the appropriate space on your answer sheet.

Example:

The region has a climate <u>so severe</u> <u>that</u> plants
                    A

<u>growing there</u> rarely <u>had been</u> more than twelve
    B   C

inches <u>high</u>. <u>No error</u>
     D   E

Ⓐ Ⓑ ● Ⓓ Ⓔ

12. I <u>have been thinking</u> lately about the monsters—<u>or</u> fantasies or
         A   B

  whatever—<u>that</u> frightened <u>myself</u> as a child. <u>No error</u>
         C   D   E

13. Postoperative patients <u>who fail</u> to exercise as <u>regular</u> as their doctors
                     A   B   C

  recommend take longer to <u>recover from</u> surgery than more active
                          D

  patients do. <u>No error</u>
         E

14. He worked in the lumber camps during the summer not because of
                                             A   B

the money but because he wanted to strengthen his muscles by
              C

doing hard physical labor. No error
       D   E

15. That book is liable to become a best seller because it is well written,
    A   B

full of suspense, and very entertaining. No error
      C   D   E

16. According to a random poll taken by *National Wildlife*, the top three
        A   B

threats to the environment is water pollution, air pollution, and
                           C

hazardous wastes. No error
    D   E

17. His three children, Ruth, Frank, and Ellis, are very talented young
sters, but the latter shows the most promise. No error
     A   B   C   D   E

18. Passing antidrug legislation, calling for more education, and to aid
    A   B

Bolivia in raids on cocaine dealers are all ways that the United States
                                    C

is fighting back against "crack" use. No error
         D   E

19. Cajun cooking, which uses special prepared spices, has always been
                          A

popular in Louisiana, but it is only now becoming known in other
                   B   C

parts of the country. No error
    D   E

20. It seems strange to realize that, when Harvey Firestone organized the
                    A   B
Firestone Tire and Rubber Company in 1900, rubber tires had been a
                                     C   D
novelty. No error
         E

21. The same laser technology that is being used on compact discs is
                                       A   B
also under application to computers to achieve additional memory.
     C   D
No error
E

22. The Philippine government changed hands when Marcos failed
                              A   B
satisfying his countrymen that he had won the presidential election,
C
and Corazon Aquino took over. No error
                        D   E

23. Was it they who were involved in the recent unruly demonstration?
    A B C   D
No error
E

24. We must regard any statement about this controversy, whatever the
      A   B
source, as gossip until they are confirmed. No error
      C   D   E

25. She is the only one of the applicants who are fully qualified for the
                  A   B   C   D
position. No error
          E

26. In order to meet publication schedules, publishers often find
        A   B

    it necessary to trim everyone's schedule and leaving room for unex-
      C   D

    pected problems. No error
                  E

27. There are probably few comeback stories as moving as
       A   B   C

    cycling's stalwart champion, Lance Armstrong. No error
           D   E

28. A hotel's ability for winning the loyalty of its guests
              A

    is primarily determined by the friendliness and courtesy of the
           B

    employees who are stationed at the front desk. No error
          C   D   E

29. While some scientists are absorbed by the philosophical question of
        A   B

    what consciousness is, but others restrict themselves to trying to
                                C

    understand what is going on at the neurological level when con-
                                       D

    sciousness is present. No error
                 E

The passage below is the unedited draft of a student's essay. Parts of the essay need to be rewritten to make the meaning clearer and more precise. Read the essay carefully.

The essay is followed by six questions about changes that might improve all or part of the organization, development, sentence structure, use of language, appropriateness to the audience, or use of standard written English. In each case, choose the answer that most clearly and effectively expresses the student's intended meaning. Indicate your choice by blackening the corresponding space on the answer sheet.

[1] When you turn on the radio or pop in a tape while the house is quiet or going to work or school in your car, you have several choices of music to listen to. [2] Although, in recent years, CDs have become the medium of choice over records and even tapes. [3] On the radio you have your rap on one station, your classical on another, your New Wave music on another, and then you have your Country. [4] Some young people feel that country is for fat old people, but it isn't. [5] It is music for all ages, fat or thin.

[6] Country music is "fun" music. [7] It has an unmistakable beat and sound that gets you up and ready to move. [8] You can really get into country, even if it is just the clapping of the hands or the stamping of the feet. [9] You can't help feeling cheerful watching the country performers, who all seem so happy to be entertaining their close "friends," although there may be 10,000 of them in the stadium or concert hall. [10] The musicians love it, and audience flips out with delight. [11] The interpersonal factors in evidence cause a sudden psychological bond to develop into a temporary, but nevertheless tightly knit, family unit. [12] For example, you can imagine June Carter Cash as your favorite aunt and Randy Travis as your long lost cousin.

[13] Some people spurn country music. [14] Why, they ask, would anyone want to listen to singers whine about their broken

marriages or their favorite pet that was run over by an 18-wheeler? [15] They claim that Willie Nelson, one of today's country legends, can't even keep his income taxes straight. [16] Another "dynamic" performer is Dolly Parton, whose most famous feature is definitely not her voice. [17] How talented could she be if her body is more famous than her singing?

[18] Loretta Lynn is the greatest. [19] Anyone's negative feelings towards country music would change after hearing Loretta's strong, emotional, and haunting voice. [20] Look, it can't hurt to give a listen. [21] You never know, you might even like it so much that you will go out, pick up a secondhand guitar and learn to strum a few chords.

30. Which is the best revision of the underlined segment of sentence 1 below?

When you turn on the radio or pop in a tape while the house is quiet or going to work or school in your car, *you* have several choices of music to listen to.

(A) while the house is quiet or in your car going to work or school
(B) driving to work or school while the house is quiet
(C) while the house is quiet or you are driving to work or school
(D) while driving to work or school in your car, and the house is quiet
(E) while there's quiet in the house or you go to work or school in your car

31. To improve the coherence of paragraph 1, which of the following sentences should be deleted?

(A) Sentence 1
(B) Sentence 2
(C) Sentence 3
(D) Sentence 4
(E) Sentence 5

32. In the context of the sentences that precede and follow sentence 8, which of the following is the best revision of sentence 8?

    (A) Clap your hands and stamp your feet is what to do to easily get into country.
    (B) You're really into country, even if it is just clapping of the hands or stamping of the feet.
    (C) You can easily get into country just by clapping your hands or stamping your feet.
    (D) One can get into country music rather easily; one must merely clap one's hands or stamp one's feet.
    (E) Getting into country is easy, just clap your hands and stamp your feet.

33. With regard to the writing style and tone of the essay, which is the best revision of sentence 11?

    (A) The interpersonal relationship that develops suddenly creates a temporary, but nevertheless a closely knit, family unit.
    (B) A family-like relationship develops quickly and rapidly.
    (C) A close family-type relation is suddenly very much in evidence between the performer and his or her audience.
    (D) All of a sudden you feel like a member of a huge, but tight, family.
    (E) A sudden bond develops between the entertainer and the audience that might most suitably be described as a "family," in the best sense of the term.

34. With regard to the essay as a whole, which of the following best describes the function of paragraph 3?

    (A) To present some objective data in support of another viewpoint
    (B) To offer a more balanced view of the essay's subject matter
    (C) To ridicule readers who don't agree with the writer
    (D) To lend further support to the essay's main idea
    (E) To divert the reader's attention from the main idea of the essay

35. Which of the following revisions of sentence 18 provides the smoothest transition between paragraphs 3 and 4?

    (A) Loretta Lynn is one of the great singers of country music.
    (B) Loretta Lynn, however, is the greatest country singer yet.
    (C) But you can bet they've never heard Loretta Lynn.
    (D) The sounds of Loretta Lynn tells a different story, however.
    (E) Loretta Lynn, on the other hand, is superb.

YOU MAY GO BACK AND REVIEW THIS SECTION IN THE
REMAINING TIME, BUT DO NOT WORK IN ANY OTHER
SECTION UNTIL TOLD TO DO SO.   **S T O P**

PRACTICE TEST 1
SECTION 6

24 Questions—25 Minutes

Select the best answer to each of the following questions; then blacken the appropriate space on your answer sheet.

Each of the following sentences contains one or two blanks; each blank indicates that a word or set of words has been left out. Below the sentence are five words or phrases, lettered A through E. Select the word or set of words that best completes the sentence.

Example:

Fame is ----; today's rising star is all too soon tomorrow's washed-up has-been.

(A) rewarding   (B) gradual   (C) essential
(D) spontaneous   (E) transitory

1. Despite the ---- of the materials with which Tiffany worked, many of his glass masterpieces have survived for more than seventy years.

(A) beauty
(B) translucence
(C) abundance
(D) majesty
(E) fragility

2. No summary of the behavior of animals toward reflected images is given, but not much else that is ---- seems missing from this comprehensive yet compact study of mirrors and mankind.

    (A) redundant
    (B) contemplative
    (C) relevant
    (D) peripheral
    (E) disputable

3. Pain is the body's early warning system: loss of ---- in the extremities leaves a person ---- injuring himself unwittingly.

    (A) agony..incapable of
    (B) sensation..vulnerable to
    (C) consciousness..desirous of
    (D) feeling..habituated to
    (E) movement..prone to

4. Much of the clown's success may be attributed to the contrast between the ---- manner he adopts and the general ---- that characterizes the circus.

    (A) giddy..sobriety
    (B) lugubrious..hilarity
    (C) gaudy..clamor
    (D) joyful..hysteria
    (E) frenetic..excitement

5. Fortunately, she was ---- her accomplishments, properly unwilling to ---- them before her friends.

    (A) excited by..parade
    (B) immodest about..discuss
    (C) deprecatory about..flaunt
    (D) uncertain of..concede
    (E) unaware of..conceal

Questions 6–9 are based on the following passages.

Passage 1

Pioneering conservationist Marjory Stoneman Douglas
called it the River of Grass. Stretching south from Lake
Okeechobee, fed by the rain-drenched Kissimmee River
Line basin, the Everglades is a water marsh, a slow-moving river
(5) of swamps and sawgrass flowing southward to the Gulf of
Mexico. It is a unique ecosystem, whose enduring value
has come from its being home to countless species of
plants and animals: cypress trees and mangroves, wood
storks and egrets, snapping turtles and crocodiles. For the
(10) past 50 years, however, this river has been shrinking. Never
a torrent, it has dwindled as engineering projects have
diverted the waters feeding it to meet agricultural and housing needs.

Passage 2

Today South Florida's sugar industry is in serious trou-
(15) ble. Responding to the concerns of the scientific community and to the mandates of the Everglades Forever Act,
local sugar producers have spent millions of dollars since
1994 to minimize the runoff of phosphorus from sugar
cane fields into the Everglades. (Phosphorus runoff, scien-
(20) tists maintain, has encouraged an invasion of cattails,
which overrun the native sawgrass and choke the flow of
water through what was once a vast sawgrass marsh.)
Sugar producers have adopted ecologically sound farming
practices and at great cost have dramatically reduced phos-
(25) phorus levels to help save the Everglades' fragile ecosystem. But who or what will help save Florida's imperiled
sugar industry?

6. The author of Passage 1 cites the conservationist Marjory Stoneman Douglas in order to

    (A) present a viewpoint
    (B) challenge an opinion
    (C) introduce a metaphor
    (D) correct a misapprehension
    (E) honor a pioneer

7. In Passage 1, the word "enduring" (line 6) most nearly means

    (A) tolerating
    (B) noteworthy
    (C) hard-won
    (D) lasting
    (E) serene

8. In lines 19–22, the author of Passage 2 uses a parenthetic remark to

    (A) cast doubt on the credibility of a statement
    (B) provide background on the reasons for a concern
    (C) demonstrate support for the scientific community
    (D) explain the usage of a technical term
    (E) justify the efforts of the sugar industry

9. On the basis of the final sentence ("But…industry") of Passage 2, the author of this passage would most likely appear to the author of Passage 1 as

    (A) strongly opposed to the Everglades cleanup
    (B) well informed concerning specific requirements of the Everglades Forever Act
    (C) inclined to overestimate the importance of the sugar industry
    (D) having a deep sympathy for environmental causes
    (E) having little understanding of scientific methods

Questions 10–15 are based on the following passage.

In this excerpt from Richard Wright's 1937 novel Black Boy, *the young African-American narrator confronts a new world in the books he illegally borrows from the "whites-only" public library.*

That night in my rented room, while letting the hot water
run over my can of pork and beans in the sink, I opened
Mencken's *A Book of Prejudices* and began to read. I was
Line jarred and shocked by the style, the clear, clean, sweeping
(5)   sentences. Why did he write like that? And how did one
write like that? I pictured the man as a raging demon,
slashing with his pen, consumed with hate, denouncing
everything American, extolling everything European, laughing at the weaknesses of people, mocking God, authority.
(10) What was this? I stood up, trying to realize what reality lay
behind the meaning of the words. Yes, this man was fighting, fighting with words. He was using words as a weapon,
using them as one would use a club. Could words be
weapons? Well, yes, for here they were. Then, maybe, per-
(15) haps, a Negro could use them as a weapon? No. It frightened me. I read on, and what amazed me was not what he
said, but how on earth anybody had the courage to say it.
What strange world was this? I concluded the book with
the conviction that I had somehow overlooked something
(20) terribly important in life. I had once tried to write, had once
reveled in feeling, had let my crude imagination roam, but
the impulse to dream had been slowly beaten out of me by
experience. Now it surged up again and I hungered for
books, new ways of looking and seeing. It was not a matter
(25) of believing or disbelieving what I read, but of feeling
something new, of being affected by something that made
the look of the world different.
As dawn broke I ate my pork and beans, feeling dopey,
sleepy. I went to work, but the mood of the book would not
(30) die; it lingered, coloring everything I saw, heard, did. I now

felt that I knew what the white men were feeling. Merely
because I had read a book that had spoken of how they
lived and thought, I identified myself with that book. I felt
vaguely guilty. Would I, filled with bookish notions, act in a
(35) manner that would make the whites dislike me?

I forged more notes and my trips to the library became
frequent. Reading grew into a passion. My first serious
novel was Sinclair Lewis's *Main Street*. It made me see my
boss, Mr. Gerald, and identify him as an American type. I
(40) would smile when I saw him lugging his golf bags into the
office. I had always felt a vast distance separating me from
the boss, and now I felt closer to him, though still distant. I
felt now that I knew him, that I could feel the very limits of
his narrow life. This had happened because I had read a
(45) novel about a mythical man called George F. Babbitt. But I
could not conquer my sense of guilt, my feeling that the
white men around me knew that I was changing, that I had
begun to regard them differently.

10. The narrator's initial reaction to Mencken's prose can best be
described as one of

(A) wrath
(B) disbelief
(C) remorse
(D) laughter
(E) disdain

11. To the narrator, Mencken appeared to be all of the following EXCEPT

(A) intrepid
(B) articulate
(C) satiric
(D) reverent
(E) opinionated

12. As used in line 30, "coloring" most nearly means

(A) reddening
(B) sketching
(C) blushing
(D) affecting
(E) lying

13. The narrator's attitude in lines 23 and 24 is best described as one of

(A) dreamy indifference
(B) sullen resentment
(C) impatient ardor
(D) wistful anxiety
(E) quiet resolve

14. The passage suggests that, when he saw Mr. Gerald carrying the golf clubs, the narrator smiled out of a sense of

(A) relief
(B) duty
(C) recognition
(D) disbelief
(E) levity

15. The passage as a whole is best characterized as

(A) an impassioned argument in favor of increased literacy for blacks
(B) a description of a youth's gradual introduction to racial prejudice
(C) a comparison of the respective merits of Mencken's and Lewis's literary styles
(D) an analysis of the impact of ordinary life on art
(E) a portrait of a youth's response to expanding intellectual horizons

Questions 16–24 are based on the following passage.

The following passage about pond-dwellers is excerpted from a classic essay on natural history written by the zoologist Konrad Lorenz.

There are some terrible robbers in the pond world, and, in our aquarium, we may witness all the cruelties of an embittered struggle for existence enacted before our very
Line eyes. If you have introduced to your aquarium a mixed
(5)   catch, you will soon see an example of such conflicts, for, amongst the new arrivals, there will probably be a larva of the water-beetle *Dytiscus.* Considering their relative size, the voracity and cunning with which these animals destroy their prey eclipse the methods of even such notorious rob-
(10) bers as tigers, lions, wolves, or killer whales. These are all as lambs compared with the *Dytiscus* larva.

It is a slim, streamlined insect, rather more than two inches long. Its six legs are equipped with stout fringes of bristles, which form broad oar-like blades that propel the
(15) animal quickly and surely through the water. The wide, flat head bears an enormous, pincer-shaped pair of jaws that are hollow and serve not only as syringes for injecting poison, but also as orifices of ingestion. The animal lies in ambush on some waterplant; suddenly it shoots at lightning
(20) speed towards its prey, darts underneath it, then quickly jerks up its head and grabs the victim in its jaws. "Prey," for these creatures, is all that moves or that smells of "animal" in any way. It has often happened to me that, while standing quietly in the water of a pond, I have been "eaten"
(25) by a *Dytiscus* larva. Even for man, an injection of the poisonous digestive juice of this insect is extremely painful.

These beetle larvae are among the few animals that digest "out of doors." The glandular secretion that they inject, through their hollow forceps, into their prey, dis-
(30) solves the entire inside of the latter into a liquid soup,

which is then sucked in through the same channel by the attacker. Even large victims, such as fat tadpoles or dragon-fly larvae, which have been bitten by a *Dytiscus* larva, stiffen after a few defensive moments, and their

(35) inside, which, as in most water animals, is more or less transparent, becomes opaque as though fixed by formalin. The animal swells up first, then gradually shrinks to a limp bundle of skin that hangs from the deadly jaws, and is finally allowed to drop. In the confines of an aquarium, a

(40) few large *Dytiscus* larvae will, within days, eat all living things over a quarter of an inch long. What happens then? They will eat each other, if they have not already done so; this depends less on who is bigger and stronger than upon who succeeds in seizing the other first. I have often seen

(45) two nearly equal sized *Dytiscus* larvae each seize the other simultaneously and both die a quick death by inner dissolution. Very few animals, even when threatened with starvation, will attack an equal sized animal of their own species with the intention of devouring it. I only know this to be

(50) definitely true of rats and a few related rodents; that wolves do the same thing, I am much inclined to doubt, on the strength of some observations of which I shall speak later. But *Dytiscus* larvae devour animals of their own breed and size, even when other nourishment is at hand, and that is

(55) done, as far as I know, by no other animal.

16. By robbers (line 1), the author refers to

(A) thieves
(B) plagiarists
(C) people who steal fish
(D) creatures that devour their prey
(E) unethical scientific observers

17. As used in lines 4 and 5, a "mixed catch" most likely is

(A) a device used to shut the aquarium lid
(B) a disturbed group of water beetle larvae
(C) a partially desirable prospective denizen of the aquarium
(D) a random batch of creatures taken from a pond
(E) a theoretical drawback that may have positive results

18. The presence of *Dytiscus* larvae in an aquarium most likely would be of particular interest to naturalists studying

(A) means of exterminating water-beetle larvae
(B) predatory patterns within a closed environment
(C) genetic characteristics of a mixed catch
(D) the effect of captivity on aquatic life
(E) the social behavior of dragon-fly larvae

19. The author's primary purpose in lines 12–18 is to

(A) depict the typical victim of a *Dytiscus* larva
(B) point out the threat to humans represented by *Dytiscus* larvae
(C) describe the physical appearance of an aquatic predator
(D) refute the notion of the aquarium as a peaceful habitat
(E) clarify the method the *Dytiscus* larva uses to dispatch its prey

20. The passage mentions all of the following facts about *Dytiscus* larvae EXCEPT that they

(A) secrete digestive juices
(B) attack their fellow larvae
(C) are attracted to motion
(D) provide food for amphibians
(E) have ravenous appetites

21. By digesting "out of doors" (line 28), the author is referring to the *Dytiscus* larva's

(A) preference for open-water ponds over confined spaces
(B) metabolic elimination of waste matter
(C) amphibious method of locomotion
(D) extreme voraciousness of appetite
(E) external conversion of food into absorbable form

22. According to the author, which of the following is (are) true of the victim of a *Dytiscus* larva?

    I.   Its interior increases in opacity.
    II. It shrivels as it is drained of nourishment.
    III. It is beheaded by the larva's jaws.

    (A) I only
    (B) II only
    (C) III only
    (D) I and II only
    (E) II and III only

23. In the final paragraph, the author mentions rats and related rodents in order to emphasize which point about *Dytiscus* larvae?

    (A) Unless starvation drives them, they will not resort to eating members of their own species.
    (B) They are reluctant to attack equal-sized members of their own breed.
    (C) They are capable of resisting attacks from much larger animals.
    (D) They are one of extremely few species given to devouring members of their own breed.
    (E) Although they are noted predators, *Dytiscus* larvae are less savage than rats.

24. The author indicates that in subsequent passages he will discuss

    (A) the likelihood of cannibalism among wolves
    (B) the metamorphosis of dragon-fly larvae into dragon-flies
    (C) antidotes to cases of *Dytiscus* poisoning
    (D) the digestive processes of killer whales
    (E) the elimination of *Dytiscus* larvae from aquariums

YOU MAY GO BACK AND REVIEW THIS SECTION IN THE
REMAINING TIME, BUT DO NOT WORK IN ANY OTHER
SECTION UNTIL TOLD TO DO SO.   **S T O P**

PRACTICE TEST 1
SECTION 7

18 Questions—25 Minutes

You have 25 minutes to answer the 8 multiple-choice questions and 10 student-produced response questions in this section. For each multiple-choice question, determine which of the five choices is correct and blacken the corresponding choice on your answer sheet. You may use any blank space on the page for your work.

Notes:
- You may use a calculator whenever you think it will be helpful.
- Only real numbers are used. No question or answer on this test involves a complex or imaginary number.
- Use the diagrams provided to help you solve the problems. Unless you see the words "<u>Note:</u> Figure not drawn to scale" under a diagram, it has been drawn as accurately as possible. Unless it is stated that a figure is three-dimensional, you may assume it lies in a plane.
- For any function, f, the domain, unless specifically restricted, is the set of all real numbers for which $f(x)$ is also a real number.

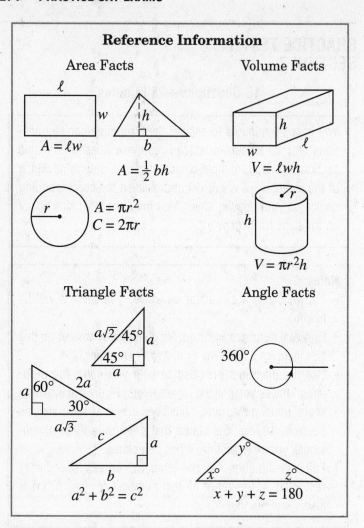

Reference Information

Area Facts

$A = \ell w$

$A = \frac{1}{2} bh$

$A = \pi r^2$
$C = 2\pi r$

Volume Facts

$V = \ell w h$

$V = \pi r^2 h$

Triangle Facts

$a^2 + b^2 = c^2$

Angle Facts

$360°$

$x + y + z = 180$

1. How many integers are solutions of the inequality $3|x| + 2 < 17$?

(A) 0
(B) 4
(C) 8
(D) 9
(E) Infinitely many

2. If a speed of 1 meter per second is equal to a speed of k kilometers per hour, what is the value of k?

(1 kilometer = 1000 meters)

(A) 0.036
(B) 0.06
(C) 0.36
(D) 0.6
(E) 3.6

3. If $f(x) = x^2 + \sqrt[3]{x}$, what is the value of $f(-8)$?

(A) −66
(B) −62
(C) 62
(D) 64
(E) 66

4. In 1994, twice as many boys as girls at Adams High School earned varsity letters. From 1994 to 2004, the number of girls earning varsity letters increased by 25% while the number of boys earning varsity letters decreased by 25%. What was the ratio in 2004 of the number of girls to the number of boys who earned varsity letters?

(A) $\dfrac{5}{3}$

(B) $\dfrac{6}{5}$

(C) $\dfrac{1}{1}$

(D) $\dfrac{5}{6}$

(E) $\dfrac{3}{5}$

5. If today is Saturday, what day will it be 500 days from today?

(A) Saturday
(B) Sunday
(C) Tuesday
(D) Wednesday
(E) Friday

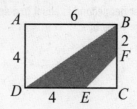

6. If a point is chosen at random from the interior of rectangle *ABCD* above, what is the probability the point will be in the shaded quadrilateral *BDEF*?

(A) $\dfrac{1}{4}$

(B) $\dfrac{1}{3}$

(C) $\dfrac{5}{12}$

(D) $\dfrac{1}{2}$

(E) $\dfrac{7}{12}$

7. If the average (arithmetic mean) of *a*, *b*, *c*, and *d* is equal to the average of *a*, *b*, and *c*, what is *d* in terms of *a*, *b*, and *c*?

(A) $a + b + c$

(B) $\dfrac{a+b+c}{3}$

(C) $\dfrac{4(a+b+c)}{3}$

(D) $\dfrac{3(a+b+c)}{4}$

(E) $\dfrac{(a+b+c)}{4}$

8. Because her test turned out to be more difficult than she intended it to be, a teacher decided to adjust the grades by deducting only half the number of points a student missed. For example, if a student missed 10 points, she received a 95 instead of a 90. Before the grades were adjusted, Meri's grade on the test was A. What was her grade after the adjustment?

(A) $50 + \dfrac{A}{2}$

(B) $\dfrac{50 + A}{2}$

(C) $100 - \dfrac{A}{2}$

(D) $\dfrac{100 - A}{2}$

(E) $A + 25$

Directions for Student-Produced Response Questions (Grid-ins)

In questions 9–18, first solve the problem, and then enter your answer on the grid provided on the answer sheet. The instructions for entering your answers are as follows:

- First, write your answer in the boxes at the top of the grid.
- Second, grid your answer in the columns below the boxes.
- Use the fraction bar in the first row or the decimal point in the second row to enter fractions and decimal answers.

Answer: $\frac{8}{15}$ Answer: 1.75

Write your → answer in the boxes.

Grid in → your answer.

Answer: 100

Either position is acceptable

- Grid only one space in each column.
- Entering the answer in the boxes is recommended as an aid in gridding, but is not required.
- The machine scoring your exam can read only what you grid, so **you must grid in your answers correctly to get credit.**
- If a question has more than one correct answer, grid in only one of these answers.
- The grid does not have a minus sign, so no answer can be negative.
- A mixed number *must* be converted to an improper fraction or a decimal before it is gridded. Enter $1\frac{1}{4}$ as 5/4 or 1.25; the machine will interpret 1 1/4 as $\frac{11}{4}$ and mark it wrong.
- **All decimals must be entered as accurately as possible.** Here are the three acceptable ways of gridding

$$\frac{3}{11} = 0.272727\ldots$$

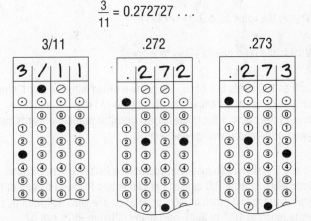

- Note that rounding to .273 is acceptable, because you are using the full grid, but you would receive **no credit** for .3 or .27, because these answers are less accurate.

9. Pencils that were selling at three for 25 cents are now on sale at five for 29 cents. How much money, in cents, would you save by buying 60 pencils at the sale price?

10. If $1 < 3x - 5 < 2$, what is one possible value for x?

11. What is the largest integer, x, such that x < 10,000 and $\dfrac{\sqrt{x}}{5}$ is an even integer?

12. Ellie is dropping marbles into a box one at a time in the following order: red, white, white, blue, blue, blue; red, white, white, blue, blue, blue; .... How many marbles will be in the box right after the 100th blue one is put in?

13. Four 3-4-5 right triangles and a square whose sides are 5 are arranged to form a second square. What is the perimeter of that square?

Questions 14 and 15 refer to the following definition.

$$\text{For any positive integer } a: <<a>> = \frac{1}{2^{a+1}}.$$

14. What is the value of $<<3>> - <<4>>$?

15. What is the ratio of $<<a + 3>>$ to $<<a>>$?

16. Each of 100 cards has none, one, or two of the letters A and C written on it. If 75 cards have the letter A, 30 have the letter C, and fewer than 15 are blank, what is the largest possible number of cards that have both A and C written on them?

17. To use a certain cash machine, you need a Personal Identification Code (PIC). If each PIC consists of two letters followed by one of the digits from 1 to 9 (such as AQ7 or BB3) or one letter followed by two digits (such as Q37 or J88), how many different PIC's can be assigned?

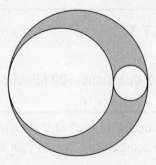

18. In the figure above, the three circles are tangent to one another. If the ratio of the diameter of the large white circle to the diameter of the small white circle is 3:1, what fraction of the largest circle has been shaded?

YOU MAY GO BACK AND REVIEW THIS SECTION IN THE REMAINING TIME, BUT DO NOT WORK IN ANY OTHER SECTION UNTIL TOLD TO DO SO.

STOP

PRACTICE TEST 1
SECTION 8

19 Questions—20 Minutes

> Select the best answer to each of the following questions; then blacken the appropriate space on your answer sheet.

> Each of the following sentences contains one or two blanks; each blank indicates that a word or set of words has been left out. Below the sentence are five words or phrases, lettered A through E. Select the word or set of words that best completes the sentence.
>
> Example:
>
>   Fame is ----; today's rising star is all too soon tomorrow's washed-up has-been.
>
>   (A) rewarding   (B) gradual   (C) essential
>   (D) spontaneous   (E) transitory
>
>

1. Although similar to mice in many physical characteristics, voles may be ---- mice by the shortness of their tails.

    (A) distinguished from
    (B) classified with
    (C) related to
    (D) categorized as
    (E) enumerated with

2. Dr. Charles Drew's technique for preserving and storing blood plasma for emergency use proved so ---- that it became the ---- for the present blood bank system used by the American Red Cross.

   (A) irrelevant..inspiration
   (B) urgent..pattern
   (C) effective..model
   (D) innocuous..excuse
   (E) complex..blueprint

3. The likenesses of language around the Mediterranean were sufficiently marked to ---- ease of movement both of men and ideas: it took relatively few alterations to make a Spanish song intelligible in Italy, and an Italian trader could, without much difficulty, make himself at home in France.

   (A) eliminate
   (B) facilitate
   (C) hinder
   (D) clarify
   (E) aggravate

4. Because he saw no ---- to the task assigned him, he worked at it in a very ---- way.

   (A) function..systematic
   (B) method..dutiful
   (C) purpose..diligent
   (D) end..rigid
   (E) point..perfunctory

5. During the Battle of Trafalgar, Admiral Nelson remained ---- , in full command of the situation in spite of the hysteria and panic all around him.

   (A) impassable
   (B) imperturbable
   (C) overbearing
   (D) frenetic
   (E) lackadaisical

6. Although he had spent many hours at the computer trying to solve the problem, he was the first to admit that the final solution was ---- and not the ---- of his labor.

(A) trivial..cause
(B) incomplete..intent
(C) adequate..concern
(D) schematic..fault
(E) fortuitous..result

The questions that follow the next two passages relate to the content of both, and to their relationship. The correct response may be stated outright in the passage or merely suggested.

Questions 7–19 are based on the following passages.

The following passages are excerpted from two recent essays that make an analogy between writing and sports. The author of Passage 1, whose manuscript has been rejected by his publisher, discusses the sorts of failures experienced by writers and ballplayers. The author of Passage 2 explores how his involvement in sports affected his writing career.

Passage 1

In consigning this manuscript to a desk drawer, I am comforted by the behavior of baseball players. There are *no* pitchers who do not give up home runs, there are *no* bat-
Line ters who do not strike out. There are *no* major league pitch-
(5) ers or batters who have not somehow learned to survive giving up home runs and striking out. That much is obvious.

What seems to me less obvious is how these "failures" must be digested, or put to use, in the overall experience of
(10) the player. A jogger once explained to me that the nerves of the ankle are so sensitive and complex that each time a

runner sets his foot down, hundreds of messages are conveyed to the runner's brain about the nature of the terrain
and the requirements for weight distribution, balance, and
(15) muscle-strength. I'm certain that the ninth-inning home run
that Dave Henderson hit off Donny Moore registered com-
plexly and permanently in Moore's mind and body and that
the next time Moore faced Henderson, his pitching was
informed by his awful experience of October 1986. Moore's
(20) continuing baseball career depended to some extent on his
converting that encounter with Henderson into something
useful for his pitching. I can also imagine such an experience destroying an athlete, registering in his mind and body
in such a negative way as to produce a debilitating fear.
(25)   Of the many ways in which athletes and artists are similar, one is that, unlike accountants or plumbers or insurance salesmen, to succeed at all they must perform at an
extraordinary level of excellence. Another is that they must
be willing to extend themselves irrationally in order to
(30) achieve that level of performance. A writer doesn't have to
write all-out all the time, but he or she must be ready to
write all-out any time the story requires it. Hold back and
you produce what just about any literate citizen can produce, a "pretty good" piece of work. Like the cautious
(35) pitcher, the timid writer can spend a lifetime in the minor
leagues.
        And what more than failure—the strike out, the crucial
home run given up, the manuscript criticized and
rejected—is more likely to produce caution or timidity? An
(40) instinctive response to painful experience is to avoid the
behavior that produced the pain. To function at the level of
excellence required for survival, writers, like athletes, must
go against instinct, must absorb their failures and become
stronger, must endlessly repeat the behavior that produced
(45) the pain.

Passage 2

The athletic advantages of this concentration, particularly for an athlete who was making up for the absence of great natural skill, were considerable. Concentration gave you an edge over many of your opponents, even your bet-
(50) ters, who could not isolate themselves to that degree. For example, in football if they were ahead (or behind) by several touchdowns, if the game itself seemed to have been settled, they tended to slack off, to ease off a little, certainly to relax their own concentration. It was then that your own
(55) unwavering concentration and your own indifference to the larger point of view paid off. At the very least you could deal out surprise and discomfort to your opponents.

But it was more than that. Do you see? The ritual of physical concentration, of acute engagement in a
(60) small space while disregarding all the clamor and demands of the larger world, was the best possible lesson in precisely the kind of selfish intensity needed to create and to finish a poem, a story, or a novel. This alone mattered while all the world going on, with and without you, did not.

(65) I was learning first in muscle, blood, and bone, not from literature and not from teachers of literature or the arts or the natural sciences, but from coaches, in particular this one coach who paid me enough attention to influence me to teach some things to myself. I was learning about art
(70) and life through the abstraction of athletics in much the same way that a soldier is, to an extent, prepared for war by endless parade ground drill. His body must learn to be a soldier before heart, mind, and spirit can.

Ironically, I tend to dismiss most comparisons of athlet-
(75) ics to art and to "the creative process." But only because, I think, so much that is claimed for both is untrue. But I have come to believe—indeed I have to believe it insofar as I believe in the validity and efficacy of art—that what comes

to us first and foremost through the body, as a sensuous
(80) affective experience, is taken and transformed by mind and
self into a thing of the spirit. Which is only to say that what
the body learns and is taught is of enormous significance—
at least until the last light of the body fails.

7. Why does the author of Passage 1 consign his manuscript to a desk
drawer?

   (A) To protect it from the inquisitive eyes of his family
   (B) To prevent its getting lost or disordered
   (C) Because his publisher wishes to take another look at it
   (D) Because he chooses to watch a televised baseball game
   (E) To set it aside as unmarketable in its current state

8. Why is the author of Passage 1 "comforted by the behavior of baseball players" (lines 1 and 2)?

   (A) He treasures the timeless rituals of America's national pastime.
   (B) He sees he is not alone in having to confront failure and move
   on.
   (C) He enjoys watching the frustration of the batters who strike out.
   (D) He looks at baseball from the viewpoint of a behavioral
   psychologist.
   (E) He welcomes any distraction from the task of revising his novel.

9. What function in the passage is served by the discussion of the
nerves in the ankle in lines 10–15?

   (A) It provides a momentary digression from the overall narrative
   flow.
   (B) It emphasizes how strong a mental impact Henderson's home
   run must have had on Moore.
   (C) It provides scientific confirmation of the neuromuscular abilities
   of athletes.
   (D) It illustrates that the author's interest in sports is not limited to
   baseball alone.
   (E) It conveys a sense of how confusing it is for the mind to deal
   with so many simultaneous messages.

10. The word "registered" in line 16 means

   (A) enrolled formally
   (B) expressed without words
   (C) corresponded exactly
   (D) made an impression
   (E) qualified officially

11. The attitude of the author of Passage 1 to accountants, plumbers, and insurance salesmen (lines 25–28) can best be described as

    (A) respectful
    (B) cautious
    (C) superior
    (D) cynical
    (E) hypocritical

12. In the final two paragraphs of Passage 1, the author appears to

    (A) romanticize the writer as someone heroic in his or her accomplishments
    (B) deprecate athletes for their inability to react to experience instinctively
    (C) minimize the travail that artists and athletes endure to do their work
    (D) advocate the importance of literacy to the common citizen
    (E) suggest that a cautious approach would reduce the likelihood of future failure

13. The author of Passage 2 prizes

    (A) his innate athletic talent
    (B) the respect of his peers
    (C) his ability to focus
    (D) the gift of relaxation
    (E) winning at any cost

14. The word "settled" in line 53 means

    (A) judged
    (B) decided
    (C) reconciled
    (D) pacified
    (E) inhabited

15. What does the author mean by "indifference to the larger point of view" (lines 55 and 56)?

    (A) Inability to see the greater implications of the activity in which you were involved
    (B) Hostility to opponents coming from larger, better trained teams
    (C) Reluctance to look beyond your own immediate concerns
    (D) Refusing to care how greatly you might be hurt by your opponents
    (E) Being more concerned with the task at hand than with whether you win or lose

16. What is the function of the phrase "to an extent" in line 71?

(A) It denies a situation.
(B) It conveys a paradox.
(C) It qualifies a statement.
(D) It represents a metaphor.
(E) It minimizes a liability.

17. The author finds it ironic that he tends to "dismiss most comparisons of athletics to art" (lines 74 and 75) because

(A) athletics is the basis for great art
(B) he finds comparisons generally unhelpful
(C) he is making such a comparison
(D) he typically is less cynical
(E) he rejects the so-called creative process

18. The authors of both passages would agree that

(A) the lot of the professional writer is more trying than that of the professional athlete
(B) athletics has little to do with the actual workings of the creative process
(C) both artists and athletes learn hard lessons in the course of mastering their art
(D) it is important to concentrate on the things that hurt us in life
(E) participating in sports provides a distraction from the isolation of a writer's life

19. How would the author of Passage 2 respond to the author of Passage 1's viewpoint that a failure such as giving up a key home run can destroy an athlete?

(A) An athlete learns through his body that failure is enormously significant and affects him both physically and spiritually.
(B) Athletes of great natural skill suffer less from the agonies of failure than less accomplished athletes do.
(C) If an athlete plays without holding back, he will surpass athletes who are more inherently adept.
(D) If the athlete focuses on the job at hand and not on past errors, he will continue to function successfully.
(E) Athletes are highly sensitive performers who need to be sheltered from the clamor and demands of the larger world.

YOU MAY GO BACK AND REVIEW THIS SECTION IN THE
REMAINING TIME, BUT DO NOT WORK IN ANY OTHER
SECTION UNTIL TOLD TO DO SO.   **S T O P**

PRACTICE TEST 1
SECTION 9

16 Questions—22 Minutes

For each problem in this section determine which of the five choices is correct and blacken the corresponding choice on your answer sheet. You may use any blank space on the page for your work.

Notes:

- You may use a calculator whenever you think it will be helpful.
- Only real numbers are used. No question or answer on this test involves a complex or imaginary number.
- Use the diagrams provided to help you solve the problems. Unless you see the words "Note: Figure not drawn to scale" under a diagram, it has been drawn as accurately as possible. Unless it is stated that a figure is three-dimensional, you may assume it lies in a plane.
- For any function, f, the domain, unless specifically restricted, is the set of all real numbers for which $f(x)$ is also a real number.

Reference Information

Area Facts

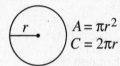

$A = \ell w$

$A = \frac{1}{2} bh$

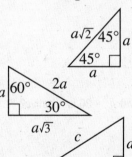

$A = \pi r^2$
$C = 2\pi r$

Volume Facts

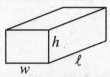

$V = \ell wh$

$V = \pi r^2 h$

Triangle Facts

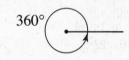

$a^2 + b^2 = c^2$

Angle Facts

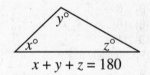

$x + y + z = 180$

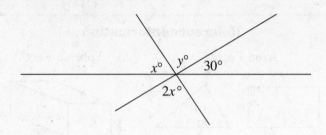

1. In the figure above, what is the value of y?

(A) 50
(B) 70
(C) 100
(D) 140
(E) It cannot be determined from the information given.

2. In a laboratory a solution was being heated. In 90 minutes, the temperature rose from $-8°$ to $7°$. What was the average hourly increase in temperature?

(A) 5°
(B) 7.5°
(C) 10°
(D) 15°
(E) 22.5°

3. For how many integers, n, is it true that $n^2 - 30$ is negative?

(A) 5
(B) 6
(C) 10
(D) 11
(E) Infinitely many

4. Which of the following is not a solution of $2a^2 + 3b = 5$?

(A) $a = 0$ and $b = \dfrac{5}{3}$
(B) $a = 1$ and $b = 1$
(C) $a = 2$ and $b = -1$
(D) $a = 3$ and $b = -4$
(E) $a = 4$ and $b = -9$

5. What is the slope of the line that passes through (0, 0) and is perpendicular to the line that passes through (−2, 2) and (3, 3)?

(A) −5

(B) $-\dfrac{1}{5}$

(C)   0

(D) $\dfrac{1}{5}$

(E)   5

6. If the measures of the angles of a triangle are in the ratio of 1:2:3, what is the ratio of the lengths of the sides?

(A) 1:2:3

(B) $1:1:\sqrt{2}$

(C) $1:\sqrt{3}:2$

(D) 3:4:5

(E) It cannot be determined from the information given.

7. A googol is the number that is written as 1 followed by 100 zeros. If g represents a googol, how many digits are there in g^2?

(A) 102

(B) 103

(C) 199

(D) 201

(E) 202

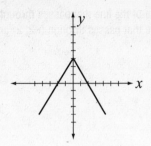

8. The figure above is the graph of $y = f(x)$. Which of the following is the graph of $y = -f(x - 3)$?

(A)

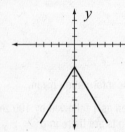

(B)

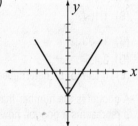

(C)

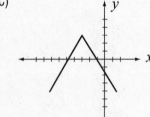

(D)

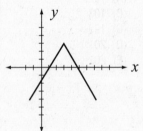

(E)

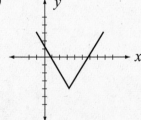

9. Which of the following expresses the area of a circle in terms of C, its circumference?

(A) $\dfrac{C^2}{4\pi}$

(B) $\dfrac{C^2}{2\pi}$

(C) $\dfrac{\sqrt{C}}{2\pi}$

(D) $\dfrac{C\pi}{4}$

(E) $\dfrac{C}{4\pi}$

10. What is the value of $\left(4^{\frac{1}{2}} \cdot 8^{\frac{1}{3}} \cdot 16^{\frac{1}{4}} \cdot 32^{\frac{1}{5}} \right)^{\frac{1}{2}}$?

(A) 2
(B) 4
(C) 8
(D) 16
(E) 64

11. If $\sqrt{x-15} - 5 = 2$ what is the value of $\sqrt{x}$?

(A) 2
(B) $\sqrt{14}$
(C) 8
(D) $\sqrt{34}$
(E) 64

12. To get to a business meeting, Joanna drove *m* miles in *h* hours, and arrived $\frac{1}{2}$ hour early. At what rate should she have driven to arrive exactly on time?

(A) $\dfrac{m}{2h}$

(B) $\dfrac{2m+h}{2h}$

(C) $\dfrac{2m-h}{2h}$

(D) $\dfrac{2m}{2h-1}$

(E) $\dfrac{2m}{2h+1}$

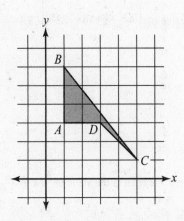

13. In the figure above, what is the area of quadrilateral *ABCD*?

(A) 4
(B) 5
(C) 5.5
(D) 6
(E) 7

14. If y is inversely proportional to x and directly proportional to z, and $x = 4$ and $z = 8$ when $y = 10$, what is the value of $x + z$ when $y = 20$?

    (A) 6
    (B) 12
    (C) 16
    (D) 18
    (E) 24

15. What is the average (arithmetic mean) of 3^{30}, 3^{60}, and 3^{90}?

    (A) 3^{60}
    (B) 3^{177}
    (C) $3^{10} + 3^{20} + 3^{30}$
    (D) $3^{27} + 3^{57} + 3^{87}$
    (E) $3^{29} + 3^{59} + 3^{89}$

16. If a and b are the lengths of the legs of a right triangle whose hypotenuse is 10 and whose area is 20, what is the value of $(a + b)^2$?

    (A) 100
    (B) 120
    (C) 140
    (D) 180
    (E) 200

YOU MAY GO BACK AND REVIEW THIS SECTION IN THE
REMAINING TIME, BUT DO NOT WORK IN ANY OTHER
SECTION UNTIL TOLD TO DO SO.   **S T O P**

PRACTICE TEST 1
SECTION 10

14 Questions—10 Minutes

For each of the following questions, select the best answer from the choices provided and fill in the appropriate circle on the answer sheet.

Some or all parts of the following sentences are underlined. The first answer choice, (A), simply repeats the underlined part of the sentence. The other four choices present four alternative ways to phrase the underlined part. Select the answer that produces the most effective sentence, one that is clear and exact, and blacken the appropriate space on your answer sheet. In selecting your choice, be sure that it is standard written English, and that it expresses the meaning of the original sentence.

Example:

The first biography of author Eudora Welty came out in 1998 and she was 89 years old at the time.

(A) and she was 89 years old at the time
(B) at the time when she was 89
(C) upon becoming an 89 year old
(D) when she was 89
(E) at the age of 89 years old

1. Unfortunately, soul singer Anita Baker's voice <u>has not weathered the years as well as other singers have.</u>
   - (A) has not weathered the years as well as other singers have
   - (B) had not weathered the years as well as other singers have
   - (C) has not been weathered by the years as well as the voices of other singers have been
   - (D) has not weathered the years as well as other singers' voices have
   - (E) has not weathered the years as good as other singers' voices have

2. <u>The mathematics teacher drew a right triangle on the blackboard, he</u> proceeded to demonstrate that we could determine the length of the longest side of the triangle if we knew the lengths of its two shorter sides.
   - (A) The mathematics teacher drew a right triangle on the blackboard, he
   - (B) The right triangle, which was drawn on the blackboard by the mathematics teacher, he
   - (C) After drawing a right triangle on the blackboard, the mathematics teacher
   - (D) A right triangle was first drawn on the blackboard by the mathematics teacher, then he
   - (E) Once a right triangle was drawn on the blackboard by the mathematics teacher, who then

3. An inside trader is <u>when a corporate officer who has access to "inside" or privileged information about a company's prospects uses that information</u> in buying or selling company shares.
   - (A) when a corporate officer who has access to "inside" or privileged information about a company's prospects uses that information
   - (B) when a corporate officer has access to "inside" or privileged information about a company's prospects and uses that information
   - (C) a corporate officer who has access to "inside" or privileged information about a company's prospects and uses that information
   - (D) a corporate officer who has accessed "inside" or privileged information about a company's prospects for use of that information
   - (E) that a corporate officer who has access to "inside" or privileged information about a company's prospects and he uses that information

4. Gymnastics students perform stretching <u>exercises to develop flexibil-</u><u>ity and to become a more agile tumbler</u>.

   (A) exercises to develop flexibility and to become a more agile tumbler
   (B) exercises for the development of flexibility and to become a more agile tumbler
   (C) exercises so that they develop flexibility, becoming a more agile tumbler
   (D) exercises to develop flexibility and to become more agile tumblers
   (E) exercises because they want to develop flexibility in becoming a more agile tumbler

5. <u>Because the Ming vase is priceless plus being highly fragile,</u> it is kept safe in a sealed display case.

   (A) Because the Ming vase is priceless plus being highly fragile,
   (B) Being that the Ming vase is priceless and also it is highly fragile,
   (C) Although the Ming vase is priceless and highly fragile,
   (D) Because the Ming vase is priceless and highly fragile is why
   (E) Because the Ming vase is both priceless and highly fragile,

6. The soft, pulpy flesh of the passion fruit possesses a flavor at once tart and <u>sweet and the flavor has captivated</u> many prominent chefs, among them Alice Waters.

   (A) sweet and the flavor has captivated
   (B) sweet that has captivated
   (C) sweet that have captivated
   (D) sweet and the flavors have captivated
   (E) sweet and the favor captivates

7. Shakespeare's acting company performed in a relatively intimate setting, <u>appearing before smaller audiences than most theaters today</u>.

   (A) appearing before smaller audiences than most theaters today
   (B) they appeared before smaller audiences than most theaters today
   (C) appearing before audiences smaller than most audiences today
   (D) having appeared before smaller audiences than most theaters today
   (E) and they appeared before audiences smaller than the ones at most theaters today

8. Observing the interactions of preschoolers in a playground setting, it can be seen that the less adults relate to the children in their charge, the more these children relate to one another.

   (A) Observing the interactions of preschoolers in a playground setting, it can be seen

   (B) Having observed the interactions of preschoolers in a playground setting, it can be seen

   (C) If one observes the interactions of preschoolers in a playground setting, you can see

   (D) Observing the interactions of preschoolers in a playground setting, we can see

   (E) Observing the interactions of preschoolers in a playground setting can be seen

9. Neither the Florida coast nor the Caribbean islands was prepared for the series of hurricanes that devastated the region in 2004.

   (A) Neither the Florida coast nor the Caribbean islands was prepared for

   (B) Neither the Florida coast nor the Caribbean islands have been prepared for

   (C) Neither the Florida coast or the Caribbean islands were prepared for

   (D) Neither the Florida coast or the Caribbean islands was prepared for

   (E) Neither the Florida coast nor the Caribbean islands were prepared for

10. Far from being mercenary ambulance chasers, trial lawyers perform a public service by forcing corporations to consider the potential financial cost of pollution, unsafe products, and mistreatment of workers.

    (A) Far from being mercenary ambulance chasers

    (B) Despite them being mercenary ambulance chasers

    (C) Far from them being mercenary ambulance chasers

    (D) Far from having been mercenary ambulance chasers

    (E) Further from being mercenary ambulance chasers

11. *Unsafe at Any Speed* is Ralph Nader's detailed <u>portrait of how the auto industry willfully resisted safety innovations and thus contributed to</u> thousands of highway deaths a year.

   (A) portrait of how the auto industry willfully resisted safety innovations and thus contributed to
   (B) portrait of when the auto industry was willful about resisting safety innovations and thus contributing to
   (C) portrait of how the auto industry fully willed themselves to resist safety innovations and thus contributed to
   (D) portrait of how the auto industry willfully resisted safety innovations in order to contribute to
   (E) portrait showing how the auto industry willfully resisted safety innovations, and they thus contributed to

12. In 1532, Francisco Pizarro and his troops arrived in Cuzco, took hostage the Incan king, <u>Atahualpa, and then they demanded ransom</u>.

   (A) Atahualpa, and then they demanded ransom
   (B) who was named Atahualpa, and then they demanded ransom
   (C) Atahualpa, it was so they could demand ransom
   (D) Atahualpa, and then there was a demand for ransom
   (E) Atahualpa, and then demanded ransom

13. <u>Although demand for cars, motorcycles, and other consumer goods are booming,</u> the economy is growing only at roughly 4 percent a year, and the unemployment rate is about 10 percent.

   (A) Although demand for cars, motorcycles, and other consumer goods are booming
   (B) Because demand for cars, motorcycles, and other consumer goods are booming
   (C) Although demand for cars, motorcycles, and other consumer goods is booming
   (D) Although demand for cars, motorcycles, and other consumer goods have been booming
   (E) Although demand of cars, motorcycles, and other consumer goods is booming

14. <u>Samuel Sewall, who was a judge in the Salem witch trials but later repented his role and, in 1700,</u> wrote the first attack on the American slave trade.

- (A) Samuel Sewall, who was a judge in the Salem witch trials but later repented his role and, in 1700,
- (B) Samuel Sewall was a judge in the Salem witch trials but who later repented his role and, in 1700,
- (C) Samuel Sewall, a judge in the Salem witch trials, but later he repented his role and, in 1700,
- (D) Samuel Sewall, a judge in the Salem witch trials who later repented his role, in 1700
- (E) Samuel Sewall, who was a judge in the Salem witch trials but who later repented his role, and who, in 1700,

YOU MAY GO BACK AND REVIEW THIS SECTION IN THE REMAINING TIME, BUT DO NOT WORK IN ANY OTHER SECTION UNTIL TOLD TO DO SO.   **STOP**

Answer Key

Section 2   Critical Reading

1. **A**	6. **A**	11. **A**	16. **E**	21. **C**
2. **D**	7. **C**	12. **C**	17. **B**	22. **C**
3. **B**	8. **C**	13. **B**	18. **D**	23. **E**
4. **D**	9. **E**	14. **C**	19. **C**	24. **B**
5. **D**	10. **B**	15. **E**	20. **A**	

Section 3   Mathematical Reasoning

1. **C**	5. **C**	9. **B**	13. **E**	17. **D**
2. **C**	6. **E**	10. **C**	14. **C**	18. **E**
3. **D**	7. **B**	11. **E**	15. **C**	19. **D**
4. **B**	8. **C**	12. **B**	16. **B**	20. **E**

Section 4   Writing Skills

1. **B**	8. **E**	15. **B**	22. **C**	29. **A**
2. **A**	9. **C**	16. **C**	23. **E**	30. **C**
3. **C**	10. **B**	17. **B**	24. **D**	31. **B**
4. **D**	11. **A**	18. **B**	25. **C**	32. **C**
5. **A**	12. **D**	19. **A**	26. **D**	33. **D**
6. **A**	13. **C**	20. **D**	27. **D**	34. **B**
7. **D**	14. **B**	21. **C**	28. **A**	35. **C**

Section 5

On this test, Section 5 was the experimental section. It could have been an extra critical reading, mathematics, or writing skills section. Remember: on the SAT you take, the experimental section may be any section from 2 to 7.

Section 6   Critical Reading

1. **E**	6. **C**	11. **D**	16. **D**	21. **E**
2. **C**	7. **D**	12. **D**	17. **D**	22. **D**
3. **B**	8. **B**	13. **C**	18. **B**	23. **D**
4. **B**	9. **C**	14. **C**	19. **C**	24. **A**
5. **C**	10. **B**	15. **E**	20. **D**	

Section 7   Mathematical Reasoning

Multiple-Choice Questions

1. **D**   3. **C**   5. **C**   7. **B**
2. **E**   4. **D**   6. **C**   8. **A**

Grid-in Questions

9.

| | 1 | 5 | 2 |

10.

| | 2 | . | 1 |

$2.01 \leq x \leq 2.33$

11.

| 8 | 1 | 0 | 0 |

12.

| 2 | 0 | 2 |

13.

| | 2 | 8 |

14.

| 1 | / | 3 | 2 |

15.

	1	/	8
	⊘	●	
⊙	⊙	⊙	⊙
	⓪	⓪	⓪
①	●	①	①
②	②	②	②
③	③	③	③
④	④	④	④
⑤	⑤	⑤	⑤
⑥	⑥	⑥	⑥
⑦	⑦	⑦	⑦
⑧	⑧	⑧	●
⑨	⑨	⑨	⑨

16.

		1	9
	⊘	⊘	
⊙	⊙	⊙	⊙
	⓪	⓪	⓪
①	①	●	①
②	②	②	②
③	③	③	③
④	④	④	④
⑤	⑤	⑤	⑤
⑥	⑥	⑥	⑥
⑦	⑦	⑦	⑦
⑧	⑧	⑧	⑧
⑨	⑨	⑨	●

17.

8	1	9	0
	⊘	⊘	
⊙	⊙	⊙	⊙
	⓪	⓪	●
①	●	①	①
②	②	②	②
③	③	③	③
④	④	④	④
⑤	⑤	⑤	⑤
⑥	⑥	⑥	⑥
⑦	⑦	⑦	⑦
●	⑧	⑧	⑧
⑨	⑨	●	⑨

18.

	3	/	8
	⊘	●	
⊙	⊙	⊙	⊙
	⓪	⓪	⓪
①	①	①	①
②	②	②	②
③	●	③	③
④	④	④	④
⑤	⑤	⑤	⑤
⑥	⑥	⑥	⑥
⑦	⑦	⑦	⑦
⑧	⑧	⑧	●
⑨	⑨	⑨	⑨

19.

or

.	3	7	5
	⊘	⊘	
●	⊙	⊙	⊙
	⓪	⓪	⓪
①	①	①	①
②	②	②	②
③	●	③	③
④	④	④	④
⑤	⑤	⑤	●
⑥	⑥	⑥	⑥
⑦	⑦	●	⑦
⑧	⑧	⑧	⑧
⑨	⑨	⑨	⑨

Section 8   Critical Reading

1. **A**	5. **B**	9. **B**	13. **C**	17. **C**
2. **C**	6. **E**	10. **D**	14. **B**	18. **C**
3. **B**	7. **E**	11. **C**	15. **E**	19. **D**
4. **E**	8. **B**	12. **A**	16. **C**	

Section 9   Mathematical Reasoning

1. **C**	5. **A**	9. **A**	13. **A**
2. **C**	6. **C**	10. **B**	14. **D**
3. **D**	7. **D**	11. **C**	15. **E**
4. **D**	8. **E**	12. **E**	16. **D**

Section 10   Writing Skills

1. **D**	4. **D**	7. **C**	10. **A**	13. **C**
2. **C**	5. **E**	8. **D**	11. **A**	14. **D**
3. **C**	6. **B**	9. **E**	12. **E**	

Answer Explanations

Section 2 Critical Reading

1. **A** Because lightning victims are so battered and confused, they seem like assault victims. Thus, they are often *mistaken for* victims of assault.   (Cause and Effect Signal)

2. **D** Anyone who has produced more than three hundred books in a single lifetime is an enormously productive or *prolific* writer. Writers are often described as prolific, but few, if any, have been as prolific as the late Dr. Asimov.
Beware of Eye-Catchers: Choice A is incorrect. *Fastidious* means painstakingly careful; it has nothing to do with writing quickly.
(Examples)

3. **B** Time limitations would cause problems for you if you were reading a *lengthy* book. To save time, you might want to read it in an *abridged* or shortened form.
Remember to watch for signal words that link one part of the sentence to another. The use of "because" in the opening clause is a cause signal.   (Cause and Effect Signal)

4. **D** Speakers wish to communicate *unambiguously* in order that there may be no *confusion* about their meaning.
Remember to watch for signal words that link one part of the sentence to another. The presence of "and" linking two items in a pair indicates that the missing word may be a synonym or near-synonym for the other linked word. In this case, *unambiguously* is a synonym for *clearly*. Similarly, the use of "so that" in the second clause signals cause and effect.   (Argument Pattern)

5. **D** Lisa was normally *gregarious* or sociable. When she unexpectedly lost her job, she became quiet and *withdrawn* (distant; unsociable). Note how the signal word *Although* indicates a contrast between her normally sociable and later unsociable states.
(Contrast Pattern)

6. **A** Wilma Mankiller, a female, heads a major American Indian tribe. She performs her role successfully: she is "increasingly popular." By her success, she has *shattered* or exploded a myth of male supremacy. (Argument Pattern)

7. **C** The commission censured or condemned the senator for doing something wrong: his expenditures of public funds were *lavish* or extravagant. He spent the public's money in an *unjustifiable*, unwarranted way. (Cause and Effect Pattern)

8. **C** A stereotyped or oversimplified portrait of a slave would lead sensitive readers to express *criticism* because the issue of slavery was treated so casually. Thus, they normally would be *detractors* of the novel. However, *Huckleberry Finn* is such a fine work that even its critics acknowledge its greatness. Signal words are helpful here. "Despite" in the first clause implies a contrast, and "even" in the second clause implies that the subjects somewhat reluctantly agree that the novel is a masterpiece.
(Contrast Signal)

9. **E** The final sentence of the passage maintains that, contrary to expectation, the jellyfish has a sophisticated or complex genetic structure.
Beware of eye-catchers. Choice B is incorrect. "Spineless" (line 1) here means invertebrate, lacking a backbone or spinal column. It does not mean cowardly.

10. **B** The second sentence of the passage states that the jellyfish "seems the most primitive of creatures." The last sentence of the passage, however, *contradicts* or denies that *assumption*.

11. **A** The human faculty for myth is the *capacity* or ability of people to invent legends.

12. **C** The fact that Raleigh is remembered more for a romantic, perhaps apocryphal, gesture than for his voyages of exploration *illustrates how legendary events outshine historical achievements in the public's mind.*

13. **B** The author is writing a book about the effect of the opening of the West on the Indians living there. As a historian, he needs primary source materials—firsthand accounts of the period written by men and women living at that time. Thus, he finds the period of 1860–1890 worth mentioning because during those years the "greatest concentration of recorded experience and observation" (the bulk of original accounts) was created.

14. **C** Only the white settlers looked on their intrusion into Indian territory as the opening of the West. To the Native Americans, it was an invasion. Thus, "opening" *from a Native American perspective is an inaccurate term.*

15. **E** Throughout the passage the author presents and comments on the nature of the original documents that form the basis for his historical narrative. Thus, it is clear that a major concern of his is to *introduce* these "sources of almost forgotten oral history" to his readers.
    Choice A is incorrect. The author clearly regrets the fate of the Indians. However, he does not take this occasion to denounce or condemn the white man.
    Choice B is incorrect. While the author discusses the various treaty councils, he does not evaluate or judge their effectiveness.
    Choice C is incorrect. The author never touches on the current treatment of Indians.
    Choice D is incorrect. The author indicates no such similarity.

16. **E** Of all the thousands of published descriptions of the opening of the West, the greatest concentration or *accumulation* of accounts dates from the period of 1860 to 1890.

17. **B** The author is describing a period in which Native Americans lost their land and much of their personal freedom to the same pioneers who supposedly revered the ideal of freedom. Thus, in describing the ideal of freedom revered by the pioneers as "personal freedom for those who already had it" (in other words, personal freedom for the pioneers, not the Indians), the author is being *ironic.*

18. **D** You can arrive at the correct choice by the process of elimination. Statement I is true. The passage states that the quality of the interviews depended on the interpreters' abilities. Inaccuracies could creep in because of the translators' lack of skill. Therefore, you can eliminate Choice B.
    Statement II is untrue. The passage indicates that the Indians sometimes exaggerated, telling the reporters tall tales. It does not indicate that the reporters in turn overstated what they had been told. Therefore, you can eliminate Choices C and E.
    Statement III is true. The passage indicates that the Indians sometimes were disinclined to speak the whole truth because they feared reprisals (retaliation) if they did. Therefore, you can eliminate choice A.
    Only Choice D is left. It is the correct answer.

19. **C** Brown speaks of the Indians who lived through the "doom period of their civilization," the victims of the conquest of the American West. In doing so, his tone can best be described as *elegiac*, expressing sadness about their fate and lamenting their vanished civilization.

20. **A** In the fifth paragraph Brown comments upon the "graphic similes and metaphors of the natural world" found in the English translations of Indian speeches. Thus, he is impressed by their *vividness of imagery*.

21. **C** Commenting about inadequate interpreters who turned eloquent Indian speeches into "flat" prose, Brown is criticizing the translations for their *pedestrian*, unimaginative quality.

22. **C** Lines 60–63 state that, as the Indian leaders became more sophisticated or knowledgeable about addressing treaty councils, "they demanded the right to choose their own interpreters and recorders." Until they had become familiar with the process, *they were unaware that they had the option to demand such services*.

23. **E** Brown has tried to create a narrative of the winning of the West from the victims' perspective. In asking his readers to read the book facing eastward (the way the Indians would have been looking when they first saw the whites headed west), he is asking them metaphorically *to identify* with *the Indians' viewpoint*.

24. **B** In the sentence immediately preceding the one in which the phrase "equated with" appears, Brown calls the Indians "true conservationists." Such conservationists know that life is *necessarily tied to* the earth and to its resources, and that by destroying these resources, by imbalancing the equation, so to speak, "the intruders from the East" would destroy life itself.

Section 3 Mathematical Reasoning

1. **C** Just quickly add up the number of miles Greg jogs each week:

$$3 + 4 + 5 + 6 + 7 + 8 + 9 = 42.$$

In 2 weeks he jogs **84** miles.

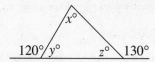

2. **C** In the figure above, $x + y + z = 180$. Also, since $y = 60$ ($180 - 120$) and $z = 50$ ($180 - 130$), then

$$x = 180 - (50 + 60) = 180 - 110 = \textbf{70}.$$

3. **D** After an increase of 75¢, a tuna fish sandwich will cost $5.00. The only sandwiches that, after a 50¢ increase, will be more expensive than the tuna fish are the **3** that now cost *more than* $4.50.

4. **B** Discard the scores of 9.2 and 9.7, and take the average of the other four scores:

$$\frac{9.4 + 9.5 + 9.6 + 9.6}{4} = \frac{38.1}{4} = \textbf{9.525}.$$

5. **C** The sum of the measures of two adjacent angles of a parallelogram is 180°. Therefore,

$$180 = 10x + 25x - 30 = 35x - 30,$$

which implies that $35x = 210$ and $x = \textbf{6}$.

6. **E** The figures below show that **all** of the choices **are possible**.

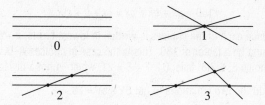

7. **B** Since $a^2 - b^2 = (a - b)(a + b)$, then:

$$20 = a^2 - b^2 = (a - b)(a + b) = 10(a + b).$$

Therefore, $a + b = 2$. Adding the equations $a + b = 2$ and $a - b = 10$ gives

$$2a = 12 \Rightarrow a = 6 \Rightarrow b = \textbf{-4}.$$

8. **C** Each year the dealer sells half of her silver, so after 1 year she owns $\left(\frac{1}{2}\right)$ 1000 ounces.

   After 2 years she owns half as many ounces:

   $$\left(\frac{1}{2}\right)\left(\frac{1}{2}(1000)\right) = \left(\frac{1}{2}\right)^2 (1000).$$

   In general, after t years, she will own 1000 $\left(\frac{1}{2}\right)^t$ ounces.
   Since $\frac{1}{2} = 2^{-1}$:

   $$\left(\frac{1}{2}\right)^t = (2^{-1})^t = 2^{-t} \text{ and } 1000 \left(\frac{1}{2}\right)^t = \mathbf{1000 \times 2^{-t}}.$$

9. **B** Since 9 is a solution of $x^2 - a = 0$, then $81 - a = 0 \Rightarrow a = 81$. Now solve the equation:

   $$x^4 - 81 = 0 \Rightarrow x^4 = 81 \Rightarrow x^2 = 9 \Rightarrow x = 3 \text{ or } \mathbf{-3}.$$

10. **C** The mode is 8, since more people earn \$8 an hour than any other salary. Also, since there are 16 employees, the median is the average of the 8th and 9th items of data: \$8 and \$10, so the median is 9. Finally, the average of 8 and 9 is **8.5**.

11. **E** If the ratio were $a:b:c$, then

    $$180 = ax + bx + cx = (a + b + c)x.$$

    Since each of the choices is written in lowest terms, $a + b + c$ must be a factor of 180. This is the case in choices A–D. Only choice E, **6:7:8**, fails: $6 + 7 + 8 = 21$, which is not a divisor of 180.

12. **B** Add the two equations to get $5x + 5y = 28$.
    Then $x + y = \dfrac{28}{5}$, and the average of x and y is

    $$\frac{x + y}{2} = \frac{\frac{28}{5}}{2} = \frac{28}{10} = \mathbf{2.8}.$$

13. **E** Since $W = 3$ and $2W = 3X$, then $3X = 6 \Rightarrow X = 2$. Therefore

    $$3 + 7 = 2 + Y \Rightarrow Y = 10 - 2 = \mathbf{8}.$$

14. **C** By definition, $W + W = X + Y \Rightarrow 2W = X + Y$; but the definition also states that $2W = 3X$, so $X = \dfrac{2}{3} W$. Therefore

$$2W = \dfrac{2}{3} W + Y \Rightarrow Y = \dfrac{4}{3} W.$$

15. **C** If the ring was originally priced at $100, it was accidentally marked $40 instead of $160. The incorrect price of $40 must be increased by $120, which is 3 times, or **300%** of, the incorrect price.

16. **B** John's average speed is calculated by dividing his total distance of 10 miles by the total time he spent riding his bicycle. Each tick mark on the horizontal axis of the graph represents 10 minutes.

    He left at 8:30 and arrived back home $1\dfrac{1}{2}$ hours later, at 10:00.

    However, he stopped for 10 minutes, from 9:20 to 9:30, so he was riding for only 1 hour and 20 minutes, or $\dfrac{4}{3}$ hours. Finally,

    $10 \div \dfrac{4}{3} = 10 \times \dfrac{3}{4} = 7\dfrac{1}{2}$.

17. **D** Assume $AB = 3$ and $BC = 5$. The least that AC can be is 2, if A is on line BC, between B and C; and the most AC can be is 8, if A is on line BC, so that B is between A and C. In fact, AC can be any length between 2 and 8.

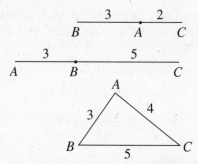

    Therefore the ratio $AB : AC$ can be any number between 3:2 (= 1.5) and 3:8 (= 0.375). In particular, it can be 1:2 (= 0.5) and 3:8. (I and III are true.) It cannot be 1:3 (= 0.333). (II is false.) Statements **I and III only** are true.

18. **E** $g(2) = f(3 \times 2) + 3 = f(6) + 3$.

    $f(6) = \sqrt{100 - 6^2} = \sqrt{100 - 36} = \sqrt{64} = 8$.

    So $g(2) = f(6) + 3 = 8 + 3 = \textbf{11}$.

19. **D** The formula for the volume of a cylinder is $V = \pi r^2 h$. Replacing r by 8 and h by π^2, we get that $V = \pi(8)^2(\pi^2) = 64\pi^3$. If e is the edge of the cube, then the volume of the cube is e^3. So $e^3 = 64\pi^3 \Rightarrow e = \textbf{4}\boldsymbol{\pi}$.

20. **E** To earn 10 points, Ellen needed to get 10 correct answers and then earn no more points on the remaining $q - 10$ questions. To earn no points on a set of questions, she had to miss 4 questions (thereby losing $4 \times \dfrac{1}{4} = 1$ point) for every 1 question she got right in that set. She answered $\dfrac{1}{5}$ of the $q - 10$ questions correctly (and $\dfrac{4}{5}$ of them incorrectly). The total number of correct answers was

    $$10 + \frac{q - 10}{5} = 10 + \frac{q}{5} - \frac{10}{5} = \textbf{8} + \frac{\boldsymbol{q}}{\textbf{5}}.$$

    <u>Alternative solution:</u> Let c be the number of questions Ellen answered correctly, and $q - c$ the number she missed. Then her raw score is

    $c - \dfrac{1}{4}(q - c)$, which equals 10, so

    $4c - q + c = 40 \Rightarrow 5c - q = 40 \Rightarrow 5c = 40 + q$

    $$\Rightarrow c = \frac{40 + q}{5} = \textbf{8} + \frac{\boldsymbol{q}}{\textbf{5}}.$$

Section 4 Writing Skills

1. **B** Choice B eliminates the excessive wordiness of the original sentence without introducing any errors in diction.

2. **A** As used in Choice A, the semicolon separating a pair of clauses is correct. Choices C–E introduce errors in parallel structure.

3. **C** Error in agreement. *Kind* is singular and requires a singular modifier (*this*).

4. **D** Choice D corrects the error in diction (*eminently*, not *imminently*) and the error in parallel structure.

5. **A** The original answer provides the most effective and concise sentence.

6. **A** The original sentence is correct. The singular pronoun *it* refers to the subject of the main clause, *fate* (singular).

7. **D** Choices A, B, C, and E suffer from errors in the sequence of tenses.

8. **E** Error in parallelism. There is a lack of parallel structure in the other four choices.

9. **C** Errors in precision and clarity.
Choice A states the result of the program rather than the goal.
Choice B results in a sentence fragment.
Choices D and E use the *was where* construction, which is unclear and should be avoided.

10. **B** Dangling modifier. Ask yourself who revised the dissertation. Clearly, *she* (the writer) did.

11. **A** Sentence is correct. *Unique* means being without a like or equal. Avoid phrases like *very unique* and *more unique* that imply there can be degrees of uniqueness.

12. **D** The reflexive pronoun *myself* cannot be used as the object of the verb *frightened*. Change *myself* to *me*.

13. **C** Adjective and adverb confusion. Change *regular* to *regularly.*

14. **B** Error in parallelism. Change *not because of the money* to *not because he needed the money* (a clause) to parallel the clause that follows *but.*

15. **B** Error in diction. Change *liable* to *likely.*

16. **C** Error in subject-verb agreement. Change *is* to *are.*

17. **B** Error in diction. *Latter* should not be used to refer to more than two items. Change *latter* to *last.*

18. **B** Error in parallelism. Change *to aid* to *aiding.*

19. **A** Adjective and adverb confusion. Change *special prepared* to *specially prepared*.

20. **D** Error in tense. Change *had been* to *were*.

21. **C** Error in parallelism. Change *under application* to *being applied*.

22. **C** Faulty verbal. Change *satisfying* to the infinitive *to satisfy*.

23. **E** Sentence is correct.

24. **D** Error in pronoun-antecedent agreement. Change *they are* to *it is*.

25. **C** Error in subject-verb agreement. The antecedent of *who* is *one*. Therefore, *who is* is correct.

26. **D** Error in parallelism. Change *and leaving room for* to *to leave room for*.

27. **D** Incomplete comparison. Compare *stories* with *stories*, not *stories* with *champion*. The sentence should read: "There are probably few comeback stories as moving as that of cycling's stalwart champion, Lance Armstrong."

28. **A** Unidiomatic preposition. Replace *ability for winning* with *ability to win*.

29. **A** Error in coordination and subordination. Remember: any sentence elements that are *not* underlined are by definition correct. Here, the coordinating conjunction *but* is not underlined. Coordinating conjunctions connect sentence elements that are grammatically equal. In this case, *but* should connect the main clause beginning "others restrict themselves" with another main clause. However, *while*, a subordinating conjunction, introduces a subordinate clause, not a main clause. To correct the error, delete *While* and begin the sentence *Some scientists are absorbed*.

30. **C** Choice A says that the house is *in your car*, an unlikely situation. Choice B contains an idea that the writer could not have intended. Choice C accurately states the intended idea. It is the best answer. Choice D, like Choice B, contains an idea that is quite absurd. Choice E is wordy and awkwardly expressed.

31. **B** All the sentences except sentence 2 contribute to the development of the essay's topic. Therefore, Choice B is the best answer.

32. **C** Choice A is awkwardly expressed.
Choice B is awkward and contains the pronoun *it*, which has no specific antecedent.
Choice C is accurately expressed and is consistent with the sentences that precede and follow sentence 8. It is the best answer.
Choice D is written in a style that is different from that of the rest of the essay.
Choice E would be a good choice, but it contains a comma splice. A comma may not be used to join two independent clauses.

33. **D** Choice A is quite formal and is not in keeping with the style and tone of the essay.
Choice B is close to the style and tone of the essay, but it contains the redundancy *quickly and rapidly*.
Choice C has a formal tone inconsistent with the rest of the essay.
Choice D uses the second-person pronoun and is consistent with the folksy, conversational style of the essay. It is the best answer.
Choice E uses an objective tone far different from the writing in the rest of the essay.

34. **B** Choice A is only partly true. While the paragraph gives another viewpoint, the data it contains are hardly objective.
Choice B accurately states the writer's intention. It is the best answer.
Choices C, D, and E in no way describe the function of paragraph 3.

35. **C** Choice A provides no particular link to the preceding paragraph.
Choice B provides a rather weak transition between paragraphs.
Choice C creates a strong bond between paragraphs by alluding to material in paragraph 3 and introducing the topic of paragraph 4. It is the best answer.
Choice D could be a good transition were it not for the error in subject-verb agreement. The subject *sounds* is plural; the verb *tells* is singular.
Choice E provides a weak transition and its writing style is not consistent with the rest of the essay.

Section 6 Critical Reading

1. **E** Tiffany's works of art have survived in spite of their *fragility* (tendency to break).
   Remember to watch for signal words that link one part of the sentence to another. The use of "despite" in the opening phrase sets up a contrast. *Despite* signals you that Tiffany's glass works were unlikely candidates to survive for several decades.

   (Contrast Signal)

2. **C** A comprehensive or thorough study would not be missing *relevant* or important material.
   Remember to watch for signal words that link one part of the sentence to another. The use of "but" in the second clause sets up a contrast.

   (Contrast Signal)

3. **B** Pain is a *sensation*. Losing the ability to feel pain would leave the body *vulnerable*, defenseless, lacking its usual warnings against impending bodily harm.
   Note how the second clause serves to clarify or explain what is meant by pain's being an "early warning system."   (Definition)

4. **B** A *lugubrious* (exaggeratedly gloomy) manner may create laughter because it is so inappropriate in the *hilarity* (noisy gaiety) of the circus. The clown's success stems from a contrast. The missing words must be antonyms or near-antonyms. You can immediately eliminate Choices C, D, and E as nonantonym pairs. In addition, you can eliminate Choice A; *sobriety* or seriousness is an inappropriate term for describing circus life.

   (Contrast Pattern)

5. **C** If she was *deprecatory about* her accomplishments (diminished them or saw nothing praiseworthy in them), she would be unwilling to boast about them or *flaunt* them. Note the use of "properly" to describe her unwillingness to do something. This suggests that the second missing word would have negative associations.   (Definition)

6. **C** The author refers to Douglas in order to introduce Douglas's metaphoric description of the Everglades as the River of Grass.

7. **D** Enduring value is value that *lasts*. The *lasting* value of the Everglades is that it provides a habitat for endangered species.

8. **B** The author's parenthetic remark serves to *provide background on the reasons* for the scientific and governmental *concern* about the dangers of phosphorus runoff.

9. **C** The author of Passage 1 is wholly concerned with the threat to the Everglades' fragile ecosystem. The environment is what is important to her. She mentions agricultural needs only in terms of how they have affected the River of Grass. Given her perspective, she would most likely view the author of Passage 2 as someone *inclined to overestimate the importance of the sugar industry*.

10. **B** The author describes himself as "jarred and shocked" (line 4). He asks himself, "What strange world was this?" His initial reaction to Mencken's prose is one of *disbelief*.
    Choice A is incorrect. Mencken rages; the narrator does not.
    Choice C is incorrect. It is unsupported by the passage.
    Choices D and E are incorrect. Again, these terms apply to Mencken, not to the narrator.

11. **D** The narrator does *not* portray Mencken as reverent or respectful of religious belief. Instead, he says that Mencken mocks God.
    Choice A is incorrect. The narrator portrays Mencken as intrepid (brave); he wonders where Mencken gets his courage.
    Choice B is incorrect. The narrator portrays Mencken as articulate (verbally expressive); he says Mencken writes clear, clean sentences.
    Choice C is incorrect. The narrator portrays Mencken as satiric (mocking); he says Mencken makes fun of people's weaknesses.
    Choice E is incorrect. The narrator portrays Mencken as opinionated (stubborn about his opinions; prejudiced). Mencken's book, after all, is *A Book of Prejudices*.
    Remember: when asked about specific information in the passage, spot key words in the question and scan the passage to find them (or their synonyms).

12. **D** The mood of the book colored or *affected* the narrator's perceptions.
    Remember: when answering a vocabulary-in-context question, test each answer choice, substituting it in the sentence for the word in quotes.

13. **C** The narrator feels a hunger for books that surges up in him. In other words, he is filled with *impatient ardor* or eagerness.
    Choice A is incorrect. The narrator has his dreams, but he is involved rather than indifferent.

Choices B and D are incorrect. There is nothing in the lines to suggest them.

Choice E is incorrect. The narrator is determined, but his resolve is active and eager rather than quiet.

Remember: when asked to determine the author's attitude or tone, look for words that convey emotion or paint pictures.

14. **C** The narrator is able to identify Mr. Gerald as an American type. He feels closer to Mr. Gerald, familiar with the limits of his life. This suggests that he smiles out of a sense of *recognition*. Choices A, B, D, and E are incorrect. There is nothing in the passage to suggest them.

Remember: when asked to make inferences, base your answers on what the passage implies, not what it states directly.

15. **E** Phrases like "of feeling something new, of being affected by something that made the look of the world different" and "filled with bookish notions" reflect the narrator's response to the new books he reads. You have here a portrait of a youth's response to his expanding intellectual horizons.

Choice A is incorrect. The narrator is not arguing in favor of a cause; he is recounting an episode from his life.

Choice B is incorrect. The narrator was aware of racial prejudice long before he read Mencken.

Choice C is incorrect. The passage is not about Mencken's and Lewis's styles; it is about their effect in opening up the world to the narrator.

Choice D is incorrect. The passage is more about the impact of art on life than about the impact of life on art.

Remember: when asked to find the main idea, be sure to check the opening and summary sentences of each paragraph.

16. **D** The terrible robbers in the pond world are the cruel creatures that, in the course of the struggle to exist, devour their fellows.

17. **D** Here, "catch" is used as in fishing: "a good catch of fish." Suppose you want to collect a sample of pond-dwellers. You lower a jar into the nearest pond and capture a random batch of creatures swimming by—fish, tadpoles, full-grown insects, larvae—in other words, a "mixed catch."

18. **B** The opening paragraph states that the introduction of the *Dytiscus* larvae to the aquarium will result in a struggle for existence in which the larvae will destroy their prey. The larvae, thus, are predators (hunters of prey). This suggests that their presence

would be of particular interest to naturalists studying predatory patterns at work within a closed environment such as an aquarium.

19. **C** The author is describing how the *Dytiscus* larva looks: slim body, six legs, flat head, huge jaws.

Choice A is incorrect. All the details indicate the author is describing the killer, not the victim.

20. **D** Though the passage mentions amphibians—tadpoles—and food, it states that the tadpoles provide food for the larvae, not vice versa. The passage nowhere states that the larvae are a source of food for amphibians.
Choice A is incorrect. The passage states that the larvae secrete digestive juices; it mentions secretion in line 28.
Choice B is incorrect. The passage states that the larvae attack one another; they seize and devour their own breed (lines 42–49).
Choice C is incorrect. The passage states that the larvae are attracted to motion; prey for them "is all that moves."
Choice E is incorrect. The passage states that the larvae have ravenous appetites: their "voracity" is unique.
Remember: when asked about specific information in the passage, spot key words in the question and scan the passage to find them (or their synonyms).

21. **E** Digesting "out of doors" refers to the larva's external conversion of food into absorbable form. Look at the sentence immediately following line 28. Break down the process step by step. The larva injects a secretion into the victim. The secretion dissolves the victim's "entire inside." That is the start of the digestive process. It takes place inside the victim's body; in other words, *outside* the larva's body—"out of doors." Only then does the larva begin to suck up the dissolved juices of his prey.

22. **D** Choice D is correct. You can arrive at it by the process of elimination. Statement I is true. The inside of the victim "becomes opaque" (line 36); it increases in opacity. Therefore, you can eliminate Choices B, C, and E. Statement II is also true. As the victim is drained, its body shrivels or "shrinks to a limp bundle of skin." Therefore, you can eliminate choice A. Statement III has to be untrue. The victim's head must stay on; otherwise, the dissolving interior would leak out. Only Choice D is left. It is the correct answer.

23. **D** The author mentions rats because a rat will attack and devour other rats. He is sure rodents do this; he's not sure any other animals do so. Thus, he mentions rats and related rodents to point up an uncommon characteristic also found in Dytiscus larvae.

24. **A** In line 52 the author mentions some "observations of which I shall speak later." These observations deal with whether wolves try to devour other wolves. Thus, the author clearly intends to discuss the likelihood of cannibalism among wolves.
    In answering questions about what may be discussed in subsequent sections of the text, pay particular attention to words that are similar in meaning to subsequent: *following, succeeding, successive, later.*

Section 7 Mathematical Reasoning

MULTIPLE-CHOICE QUESTIONS

1. **D** $3|x| + 2 < 17 \Rightarrow 3|x| < 15 \Rightarrow |x| < 5$. There are **9** integers whose absolute values are less than 5: $-4, -3, -2, -1, 0, 1, 2, 3, 4$.

2. **E** Set up a proportion:

$$\frac{1 \text{ meter}}{1 \text{ second}} = \frac{k \text{ kilometers}}{1 \text{ hour}} = \frac{1000k \text{ meters}}{60 \text{ minutes}} =$$

$$\frac{1000k \text{ meters}}{3600 \text{ seconds}} = \frac{10k \text{ meters}}{36 \text{ seconds}}$$

   Cross-multiplying the first and last ratios, you get $10k = 36$, and so $k = \mathbf{3.6}$.

3. **C** $f(-8) = (-8)^2 + \sqrt[3]{-8} = 64 + (-2) = \mathbf{62}$

4. **D** Pick easy-to-use numbers. Assume that, in 1994, 200 boys and 100 girls earned varsity letters. Then, in 2004, there were 150 boys and 125 girls. The ratio of girls to boys was

$$125{:}150 = 5{:}6 \text{ or } \frac{5}{6}.$$

5. **C** The days of the week form a repeating sequence with 7 terms in the set that repeats. The nth term is the same as the rth term, where r is the remainder when n is divided by 7.

   $500 \div 7 = 71.428\ldots \Rightarrow$ the quotient is 71.

   $71 \times 7 = 497$ and $500 - 497 = 3 \Rightarrow$ the remainder is 3.

   Therefore, 500 days from Saturday will be the same day as 3 days from Saturday, namely **Tuesday**.

6. **C** The area of rectangle $ABCD = (4)(6) = 24$.

   The area of right triangle $DAB = \frac{1}{2}(4)(6) = 12$, and the area of right triangle $ECF = \frac{1}{2}(2)(2) = 2$.

   Therefore, the area of quadrilateral $BDEF = 24 - 12 - 2 = 10$. Then the shaded area is $\frac{10}{24} = \frac{5}{12}$ the area of the rectangle, and so the required probability is $\frac{5}{12}$.

7. **B** The easiest observation is that, if adding a fourth number, d, to a set doesn't change the average, then d is equal to the existing average. If you don't realize that, solve for d:

   $$\frac{a+b+c+d}{4} = \frac{a+b+c}{3} \Rightarrow$$
   $$3a + 3b + 3c + 3d = 4a + 4b + 4c \Rightarrow$$
   $$3d = a + b + c \Rightarrow d = \frac{a+b+c}{3}.$$

8. **A** If Meri earned a grade of A, she missed $(100 - A)$ points. In adjusting the grades, the teacher decided to deduct only half that number:

   $\frac{100-A}{2}$, so Meri's new grade was

   $$100 - \left(\frac{100-A}{2}\right) = 100 - 50 + \frac{A}{2} = 50 + \frac{A}{2}.$$

GRID-IN QUESTIONS

9. (152)   Normally, to get 60 pencils you would need to buy 20 sets of three at 25 cents per set, a total expenditure of $20 \times 25 = 500$ cents. On sale, you could get 60 pencils by buying 12 sets of five at 29 cents per set, for a total cost of $12 \times 29 = 348$ cents. This is a savings of $500 - 348 = \textbf{152}$ cents.

10. (any decimal between 2.01 and 2.33 or $\frac{13}{6}$)

It is given that: $1 < 3x - 5 < 2$

Add 5 to each expression: $6 < 3x < 7$

Divide each expression by 3: $2 < x < \frac{7}{3}$

Grid in any decimal number or fraction between 2 and 2.33: **2.1**, for example, or

$\frac{\textbf{13}}{\textbf{6}}$, which is the average of $2 = \frac{12}{6}$ and $\frac{7}{3} = \frac{14}{6}$.

11. (8100) $x < 10,000 \Rightarrow \sqrt{x} < \sqrt{10,000} = 100 \Rightarrow$

$$\frac{\sqrt{x}}{5} < \frac{100}{5} = 20$$

Since $\frac{\sqrt{x}}{5}$ must be an even integer, the greatest possible value

of $\frac{\sqrt{x}}{5}$ is 18:

$$\frac{\sqrt{x}}{5} = 18 \Rightarrow \sqrt{x} = 90 \Rightarrow x = \textbf{8100}.$$

12. (202)   After 33 repetitions of the pattern—red, white, white, blue, blue, blue—there will be $6 \times 33 = 198$ marbles in the box, of which 99 will be blue. When these are followed by 4 more marbles (1 red, 2 whites, and 1 blue), there will be 100 blue marbles, and a total of $198 + 4 = \textbf{202}$ marbles in all.

13. (28) Whether or not you can visualize (or draw) the second (large) square, you can calculate its area. The area of each of the four triangles is $\frac{1}{2}(3)(4) = 6$, for a total of 24, and the area of the 5×5 square is 25. Then, the area of the large square is $24 + 25 = 49$. Each side of the square is 7, and the perimeter is **28**.

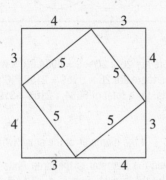

14. $\left(\dfrac{1}{32}\right)$ $\ll 3 \gg - \ll 4 \gg = \dfrac{1}{2^{3+1}} - \dfrac{1}{2^{4+1}} = \dfrac{1}{2^4} - \dfrac{1}{2^5} =$

$$\frac{1}{16} - \frac{1}{32} = \frac{1}{\mathbf{32}}.$$

15. $\left(\dfrac{1}{8}\right)$ $\ll a + 3 \gg \, : \, \ll a \gg = \dfrac{1}{2^{(a+3)+1}} : \dfrac{1}{2^{a+1}} = \dfrac{1}{2^{a+4}} : \dfrac{1}{2^{a+1}} =$

$$\frac{1}{2^{a+4}} \div \frac{1}{2^{a+1}} = \frac{1}{2^{a+4}} \times \frac{2^{a+1}}{1} = \frac{1}{2^3} = \frac{1}{\mathbf{8}}.$$

16. (19) There are at most 14 blank cards, so at least 86 of the 100 cards have one or both of the letters A and C on them. If x is the number of cards with both letters on them, then

$$75 + 30 - x \leq 86 \implies x \leq 105 - 86 = \mathbf{19}.$$

This is illustrated in the Venn diagram below.

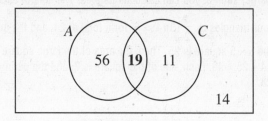

17. (8190)   There are $26 \times 26 \times 9 = 6084$ PIC's with two letters and one digit, and there are $26 \times 9 \times 9 = 2106$ PIC's with one letter and two digits, for a total of $6084 + 2106 = $ **8190**.

18. $\left(\dfrac{3}{8} \text{ or } .375 \right)$ If the diameter of the small white circle is d, then the diameter of the large white circle is $3d$, and the diameter of the largest circle is $d + 3d = 4d$. Then the ratio of the diameters, and hence of the radii, of the three circles is 4:3:1. Assume the radii are 4, 3, and 1. Then the areas of the circles are 16π, 9π, and π. The sum of the areas of the white circles is 10π, the shaded region is $16\pi - 10\pi = 6\pi$, and $\dfrac{6\pi}{16\pi} = \dfrac{3}{8}$.

Section 8 Critical Reading

1. **A** Voles are similar to mice; however, they are also different from them, and so may be *distinguished from* them.
   Note how the use of "although" in the opening phrase sets up the basic contrast here.   (Contrast Signal)

2. **C** Because Dr. Drew's method proved *effective*, it became a *model* for other systems.
   Remember to watch for signal words that link one part of the sentence to another. The "so...that" structure signals cause and effect.   (Cause and Effect Signal)

3. **B** The fact that the languages of the Mediterranean area were markedly (strikingly) alike eased or *facilitated* the movement of people and ideas from country to country.
   Note how the specific examples in the second part of the sentence clarify the idea stated in the first part.   (Examples)

4. **E** Feeling that a job has *no point* might well lead a person to perform it in a *perfunctory* (indifferent or mechanical) manner. Remember: watch for signal words that link one part of the sentence to another. "Because" in the opening clause is a cause signal. (Cause and Effect Signal)

5. **B** Nelson remained calm; he was in control in spite of the panic of battle. In other words, he was *imperturbable*, not capable of being agitated or perturbed.
Note how the phrase "in spite of" signals the contrast between the subject's calm and the surrounding panic. (Contrast Signal)

6. **E** Despite his hard work trying to solve the problem, the solution was not the *result* or outcome of his labor. Instead, it was *fortuitous* or accidental.
Remember to watch for signal words that link one part of the sentence to another. The use of the "was...and not..." structure sets up a contrast. The missing words must be antonyms or near-antonyms. (Contrast Pattern)

7. **E** The italicized introduction states that the author has had his manuscript rejected by his publisher. He is consigning or committing it to a desk drawer *to set it aside as unmarketable.*

8. **B** The rejected author identifies with these baseball players, who constantly must face "failure." *He sees he is not alone in having to confront failure and move on.*

9. **B** The author uses the jogger's comment to make a point about the *mental impact Henderson's home run must have had on Moore.* He reasons that, if each step a runner takes sends so many complex messages to the brain, then Henderson's ninth-inning home run must have flooded Moore's brain with messages, impressing its image indelibly in Moore's mind.

10. **D** The author is talking of the impact of Henderson's home run on Moore. Registering in Moore's mind, the home run *made an impression* on him.

11. **C** The author looks on himself as someone who "to succeed at all...must perform at an extraordinary level of excellence." This level of achievement, he maintains, is not demanded of accountants, plumbers, and insurance salesmen, and he seems to pride himself on belonging to a profession that requires excellence. Thus, his attitude to members of less demanding professions can best be described as *superior.*

12. **A** The description of the writer defying his pain and extending himself irrationally to create a "masterpiece" despite the rejections of critics and publishers is a highly romantic one that elevates *the writer as someone heroic in his or her accomplishments.*

13. **C** The author of Passage 2 discusses the advantages of his ability to concentrate. Clearly, he prizes *his ability to focus* on the task at hand.

14. **B** When one football team is ahead of another by several touchdowns and there seems to be no way for the second team to catch up, the outcome of the game appears *decided* or settled.

15. **E** The "larger point of view" focuses on what to most people is the big question: the outcome of the game. The author is indifferent to this larger point of view. Concentrating on his own performance, he is *more concerned with the task at hand than with* winning or losing the game.

16. **C** Parade ground drill clearly does not entirely prepare a soldier for the reality of war. It does so only "to an extent." By using this phrase, the author *qualifies* his *statement*, making it less absolute.

17. **C** One would expect someone who dismisses or rejects most comparisons of athletics to art to avoid making such comparisons. The author, however, *is making such a comparison.* This reversal of what would have been expected is an instance of irony.

18. **C** To learn to overcome failure, to learn to give one's all in performance, to learn to focus on the work of the moment, to learn to have "the selfish intensity" that can block out the rest of the world—these are *hard lessons* that *both athletes and artists learn.*

19. **D** Throughout Passage 2, the author stresses the advantages and the power of concentration. He believes that a person who *focuses on the job at hand*, rather than dwelling on past failures, will continue to function successfully. Thus, this author is not particularly swayed by the Passage 1 author's contention that a failure such as giving up a key home run can destroy an athlete.

Section 9 Mathematical Reasoning

1. **C** Replacing y by $2x$ in the equation $x + y + 30 = 180$, you get

   $x + 2x + 30 = 180 \Rightarrow 3x = 150 \Rightarrow x = 50 \Rightarrow y = 2x = \mathbf{100}$.

2. **C** The temperature rose $8 - (-7) = 8 + 7 = 15°$ in 1.5 hours. The average hourly increase was $15° \div 1.5 = \mathbf{10°}$.

3. **D** The expression $n^2 - 30$ is negative whenever $n^2 < 30$. This is true for all integers between -5 and 5 inclusive, **11** in all.

4. **D** The only thing to do is to test each set of values to see which ones work and which one doesn't. In this case, choice D, $\boldsymbol{a = 3}$ **and** $\boldsymbol{b = -4}$, does not work:
   $2(3)^2 + 3(-4) = 18 - 12 = 6$, not 5.
   The other choices all work.

5. **A** The slope of the line, ℓ, that passes through $(-2, 2)$ and $(3, 3)$ is

   $\dfrac{3 - 2}{3 - (-2)} = \dfrac{1}{5}$. The slope of any line perpendicular to ℓ is **−5**.

6. **C** For some number x, the measures of the angles are x, $2x$, and $3x$; so

   $$180 = x + 2x + 3x = 6x \Rightarrow x = 30.$$

   Therefore, the triangle is a 30-60-90 triangle, and the ratio of the sides is **1**: $\sqrt{3}$:**2**.

7. **D** By definition, a googol is equal to 10^{100}. Therefore,

   $g^2 = 10^{100} \times 10^{100} = 10^{200}$, which, when it is written out, is the digit 1 followed by 200 zeros, creating an integer with **201** digits.

8. **E** The graph of $y = f(x - 3)$ is the graph of $y = f(x)$ shifted 3 units to the right, as shown in Choice D. The graph of $y = -f(x - 3)$ reflects Choice D in the x-axis, resulting in graph **E**.

9. **A** Since $C = 2\pi r$, then $r = \dfrac{C}{2\pi}$, and the area of the circle is

   $$\pi r^2 = \pi \left(\dfrac{C}{2\pi} \right)^2 = \pi \left(\dfrac{C^2}{4\pi^2} \right) = \dfrac{C^2}{4\pi}.$$

10. **B** $\left(4^{\frac{1}{2}} \cdot 8^{\frac{1}{3}} \cdot 16^{\frac{1}{4}} \cdot 32^{\frac{1}{5}}\right)^{\frac{1}{2}} = (\sqrt{4} \cdot \sqrt[3]{8} \cdot \sqrt[4]{16} \cdot \sqrt[5]{32})^{\frac{1}{2}} =$

$= (2 \cdot 2 \cdot 2 \cdot 2)^{\frac{1}{2}} = 16^{\frac{1}{2}} = \sqrt{16} = \mathbf{4}.$

11. **C** $\sqrt{x - 15} - 5 = 2 \Rightarrow \sqrt{x - 15} = 7 \Rightarrow x - 15 = 49 \Rightarrow$

$x = 64 \Rightarrow \sqrt{x} = \sqrt{64} = \mathbf{8}.$

12. **E** Joanna needed to drive the m miles in $h + \dfrac{1}{2}$ hours. Since $r = \dfrac{d}{t}$,

to find her rate, you divide the distance, m, by the time,

$\left(h + \dfrac{1}{2}\right)$:

$$\frac{m}{h + \dfrac{1}{2}} = \frac{2m}{2h + 1}.$$

13. **A** In the figure below, the area of $\triangle BFC$ is $\dfrac{1}{2}(4)(5) = 10$. Then the

area of the shaded quadrilateral is 10 minus the areas of square
$ADEF\,(4)$ and triangle $CDE\,(2)$: $10 - 4 - 2 = \mathbf{4}.$

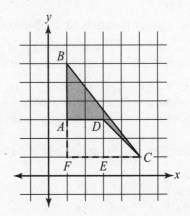

14. **D** Since y is inversely proportional to x, there is a constant k such that $xy = k$. Then $k = (4)(10) = 40$, and $40 = x(20) \Rightarrow x = 2$.

Also, since y is directly proportional to z, there is a constant m such that $\dfrac{y}{z} = m$, so $m = \dfrac{10}{8} = \dfrac{5}{4}$.

Then
$$\frac{5}{4} = \frac{20}{z} \Rightarrow 5z = 80 \Rightarrow z = 16,$$
and so
$$x + z = 2 + 16 = \mathbf{18}.$$

15. **E** To find the average of three numbers, divide their sum by 3:

$\dfrac{3^{30} + 3^{60} + 3^{90}}{3}$. To simplify this fraction, divide each term in

the numerator by 3:
$$\frac{3^{30} + 3^{60} + 3^{90}}{3} = \mathbf{3^{29} + 3^{59} + 3^{89}}.$$

16. **D**

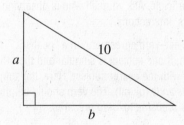

By the Pythagorean theorem,
$$a^2 + b^2 = 10^2 = 100;$$

and since the area is 20, $\dfrac{1}{2} ab = 20 \Rightarrow ab = 40$, and $2ab = 80$.

Expand:
$$(a + b)^2 = a^2 + 2ab + b^2 = (a^2 + b^2) + 2ab.$$

Then
$$(a^2 + b^2) + 2ab = 100 + 80 = \mathbf{180}.$$

Section 10 Writing Skills

1. **D** Error in logical comparison. Compare voices with voices, not voices with singers.

2. **C** Run-on sentence. Choice C corrects the error by turning the initial clause ("The ... blackboard") into a participial phrase ("After ... blackboard") and changing the subject of the main clause from *he* to *the mathematics teacher*.

3. **C** Error in usage. Do not use *when* after *is* in making a definition.

4. **D** Shift in number. The subject, *students,* is plural; the subject complement should be plural as well. Change *tumbler* to *tumblers*.

5. **E** Lack of parallelism. The "both ... and" construction provides parallel structure.

6. **B** Wordiness. Choice B makes the writer's point simply and concisely.

7. **C** Error in logical comparison. Compare audiences with audiences, not with theaters.

8. **D** Dangling participle. Ask yourself who is observing the preschoolers' interactions.

9. **E** Error in subject–verb agreement. In a "neither ... nor" construction, if one subject is singular and the other is plural, the verb agrees with the nearer subject. Here, the subject nearer to the verb is *islands* (plural). The verb should be plural as well. Change *was prepared* to *were prepared*.

10. **A** Sentence is correct.

11. **A** Sentence is correct.

12. **E** Lack of parallelism. Choice E has parallel structure.

13. **C** Error in subject–verb agreement. The subject, *demand*, is singular; the verb should be singular as well. Change *are* to *is*.

14. **D** Sentence fragment. Choice D economically corrects the fragment.

ANSWER SHEETS—TEST 2

Section 1

To write your essay, use the front and back of one sheet of standard-ruled loose-leaf paper.

If any section has more answer spaces than questions, leave the extra spaces blank.

Section 2

1 Ⓐ Ⓑ Ⓒ Ⓓ Ⓔ	10 Ⓐ Ⓑ Ⓒ Ⓓ Ⓔ	19 Ⓐ Ⓑ Ⓒ Ⓓ Ⓔ
2 Ⓐ Ⓑ Ⓒ Ⓓ Ⓔ	11 Ⓐ Ⓑ Ⓒ Ⓓ Ⓔ	20 Ⓐ Ⓑ Ⓒ Ⓓ Ⓔ
3 Ⓐ Ⓑ Ⓒ Ⓓ Ⓔ	12 Ⓐ Ⓑ Ⓒ Ⓓ Ⓔ	21 Ⓐ Ⓑ Ⓒ Ⓓ Ⓔ
4 Ⓐ Ⓑ Ⓒ Ⓓ Ⓔ	13 Ⓐ Ⓑ Ⓒ Ⓓ Ⓔ	22 Ⓐ Ⓑ Ⓒ Ⓓ Ⓔ
5 Ⓐ Ⓑ Ⓒ Ⓓ Ⓔ	14 Ⓐ Ⓑ Ⓒ Ⓓ Ⓔ	23 Ⓐ Ⓑ Ⓒ Ⓓ Ⓔ
6 Ⓐ Ⓑ Ⓒ Ⓓ Ⓔ	15 Ⓐ Ⓑ Ⓒ Ⓓ Ⓔ	24 Ⓐ Ⓑ Ⓒ Ⓓ Ⓔ
7 Ⓐ Ⓑ Ⓒ Ⓓ Ⓔ	16 Ⓐ Ⓑ Ⓒ Ⓓ Ⓔ	25 Ⓐ Ⓑ Ⓒ Ⓓ Ⓔ
8 Ⓐ Ⓑ Ⓒ Ⓓ Ⓔ	17 Ⓐ Ⓑ Ⓒ Ⓓ Ⓔ	
9 Ⓐ Ⓑ Ⓒ Ⓓ Ⓔ	18 Ⓐ Ⓑ Ⓒ Ⓓ Ⓔ	

Section 3

1 Ⓐ Ⓑ Ⓒ Ⓓ Ⓔ	10 Ⓐ Ⓑ Ⓒ Ⓓ Ⓔ	19 Ⓐ Ⓑ Ⓒ Ⓓ Ⓔ
2 Ⓐ Ⓑ Ⓒ Ⓓ Ⓔ	11 Ⓐ Ⓑ Ⓒ Ⓓ Ⓔ	20 Ⓐ Ⓑ Ⓒ Ⓓ Ⓔ
3 Ⓐ Ⓑ Ⓒ Ⓓ Ⓔ	12 Ⓐ Ⓑ Ⓒ Ⓓ Ⓔ	21 Ⓐ Ⓑ Ⓒ Ⓓ Ⓔ
4 Ⓐ Ⓑ Ⓒ Ⓓ Ⓔ	13 Ⓐ Ⓑ Ⓒ Ⓓ Ⓔ	22 Ⓐ Ⓑ Ⓒ Ⓓ Ⓔ
5 Ⓐ Ⓑ Ⓒ Ⓓ Ⓔ	14 Ⓐ Ⓑ Ⓒ Ⓓ Ⓔ	23 Ⓐ Ⓑ Ⓒ Ⓓ Ⓔ
6 Ⓐ Ⓑ Ⓒ Ⓓ Ⓔ	15 Ⓐ Ⓑ Ⓒ Ⓓ Ⓔ	24 Ⓐ Ⓑ Ⓒ Ⓓ Ⓔ
7 Ⓐ Ⓑ Ⓒ Ⓓ Ⓔ	16 Ⓐ Ⓑ Ⓒ Ⓓ Ⓔ	25 Ⓐ Ⓑ Ⓒ Ⓓ Ⓔ
8 Ⓐ Ⓑ Ⓒ Ⓓ Ⓔ	17 Ⓐ Ⓑ Ⓒ Ⓓ Ⓔ	
9 Ⓐ Ⓑ Ⓒ Ⓓ Ⓔ	18 Ⓐ Ⓑ Ⓒ Ⓓ Ⓔ	

ANSWER SHEETS—TEST 2

Section 4

1 Ⓐ Ⓑ Ⓒ Ⓓ Ⓔ	13 Ⓐ Ⓑ Ⓒ Ⓓ Ⓔ	25 Ⓐ Ⓑ Ⓒ Ⓓ Ⓔ
2 Ⓐ Ⓑ Ⓒ Ⓓ Ⓔ	14 Ⓐ Ⓑ Ⓒ Ⓓ Ⓔ	26 Ⓐ Ⓑ Ⓒ Ⓓ Ⓔ
3 Ⓐ Ⓑ Ⓒ Ⓓ Ⓔ	15 Ⓐ Ⓑ Ⓒ Ⓓ Ⓔ	27 Ⓐ Ⓑ Ⓒ Ⓓ Ⓔ
4 Ⓐ Ⓑ Ⓒ Ⓓ Ⓔ	16 Ⓐ Ⓑ Ⓒ Ⓓ Ⓔ	28 Ⓐ Ⓑ Ⓒ Ⓓ Ⓔ
5 Ⓐ Ⓑ Ⓒ Ⓓ Ⓔ	17 Ⓐ Ⓑ Ⓒ Ⓓ Ⓔ	29 Ⓐ Ⓑ Ⓒ Ⓓ Ⓔ
6 Ⓐ Ⓑ Ⓒ Ⓓ Ⓔ	18 Ⓐ Ⓑ Ⓒ Ⓓ Ⓔ	30 Ⓐ Ⓑ Ⓒ Ⓓ Ⓔ
7 Ⓐ Ⓑ Ⓒ Ⓓ Ⓔ	19 Ⓐ Ⓑ Ⓒ Ⓓ Ⓔ	31 Ⓐ Ⓑ Ⓒ Ⓓ Ⓔ
8 Ⓐ Ⓑ Ⓒ Ⓓ Ⓔ	20 Ⓐ Ⓑ Ⓒ Ⓓ Ⓔ	32 Ⓐ Ⓑ Ⓒ Ⓓ Ⓔ
9 Ⓐ Ⓑ Ⓒ Ⓓ Ⓔ	21 Ⓐ Ⓑ Ⓒ Ⓓ Ⓔ	33 Ⓐ Ⓑ Ⓒ Ⓓ Ⓔ
10 Ⓐ Ⓑ Ⓒ Ⓓ Ⓔ	22 Ⓐ Ⓑ Ⓒ Ⓓ Ⓔ	34 Ⓐ Ⓑ Ⓒ Ⓓ Ⓔ
11 Ⓐ Ⓑ Ⓒ Ⓓ Ⓔ	23 Ⓐ Ⓑ Ⓒ Ⓓ Ⓔ	35 Ⓐ Ⓑ Ⓒ Ⓓ Ⓔ
12 Ⓐ Ⓑ Ⓒ Ⓓ Ⓔ	24 Ⓐ Ⓑ Ⓒ Ⓓ Ⓔ	

Section 6

1 Ⓐ Ⓑ Ⓒ Ⓓ Ⓔ	4 Ⓐ Ⓑ Ⓒ Ⓓ Ⓔ	7 Ⓐ Ⓑ Ⓒ Ⓓ Ⓔ
2 Ⓐ Ⓑ Ⓒ Ⓓ Ⓔ	5 Ⓐ Ⓑ Ⓒ Ⓓ Ⓔ	8 Ⓐ Ⓑ Ⓒ Ⓓ Ⓔ
3 Ⓐ Ⓑ Ⓒ Ⓓ Ⓔ	6 Ⓐ Ⓑ Ⓒ Ⓓ Ⓔ	

ANSWER SHEETS—TEST 2

Section 6 (continued)

9

10

11

12

13

14

15

16

ANSWER SHEETS—TEST 2

Section 6 (continued)

17

	⊘	⊘	
⊙	⊙	⊙	⊙
	⓪	⓪	⓪
①	①	①	①
②	②	②	②
③	③	③	③
④	④	④	④
⑤	⑤	⑤	⑤
⑥	⑥	⑥	⑥
⑦	⑦	⑦	⑦
⑧	⑧	⑧	⑧
⑨	⑨	⑨	⑨

18

	⊘	⊘	
⊙	⊙	⊙	⊙
	⓪	⓪	⓪
①	①	①	①
②	②	②	②
③	③	③	③
④	④	④	④
⑤	⑤	⑤	⑤
⑥	⑥	⑥	⑥
⑦	⑦	⑦	⑦
⑧	⑧	⑧	⑧
⑨	⑨	⑨	⑨

Section 7

1 Ⓐ Ⓑ Ⓒ Ⓓ Ⓔ   10 Ⓐ Ⓑ Ⓒ Ⓓ Ⓔ   19 Ⓐ Ⓑ Ⓒ Ⓓ Ⓔ
2 Ⓐ Ⓑ Ⓒ Ⓓ Ⓔ   11 Ⓐ Ⓑ Ⓒ Ⓓ Ⓔ   20 Ⓐ Ⓑ Ⓒ Ⓓ Ⓔ
3 Ⓐ Ⓑ Ⓒ Ⓓ Ⓔ   12 Ⓐ Ⓑ Ⓒ Ⓓ Ⓔ   21 Ⓐ Ⓑ Ⓒ Ⓓ Ⓔ
4 Ⓐ Ⓑ Ⓒ Ⓓ Ⓔ   13 Ⓐ Ⓑ Ⓒ Ⓓ Ⓔ   22 Ⓐ Ⓑ Ⓒ Ⓓ Ⓔ
5 Ⓐ Ⓑ Ⓒ Ⓓ Ⓔ   14 Ⓐ Ⓑ Ⓒ Ⓓ Ⓔ   23 Ⓐ Ⓑ Ⓒ Ⓓ Ⓔ
6 Ⓐ Ⓑ Ⓒ Ⓓ Ⓔ   15 Ⓐ Ⓑ Ⓒ Ⓓ Ⓔ   24 Ⓐ Ⓑ Ⓒ Ⓓ Ⓔ
7 Ⓐ Ⓑ Ⓒ Ⓓ Ⓔ   16 Ⓐ Ⓑ Ⓒ Ⓓ Ⓔ   25 Ⓐ Ⓑ Ⓒ Ⓓ Ⓔ
8 Ⓐ Ⓑ Ⓒ Ⓓ Ⓔ   17 Ⓐ Ⓑ Ⓒ Ⓓ Ⓔ
9 Ⓐ Ⓑ Ⓒ Ⓓ Ⓔ   18 Ⓐ Ⓑ Ⓒ Ⓓ Ⓔ

ANSWER SHEETS—TEST 2

Section 8

1 Ⓐ Ⓑ Ⓒ Ⓓ Ⓔ	10 Ⓐ Ⓑ Ⓒ Ⓓ Ⓔ	19 Ⓐ Ⓑ Ⓒ Ⓓ Ⓔ
2 Ⓐ Ⓑ Ⓒ Ⓓ Ⓔ	11 Ⓐ Ⓑ Ⓒ Ⓓ Ⓔ	20 Ⓐ Ⓑ Ⓒ Ⓓ Ⓔ
3 Ⓐ Ⓑ Ⓒ Ⓓ Ⓔ	12 Ⓐ Ⓑ Ⓒ Ⓓ Ⓔ	21 Ⓐ Ⓑ Ⓒ Ⓓ Ⓔ
4 Ⓐ Ⓑ Ⓒ Ⓓ Ⓔ	13 Ⓐ Ⓑ Ⓒ Ⓓ Ⓔ	22 Ⓐ Ⓑ Ⓒ Ⓓ Ⓔ
5 Ⓐ Ⓑ Ⓒ Ⓓ Ⓔ	14 Ⓐ Ⓑ Ⓒ Ⓓ Ⓔ	23 Ⓐ Ⓑ Ⓒ Ⓓ Ⓔ
6 Ⓐ Ⓑ Ⓒ Ⓓ Ⓔ	15 Ⓐ Ⓑ Ⓒ Ⓓ Ⓔ	24 Ⓐ Ⓑ Ⓒ Ⓓ Ⓔ
7 Ⓐ Ⓑ Ⓒ Ⓓ Ⓔ	16 Ⓐ Ⓑ Ⓒ Ⓓ Ⓔ	25 Ⓐ Ⓑ Ⓒ Ⓓ Ⓔ
8 Ⓐ Ⓑ Ⓒ Ⓓ Ⓔ	17 Ⓐ Ⓑ Ⓒ Ⓓ Ⓔ	
9 Ⓐ Ⓑ Ⓒ Ⓓ Ⓔ	18 Ⓐ Ⓑ Ⓒ Ⓓ Ⓔ	

Section 9

1 Ⓐ Ⓑ Ⓒ Ⓓ Ⓔ	8 Ⓐ Ⓑ Ⓒ Ⓓ Ⓔ	15 Ⓐ Ⓑ Ⓒ Ⓓ Ⓔ
2 Ⓐ Ⓑ Ⓒ Ⓓ Ⓔ	9 Ⓐ Ⓑ Ⓒ Ⓓ Ⓔ	16 Ⓐ Ⓑ Ⓒ Ⓓ Ⓔ
3 Ⓐ Ⓑ Ⓒ Ⓓ Ⓔ	10 Ⓐ Ⓑ Ⓒ Ⓓ Ⓔ	17 Ⓐ Ⓑ Ⓒ Ⓓ Ⓔ
4 Ⓐ Ⓑ Ⓒ Ⓓ Ⓔ	11 Ⓐ Ⓑ Ⓒ Ⓓ Ⓔ	18 Ⓐ Ⓑ Ⓒ Ⓓ Ⓔ
5 Ⓐ Ⓑ Ⓒ Ⓓ Ⓔ	12 Ⓐ Ⓑ Ⓒ Ⓓ Ⓔ	19 Ⓐ Ⓑ Ⓒ Ⓓ Ⓔ
6 Ⓐ Ⓑ Ⓒ Ⓓ Ⓔ	13 Ⓐ Ⓑ Ⓒ Ⓓ Ⓔ	20 Ⓐ Ⓑ Ⓒ Ⓓ Ⓔ
7 Ⓐ Ⓑ Ⓒ Ⓓ Ⓔ	14 Ⓐ Ⓑ Ⓒ Ⓓ Ⓔ	

Section 10

1 Ⓐ Ⓑ Ⓒ Ⓓ Ⓔ	6 Ⓐ Ⓑ Ⓒ Ⓓ Ⓔ	11 Ⓐ Ⓑ Ⓒ Ⓓ Ⓔ
2 Ⓐ Ⓑ Ⓒ Ⓓ Ⓔ	7 Ⓐ Ⓑ Ⓒ Ⓓ Ⓔ	12 Ⓐ Ⓑ Ⓒ Ⓓ Ⓔ
3 Ⓐ Ⓑ Ⓒ Ⓓ Ⓔ	8 Ⓐ Ⓑ Ⓒ Ⓓ Ⓔ	13 Ⓐ Ⓑ Ⓒ Ⓓ Ⓔ
4 Ⓐ Ⓑ Ⓒ Ⓓ Ⓔ	9 Ⓐ Ⓑ Ⓒ Ⓓ Ⓔ	14 Ⓐ Ⓑ Ⓒ Ⓓ Ⓔ
5 Ⓐ Ⓑ Ⓒ Ⓓ Ⓔ	10 Ⓐ Ⓑ Ⓒ Ⓓ Ⓔ	15 Ⓐ Ⓑ Ⓒ Ⓓ Ⓔ

PRACTICE TEST 2
SECTION 1

ESSAY
Time allowed: 25 Minutes

Turn to your answer sheet and write your essay on the lined portion of the page. To receive credit, you must write your essay in the area provided.

Write on the assigned topic below. If you write on any other topic, your essay will be given a score of zero.

Write or print legibly: your readers will be unfamiliar with your handwriting, and you want them to be able to read what you write.

The excerpt appearing below makes a point about a particular topic. Read the passage carefully, and think about the assignment that follows.

Each fresh crisis we encounter is an opportunity in disguise.

ASSIGNMENT: What are your thoughts on the statement above? Compose an essay in which you express your views on this topic. Your essay may support, refute, or qualify the view expressed in the statement. What you write, however, must be relevant to the topic under discussion. Additionally, you must support your viewpoint, indicating your reasoning and providing examples based on your studies and/or experience.

PRACTICE TEST 2
SECTION 2

24 Questions—25 Minutes

Select the best answer to each of the following questions; then blacken the appropriate space on your answer sheet.

Each of the following sentences contains one or two blanks; each blank indicates that a word or set of words has been left out. Below the sentence are five words or phrases, lettered A through E. Select the word or set of words that best completes the sentence.

Example:

Fame is ----; today's rising star is all too soon. tomorrow's washed-up has-been.

(A) rewarding   (B) gradual   (C) essential
(D) spontaneous   (E) transitory

1. Archaeologists are involved in ---- Mayan temples in Central America, uncovering the old ruins in order to learn more about the civilization they represent.

(A) demolishing   (B) incapacitating   (C) excavating
(D) worshiping   (E) adapting

2. Afraid that the ---- nature of the plays being presented would corrupt the morals of their audiences, the Puritans closed the theaters in 1642.

   (A) mediocre
   (B) fantastic
   (C) profound
   (D) lewd
   (E) witty

3. The governor's imposition of martial law on the once-peaceful community was the last straw, so far as the lawmakers were concerned: the legislature refused to function until martial law was ----.

   (A) reaffirmed   (B) reiterated   (C) inaugurated
     (D) rescinded   (E) prolonged

4. The sergeant suspected that the private was ---- in order to avoid going on the ---- march scheduled for that morning.

   (A) malingering..arduous
   (B) proselytizing..interminable
   (C) invalidating..threatened
   (D) exemplary..leisurely
   (E) disgruntled..strenuous

5. The incidence of smoking among women, formerly ----, has grown to such a degree that lung cancer, once a minor problem, has become the chief ---- of cancer-related deaths among women.

   (A) negligible..cause
   (B) minor..antidote
   (C) preeminent..cure
   (D) relevant..modifier
   (E) pervasive..opponent

6. The columnist was almost ---- when he mentioned his friends, but he was unpleasant and even ---- when he discussed people who irritated him.

   (A) recalcitrant..laconic
   (B) reverential..acrimonious
   (C) sensitive..remorseful
   (D) insipid..militant
   (E) benevolent..stoical

7. An experienced politician who knew better than to launch a campaign in troubled political waters, she intended to wait for a more ---- occasion before she announced her plans.

   (A) propitious
   (B) provocative
   (C) unseemly
   (D) questionable
   (E) theoretical

8. In one instance illustrating Metternich's consuming ----, he employed several naval captains to purchase books abroad for him, eventually adding an entire Oriental library to his ---- collection.

   (A) foresight..indifferent
   (B) altruism..eclectic
   (C) bibliomania..burgeoning
   (D) avarice..inadvertent
   (E) egocentricity..magnanimous

Read each of the passages below, and then answer the questions that follow the passage. The correct response may be stated outright or merely suggested in the passage.

Questions 9 and 10 are based on the following passage.

> After the mine owner had stripped the vegetation from
> twelve acres of extremely steep land at a creek head, a flash
> flood tumbled masses of mining debris into the swollen
> Line   stream. Though no lives were lost, the flood destroyed all
> (5)   the homes in the valley. When damage suits brought sub-
> stantial verdicts favoring the victims, the company took its
> case to the more sympathetic tribunal at Frankfort. The
> state judges proclaimed that the masses of soil, uprooted
> trees, and slabs of rock had been harmless until set in
> (10)   motion by the force of water; thus they solemnly declared
> the damage an act of God—for which no coal operator,
> God-fearing or otherwise, could be held responsible.

9. As used in line 7, the word "sympathetic" most nearly means

    (A) sensitive
    (B) favorably inclined
    (C) showing empathy
    (D) humanitarian
    (E) dispassionate

10. In describing the coal operator as "God-fearing or otherwise" (line 12), the author is most likely being

    (A) reverent
    (B) pragmatic
    (C) fearful
    (D) ironic
    (E) naive

Questions 11 and 12 are based on the following passage.

In this excerpt from Jane Austen's The Watsons, the elderly Mr. Watson discusses a visit to church.

       "I do not know when I have heard a discourse more to my mind," continued Mr. Watson, "or one better delivered. He reads extremely well, with great propriety and in a very

Line impressive manner; and at the same time without any the-
(5) atrical grimace or violence. I own, I do not like much action in the pulpit. I do not like the studied air and artificial inflec-tions of voice, which your very popular preachers have. A simple delivery is much better calculated to inspire devo-tion, and shows a much better taste. Mr. Howard read like a

(10) scholar and a gentleman."

11. The passage suggests that Mr. Watson would most likely agree with which statement?

    (A) A dramatic style of preaching appeals most to discerning listeners.
    (B) Mr. Howard is too much the gentleman-scholar to be a good preacher.
    (C) A proper preacher avoids extremes in delivering his sermons.
    (D) There is no use preaching to anyone unless you happen to catch him when he is ill.
    (E) A man often preaches his beliefs precisely when he has lost them.

12. The word "studied" (line 6) most nearly means

(A) affected
(B) academic
(C) amateurish
(D) learned
(E) diligent

Questions 13–24 are based on the following passage.

Rock musicians often affect the role of social revolutionaries. The following passage is taken from an unpublished thesis on the potential of rock and roll music to contribute to political and social change.

It should be clear from the previous arguments that rock and roll cannot escape its role as a part of popular culture. One important part of that role is its commercial
Line nature. Rock and roll is "big corporation business in
(5) America and around the globe. As David De Voss has noted: 'Over fifty U.S. rock artists annually earn from $2 million to $6 million. At last count, thirty-five artists and fifteen additional groups make from three to seven times more than America's highest paid business executive.'"
(10)   Perhaps the most damning argument against rock and roll as a political catalyst is suggested by John Berger in an essay on advertising. Berger argues that "publicity turns consumption into a substitute for democracy. The choice of what one eats (or wears or drives) takes the place of signif-
(15) icant political choice." To the extent that rock and roll is big business, and that it is marketed like other consumer goods, rock and roll also serves this role. Our freedom to choose the music we are sold may be distracting us from more important concerns. It is this tendency of rock and
(20) roll, fought against but also fulfilled by punk, that Julie Burchill and Tony Parsons describe in *The Boy Looked at Johnny: The Obituary of Rock and Roll.*

Never mind, kid, there'll soon be another washing-
machine/spot-cream/rock-band on the market to
(25)   solve all your problems and keep you quiet/off the
street/distracted from the real enemy/content till the
next pay-day.
Anyhow, God Save Rock and Roll. . . it made you a
consumer, a potential Moron. . .
(30)   IT'S ONLY ROCK AND ROLL AND IT'S PLASTIC,
PLASTIC, YES IT IS!!!!!!
   This is a frustrating conclusion to reach, and it is
especially frustrating for rock and roll artists who are dissatisfied with the political systems in which they live. If
(35) rock and roll's ability to promote political change is ham-
pered by its popularity, the factor that gives it the potential
to reach significant numbers of people, to what extent can
rock and roll artists act politically? Apart from charitable
endeavors, with which rock and roll artists have been quite
(40) successful at raising money for various causes, the potential for significant political activity promoting change
appears quite limited.
   The history of rock and roll is filled with rock artists
who abandoned, at least on vinyl, their political commit-
(45) ment. Bob Dylan, who, by introducing the explicit politics of
folk music to rock and roll, can be credited with introducing
the political rock and roll of the sixties, quickly abandoned
politics for more personal issues. John Lennon, who was
perhaps more successful than any other rock and roll artist
(50) at getting political material to the popular audience, still had
a hard time walking the line between being overtly political
but unpopular and being apolitical and extremely popular.
In 1969 "Give Peace a Chance" reached number fourteen
on the Billboard singles charts. 1971 saw "Power to the
(55) People" at number eleven. But the apolitical "Instant
Karma" reached number three on the charts one year earlier. "Imagine," which mixed personal and political

concerns, also reached number three one year later.
Lennon's most political album, *Some Time in New York*
(60) *City*, produced no hits. His biggest hits, "Whatever Gets
You Through the Night" and "Starting Over," which both
reached number one on the charts, are apolitical. Jon
Wiener, in his biography of Lennon, argues that on
"Whatever Gets You Through the Night," "it seemed like
(65) John was turning himself into Paul, the person without
political values, who put out Number One songs and who
managed to sleep soundly. Maybe that's why John
(Lennon) told Elton John that 'Whatever Gets You Through
the Night' was 'one of my least favorites.'" When, after
(70) leaving music for five years, Lennon returned in 1980 with
the best-selling *Double Fantasy* album, the subject of his
writing was "caring, sharing, and being a whole person."

The politically motivated rock and roll artist's other
option is to maintain his political commitment without fool-
(75) ing himself as to the ultimate impact his work will have. If
his music is not doomed to obscurity by the challenge it
presents to its listeners the artist is lucky. But even such
luck can do nothing to protect his work from the misinterpretation it will be subjected to once it is popular. Tom
(80) Greene of the Mekons expresses the frustration such artists
feel when he says, "You just throw your hands up in horror
and try and . . . I don't know. I mean, what can you do?

How can you possibly avoid being a part of the power
relations that exist?" The artist's challenge is to try to com-
(85) municate with his audience. But he can only take responsibility for his own intentions. Ultimately, it is the popular
audience that must take responsibility for what it does with
the artist's work. The rock and roll artist cannot cause political change. But, if he is very lucky, the popular audience
(90) might let him contribute to the change it makes.

13. De Voss's comparison of the salaries of rock stars and corporate executives (lines 6–9) is cited primarily in order to

   (A) express the author's familiarity with current pay scales
   (B) argue in favor of higher pay for musical artists
   (C) refute the assertion that rock and roll stars are underpaid
   (D) support the view that rock and roll is a major industry
   (E) indicate the lack of limits on the wages of popular stars

14. The word "consumption" in line 13 means

   (A) supposition
   (B) beginning a task
   (C) using up goods
   (D) advertising a product
   (E) culmination

15. In the quotation cited in lines 23–31, Burchill and Parsons most likely run the words "washing-machine/spot-cream/rock-band" together to indicate that

   (A) to the consumer they are all commodities
   (B) they are products with universal appeal
   (C) advertisers need to market them differently
   (D) rock music eliminates conventional distinctions
   (E) they are equally necessary parts of modern society

16. The word "plastic" in the Burchill and Parsons quotation (line 31) is being used

   (A) lyrically
   (B) spontaneously
   (C) metaphorically
   (D) affirmatively
   (E) skeptically

17. Their comments in lines 28 and 29 suggest that Burchill and Parsons primarily regard consumers as

   (A) invariably dimwitted
   (B) markedly ambivalent
   (C) compulsively spendthrift
   (D) unfamiliar with commerce
   (E) vulnerable to manipulation

18. The author's comments about Bob Dylan (lines 45–48) chiefly suggest that

(A) Dylan readily abandoned political rock and roll for folk music

(B) folk music gave voice to political concerns long before rock and roll music did

(C) rock and roll swiftly replaced folk music in the public's affections

(D) Dylan lacked the necessary skills to convey his political message musically

(E) Dylan betrayed his fans' faith in him by turning away from political commentary

19. Wiener's statement quoted in lines 64–69 suggests that

(A) John had no desire to imitate more successful performers

(B) John was unable to write Number One songs without help from Paul

(C) because Paul lacked political values, he wrote fewer Number One songs than John did

(D) as an apolitical performer, Paul suffered less strain than John did

(E) John disliked "Whatever Gets You Through the Night" because it had been composed by Paul

20. In lines 60–72, "Starting Over" and the *Double Fantasy* album are presented as examples of

(A) bold applications of John's radical philosophy

(B) overtly political recordings without general appeal

(C) profitable successes lacking political content

(D) uninspired and unpopular rock and roll records

(E) unusual recordings that effected widespread change

21. The word "maintain" in line 74 means

(A) repair   (B) contend   (C) subsidize
(D) brace   (E) keep

22. As quoted in lines 81–82, Tom Greene of the Mekons feels particularly frustrated because

(A) his work has lost its initial popularity

(B) he cannot escape involvement in the power structure

(C) his original commitment to political change has diminished

(D) he lacks the vocabulary to make coherent political statements

(E) he is horrified by the price he must pay for political success

23. The author attributes the success of the politically motivated rock and roll artist to

(A) political influence
(B) challenging material
(C) good fortune
(D) personal contacts
(E) textual misinterpretation

24. In the last paragraph, the author concludes that the rock and roll artist's contribution to political change is

(A) immediate
(B) decisive
(C) indirect
(D) irresponsible
(E) blatant

YOU MAY GO BACK AND REVIEW THIS SECTION IN THE
REMAINING TIME, BUT DO NOT WORK IN ANY OTHER
SECTION UNTIL TOLD TO DO SO.   **S T O P**

PRACTICE TEST 2
SECTION 3

20 Questions—25 Minutes

For each problem in this section determine which of the five choices is correct and blacken the corresponding choice on your answer sheet. You may use any blank space on the page for your work.

Notes:
- You may use a calculator whenever you think it will be helpful.
- Only real numbers are used. No question or answer on this test involves a complex or imaginary number.
- Use the diagrams provided to help you solve the problems. Unless you see the words "Note: Figure not drawn to scale" under a diagram, it has been drawn as accurately as possible. Unless it is stated that a figure is three-dimensional, you may assume it lies in a plane.
- For any function f, the domain, unless specifically restricted, is the set of all real numbers for which $f(x)$ is also a real number.

Reference Information

Area Facts

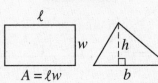

$A = \ell w$

$A = \frac{1}{2} bh$

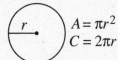

$A = \pi r^2$
$C = 2\pi r$

Volume Facts

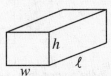

$V = \ell wh$

$V = \pi r^2 h$

Triangle Facts

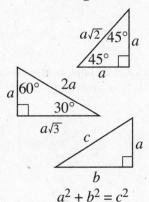

$a^2 + b^2 = c^2$

Angle Facts

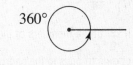

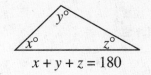

$x + y + z = 180$

---

1. If $3x = 12$, $5x =$

(A) 2.4
(B) 14
(C) 15
(D) 20
(E) 60

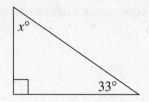

2. In the figure above, $x =$

    (A) 33
    (B) 57
    (C) 67
    (D) 123
    (E) 147

3. If $8 - (8 - m) = 8$, then $m =$

    (A) −16
    (B) −8
    (C)   0
    (D)   8
    (E) 16

4. If $\dfrac{5}{9}$ of the members of the school chorus are boys, what is the ratio of girls to boys in the chorus?

    (A) $\dfrac{4}{9}$

    (B) $\dfrac{4}{5}$

    (C) $\dfrac{5}{4}$

    (D) $\dfrac{9}{4}$

    (E) It cannot be determined from the information given.

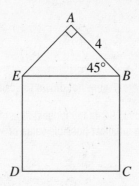

5. In the figure above, what is the perimeter of pentagon *ABCDE*, formed by right triangle *EAB* and square *BCDE*?

   (A) 20
   (B) $8 + 12\sqrt{2}$

   (C) $8 + 16\sqrt{2}$

   (D) $8 + 12\sqrt{3}$
   (E) 32

6. If $x^4 = 10$, what is x^6?

   (A) $10\sqrt{10}$
   (B) 100
   (C) $100\sqrt{10}$
   (D) 1000
   (E) $1000\sqrt{10}$

<u>Note</u>: Figure not drawn to scale

7. If, in the figure above, $\overline{BC}$ is the longest side of $\triangle ABC$ and x is an integer, what is the smallest possible value of x?

(A) 100
(B) 130
(C) 141
(D) 160
(E) 161

8. If $\dfrac{a+3}{5}$ is an integer, what is the remainder when a is divided by 5?

(A) 1
(B) 2
(C) 3
(D) 4
(E) It cannot be determined from the information given.

9. Brigitte's average (arithmetic mean) on her six math tests this marking period is 75. Fortunately for Brigitte, her teacher drops each student's lowest grade, thus raising Brigitte's average to 85. What was her lowest grade?

(A) 20
(B) 25
(C) 30
(D) 40
(E) 50

10. If m is an integer, which of the following could be true?

   I. $\dfrac{17}{m}$ is an even integer.

   II. $\dfrac{m}{17}$ is an even integer.

   III. $17m$ is a prime.

(A) I only
(B) II only
(C) III only
(D) I and II only
(E) II and III only

11. Max purchased some shares of stock at $10 per share. Six months later the stock was worth $20 per share. What was the percent increase in the value of Max's investment?

   (A) 20%
   (B) 50%
   (C) 100%
   (D) 200%
   (E) The answer depends on the number of shares purchased.

12. Benjamin can type a full report in h hours. At this rate, how many reports can he type in m minutes?

   (A) $\dfrac{mh}{60}$

   (B) $\dfrac{60m}{h}$

   (C) $\dfrac{m}{60h}$

   (D) $\dfrac{60h}{m}$

   (E) $\dfrac{h}{60m}$

13. The estate of a wealthy man was distributed as follows: 10% to his wife, 5% divided equally among his three children, 5% divided equally among his five grandchildren, and the balance to a charitable trust. If the trust received $1,000,000, how much did each grandchild inherit?

   (A) $10,000
   (B) $12,500
   (C) $20,000
   (D) $62,500
   (E) $100,000

14. If A, B, C, and D lie on the same straight line, and if $AC = 2CD = 3BD$, what is the value of the ratio $\dfrac{BC}{CD}$?

(A) $\dfrac{1}{6}$

(B) $\dfrac{1}{3}$

(C) $\dfrac{1}{2}$

(D) $\dfrac{5}{3}$

(E) It cannot be determined from the information given.

15. A car going 40 miles per hour set out on an 80-mile trip at 9:00 a.m. Exactly 10 minutes later, a second car left from the same place and followed the same route. How fast, in miles per hour, was the second car going if it caught up with the first car at 10:30 a.m.?

(A) 45
(B) 50
(C) 53
(D) 55
(E) 60

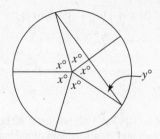

16.   In the figure above, what is the ratio of *y* to *x*?

(A) $\dfrac{1}{5}$

(B) $\dfrac{1}{4}$

(C) $\dfrac{1}{3}$

(D) $\dfrac{1}{2}$

(E) It cannot be determined from the information given.

Questions 17 and 18 refer to the following definition.

For any positive integer *n*, $\boxed{n}$ represents the sum of the integers

from 1 to n. For example, $\boxed{5}$ = 1 + 2 + 3 + 4 + 5 = 15.

17.   Which of the following is equal to $\boxed{10}$ – $\boxed{9}$?

(A) $\boxed{1}$

(B) $\boxed{2}$

(C) $\boxed{3}$

(D) $\boxed{4}$

(E) $\boxed{5}$

18. If $\boxed{1000}$ = 50,500 and $\boxed{10}$ = 55, what is the value of $\boxed{1010}$?

(A) 50,555
(B) 55,555
(C) 60,500
(D) 60,555
(E) 65,555

19. A school's honor society has 100 members: 40 boys and 60 girls, of whom 30 are juniors and 70 are seniors. What is the smallest possible number of senior boys in the society?

(A) 0
(B) 5
(C) 10
(D) 15
(E) 20

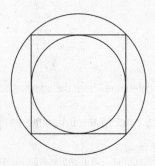

20. In the figure above, the small circle is inscribed in the square, which is inscribed in the large circle. What is the ratio of the area of the large circle to the area of the small circle?

(A) $\sqrt{2} : 1$

(B) $\sqrt{3} : 1$
(C) $2 : 1$

(D) $2\sqrt{2} : 1$

(E) It cannot be determined from the information given.

YOU MAY GO BACK AND REVIEW THIS SECTION IN THE
REMAINING TIME, BUT DO NOT WORK IN ANY OTHER
SECTION UNTIL TOLD TO DO SO.   **S T O P**

PRACTICE TEST 1
SECTION 4

35 Questions—25 Minutes

Select the best answer to each of the following questions; then blacken the appropriate space on your answer sheet.

Some or all parts of the following sentences are underlined. The first answer choice, (A), simply repeats the underlined part of the sentence. The other four choices present four alternative ways to phrase the underlined part. Select the answer that produces the most effective sentence, one that is clear and exact, and blacken the appropriate space on your answer sheet. In selecting your choice, be sure that it is standard written English, and that it expresses the meaning of the original sentence.

Example:

The first biography of author Eudora Welty came out in 1998 <u>and she was 89 years old at the time.</u>

(A) and she was 89 years old at the time
(B) at the time when she was 89
(C) upon becoming an 89 year old
(D) when she was 89
(E) at the age of 89 years old

1. By the time we arrive in Italy, we have traveled through four countries.

   (A) we have traveled through four countries
   (B) we had traveled through four countries
   (C) we will have traveled through four countries
   (D) four countries will have been traveled through
   (E) we through four countries shall have traveled

2. To say "My lunch was satisfactory" is complimentary, to say "My lunch was adequate" is not.

   (A) complimentary, to say
   (B) complementary, to say
   (C) complementary, however, to say
   (D) complimentary, but to say
   (E) complementary to saying

3. When one debates the merits of the proposed reduction in our tax base, you should take into consideration the effect it will have on the schools and the other public services.

   (A) you should take into consideration the effect
   (B) you should consider the effect
   (C) one should take the affect
   (D) one takes into consideration the affect
   (E) one should take into consideration the effect

4. We were afraid of the teacher's wrath, due to his statement that he would penalize anyone who failed to hand in his term paper on time.

   (A) wrath, due to his statement that
   (B) wrath due to his statement that,
   (C) wrath, inasmuch as his statement that,
   (D) wrath because of his statement that
   (E) wrath and his statement that,

5. Because the sports industry has become so <u>popular is the reason that</u> <u>some universities have created new courses in sports marketing and</u> <u>event planning.</u>

    (A) popular is the reason that some universities have created new courses in sports marketing and event planning
    (B) popular, some universities have created new courses in sports marketing and event planning
    (C) popular, there have been new courses in sports marketing and event planning created by some universities
    (D) popular is the reason that new courses in sports marketing and event planning have been created by some universities
    (E) popular, they have created new courses in sports marketing and event planning at some universities

6. I have discovered that the subways in New York are <u>as clean as any</u> <u>other city I have visited.</u>

    (A) as clean as any other city I have visited
    (B) as clean as those in any other city I have visited
    (C) as clean as those in any city I visited
    (D) cleaner than any city I visited
    (E) cleaner than any other city I have visited

7. Inflation in the United States <u>has not and, we hope, never will reach</u> a rate of 20 percent a year.

    (A) has not and, we hope, never will reach
    (B) has not reached and, we hope, never will
    (C) has not and hopefully never will reach
    (D) has not reached and, we hope, never will reach
    (E) has not reached and hopefully never will

8. *Godard* is part biography, part cultural <u>analysis, and it partly pays</u> <u>tribute to an artist</u> who, the author believes, is one of the most influential of his time.

    (A) analysis, and it partly pays tribute to an artist
    (B) analysis, and part tribute to an artist
    (C) analysis, and partly a payment of tribute to an artist
    (D) analysis, also it partly pays tribute to an artist
    (E) analysis, but there is a part that is a tribute to an artist

9. Embarrassment over the discovery of element 118, announced with great fanfare and then retracted amid accusations of scientific fraud, has left the nuclear physics community feeling bruised.

   (A) element 118, announced with great fanfare and then retracted amid accusations of scientific fraud, has left

   (B) element 118, which was announced with great fanfare and afterwards which was retracted amid accusations of scientific fraud, has left

   (C) element 118, announced with great fanfare and then retracted amid accusations of scientific fraud, have left

   (D) element 118 was announced with great fanfare and then was retracted amid accusations of scientific fraud, it has left

   (E) element 118, it having been announced with great fanfare and then it was retracted amidst accusations of scientific fraud, has left

10. Life on Earth has taken a tremendous range of forms, but all species arise from the same molecular ingredients, these ingredients limit the chemical reactions that can occur within cells and so constrain what life can do.

   (A) ingredients, these ingredients limit the chemical reactions that can occur within cells

   (B) ingredients, these are ingredients that limit the chemical reactions that can occur within cells

   (C) ingredients, these ingredients limit the chemical reactions that could occur within cells

   (D) ingredients, which limit the chemical reactions that can occur within cells

   (E) ingredients; but these ingredients limit the chemical reactions that can occur within cells

11. Thompson's fictional retelling of Ignaz Semmelweis's battle to eradicate childbed fever proved to at least one adolescent reader that taking a stand against the establishment, no matter the consequences, is worth the struggle.

   (A) taking a stand against the establishment, no matter the consequences, is worth the struggle

   (B) to take a stand against the establishment, it does not matter what the consequences are, is worth the struggle

   (C) taking a stand against the establishment, despite the consequences, are worth the struggle

   (D) if one takes a stand against the establishment, no matter the consequences, you will find it worth the trouble

   (E) taking a stand against the establishment, irregardless of the consequences, is worth the trouble

The sentences in this section may contain errors in grammar, usage, choice of words, or idioms. Either there is just one error in a sentence or the sentence is correct. Some words or phrases are underlined and lettered; everything else in the sentence is correct.

If an underlined word or phrase is incorrect, choose that letter; if the sentence is correct, select No error. Then blacken the appropriate space on your answer sheet.

Example:

The region has a climate so severe that plants
                                 A

growing there rarely had been more than twelve
          B   C

inches high. No error
         D   E

Ⓐ Ⓑ ● Ⓓ Ⓔ

12. The lieutenant reminded his men that the only information
                        A

    to be given the captors was each individual's name, rank, and what
          B   C   D

    his serial number was. No error
            D   E

13. When the teacher ordered the student to go to the dean's office
              A   B

    as a result of the class disruption, she surprised us because she
            C

    usually will handle her own discipline problems. No error
            D   E

14. He was the author whom I believed was most likely to receive the
                        A   B   C

    coveted award. No error
         D   E

15. Please give this scholarship to whoever in the graduating class
                              —————
                                A
    has done the most to promote goodwill in the community. No error
    —————   ——————— ————————   ————
      B   C   D   E

16. The two lawyers interpreted the statute differently, and they needed a
                    ——————————   —————————— ———
                        A   B   C
    judge to settle its dispute. No error
                    ———   ————
                     D   E

17. All of the team members, except him, has anticipated interest from
                                   ——— ———   ——————————
                                    A   B   C
    the national leagues, and now practice twice as long. No error
                                           ——————————   ————
                                              D   E

18. Everybody but him has paid their dues; we must seek ways to make
             ———   —————   ——————————
              A   B   C
    him understand the need for prompt payment. No error
    —————————————   ————
         D   E

19. In order to be sure that the mattress was firm before placing an
    ———————   ————
       A   B
    order, the man gingerly sat down and laid back. No error
                            ———————   ————————— ————
                              C   D   E

20. The data that he presented was not pertinent to the matter
        ————   ———   ——————————
         A   B   C
    under discussion. No error
    ———————————   ————
         D   E

21. In order for she and I to be able to attend, we will need to receive
    —————————   ———   —————— ————————
        A   B   C   D
    tickets within the week. No error
                            ————
                             E

22. I feel badly about the present conflict because I do not know how to
           ———————   ——————————
              A   B
    resolve it without hurting either you or him. No error
                       ———————   ————
                          C   D   E

23. A new production of the opera *Aida* has just been announced; it
                                          ———————————
                                              A   B
    will be sang on an outdoor stage with live animals. No error
            —————   ————   ————
             C   D   E

24. Unless two or more members object to him joining the club, we shall
    A ‾‾‾‾‾‾‾‾‾‾‾   B
have to accept his application for membership. No error
    C ‾‾‾‾‾‾‾   D ‾‾‾   E

25. Thurgood Marshall made history by becoming the first black
                      A ‾‾‾‾‾‾‾   B
Supreme Court Justice when he was appointed of this position by
                      C ‾‾‾‾‾   D ‾‾‾‾‾‾‾
President Lyndon Johnson. No error
                      E

26. Chinese scientists analyzing the genome of the SARS virus

have documented the immense rapidity with which it evolved off an
    A ‾‾‾‾‾‾‾   B ‾‾‾‾‾   C ‾‾‾‾‾
animal pathogen into one capable of infecting human cells. No error
                      D ‾‾‾‾‾   E

27. When Freud introduced the notion that most mental processes that
                                      A ‾‾‾‾

determine our everyday thoughts, feelings, and what we wish occur
                                      B ‾‾‾‾‾
unconsciously, his contemporaries rejected it as impossible. No error
    C ‾‾‾‾‾   D ‾‾   E

28. Artesian water comes from an artesian well, a well that taps a water-
                      A ‾‾‾‾‾   B ‾‾‾‾
bearing layer of rock or sand, in which the water level stands above
                      C ‾‾‾‾‾   D ‾‾‾‾‾
the top of the aquifer. No error
                      E

29. During the Cultural Revolution in China, Li Huayi has labored as a
    A ‾‾‾   B ‾‾‾‾‾
"worker-artist," painting government propaganda posters, while in
                      C ‾‾‾‾
private he developed his own artistic style. No error
                      D ‾‾‾‾   E

> The passage below is the unedited draft of a student's essay. Parts of the essay need to be rewritten to make the meaning clearer and more precise. Read the essay carefully.
>
> The essay is followed by six questions about changes that might improve all or part of the organization, development, sentence structure, use of language, appropriateness to the audience, or use of standard written English. In each case, choose the answer that most clearly and effectively expresses the student's intended meaning. Indicate your choice by blackening the corresponding space on the answer sheet.

[1] From the colonial times until today, the appeal of the underdog has retained a hold on Americans. [2] It is a familiar sight today to see someone rooting for the underdog while watching a sports event on television. [3] Though that only happens if they don't already have a favorite team. [4] Variations of the David and Goliath story are popular in both fact and fiction. [5] Horatio Alger stories, wondrous tales of conquering the West, and the way that people have turned rags-to-riches stories such as Vanderbilt into national myths are three examples of America's fascination with the underdog.

[6] This appeal has been spurred by American tradition as well as an understandably selfish desire to feel good about oneself and life. [7] Part of the aura America has held since its creation is that the humblest and poorest person can make it here in America. [8] That dream is ingrained in the history of America. [9] America is made up of immigrants. [10] Most were poor when they came here. [11] They thought of America as the land of opportunity, where any little guy could succeed. [12] All it took was the desire to lift oneself up and some good honest work. [13] Millions succeeded on account of the American belief to honor and support the underdog in all its efforts.

[14] The underdog goes against all odds and defeats the stronger opponent with hope. [15] It makes people feel that maybe one day they too will triumph against the odds. [16] It changes their view of life's struggles because they trust that in the end all their hardships will amount to something. [17] Despair has no place in a society where everyone knows that they can succeed. [18] It's no wonder that the underdog has always had a tight hold upon American hopes and minds.

30. Which of the following is the best revision of the underlined sections of sentences 1 and 2 (below), so that the two sentences are combined into one?

From the colonial times until today, the appeal of the underdog has retained a hold on Americans. It is a familiar sight today to see someone rooting for the underdog while watching a sports event on television.

(A) the appeal of the underdog has retained a hold on Americans, and it is a familiar sight today to see underdogs being the one rooted for

(B) the appeal of the underdog has retained a hold on Americans, but it is a familiar sight today to see someone rooting for the underdog

(C) the underdog has retained a hold on Americans, who commonly root for the underdog, for example,

(D) the underdog has retained a hold on Americans, commonly rooting for the underdog

(E) the underdog's appeal has retained a hold on Americans, for example, they commonly root for the underdog

31. To improve the coherence of paragraph 1, which of the following sentences should be deleted?

(A) Sentence 1
(B) Sentence 2
(C) Sentence 3
(D) Sentence 4
(E) Sentence 5

32. Considering the content of paragraph 2, which of the following is the best revision of the paragraph's topic sentence, sentence 6?

(A) This appeal got spurred by American tradition as well as by an understandably selfish desire to feel good about oneself and one's life.

(B) The appeal of the underdog has been spurred by American tradition.

(C) The appeal has been spurred by Americans' traditional and selfish desire to feel good about themselves and life.

(D) American tradition as well as Americans' desire to feel good about oneself and their life has spurred the appeal of underdogs.

(E) American traditions include an understandably selfish desire to feel good about themselves and the appeal of the underdog.

33. In the context of paragraph 2, which of the following is the best way to combine sentences 8, 9, 10, and 11?

(A) That dream is ingrained in the experience of America, a country made up of poor immigrants who believed that in this land of opportunity any little guy had a chance to succeed.

(B) That dream was ingrained in our history, a country made up of immigrants, poor and hopeful that any little guy is able to succeed in America, the land of opportunity.

(C) That dream has been ingrained America's history that poor immigrants look on America as a land of opportunity, which any little guy had been able to succeed in.

(D) The American experience has ingrained in it the dream that by immigrants coming to this country poorly could succeed because America is the land of opportunity.

(E) Ingrained in the American experience is the dream of poor immigrants that they could succeed here, after all, this is the land of opportunity.

34. In view of the sentences that precede and follow sentence 13, which of the following is the most effective revision of sentence 13?

(A) Americans believe that the underdog should be honored and supported, which led to their success.

(B) Because America believed in honoring and supporting the underdog, they succeed.

(C) And succeed they did because of America's commitment to honor and support the underdog.

(D) Honoring and supporting underdogs is a firmly held value in America, and it led to the success of underdogs.

(E) They succeeded with their efforts to be supported and honored by America.

35. Which of the following revisions of sentence 14 is the best transition between paragraphs 3 and 4?

(A) Underdogs, in addition, went against all odds and with hope defeat stronger opponents.

(B) The underdog, feeling hopeful, going against all odds, and defeating stronger opponents.

(C) It is the hope of the underdog who goes against the odds and defeats the stronger opponent.

(D) The triumph of the underdog over a strong opponent inspires hope.

(E) The underdog triumphs against all odds and defeats the stronger opponents.

YOU MAY GO BACK AND REVIEW THIS SECTION IN THE REMAINING TIME, BUT DO NOT WORK IN ANY OTHER SECTION UNTIL TOLD TO DO SO.

S T O P

PRACTICE TEST 2
SECTION 6

24 Questions—25 Minutes

Select the best answer to each of the following questions; then blacken the appropriate space on your answer sheet.

Each of the following sentences contains one or two blanks; each blank indicates that a word or set of words has been left out. Below the sentence are five words or phrases, lettered A through E. Select the word or set of words that best completes the sentence.

Example:

Fame is ----; today's rising star is all too soon tomorrow's washed-up has-been.

(A) rewarding   (B) gradual   (C) essential
(D) spontaneous   (E) transitory

1. The civil rights movement did not emerge from obscurity into national prominence overnight; on the contrary, it captured the public's imagination only ----.
   (A) fruitlessly
   (B) unimpeachably
   (C) momentarily
   (D) expeditiously
   (E) gradually

2. The seventeenth-century writer Mary Astell was a rare phenomenon, a single woman who maintained and even ---- a respectable reputation while earning a living by her pen.

   (A) eclipsed   (B) impaired   (C) decimated
      (D) avoided   (E) enhanced

3. An optimistic supporter of the women's movement, Kubota contends that recent ---- by Japanese women in the business world are meaningful and indicative of ---- opportunity to come.

   (A) advances..diminished
   (B) strides..greater
   (C) innovations..marginal
   (D) retreats..theoretical
   (E) failures..hidden

4. The ---- ambassador was but ---- linguist; yet he insisted on speaking to foreign dignitaries in their own tongues without resorting to a translator's aid.

   (A) eminent..an indifferent
   (B) visiting..a notable
   (C) revered..a talented
   (D) distinguished..a celebrated
   (E) ranking..a sensitive

5. Nowadays life models—men and women who pose in the nude for artists—seem curiously ----, relics of a bygone age when art students labored amid skeletons and anatomical charts, learning to draw the human body as painstakingly as medical students learn to ---- it.

   (A) anachronistic..sketch
   (B) archaic..dissect
   (C) contemporary..diagnose
   (D) stereotyped..examine
   (E) daring..cure

Read the passages below, and then answer the questions
that follow them. The correct response may be stated outright or merely suggested in the passages.

Questions 6–9 are based on the following passages.

Passage 1

It was the voyageur who struck my imagination—the
canoe man who carried loads of hundreds of pounds and
paddled 18 hours a day fighting waves and storms. His
Line muscle and brawn supplied the motive power for French-
(5) Canadian exploration and trade, but despite the harshness
of his life—the privation, suffering, and constant threat of
death by exposure, drowning, and Indian attack—he developed an unsurpassed nonchalance and joy in the wilderness. These exuberant men, wearing red sashes and caps
(10) and singing in the face of disaster, were the ones who
stood out.

Passage 2

The French *voyageurs* ("travelers") in essence were
fur traders, commercial agents hired by a merchant company to conduct trade on its behalf. In Canada, the French
(15) fur trade in Montreal was taken over by British fur traders,
who provided the capital for the enterprise. The voyageurs,
for their part, supplied their knowledge of Indian tribal cus-
toms and wilderness trails, as well as their expertise in
traveling by canoe. They established a system of canoe
(20) convoys between fur-trading posts that ran from Montreal
to the western plains, well into the region now known as
Canada's North West Territories.

6. As used in Passage 1, the word "struck" (line 1) most nearly means

   (A) picketed
   (B) inflicted
   (C) impressed
   (D) dismantled
   (E) overthrew

7. The author of Passage 1 is most affected by the voyageur's

   (A) inventiveness
   (B) hardships
   (C) strength
   (D) zest
   (E) diligence

8. Compared to the author of Passage 2, the author of Passage 1 regards the voyageurs with more

   (A) overt cynicism
   (B) objective detachment
   (C) open admiration
   (D) misguided affection
   (E) marked ambivalence

9. Unlike the author of Passage 2, the author of Passage 1 makes use of

   (A) direct quotation
   (B) historical research
   (C) literary references
   (D) statistical data
   (E) personal voice

Questions 10–15 are based on the following passage.

The following passage on the formation of oil is excerpted from a novel about oil exploration written by Alistair MacLean.

Five main weather elements act upon rock. Frost and
ice fracture rock. It can be gradually eroded by airborne
dust. The action of the seas, whether through the constant
Line movement of tides or the pounding of heavy storm waves,
(5) remorselessly wears away the coastlines. Rivers are
immensely powerful destructive agencies—one has but to
look at the Grand Canyon to appreciate their enormous

power. And such rocks as escape all these influences are worn away over the eons by the effect of rain.

(10)   Whatever the cause of erosion, the net result is the same. The rock is reduced to its tiniest possible con-stituents—rock particles or, simply, dust. Rain and melting snow carry this dust down to the tiniest rivulets and the mightiest rivers, which, in turn, transport it to lakes, inland

(15) seas and the coastal regions of the oceans. Dust, however fine and powdery, is still heavier than water, and whenever the water becomes sufficiently still, it will gradually sink to the bottom, not only in lakes and seas but also in the slug-gish lower reaches of rivers and where flood conditions

(20) exist, in the form of silt.

And so, over unimaginably long reaches of time, whole mountain ranges are carried down to the seas, and in the process, through the effects of gravity, new rock is born as layer after layer of dust accumulates on the bottom, building

(25) up to a depth of ten, a hundred, perhaps even a thousand feet, the lowermost layers being gradually compacted by the immense and steadily increasing pressures from above, until the particles fuse together and reform as a new rock.

It is in the intermediate and final processes of the new

(30) rock formation that oil comes into being. Those lakes and seas of hundreds of millions of years ago were almost choked by water plants and the most primitive forms of aquatic life. On dying, they sank to the bottom of the lakes and seas along with the settling dust particles and were

(35) gradually buried deep under the endless layers of more dust and more aquatic and plant life that slowly accumu-lated above them. The passing of millions of years and the steadily increasing pressures from above gradually changed the decayed vegetation and dead aquatic life into oil.

(40)   Described this simply and quickly, the process sounds reasonable enough. But this is where the gray and disputa-tious area arises. The conditions necessary for the forma-

tion of oil are known; the cause of the metamorphosis is
not. It seems probable that some form of chemical catalyst
(45) is involved, but this catalyst has not been isolated. The first
purely synthetic oil, as distinct from secondary synthetic
oils such as those derived from coal, has yet to be produced. We just have to accept that oil is oil, that it is there,
bound up in rock strata in fairly well-defined areas through-
(50) out the world but always on the sites of ancient seas and
lakes, some of which are now continental land, some
buried deep under the encroachment of new oceans.

10. According to the author, which of the following statements is (are)
    true?

    I. The action of the seas is the most important factor in erosion of
    Earth's surface.
   II. Scientists have not been able to produce a purely synthetic oil in
    the laboratory.
 III. Gravity plays an important role in the formation of new rock.

    (A) I only
    (B) II only
    (C) III only
    (D) I and III only
    (E) II and III only

11. The Grand Canyon is mentioned in the first paragraph to illustrate

    (A) the urgent need for dams
    (B) the devastating impact of rivers
    (C) the effect of rain
    (D) a site where oil may be found
    (E) the magnificence of nature

12. According to the author, our understanding of the process by which
    oil is created is

    (A) biased   (B) systematic   (C) erroneous
     (D) deficient   (E) adequate

13. We can infer that prospectors should search for oil deposits

    (A) wherever former seas existed
    (B) in mountain streambeds
    (C) where coal deposits are found
    (D) in the Grand Canyon
    (E) in new rock formations

14. The author does all of the following EXCEPT

(A) describe a process
(B) state a possibility
(C) cite an example
(D) propose a solution
(E) mention a limitation

15. The word "reaches" in line 19 means

(A) grasps
(B) unbroken stretches
(C) range of knowledge
(D) promontories
(E) juxtapositions

Questions 16–24 are based on the following passage.

The following passage is excerpted from a book on the meaning and importance of fairy tales by noted child psychologist Bruno Bettelheim.

Plato—who may have understood better what forms the mind of man than do some of our contemporaries who want their children exposed only to "real" people and every-
Line day events—knew what intellectual experiences make for
(5) true humanity. He suggested that the future citizens of his ideal republic begin their literary education with the telling of myths, rather than with mere facts or so-called rational teachings. Even Aristotle, master of pure reason, said: "The friend of wisdom is also a friend of myth."
(10)   Modern thinkers who have studied myths and fairy tales from a philosophical or psychological viewpoint arrive at the same conclusion, regardless of their original persua-sion. Mircea Eliade, for one, describes these stories as "models for human behavior [that,] by that very fact, give
(15) meaning and value to life." Drawing on anthropological par-allels, he and others suggest that myths and fairy tales were derived from, or give symbolic expression to, initia-tion rites or other *rites of passage*—such as metaphoric

death of an old, inadequate self in order to be reborn on a
(20) higher plane of existence. He feels that this is why these
tales meet a strongly felt need and are carriers of such
deep meaning.

Other investigators with a depth-psychological orienta-
tion emphasize the similarities between the fantastic events
(25) in myths and fairy tales and those in adult dreams and day-
dreams—the fulfillment of wishes, the winning out over all
competitors, the destruction of enemies—and conclude
that one attraction of this literature is its expression of that
which is normally prevented from coming to awareness.

(30) There are, of course, very significant differences
between fairy tales and dreams. For example, in dreams
more often than not the wish fulfillment is disguised, while
in fairy tales much of it is openly expressed. To a considerable degree, dreams are the result of inner pressures that
(35) have found no relief, of problems that beset a person to
which he knows no solution and to which the dream finds
none. The fairy tale does the opposite: it projects the relief
of all pressures and not only offers ways to solve problems
but promises that a "happy" solution will be found.

(40) We cannot control what goes on in our dreams.
Although our inner censorship influences what we may
dream, such control occurs on an unconscious level. The
fairy tale, on the other hand, is very much the result of
common conscious and unconscious content having been
(45) shaped by the conscious mind, not of one particular person, but the consensus of many in regard to what they view
as universal human problems, and what they accept as
desirable solutions. If all these elements were not present
in a fairy tale, it would not be retold by generation after
(50) generation. Only if a fairy tale met the conscious and
unconscious requirements of many people was it repeatedly retold, and listened to with great interest. No dream of
a person could arouse such persistent interest unless it

was worked into a myth, as was the story of the pharaoh's
(55) dream as interpreted by Joseph in the Bible.

There is general agreement that myths and fairy tales
speak to us in the language of symbols representing
unconscious content. Their appeal is simultaneously to our
conscious mind, and to our need for ego-ideals as well.
(60) This makes it very effective; and in the tales' content, inner
psychological phenomena are given body in symbolic form.

16. In the opening paragraph, the author quotes Plato and Aristotle primarily in order to

   (A) define the nature of myth
   (B) contrast their opposing points of view
   (C) support the point that myths are valuable
   (D) prove that myths originated in ancient times
   (E) give an example of depth psychology

17. The author's comment about people who wish their children exposed only to actual historic persons and commonplace events (lines 3 and 4) suggests he primarily views such people as

   (A) considerate of their children's welfare
   (B) misguided in their beliefs
   (C) determined to achieve their ends
   (D) more rational than the ancients
   (E) optimistic about human nature

18. By "Plato . . . knew what intellectual experiences make for true humanity" (lines 1–5), the author means that

   (A) Plato comprehended the effects of the intellectual life on real human beings
   (B) Plato realized how little a purely intellectual education could do for people's actual well-being
   (C) Plato grasped which sorts of experiences helped promote the development of truly humane individuals
   (D) actual human beings are transformed by reading the scholarly works of Plato
   (E) human nature is a product of mental training according to the best philosophical principles

19. The word "persuasion" in lines 12 and 13 means

(A) enticement
(B) convincing force
(C) political party
(D) opinion
(E) gullibility

20. Lines 10–15 suggest that Mircea Eliade is most likely

(A) a writer of children's literature
(B) a student of physical anthropology
(C) a twentieth century philosopher
(D) an advocate of practical education
(E) a contemporary of Plato

21. In line 58, the word "appeal" most nearly means

(A) plea
(B) wistfulness
(C) prayer
(D) request
(E) attraction

22. It can be inferred from the passage that the author's interest in fairy tales centers chiefly on their

(A) literary qualities
(B) historical background
(C) factual accuracy
(D) psychological relevance
(E) ethical weakness

23. Which of the following best describes the author's attitude toward fairy tales?

(A) Reluctant fascination
(B) Wary skepticism
(C) Scornful disapprobation
(D) Indulgent tolerance
(E) Open approval

24. According to the passage, fairy tales differ from dreams in which of the following characteristics?

    I. The shared nature of their creation
    II. The convention of a happy ending
    III. Enduring general appeal

(A) I only
(B) II only
(C) I and II only
(D) II and III only
(E) I, II, and III

YOU MAY GO BACK AND REVIEW THIS SECTION IN THE
REMAINING TIME, BUT DO NOT WORK IN ANY OTHER
SECTION UNTIL TOLD TO DO SO.   **STOP**

PRACTICE TEST 2
SECTION 7

18 Questions—25 Minutes

You have 25 minutes to answer the 8 multiple-choice questions and 10 student-produced response questions in this section. For each multiple-choice question, determine which of the five choices is correct and blacken the corresponding choice on your answer sheet. You may use any blank space on the page for your work.

Notes:

- You may use a calculator whenever you think it will be helpful.
- Only real numbers are used. No question or answer on this test involves a complex or imaginary number.
- Use the diagrams provided to help you solve the problems. Unless you see the words "Note: Figure not drawn to scale" under a diagram, it has been drawn as accurately as possible. Unless it is stated that a figure is three-dimensional, you may assume it lies in a plane.
- For any function f, the domain, unless specifically restricted, is the set of all real numbers for which $f(x)$ is also a real number.

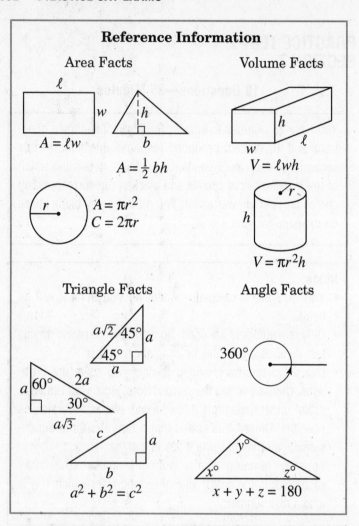

Reference Information

Area Facts

$A = \ell w$

$A = \frac{1}{2} bh$

$A = \pi r^2$
$C = 2\pi r$

Volume Facts

$V = \ell wh$

$V = \pi r^2 h$

Triangle Facts

$a^2 + b^2 = c^2$

Angle Facts

360°

$x + y + z = 180$

---

1. In a class, 20 children were sharing equally the cost of a present for their teacher. When 4 of the children decided not to contribute, each of the other children had to pay $1.50 more. How much, in dollars, did the present cost?

(A)   50
(B)   80
(C)   100
(D)   120
(E)   150

2. If Wally's Widget Works is open exactly 20 days each month and produces 80 widgets each day it is open, how many years will it take to produce 96,000 widgets?

    (A) less than 5
    (B) 5
    (C) more than 5 but less than 10
    (D) 10
    (E) more than 10

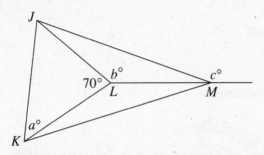

3. In the figure above, $JL = KL = LM$ and $m\angle JLK = 70$. This information is sufficient to determine the value of which of the following?

    (A) a only
    (B) b only
    (C) a and b only
    (D) b and c only
    (E) a, b, and c

4. The equation $\left| 10 - \sqrt{x} \right| = 7$ has two solutions. What is the sum of these solutions?

    (A) 0
    (B) 9
    (C) 18
    (D) 20
    (E) 298

5. A (5, 1) lies on a circle whose center is O (1, 5). If $\overline{AB}$ is a diameter, what are the coordinates of B?

    (A) (3, 3)
    (B) (6, 6)
    (C) (−1, 5)
    (D) (−1, 10)
    (E) (−3, 9)

6. What is the volume, in cubic inches, of a cube whose total surface area is 216 square inches?

(A) 6
(B) 18
(C) 36
(D) 216
(E) 1296

7. For how many integers, x, is the function $f(x) = \sqrt{x^2 - 9}$ undefined?

(A) None
(B) 4
(C) 5
(D) 7
(E) Infinitely many

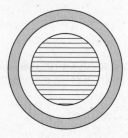

The three circles have the same center. The radii of the circles are 3, 4, and 5.

8. If a point in the figure above is chosen at random, what is the probability that the point lies in the shaded outer ring?

(A) $\dfrac{1}{5}$

(B) $\dfrac{7}{25}$

(C) $\dfrac{1}{3}$

(D) $\dfrac{8}{25}$

(E) $\dfrac{9}{25}$

Directions for Student-Produced Response Questions (Grid-ins)

In questions 9–18, first solve the problem, and then enter your answer on the grid provided on the answer sheet. The instructions for entering your answers are as follows:

- First, write your answer in the boxes at the top of the grid.
- Second, grid your answer in the columns below the boxes.
- Use the fraction bar in the first row or the decimal point in the second row to enter fractions and decimal answers.

Answer: $\frac{8}{15}$ Answer: 1.75

Write your →
answer in
the boxes.

Grid in →
your
answer.

Answer: 100

Either position is acceptable

- Grid only one space in each column.
- Entering the answer in the boxes is recommended as an aid in gridding, but is not required.
- The machine scoring your exam can read only what you grid, so **you must grid in your answers correctly to get credit.**
- If a question has more than one correct answer, grid in only one of these answers.
- The grid does not have a minus sign, so no answer can be negative.
- A mixed number *must* be converted to an improper fraction or a decimal before it is gridded. Enter $1\frac{1}{4}$ as 5/4 or 1.25; the machine will interpret 1 1/4 as $\frac{11}{4}$ and mark it wrong.
- **All decimals must be entered as accurately as possible.** Here are the three acceptable ways of gridding

$$\frac{3}{11} = 0.272727\ldots$$

3/11   .272   .273

- Note that rounding to .273 is acceptable, because you are using the full grid, but you would receive **no credit** for .3 or .27, because these answers are less accurate.

9. If $a = 3$ and $b = -3$, what is the value of $3a - 2b$?

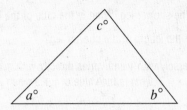

10. If $a:b:c = 6:7:11$, what is the value of $c - a$?

11. What is the perimeter of a right triangle if the lengths of its two smallest sides are 15 and 36?

12. There are 250 people on a line outside a theater. If Jack is the 25th person from the front, and Jill is the 125th person from the front, how many people are between Jack and Jill?

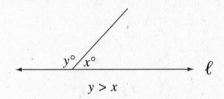

$y > x$

Note: Figure not drawn to scale

13. In the figure above, x and y are integers. What is the largest possible value of x?

14. Five people shared a prize of $100. Each one received a whole number of dollars, and no two people received the same amount. If the largest share was $30 and the smallest share was $15, what is the most money that the person with the third largest share could have received? (Grid in your answer without a dollar sign.)

15. The average (arithmetic mean) of a set of 9 numbers is 99. After one of the numbers is deleted from the set, the average of the remaining numbers is 89. What number was deleted?

16. The sum of three different positive integers is 12. Let g be the greatest possible product of the three integers, and let ℓ be the least possible product of the integers. What is the value of $g - \ell$?

17. In a right triangle, $\frac{1}{4}$ of the length of the longer leg is equal to $\frac{3}{5}$ of the length of the shorter leg. What is the ratio of the length of the hypotenuse to the length of the shorter leg?

18. If x varies inversely with y and varies directly with z, and if y and z are both 12 when $x = 3$, what is the value of $y + z$ when $x = 4$?

YOU MAY GO BACK AND REVIEW THIS SECTION IN THE
REMAINING TIME, BUT DO NOT WORK IN ANY OTHER
SECTION UNTIL TOLD TO DO SO.   **S T O P**

PRACTICE TEST 2
SECTION 8

19 Questions—20 Minutes

Select the best answer to each of the following questions; then blacken the appropriate space on your answer sheet.

Each of the following sentences contains one or two blanks; each blank indicates that a word or set of words has been left out. Below the sentence are five words or phrases, lettered A through E. Select the word or set of words that best completes the sentence.

Example:

Fame is ----; today's rising star is all too soon tomorrow's washed-up has-been.

 (A) rewarding   (B) gradual   (C) essential
   (D) spontaneous   (E) transitory

1. Most of the settlements that grew up near the logging camps were ---- affairs, thrown together in a hurry because people needed to live on the job.

   (A) protracted   (B) unobtrusive   (C) nomadic
    (D) ramshackle   (E) banal

2. Quick-breeding and immune to most pesticides, cockroaches are so ---- that even a professional exterminator may fail to ---- them.

   (A) vulnerable..eradicate
   (B) widespread..discern
   (C) fragile..destroy
   (D) hardy..eliminate
   (E) numerous..detect

3. The patient bore the pain ----, neither wincing nor whimpering when the incision was made.

(A) histrionically (B) stoically (C) sardonically
  (D) poorly (E) marginally

4. The actor's stories of backstage feuds and rivalry might be thought ---- were there not so many corroborating anecdotes from other theatrical personalities.

(A) pantomime (B) ambiguity (C) approbation
  (D) hyperbole (E) vainglory

5. Wemmick, the soul of kindness in private, is obliged in ---- to be uncompassionate and even ---- on behalf of his employer, the harsh lawyer Jaggers.

(A) conclusion..careless
(B) principle..contradictory
(C) theory..esoteric
(D) court..judicious
(E) public..ruthless

6. Although Roman original contributions to government, jurisprudence, and engineering are commonly acknowledged, the artistic legacy of the Roman world continues to be judged widely as ---- the magnificent Greek traditions that preceded it.

(A) an improvement on
(B) an echo of
(C) a resolution of
(D) a precursor of
(E) a consummation of

The questions that follow the next two passages relate to the content of both, and to their relationship. The correct response may be stated outright in the passage or merely suggested.

Questions 7–19 are based on the following passages.

The following passages are taken from memoirs by two young American writers, each of whom records his reaction to the prospect of visiting his ancestral homeland.

Passage 1

Thomas Wolfe said that going home again is like step-ping into a river. You cannot step into the same river twice; you cannot go home again. After a very long time away,
Line you will not find the same home you left behind. It will be
(5) different, and so will you. It is quite possible that home will not be home at all, meaningless except for its sentimental place in your heart. At best it will point the long way back to where you started, its value lying in how it helped to shape you and in the part of home you have carried away.
(10) Alex Haley went to Africa in the mid-sixties. Somehow he had managed to trace his roots back to a little village called Juffure, upriver from Banjul in the forests of The Gambia. It was the same village from which his ancestors had been stolen and forced into slavery. In some way Haley
(15) must have felt he was returning home: a flood of emotions, an awakening of the memories hidden in his genes.

Those were the two extremes between which I was trapped. I could not go home again, yet here I was. Africa was so long ago the land of my ancestors that it held for
(20) me only a symbolic significance. Yet there was enough to remind me that what I carry as a human being has come in

part from Africa. I did not feel African, but was beginning to
feel not wholly American anymore either. I felt like an
orphan, a waif without a home.

(25)   I was not trying to find the village that had once been
home to my people, nor would I stand and talk to people
who could claim to be my relatives, as Haley had done. The
thought of running into someone who looked like a relative
terrified me, for that would have been too concrete, too
(30) much proof. My Africanism was abstract and I wanted it to
remain so. I did not need to hear the names of my ancient
ancestors or know what they looked like. I had seen the
ways they loved their children in the love of my father. I
would see their faces and their smiles one day in the eyes
(35) of my children.

Haley found what he was seeking. I hardly knew what I
was looking for, except perhaps to know where home once
was, to know how much of me is really me, how much of
being black has been carried out of Africa.

Passage 2

(40)   I am a *Sansei*, a third-generation Japanese-American.
In 1984, through luck and through some skills as a poet, I
traveled to Japan. My reasons for going were not very
clear.

At the time, I'd been working as an arts administrator
(45) in the Writers-in-the-Schools program, sending other writers to grade schools and high schools throughout
Minnesota. It wasn't taxing, but it didn't provide the long
stretches needed to plunge into my own work. I had applied
for a U.S./Japan Creative Artist Exchange Fellowship mainly
(50) because I wanted time to write.

Japan? That was where my grandparents came from;
it didn't have much to do with my present life.

For me Japan was cheap baseballs, Godzilla, weird
sci-fi movies like *Star Man*, where you could see the strings
(55) that pulled him above his enemies, flying in front of a back-
drop so poorly made even I, at eight, was conscious of the
fakery. Then there were the endless hordes storming GI's in
war movies. Before the television set, wearing my ever-
present Cubs cap, I crouched near the sofa, saw the enemy
(60) surrounding me. I shouted to my men, hurled a grenade. I
fired my gun. And the Japanese soldiers fell before me,
one by one.

So, when I did win the fellowship, I felt I was going
not as an ardent pilgrim, longing to return to the land of his
(65) grandparents, but more like a contestant on a quiz show
who finds himself winning a trip to Bali or the Bahamas. Of
course, I was pleased about the stipend, the plane fare for
me and my wife, and the payments for Japanese lessons,
both before the trip and during my stay. I was also excited
(70) that I had beat out several hundred candidates in literature
and other fields for one of the six spots. But part of me
wished the prize was Paris, not Tokyo. I would have preferred French bread and Brie over *sashimi* and rice,
Baudelaire and Proust over Basho and Kawabata, struc-
(75) turalism and Barthes over Zen and D. T. Suzuki.

This contradiction remained. Much of my life I had
insisted on my Americanness, had shunned most connections with Japan and felt proud I knew no Japanese; yet I
was going to Japan as a poet, and my Japanese ancestry
(80) was there in my poems—my grandfather, the relocation
camps, the hibakusha (victims of the atomic bomb), a pic-
nic of Nisei (second-generation Japanese-Americans), my
uncle who fought in the 442nd. True, the poems were written in blank verse, rather than haiku, tanka, or haibun. But
(85) perhaps it's a bit disingenuous to say that I had no longing
to go to Japan; it was obvious my imagination had been
traveling there for years, unconsciously swimming the

Pacific, against the tide of my family's emigration, my par-
(90) ents' desire, after the internment camps, to forget the past.

7. Wolfe's comment referred to in lines 1–5 represents

(A) a digression from the author's thesis
(B) an understatement of the situation
(C) a refutation of the author's central argument
(D) a figurative expression of the author's point
(E) an example of the scientific method

8. According to lines 7–9, the most positive outcome of attempting to go home again would be for you to

(A) find the one place you genuinely belong
(B) recognize the impossibility of the task
(C) grasp how your origins have formed you
(D) reenter the world of your ancestors
(E) decide to stay away for shorter periods of time

9. Throughout Passage 1, the author seeks primarily to convey

(A) his resemblance to his ancestors
(B) his ambivalence about his journey
(C) the difficulties of traveling in a foreign country
(D) his need to deny his American origins
(E) the depth of his desire to track down his roots

10. The statement "I could not go home again, yet here I was" (line 18) represents

(A) a paradox
(B) a prevarication
(C) an interruption
(D) an analogy
(E) a fallacy

11. The word "held" in line 19 means

(A) grasped
(B) believed
(C) absorbed
(D) accommodated
(E) possessed

12. By "my own work" (line 48), the author of Passage 2 refers to

(A) seeking his ancestral roots
(B) teaching in high school
(C) writing a travel narrative
(D) creating poetry
(E) directing art programs

13. The word "taxing" in line 47 means

(A) imposing
(B) obliging
(C) demanding
(D) accusatory
(E) costly

14. The author's purpose in describing the war movie incident (lines 57–62) most likely is to

(A) indicate the depth of his hatred for the Japanese
(B) show the extent of his self-identification as an American
(C) demonstrate the superiority of American films to their Japanese counterparts
(D) explore the range of his interest in contemporary art forms
(E) explain why he had a particular urge to travel to Japan

15. By "a trip to Bali or the Bahamas" (line 66) the author wishes to convey

(A) his love for these particular vacation sites
(B) the impression that he has traveled to these places before
(C) his preference for any destination other than Japan
(D) his sense of Japan as just another exotic destination
(E) the unlikelihood of his ever winning a second trip

16. The author's attitude toward winning the fellowship can best be described as one of

(A) graceful acquiescence
(B) wholehearted enthusiasm
(C) unfeigned gratitude
(D) frank dismay
(E) marked ambivalence

17. The author concludes Passage 2 with

  (A) a rhetorical question
  (B) a eulogy
  (C) an epitaph
  (D) an extended metaphor
  (E) a literary allusion

18. Both passages are concerned primarily with the subject of

  (A) ethnic identity
  (B) individual autonomy
  (C) ancestor worship
  (D) racial purity
  (E) genealogical research

19. For which of the following statements or phrases from Passage 1 is a parallel idea not conveyed in Passage 2?

  (A) Africa "held for me only a symbolic significance" (lines 19 and 20)
  (B) "I did not feel African" (line 22)
  (C) "I felt like an orphan, a waif without a home" (lines 23 and 24)
  (D) "I hardly knew what I was looking for" (lines 36 and 37)
  (E) "An awakening of the memories hidden in his genes" (line 16)

YOU MAY GO BACK AND REVIEW THIS SECTION IN THE
REMAINING TIME, BUT DO NOT WORK IN ANY OTHER
SECTION UNTIL TOLD TO DO SO.   **S T O P**

PRACTICE TEST 2
SECTION 9

16 Questions—20 Minutes

For each problem in this section determine which of the five choices is correct and blacken the corresponding choice on your answer sheet. You may use any blank space on the page for your work.

Notes:

- You may use a calculator whenever you think it will be helpful.
- Only real numbers are used. No question or answer on this test involves a complex or imaginary number.
- Use the diagrams provided to help you solve the problems. Unless you see the words "Note: Figure not drawn to scale" under a diagram, it has been drawn as accurately as possible. Unless it is stated that a figure is three-dimensional, you may assume it lies in a plane.
- For any function f, the domain, unless specifically restricted, is the set of all real numbers for which $f(x)$ is also a real number.

Reference Information

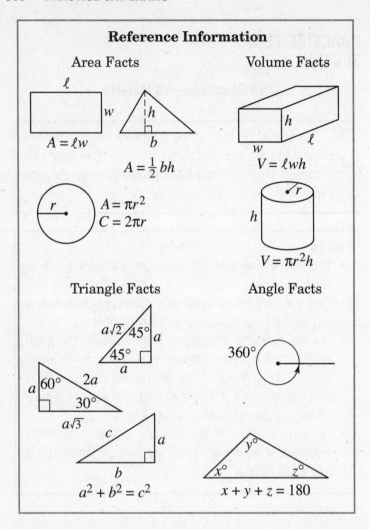

Area Facts

$A = \ell w$

$A = \frac{1}{2} bh$

$A = \pi r^2$
$C = 2\pi r$

Volume Facts

$V = \ell wh$

$V = \pi r^2 h$

Triangle Facts

$a\sqrt{2}$, $45°$, a, $45°$, a

a, $60°$, $2a$, $30°$, $a\sqrt{3}$

c, a, b
$a^2 + b^2 = c^2$

Angle Facts

$360°$

$y°$, $x°$, $z°$
$x + y + z = 180$

1. If $3x = 36$, then $\dfrac{x}{3} =$

(A) 3
(B) 4
(C) 6
(D) 9
(E) 12

2. If $a\left(\dfrac{7}{11}\right) = \left(\dfrac{7}{11}\right) b$, then $\dfrac{a}{b} =$

(A) $\dfrac{49}{121}$

(B) $\dfrac{7}{11}$

(C) 1

(D) $\dfrac{11}{7}$

(E) $\dfrac{121}{49}$

3. The weights, in kilograms, of five students are 48, 56, 61, 52, and 57. If 1 kilogram = 2.2 pounds, how many of the students weigh over 120 pounds?

(A) 1
(B) 2
(C) 3
(D) 4
(E) 5

4. From 1980 to 1990, the value of a share of stock of XYZ Corporation doubled every year. If in 1990 a share of the stock was worth $80, in what year was it worth $10?

(A) 1984
(B) 1985
(C) 1986
(D) 1987
(E) 1988

5. The average (arithmetic mean) of two numbers is a. If one of the numbers is 10, what is the other?

(A) $2a + 10$

(B) $2a - 10$

(C) $2(a - 10)$

(D) $\dfrac{10 + a}{2}$

(E) $\dfrac{10 - a}{2}$

6. The chart below shows the value of an investment on January 1 of each year from 1990 to 1995. During which year was the percent increase in the value of the investment the greatest?

Year	Value
1990	$150
1991	$250
1992	$450
1993	$750
1994	$1200
1995	$1800

(A) 1990

(B) 1991

(C) 1992

(D) 1993

(E) 1994

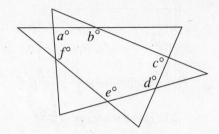

7. In the figure above, what is the value of $a + b + c + d + e + f$?

    (A) 360
    (B) 540
    (C) 720
    (D) 900
    (E) It cannot be determined from the information given.

8. If the circumference of a circle is equal to the perimeter of a square whose sides are π, what is the radius of the circle?

    (A) 1
    (B) 2
    (C) 4
    (D) π
    (E) 2π

9. The first term of a sequence is 1 and every term after the first one is 1 more than the square of the preceding term. What is the fifth term?

    (A) 25
    (B) 26
    (C) 256
    (D) 676
    (E) 677

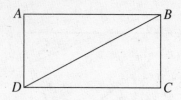

Note: Figure not drawn to scale

10. If the perimeter of rectangle *ABCD* above is 14, what is the perimeter of △*BCD*?

(A) 7

(B) 12

(C) $7 + \sqrt{29}$

(D) $7 + \sqrt{37}$

(E) It cannot be determined from the information given.

11. Jordan has taken five math tests so far this semester. If he gets a 70 on his next test, that grade will lower his test average (arithmetic mean) by 4 points. What is his average now?

(A) 74

(B) 85

(C) 90

(D) 94

(E) 95

12. If $f(x) = x^2 - 3x$ and $g(x) = f(3x)$, what is $g(-10)$?

(A) 210

(B) 390

(C) 490

(D) 810

(E) 990

13. The expression $\dfrac{12a^2 b^{-\frac{1}{2}} c^6}{4a^{-2} b^{\frac{1}{2}} c^2}$ is equivalent to which of the following?

(A) $\dfrac{3a^4 c^4}{b}$

(B) $\dfrac{3c^3}{ab}$

(C) $\dfrac{3bc^4}{a^4}$

(D) $\dfrac{a^4 c^3}{3b}$

(E) $3c^4$

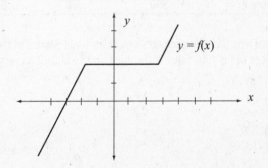

14. The figure above is the graph of the function $y = f(x)$. What are the *x*-coordinates of the points where the graph of $y = f(x - 2)$ intersects the *x*-axis?

(A) Only −5

(B) Only −1

(C) −5 and −1

(D) All numbers between −2 and 3

(E) The graph of $y = f(x - 2)$ does not intersect the *x*-axis.

15. Store 1 is a full-service retail store that charges regular prices. Store 2 is a self-service factory-outlet store that sells all items at a reduced price. In January 2004, each store sold three brands of DVD players. The numbers of DVD players sold and their prices are shown in the following tables.

Number of DVD Players Sold		
	Store 1	Store 2
Brand *A*	10	30
Brand *B*	20	40
Brand *C*	20	20

Prices of DVD Players			
	Brand *A*	Brand *B*	Brand *C*
Store 1	$80	$100	$150
Store 2	$50	$80	$120

What was the difference between Store 1 and Store 2 in the dollar values of the total sales of the three brands of DVD players?

(A) 40
(B) 80
(C) 140
(D) 330
(E) 1300

16. $A = \{2, 3\}$ $B = \{4, 5\}$ $C = \{6, 7\}$

In how many ways is it possible to pick 1 number from each set, so that the 3 numbers could be the lengths of the three sides of a triangle?

(A) 0
(B) 2
(C) 4
(D) 6
(E) 8

YOU MAY GO BACK AND REVIEW THIS SECTION IN THE
REMAINING TIME, BUT DO NOT WORK IN ANY OTHER
SECTION UNTIL TOLD TO DO SO.   **S T O P**

PRACTICE TEST 2
SECTION 10

14 Questions—10 Minutes

For each of the following questions, select the best answer from the choices provided and fill in the appropriate circle on the answer sheet.

Some or all parts of the following sentences are underlined. The first answer choice, (A), simply repeats the underlined part of the sentence. The other four choices present four alternative ways to phrase the underlined part. Select the answer that produces the most effective sentence, one that is clear and exact, and blacken the appropriate space on your answer sheet. In selecting your choice, be sure that it is standard written English, and that it expresses the meaning of the original sentence.

Example:

The first biography of author Eudora Welty came out in 1998 and she was 89 years old at the time.

(A) and she was 89 years old at the time
(B) at the time when she was 89
(C) upon becoming an 89 year old
(D) when she was 89
(E) at the age of 89 years old

1. Jane Austen wrote <u>novels and they depicted</u> the courtships and eventual marriages of members of the middle classes.

   (A) novels and they depicted
   (B) novels, being depictions of
   (C) novels, they depicted
   (D) novels that depict
   (E) novels, and depictions in them

2. The princess, <u>together with the members of her retinue, are scheduled</u> to attend the opening ceremonies.

   (A) together with the members of her retinue, are scheduled
   (B) together with the members of her retinue, were scheduled
   (C) along with the members of the retinue, are scheduled
   (D) together with the members of her retinue, is scheduled
   (E) being together with the members of her retinue, is scheduled

3. Dog experts describe the chihuahua as <u>the smallest dog, and also the most truculent of them</u>.

   (A) the smallest dog, and also the most truculent of them
   (B) the smallest and yet the most truculent of dogs
   (C) the smallest dog at the same time it is the most truculent dog
   (D) not only the smallest dog, but also more truculent than any
   (E) the smallest of dogs in spite of being the most truculent of them

4. Painters of the Art Deco period took motifs from the art of Africa, South America, and the Far East <u>as well as incorporating</u> them with the sleek lines of modern industry.

   (A) as well as incorporating
   (B) they also incorporated
   (C) and incorporated
   (D) likewise they incorporated
   (E) furthermore incorporating

5. The university reserves the right to sublet <u>students' rooms who are</u> away on leave.

   (A) students' rooms who are
   (B) students whose rooms are
   (C) the rooms of students who are
   (D) the rooms of students which are
   (E) students' rooms which are

6. High school students at the beginning of the twenty-first century ate more fast food than the middle of the twentieth century.

   (A) than
   (B) than the high schools during
   (C) than occurred in
   (D) than did students in
   (E) than did

7. Her thesis explained what motivated Stiller and Meara to give up their separate theatrical careers <u>to become comedy duos</u> in the late 1960s.

   (A) to become comedy duos
   (B) when they will become comedy duos
   (C) that they had become a comedy duo
   (D) in favor of becoming comedy duos
   (E) to become a comedy duo

8. <u>Writing a review of opening night, the production was panned by the *Chronicle*'s theater critic.</u>

   (A) Writing a review of opening night, the production was panned by the *Chronicle*'s theater critic.
   (B) Because he was writing a review of opening night, the production was panned by the *Chronicle*'s theater critic.
   (C) Writing a review of opening night, the *Chronicle*'s theater critic panned the production.
   (D) In a written review of opening night, the production by the *Chronicle*'s theater critic was being panned.
   (E) Having written a review of opening night, the production was panned by the *Chronicle*'s theater critic.

9. Frightened of meeting anyone outside her immediate family circle, <u>it was only after Elizabeth Barrett had eloped with Robert Browning that she grew to enjoy herself in society</u>.

   (A) it was only after Elizabeth Barrett had eloped with Robert Browning that she grew to enjoy herself in society.
   (B) it was only after eloping with Robert Browning that Elizabeth Barrett grew to enjoy herself in society.
   (C) Elizabeth Barrett grew to enjoy herself in society only after she had eloped with Robert Browning.
   (D) it was only after Elizabeth Barrett had eloped with Robert Browning that she had grown to enjoy herself in society.
   (E) Elizabeth Barrett grew to enjoy herself in society, however it was only after her eloping with Robert Browning.

10. Many of the students found the visiting professor the greatest lec-
turer they had ever heard, <u>but for others they found him</u> a deadly
bore with little of interest to impart.

(A) but for others they found him
(B) except others that found him
(C) however, others found him
(D) but others found him
(E) others they found him

11. Visitors to Yosemite National Park encounter a landscape of great
ruggedness and <u>majesty and the landscape has</u> inspired many pho-
tographers, above all Ansel Adams.

(A) majesty and the landscape has
(B) majesty, the reason being that the landscape has
(C) majesty, but the landscape has
(D) majesty, a landscape that has
(E) majesty, it has

12. <u>If we compare the number of station wagons on the road with the
minivan, we see that the minivan is</u> currently in the ascendant.

(A) If we compare the number of station wagons on the road with
the minivan, we see that the minivan is
(B) To compare the station wagons on the road with minivans is to
show that the minivan is
(C) In comparison with the station wagons on the road, the number
of minivans is
(D) A comparison of the numbers of station wagons and minivans on
the road indicates that minivans are
(E) Comparing the numbers of station wagons and minivans on the
road, it can be seen that the minivan is

13. Despite all his attempts <u>to ingratiate himself with his prospective father-in-law, the young man found he could hardly do nothing to please him</u>.

(A) to ingratiate himself with his prospective father-in-law, the young man found he could hardly do nothing to please him

(B) to ingratiate himself to his prospective father-in-law, the young man found he could hardly do nothing to please him

(C) to ingratiate himself with his prospective father-in-law, the young man found he could hardly do anything to please him

(D) to be ingratiating toward his prospective father-in-law, the young man found he could hardly do nothing to please him

(E) to ingratiate himself with his prospective father-in-law, the young man had found he could hardly do nothing to please him

14. Of all the cities competing to host the 2012 Olympic Games, <u>the mayor of New York was the only one to lack the funds</u> to build a new stadium.

(A) the mayor of New York was the only one to lack the funds

(B) New York's mayor only lacked the funds

(C) New York was the only one whose mayor lacked the funds

(D) the mayor of New York lacked only the funds

(E) New York had a mayor who was the only one who was lacking the funds

Answer Key

Section 2   Critical Reading

1. C	6. B	11. C	16. C	21. E
2. D	7. A	12. A	17. E	22. B
3. D	8. C	13. D	18. B	23. C
4. A	9. B	14. C	19. D	24. C
5. A	10. D	15. A	20. C	

Section 3   Mathematical Reasoning

1. D	5. B	9. B	13. B	17. D
2. B	6. A	10. E	14. E	18. D
3. D	7. E	11. C	15. A	19. C
4. B	8. B	12. C	16. B	20. C

Section 4   Writing Skills

1. C	8. B	15. E	22. A	29. B
2. D	9. A	16. D	23. C	30. C
3. E	10. D	17. B	24. B	31. C
4. D	11. A	18. B	25. D	32. B
5. B	12. D	19. D	26. C	33. A
6. B	13. D	20. B	27. B	34. C
7. D	14. A	21. B	28. E	35. D

Section 5

On this test, Section 5 was the experimental section. It could have been an extra critical reading, mathematics, or writing skills section. Remember: on the SAT you take, the experimental section may be any section from 2 to 7.

Section 6   Critical Reading

1. E	6. C	11. B	16. C	21. E
2. E	7. D	12. D	17. B	22. D
3. B	8. C	13. A	18. C	23. E
4. A	9. E	14. D	19. D	24. E
5. B	10. E	15. B	20. C	

Section 7   Mathematical Reasoning

Multiple-Choice Questions

1. **D**	3. **A**	5. **E**	7. **C**
2. **B**	4. **E**	6. **D**	8. **E**

Grid-in Questions

9. **15**

10. **37.5**

11. **90**

12. **99**

13. **89**

14. **19**

15. **179**

16. **42**

17. **13/5**

or 2.6

18. **25**

Section 8   Critical Reading

1. **D**	5. **E**	9. **B**	13. **C**	17. **D**
2. **D**	6. **B**	10. **A**	14. **B**	18. **A**
3. **B**	7. **D**	11. **E**	15. **D**	19. **C**
4. **D**	8. **C**	12. **D**	16. **E**	

Section 9   Mathematical Reasoning

1. **B**	5. **B**	9. **E**	13. **A**
2. **C**	6. **B**	10. **E**	14. **B**
3. **C**	7. **C**	11. **D**	15. **E**
4. **D**	8. **B**	12. **E**	16. **C**

Section 10   Writing Skills

1. **D**	4. **C**	7. **E**	10. **D**	13. **C**
2. **D**	5. **C**	8. **C**	11. **D**	14. **C**
3. **B**	6. **D**	9. **C**	12. **D**	

Answer Explanations

Section 2 Critical Reading

1. **C** To uncover buried ruins is to *excavate* them. Notice the use of the comma to set off the phrase that defines the missing word.

(Definition)

2. **D** Puritans (members of a religious group following a pure standard of morality) would be offended by *lewd* (lecherous, obscene) material and would fear it might corrupt theatergoers.

(Argument Pattern)

3. **D** *Rescind* means to cancel or withdraw. The lawmakers were so angered by the governor's enactment of martial law that they refused to work until it was canceled.
The phrase "the last straw" refers to the straw that broke the camel's back. *Because* the governor had exceeded his bounds, the lawmakers essentially went on strike.

(Cause and Effect Pattern)

4. **A** *Malingering* means pretending illness to avoid duty. Faced with an *arduous* (hard) march, a private might well try to get out of it.

(Argument Pattern)

5. **A** What was once a minor problem is now a major cause of death; what was formerly *negligible* (insignificant; minor and thus of no consequence) has become the chief *cause* of cancer-related deaths. Note how the two phrases set off by commas ("formerly..."; "once...") balance one another and are similar in meaning.
Remember: in double-blank sentences, go through the answer choices, testing the *first* word in each choice and eliminating the ones that don't fit.

(Argument Pattern)

6. **B** The columnist was almost *reverential* (worshipful) in what he wrote about those he liked, but he savagely attacked those he disliked. "Even" here serves as an intensifier. *Acrimonious* (stinging or bitter in nature) is a stronger word than *unpleasant*. It emphasizes how *very* unpleasant the columnist could become.

(Contrast Signal)

7. **A** *Propitious* means favorable. It would be sensible to wait for a favorable moment to reveal plans. Remember: before you look at the choices, read the sentence and think of a word that makes sense.

Likely Words: appropriate, fitting, favorable. (Examples)

8. **C** Metternich hires ships' captains to buy books to add to his growing (*burgeoning*) collection. This is an example of his great passion for books (*bibliomania*).

Word Parts Clue: *Biblio-* means book; *mania* means passion or excessive enthusiasm. (Example)

9. **B** The coal-mining company naturally sought a court that it expected to be *favorably inclined* toward its case.

10. **D** The author, alluding to the judges' ruling that the damage had been an act of God, is being *ironic* in describing the coal operator as God-fearing or perhaps not so God-fearing after all. Certainly the coal operator does not fear God enough to recompense the people who suffered because of his actions.

11. **C** Mr. Watson dislikes theatricality and violence in sermons. His notion of a proper preacher is one who *avoids extremes in delivering his sermons.*

12. **A** Mr. Watson likes simplicity in preaching. Thus, he condemns artificiality and a studied or *affected* (phony, pretentious) attitude.

13. **D** The sentence immediately preceding the De Voss quotation asserts that rock and roll is "big corporation business." The De Voss quote is used to support this view that *rock and roll is a major industry*, for, by showing that many rock stars earn far more than major corporate executives do, it indicates the impact that the music business has on America's economy.

14. **C** *Consumption* here refers to *using up* [*consumer*] *goods*, such as foodstuffs, clothes, and cars.

15. **A** The washing machine, spot cream, and rock band are all "on the market" (lines 23 and 24): they are all being marketed as *commodities*, and they all serve equally well to distract the consumer from more essential concerns.

16. **C** "Plastic" here is being used *metaphorically* or figuratively. It creates an image of rock and roll as somehow synthetic, dehumanized, even mercenary, as in *plastic smiles* or *plastic motel rooms* or *plastic money*.

17. **E** To Burchill and Parsons, the consumer is "a potential Moron" who can be kept quiet and content by being handed consumer goods as a distraction. Thus, the consumer is someone who is *vulnerable to manipulation* by the enemy.

18. **B** Dylan is given credit for "introducing the explicit politics of folk music to rock and roll." Clearly, this implies that, at the time Dylan introduced politics to rock, folk music was already an openly political medium through which artists expressed their convictions. It was only after Dylan's introduction of political ideas into his lyrics that other rock and roll artists began to deal with political materials. In other words, *folk music gave voice to political concerns long before rock and roll music did.*

19. **D** Wiener makes three points about Paul: he lacked political values (was *apolitical*), wrote highly successful nonpolitical songs ("Number One hits"), and managed to sleep soundly. Clearly, this suggests that John, who attempted to express his political values through his songs and as a result had difficulty putting out Number One hits, didn't always sleep soundly. This in turn implies that, as *an apolitical performer* who had a relatively easy time turning out hits, *Paul suffered less strain than John did.*

20. **C** The author describes Lennon's apolitical "Starting Over" as one of his "biggest hits" (line 61). Similarly, she describes the highly personal *Double Fantasy* album as "best-selling" (line 71). Thus, she clearly offers them as examples of *profitable successes lacking political content.*

21. **E** The artist's task is to *keep* or preserve his political commitment without deluding himself about how much influence his songs will have.
Treat vocabulary-in-context questions as if they are sentence completion exercises. Always substitute each of the answer choices in place of the quoted word in the original sentence.

22. **B** Greene asks how one can "possibly avoid being a part of the power relations that exist." He feels trapped. The more popular his music is, the more his work is subject to misinterpretation, and the more he is involved in the power relations of the music industry. As a politically committed artist, he is frustrated because *he cannot escape involvement* in the very power relations he condemns.

23. **C** Throughout the last paragraph, the author reiterates that the politically motivated artist, given the difficulty of his material, is lucky to gain any degree of popular success. She clearly attributes any such success to pure luck or *good fortune*.

24. **C** The author states that the "rock and roll artist cannot cause political change" (lines 88 and 89). In other words, he has no direct, immediate effect on the political situation. However, he may be able to make an *indirect* contribution to political change by influencing his audience and thus contributing to any change it makes.

Section 3 Mathematical Reasoning

In each mathematics section, for many problems, an alternative solution, indicated by two asterisks (**), follows the first solution. When this occurs, one of the solutions is the direct mathematical one and the other is based on one of the tactics discussed in Chapter 6.

1. **D** $3x = 12 \Rightarrow x = 4 \Rightarrow 5x = $ **20**.

2. **B** The sum of the measures of the three angles in any triangle is 180° (FACT 41), so

$$90 + 33 + x = 180 \Rightarrow 123 + x = 180 \Rightarrow x = \mathbf{57}.$$

3. **D** Clearing the parentheses in the original equation gives $8 - 8 + m = 8$, so $m = $ **8**.

   Use TACTIC 10: backsolve. Replace m by 0, choice C: $8 - (8 - 0) = 8 - 8 = 0$. This is too small; eliminate A, B, C. Let $m = $ **8, choice D. It works!

4. **B** Use TACTIC 11: pick an easy-to-use number.

   Since $\frac{5}{9}$ of the members are boys, assume there are 9 members,

   5 of whom are boys. Then the other 4 are girls, and the ratio of

   girls to boys is 4 to 5, or $\frac{4}{5}$.

5. **B** Triangle *EAB* is a 45-45-90 triangle;

   then by FACT 46, $AE = 4$ and

   $BE = 4\sqrt{2}$. Since *BCDE* is a square,

   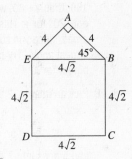

   each of its other sides is also equal to

   $4\sqrt{2}$, so the perimeter is

   $4 + 4 + 4\sqrt{2} + 4\sqrt{2} + 4\sqrt{2} = \mathbf{8 + 12\sqrt{2}}$.

   **Use TACTIC 2: trust the diagram.

    $\overline{BC}$ is clearly longer than $\overline{AB}$, which is 4, but not nearly twice as
   long. A good guess would be between 5 and 6. Then the perimeter is
   between 23 and 26. Now, use your calculator; to the nearest whole
   number, the five choices are: 20, 25, 31, 29, 32. Obviously, the right
   one is **B**.

6. **A** If $x^4 = 10$, then (taking the square root of each side) $x^2 = \sqrt{10}$,
   and $x^6 = x^4 \cdot x^2 = \mathbf{10\sqrt{10}}$.

   **If $x^4 = 10$, then $x^8 = x^4 \cdot x^4 = 10 \times 10 = 100$, so x^6 is surely less.
   Only $10\sqrt{10}$ is less than 100.

    **Use your calculator. The fourth root of 10, $(10^{.25})$, is
   approximately 1.78, which, when raised to the sixth power (1.78^6),
   is approximately 32. Only $\mathbf{10\sqrt{10}}$ is anywhere near 32.

7. **E** Since $BC > AC$, $y > 80$ (FACT 43), but $y + z = 100$. Therefore, $z < 20$, meaning that x must be greater than 160. Since x is an integer, it must be at least **161**.

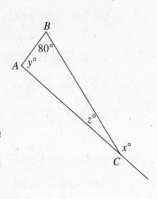

**Use TACTIC 10: backsolve. Start with 100, the smallest choice. If $x = 100$, then $z = 80$, which would leave only 20° for y. This is *way too small*, since y is supposed to be the largest angle. Try something much bigger for x.

8. **B** Pick an integer, 2 say. Then

$$\frac{a+3}{5} = 2 \Rightarrow a + 3 = 10 \Rightarrow a = 7,$$

and 5 goes into 7 once with a remainder of **2**.

9. **B** On six tests combined, Brigitte earned a total of $6 \times 75 = 450$ points (FACT 31). The total of her five best grades is $5 \times 85 = 425$ points, so her lowest grade was $450 - 425 = $ **25**.

**Assume that Brigitte's five best grades were each 85. Then each one has a deviation of 10 points above the average of 75, and the total deviation above 75 is $5 \times 10 = 50$ points. Therefore, her one bad grade must have been 50 points below 75.

10. **E** Check each statement. The only factors of 17 are ±1 and ±17. If m is any of these, $\dfrac{17}{m}$ is an odd integer. (I is false.) Eliminate A and D.

Could $\dfrac{m}{17}$ be an even integer? Sure, it could be *any* even integer; for example, if $m = 34$, $\dfrac{m}{17} = 2$, and if $m = 170$, $\dfrac{m}{17} = 10$. (II is true.) Eliminate C.

Could $17m$ be a prime? Yes, if $m = 1$. (III is true.) The true statements are **II and III only**.

11. **C** The percent increase in Max's investment is

$\dfrac{\text{actual increase}}{\text{original value}} \times 100\%$. Each share was originally worth \$10, and the actual increase in value of each share was $10. Max's

percent increase in value = $\frac{10}{10} \times 100\%$ = **100%**.

12. **C** The number, n, of reports Benjamin can type is equal to the rate, in reports *per minute*, at which he types times the number of minutes he types. Then

$$n = \frac{1 \text{ report}}{h \text{ hours}} \times m \text{ minutes}$$

$$= \frac{1 \text{ report}}{60h \text{ minutes}} \times m \text{ minutes} = \frac{m}{60h} \text{ reports.}$$

**Use TACTIC 11: pick some easy-to-use numbers. Suppose Benjamin can type 1 report every 2 hours, and he types for 60 minutes; he will complete half of a report. Which of the five

choices equals $\frac{1}{2}$ when $h = 2$ and $m = 60$? Only $\frac{m}{60h}$.

13. **B** The trust received 80% of the estate (10% went to the man's wife, 5% to his children, and 5% to his grandchildren). If E represents the value of the estate, then

$$0.80E = 1,000,000$$

$$E = 1,000,000 \div 0.80 = 1,250,000.$$

Each grandchild received 1% (one-fifth of 5%) of the estate, or **$12,500**.

14. **E** Use TACTIC 1: draw a diagram. Since this is a ratio problem, immediately plug in a number. To avoid fractions, use 6, the LCM of the numbers in the question. Let $AC = 6$; then $CD = 3$, with D on either side of C. $BD = 2$, but B could be on either side of D, and so we have no way of knowing length BC. The

value of the ratio $\frac{BC}{CD}$

cannot be determined from the information given.

15. **A** At 10:30 A.M. the first car had been going 40 miles per hour for 1.5 hours, and so had gone $40 \times 1.5 = 60$ miles. The second car covered the same 60 miles in 1 hour and 20 minutes, or $1\frac{1}{3} = \frac{4}{3}$ hours. Therefore, its rate was $60 \div \frac{4}{3} = 60 \times \frac{3}{4} = \mathbf{45}$ miles per hour.

16. **B** Since $5x = 360$ (FACT 37), $x = 72$ and $m\angle AOB = 2x = 144$. Since $OA = OB$ (they are both radii), $\triangle AOB$ is isosceles:

$2y + 144 = 180 \Rightarrow$
$2y = 36 \Rightarrow y = 18.$

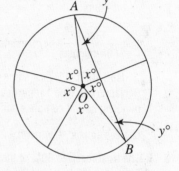

Then $\dfrac{y}{x} = \dfrac{18}{72} = \dfrac{1}{4}$.

**It should be clear that the values of x and y can be determined, so eliminate E, and use TACTIC 2: trust the diagram; x appears to be about 70 and y about 20. Then,

$\dfrac{y}{x} \approx \dfrac{20}{70} = \dfrac{1}{3.5}$, and you should *guess* between $\dfrac{1}{3}$ and $\dfrac{1}{4}$.

17. **D** It's not hard to calculate $\boxed{10}$ and $\boxed{9}$, but you don't have to. Here,

$$\boxed{10} - \boxed{9} = (1 + 2 + \cdots + 9 + 10) - (1 + 2 + \cdots + 9) = 10.$$

Now, calculate the choices: Only $\boxed{4} = 1 + 2 + 3 + 4 = 10.$

18. **D** $\boxed{1010} = (1 + 2 + ... + 1000) + (1001 + 1002 + ... + 1010)$. The sum in the first parentheses is just $\boxed{1000} = 50,500$. The sum in the second parentheses is

$$(1000 + 1) + (1000 + 2) + ... + (1000 + 10),$$

which can be written as

$$(1000 + 1000 + ... + 1000) + (1 + 2 + ... + 10) = 10,000 + 55.$$

The total is $50,500 + 10,000 + 55 = \mathbf{60,555}$.

19. **C** Draw a Venn diagram and label each region. Let *x* be the number of senior boys. Then 40 − *x* is the number of boys who are not seniors (i.e., are juniors), and 70 − *x* is the number of seniors who are not boys (i.e., are girls).

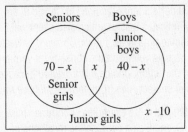

Then the number of junior girls is
$100 − [(40 − x) + x + (70 − x)] = 100 − [110 − x] = x − 10$.

Since the number of junior girls must be at least 0,
$x − 10 ≥ 0 \Rightarrow x ≥ \mathbf{10}$.

Use TACTIC 10: backsolve; but since you want the smallest number, start with A. If there are no senior boys, then all 40 boys are juniors and all 70 seniors are girls; but that's 110 people. Eliminate A. If there are 5 senior boys, there will be 35 junior boys and 65 senior girls, a total of 105. Finally, check **10, which works.

20. **C** Let *r* and *R* be the radii of the two circles. From the figure, you can see that △*OAB* is a 45-45-90 right triangle, and so $R = r\sqrt{2}$ (FACT 46). Therefore,

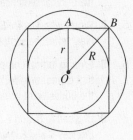

$$\frac{\text{area of large circle}}{\text{area of small circle}} = \frac{\pi R^2}{\pi r^2} = \frac{\pi (r\sqrt{2})^2}{\pi r^2} = \frac{2\pi r^2}{\pi r^2} = 2.$$

The ratio is **2:1**.

**Do exactly the same thing except let *r* = 1; then $R = \sqrt{2}$, and the ratio is

$$\frac{\pi(\sqrt{2})^2}{\pi(1)^2} = \frac{2\pi}{\pi} = \mathbf{2:1}.$$

Section 4 Writing Skills

1. **C** Error in sequence of tenses. This sentence illustrates the use of the future perfect tense. The present perfect tense, as used in Choice A, and the past perfect tense, as used in Choice B, are incorrect. Choice C correctly indicates that an anticipated event will be completed before a definite time in the future. Choice D is weak because of the use of the passive voice and the consequent vagueness as to who is performing the action. Choice E is awkward because of the needless separation of subject (*we*) from verb (*shall have traveled*).

2. **D** Choices A, B, and C are examples of comma splice sentences. Choices B, C, and E also confuse the meanings of *complementary* and *complimentary*. Choice E leaves the verb *is not* without a subject. Choice D corrects the comma splice and adds no other errors.

3. **E** Shift of personal pronoun. In Choices A and B there is an unwarranted shift from the third person pronoun *one* to the second person pronoun *you*. Choices C and D improperly use *affect* instead of *effect*.

4. **D** Error in diction. Choices A and B illustrate the incorrect use of *due to*. The change to *inasmuch* in Choice C creates a sentence fragment. Choice E is poor because it omits the causal relationship implied by the original sentence.

5. **B** Wordiness. Choice B cuts out the unnecessary words and creates a clear, effective sentence.

6. **B** Error in logical comparison. Choices A, D, and E compare two things that cannot be directly compared—subways and cities. In Choice D, the omission of *other* changes the meaning of the sentence.

7. **D** Choices A, B, and E omit important parts of the verb. *Hopefully* in Choices C and E is wrong; although many people use it this way, most grammarians do not accept it as a substitute for *we hope*. (Strictly speaking, *hopefully* should only be used to mean *in a hopeful way*, as in *The farmer searched the skies hopefully looking for signs of rain.*)

8. **B** Lack of parallelism. Change *it partly pays tribute* to *part tribute*.

9. **A** Sentence is correct.

10. **D** Run-on sentence. Choice D provides a replacement that is both grammatical and concise.

11. **A** Sentence is correct.

12. **D** Error in parallelism. Change the clause *what his serial number was* to a noun (*serial number*) to match the other items in the list.

13. **D** Error in tense. Change *will handle* to *handled*.

14. **A** Error in pronoun case. Change *whom* to *who*.

15. **E** Sentence is correct.

16. **D** Error in pronoun number agreement. Since the antecedent of the pronoun is *lawyers*, change *its* to *their*.

17. **B** Error in tense. Delete the word *has* to make the verb *anticipated*.

18. **B** Error in pronoun number agreement. *Everybody* is a singular pronoun. Change *their* to *his* or *her*.

19. **D** Error in diction. The verb *to lay* (past tense is *laid*) means to put or to place; the verb *to lie* (past tense is *lay*) means to recline. Therefore, change *laid back* to *lay back*.

20. **B** Error in subject-verb agreement. *Data* is a plural noun. Change *was* to *were*.

21. **B** Error in pronoun case. Change *she and I* to *us*.

22. **A** Adjective and adverb confusion. The verb *feels* should be followed by an adjective (*bad*).

23. **C** Error in verb form. Change *will be sang* to *will be sung*.

24. **B** Error in pronoun case. Gerunds (verb forms ending in -*ing* that function as nouns) take the possessive pronoun. Change *him joining* to *his joining*.

25. **D** Error in idiom. Change *appointed of* to *appointed to*.

26. **C** Unidiomatic preposition choice. The verb *evolve* customarily is paired with the preposition *from*. Change *evolved off* to *evolved from*.

27. **B** Lack of parallelism. Change *what we wish* to the plural noun *wishes*.

28. **E** Sentence is correct.

29. **B** Error in sequence of tenses. Change *has labored* to *labored*.

30. **C** Choice A contains the extremely awkward phrase *to see underdogs being the one rooted for.* Choice B uses the coordinating conjunction *but*, which makes no sense in the context. It also contains the redundant phrase "sight . . . to see." Choice C clearly and concisely

combines the thoughts contained in the two sentences. It is the best answer. Choice D contains a clause and a phrase that have no grammatical relationship. Choice E contains a comma splice between *Americans* and *for example*.

31. **C** All sentences except 3 contribute to the discussion of the underdog. Sentence 3 is an unnecessary digression. Therefore, Choice C is the best answer.

32. **B** Choice A is grammatically correct, but it refers to Americans' desire to feel good, a topic not discussed in paragraph 2. Choice B accurately introduces the topic of the paragraph. It is the best answer. Choices C and D are similar to A. Choice E is awkwardly expressed and contains the pronoun *themselves*, which refers grammatically to *traditions* instead of to *Americans*.

33. **A** Choice A clearly and accurately combines the sentences. It is the best answer. Choice B is awkward and cumbersome. Choice C contains an awkward shift in verb tense from present (*look*) to past perfect (*had been*). Choice D contains the adverb *poorly*, which should be an adjective and should modify *immigrants* instead of *coming*.

34. **C** Choice A is not an effective revision. It changes the focus of the discussion and contains the pronoun *their*, which refers grammatically to *Americans* instead of to *underdog*. Choice B contains an awkward shift in verb tense from past (*believed*) to present (*succeed*). Choice C follows naturally from the preceding sentence and is accurately expressed. It is the best answer. Choice D is grammatical, but it shifts the focus of the discussion. Choice E is confusing and contains the pronouns *they* and *their*, which lack a specific referent.

35. **D** Choice A contains some transitional material but shifts verb tenses from past (*went*) to present (*defeat*). Choice B, which lacks a main verb, is a sentence fragment. Choice C, although grammatically correct, seems incomplete because the pronoun *it* lacks a specific referent. Choice D provides a smooth transition between paragraphs and introduces the topic of paragraph 3. It is the best answer. Choice E lacks any meaningful transitional material.

Section 6 Critical Reading

1. **E** The first clause states that the movement did not become famous instantly or "overnight." Instead, it gained fame step by step, or *gradually*.
    Remember to watch for signal words that link one part of the sentence to another. The use of "on the contrary" here sets up a contrast. The missing word must be an antonym for *overnight*.
    (Contrast Signal)

2. **E** The intensifier "even" indicates that Astell did more than merely maintain a good reputation; she improved or *enhanced* it.
    (Intensifier Signal)

3. **B** Kubota is hopeful about the success of the women's movement. Thus, she maintains that the recent forward steps or *strides* made by Japanese women in business mean even *greater* chances for women in future days. (Support Signal)

4. **A** This is a case in which you can't eliminate any of the answer choices by checking the first word of each answer pair: all are terms that could describe an ambassador. In this case, the *eminent* ambassador was only an *indifferent* (mediocre) linguist; nevertheless, he insisted on trying to speak foreign languages without help.
    Remember to watch for signal words that link one part of the sentence to another. The use of "yet" in the second clause sets up a contrast.
    Note that "but" here means "only." That's your clue to be on the lookout for a belittling or negative word. (Contrast Signal)

5. **B** To the author, nude models seem *archaic*, suited to an earlier day when art students spent as much time learning to draw the human body as medical students today spend learning to *dissect* or cut it up.
    Remember: in double-blank sentences, go through the answer choices, testing the *first* word in each choice and eliminating the ones that don't fit. By definition, a relic or remnant of a bygone age is outdated or old-fashioned. You can immediately eliminate Choices C and E. (Definition)

6. **C** In stating that the voyageur struck his imagination, the narrator indicates that the voyageur *impressed* him.

7. **D** Although the narrator comments on the voyageur's strength and on the hardships and dangers he faces on the trail, the narrator is most impressed by the voyageur's "unsurpassed nonchalance and joy in

the wilderness." To the narrator, this exuberance or *zest* is the voyageur's outstanding quality.

8. **C** Although both authors clearly appreciate the contribution of the voyageur to Canadian exploration and trade, the author of Passage 1 shows a greater degree of *open admiration* of the voyageur than does the author of Passage 2. Beware of eye-catchers. While the author of Passage 1 may feel some degree of affection for the colorful voyageur, nothing in Passage 1 suggests that such affection may be *misguided*.

9. **E** The author of Passage 1 describe the personal impression made upon him by the voyageur: "It was the voyageur who struck my imagination." Compared to the author of Passage 2, he writes personally rather than impersonally, making use of his *personal voice*.

10. **E** You can arrive at the correct answer by the process of elimination. Statement I is false. While sea action plays a part in erosion, the author does not say it is the most important factor in erosion. Therefore, you can eliminate Choices A and D.
Statement II is true. "The first purely synthetic oil . . . has yet to be produced." Therefore, you can eliminate Choice C.
Statement III is true. New rock is born or created "through the effects of gravity." Therefore, you can eliminate Choice B.
Only Choice E is left. It is the correct answer.

11. **B** The author mentions the Grand Canyon while speaking of rivers as "immensely powerful destructive agencies." The dramatic canyon illustrates the *devastating impact* a river can have.

12. **D** In the last paragraph the author states that "the cause of the metamorphosis" of decayed vegetation and dead aquatic life into oil is not known. We lack full understanding of the process by which oil is created; therefore, our understanding is *deficient*.
Choice C is incorrect. Our knowledge is not *erroneous* or false; it is simply incomplete.

13. **A** The last sentence states that oil is always found "on the sites of ancient seas and lakes."

14. **D** The author describes several processes (erosion, rock formation, oil formation). He states the possibility that a chemical catalyst is involved in oil formation. He cites the Grand Canyon as an example of what a river can do to the land. He mentions the limitation of our

ability to produce oil synthetically. However, he never proposes a solution to any problem.

15. **B** The term "reaches" here refers to the vast, *unbroken stretches* of time required for the mountains to erode and, out of their dust, for new rock to be formed at the bottom of the sea.

16. **C** The author presents these favorable comments about myths in order to support his general thesis that myths and fairy tales perform valuable psychological and educational functions, that is, *are valuable*.

17. **B** The author looks on contemporary parents who want their children exposed only to "real" people and everyday events as mistaken. Stating that Plato may have known more about what shapes people's minds than these modern parents do, he suggests that his contemporaries may be *misguided in their beliefs*.

18. **C** As used in this sentence, "make for" means help to promote or maintain. The author is asserting that Plato understood which sorts of experiences worked to *promote the development of* true humanity.

19. **D** No matter what they originally believe—regardless of their original persuasion or *opinion*—contemporary theorists who study myths and fairy tales come to the same conclusion.
Remember: when answering a vocabulary-in-context question, test each answer choice by substituting it in the sentence for the word in quotes.

20. **C** The opening sentences of the second paragraph suggest that Eliade is a modern thinker who has studied myths from a philosophical or psychological view.
Note the use of the phrase "for one" in the sentence describing Eliade. "For one" indicates that Eliade is one of a group. In this case he is one example of the group of *twentieth century philosophers* who have explored the nature of myths.

21. **E** The author has been discussing what there is about fairy tales that attracts and holds an audience's interest. He concludes that their *attraction* or appeal is at one and the same time to our conscious mind and to our unconscious mind as well.
Again, when answering a vocabulary-in-context question, test each answer choice by substituting it in the sentence for the word in quotes.

22. **D** Like Eliade and other modern thinkers, the author is concerned with
the tales' meeting strongly felt needs and providing desirable
solutions to human problems—in other words, their *psychological
relevance.*

23. **E** The author's citation of the favorable comments of Plato, Aristotle,
and Eliade (and his lack of citation of any unfavorable comments)
indicates his attitude is one of *approval.*

24. **E** Use the process of elimination to answer this question.
Characteristic I illustrates a way in which fairy tales differ from
dreams. Fairy tales are shaped by the conscious minds of many
people (*shared creation*). Dreams, however, are created by an
individual's unconscious mind. Therefore, you can eliminate Choices
B and D.
Characteristic II illustrates a second way in which fairy tales differ
from dreams. Fairy tales promise a happy solution to problems
(*happy ending*). Dreams, on the other hand, do not necessarily offer
any solutions to problems. Therefore, you can eliminate Choice A.
Characteristic III illustrates a third way in which fairy tales differ from
dreams. Unlike dreams, which usually interest only the dreamer, fairy
tales arouse persistent interest in many people (*general appeal*).
Therefore, you can eliminate Choice C.
Only Choice E is left. It is the correct answer.

Section 7 Mathematical Reasoning

MULTIPLE-CHOICE QUESTIONS

1. **D** Let x be the amount, in dollars, that each of the 20 children was
going to contribute; then $20x$ represents the cost of the present.
When 4 children dropped out, the remaining 16 each had to pay
$(x + 1.50)$ dollars, so

$$16(x + 1.5) = 20x \Rightarrow 16x + 24 = 20x \Rightarrow 24 = 4x \Rightarrow x = 6,$$

and so the cost of the present was $20 \times 6 =$ **120** dollars.

Use TACTIC 6: backsolve. Try choice C, 100. If the present cost
$100, then each of the 20 children would have had to pay $5. When
4 dropped out, the remaining 16 would have had to pay $100 \div 16 =$
$6.25 apiece, an increase of $1.25. Since the actual increase was
$1.50, the gift was more expensive. Eliminate A, B, and C. Try D,
120; it works.

2. **B** Wally produces 80 widgets per day × 20 days per month × 12 months per year = 19,200 widgets per year; 96,000 ÷ 19,200 = **5.**

3. **A** Since $JL = KL$, the angles opposite them have the same measure (FACT 43). Then, $d = a$, and we *can* find the value of a ($a + a + 70 = 180$), but that's it. Since b and e are not necessarily equal (see the diagram), we *cannot* determine b or c. The answer is *a* **only**.

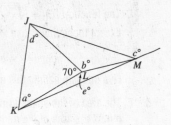

4. **E** If $\left|10 - \sqrt{x}\right| = 7$, then either

$$10 - \sqrt{x} = 7 \qquad \text{or} \qquad \sqrt{x} = -7$$

$$-\sqrt{x} = -3 \qquad \text{or} \qquad -\sqrt{x} = -17$$

$$\sqrt{x} = 3 \qquad \text{or} \qquad \sqrt{x} = 17$$

$$x = 9 \qquad \text{or} \qquad x = 289$$

The sum of the two solutions is $9 + 289 = $ **298.**

5. **E** O is the midpoint of $\overline{AB}$. Let B have coordinates (x, y).

$$(1, 5) = \left(\frac{x + 5}{2}, \frac{y + 1}{2} \right).$$

Therefore, $1 = \dfrac{x + 5}{2} \Rightarrow 2 = x + 5 \Rightarrow x = -3$,

and $5 = \dfrac{y + 1}{2} \Rightarrow 10 = y + 1 \Rightarrow y = 9$.

Therefore, B has coordinates **(−3, 9)**.

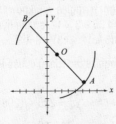

Even a rough sketch will indicate that B is in Quadrant II, and y is surely greater than 5. Only choices D and E are even plausible. A *good* sketch will lead to choice **E.

6. **D** If the total surface area of the cube is 216, then the area of each of the 6 faces is $216 \div 6 = 36$. Since each face is a square of area 36, each edge is 6. Finally, the volume of the cube is $6^3 = \mathbf{216}$.

7. **C** The function $f(x) = \sqrt{x^2 - 9}$ is defined for all real numbers except those that cause $x^2 - 9$ to be negative.

    $$x^2 < 9 \Rightarrow -3 < x < 3.$$

    Five integers satisfy this inequality: $-2, -1, 0, 1, 2$.

8. **E** The area of the shaded ring is the area of the large circle, 25π, minus the area of the middle circle, 16π:

    $$\text{Area of shaded ring} = 25\pi - 16\pi = 9\pi.$$

    The probability that the point is in that ring is $\dfrac{9\pi}{25\pi} = \dfrac{\mathbf{9}}{\mathbf{25}}$.

GRID-IN QUESTIONS

9. (15) Evaluate $3a - 2b$: $3(3) - 2(-3) = 3(3) + 2(3) = 9 + 6 = \mathbf{15}$.

10. (37.5) In a ratio problem write the letter x after each number. Then, $a = 6x$, $b = 7x$, and $c = 11x$; and since the sum of the measures of the angles of a triangle is 180°:

    $$6x + 7x + 11x = 180 \Rightarrow 24x = 180 \Rightarrow x = 7.5.$$

    Then $c - a = 11x - 6x = 5x = 5(7.5) = \mathbf{37.5}$. [Note that we did *not* have to find the value of any of the angles.]

11. (90) Draw a right triangle and label the two legs 15 and 36. To calculate the perimeter, you need only find the length of the hypotenuse and then add the lengths of the three sides. Before using the Pythagorean theorem, ask yourself whether this is a multiple of one of the basic right triangles you know: 3-4-5 or 5-12-13. It is: $15 = 3 \times 5$ and $36 = 3 \times 12$, so the hypotenuse is $3 \times 13 = 39$. The perimeter is $3(5 + 12 + 13) = 3 \times 30 = \mathbf{90}$.

 **If you don't recognize the triangle, use Pythagoras and your calculator:

$$15^2 + 36^2 = c^2 \Rightarrow c^2 = 225 + 1296 = 1521 \Rightarrow c = 39.$$

The perimeter is $15 + 36 + 39 = \mathbf{90}$.

12. (99) From the 124 people in front of Jill, remove Jack plus the 24 people in front of Jack: 124 − 25 = **99**.

**It may be easier for you to see this if you draw a diagram (TACTIC 1):

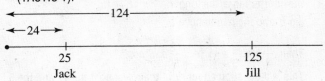

13. (89) Since $y > x$, then y must be greater than 90 and x less than 90. The largest integer less than 90 is **89**.

14. (19) Draw a diagram. For the third-place share to be as large as possible, the fourth-place share must be as small as possible. However, it must be more than $15, so let it be $16. Then the amount, in dollars, left for second and third places is 100 − (30 + 16 +15) = 100 − 61 = 39. The second-place share could be $20, and the third-place share **$19**.

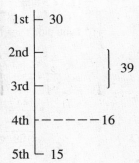

**Use TACTIC 11. Try a number.
Third place must be less than 30 and more than 15; try 20. Then second place must be at least 21 and fourth place at least 16. But 30 + 21 + 20 + 16 + 15 = 102, which is a *little* too big. Try a little smaller number, such as **19**, which works.

15. (179) If the average of a set of 9 numbers is 99, their sum is $9 \times 99 = 891$. If deleting 1 number reduces the average of the remaining 8 numbers to 89, the sum of those 8 numbers must be $8 \times 89 = 712$. The deleted number was 891 − 712 = **179**.

16. (42) Systematically list all the ways of expressing 12 as the sum of three different positive integers, and calculate each product.

Integers	Product	Integers	Product
9, 2, 1	18	6, 5, 1	30
8, 3, 1	24	6, 4, 2	48
7, 4, 1	28	5, 4, 3	60
7, 3, 2	42		

Then $g = 60$, $\ell = 18$, and $g - \ell = $ **42**.

17. $\left(\dfrac{13}{5}\ \text{or}\ 2.6\right)$ Use TACTIC 1.
Draw a right triangle, and label the shorter leg a, the longer leg b, and the hypotenuse c.

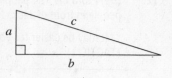

Then $\dfrac{1}{4}b = \dfrac{3}{5}a \Rightarrow b = \dfrac{12}{5}a.$ *Stop.*

This is a question about right triangles, so if the 12 and the 5 in that fraction make you think of a 5-12-13 triangle, check it out:

$\dfrac{1}{4}(12) = 3$ and $\dfrac{3}{5}(5) = 3$. It works. The ratio is $\dfrac{\mathbf{13}}{\mathbf{5}}$.

**If you didn't see that, use the Pythagorean theorem:

$$c^2 = a^2 + \left(\dfrac{12}{5}a\right)^2 =$$

$$a^2 + \dfrac{144}{25}a^2 = \dfrac{25}{25}a^2 + \dfrac{144}{25}a^2 = \dfrac{169}{25}a^2 \Rightarrow$$

$$c = \sqrt{\dfrac{169}{25}a^2} = \dfrac{13}{5}a \Rightarrow \dfrac{c}{a} = \dfrac{\mathbf{13}}{\mathbf{5}}.$$

18. **(25)** Since x varies inversely with y, there is a constant k such that $xy = k$. Then $k = (3)(12) = 36$, and, when $x = 4$, $4y = 36 \Rightarrow y = 9$. Also, since x varies directly with z, there is a constant m such that $\dfrac{x}{z} = m$. Then $m = \dfrac{3}{12} = \dfrac{1}{4}$, and when $x = 4$, $\dfrac{4}{z} = \dfrac{1}{4} \Rightarrow$ $z = 16$. Finally, $9 + 16 = \mathbf{25}$.

Section 8 Critical Reading

1. **D** Buildings constructed in such a hurry would tend to be *ramshackle* (loosely held together) affairs.   (Definition)

2. **D** Immune to most pesticides, cockroaches are thus tough or *hardy* and hard to *eliminate*.
    Remember: in double-blank sentences, go through the answer choices, testing the *first* word in each choice and eliminating those that don't fit. You can immediately eliminate Choices A and C.
                                                        (Cause and Effect Pattern)

3. **B** *Stoically* means that a person bears pain with great courage. The presence of *and* linking the two clauses indicates that the missing word continues the thought expressed in the phrase "did not wince or whimper."   (Support Signal)

4. **D** Note the use of "might." Without the support of other stories, the actor's stories might not be believed. If people need such supporting testimony, their first response to the stories must be disbelief. They must think them exaggerations or *hyperbole*. "Were there not" is a short way of saying "If there were not."
                    (Argument)

5. **E** Wemmick's private kindness is contrasted with his *public* harshness. Note here the use of "even" as an intensifier: to be *ruthless* or relentless is more blameworthy than merely to be *uncompassionate* or hard-hearted.   (Contrast Pattern)

6. **B** The view of Rome's contributions to government, law, and engineering is wholly positive: these additions to human knowledge are generally acknowledged. *In contrast,* Rome's original contributions to art are *not* recognized: they are seen as just *an echo* or imitation *of* the art of ancient Greece.
   Note that "although" sets up a contrast.   (Contrast Signal)

7. **D** Wolfe is making a point through a simile, a type of *figurative expression.* Going home again, he says, is *like* stepping into a river, through which new water constantly flows. Each time you step into the river, it will be different; each time you try to return home, it too will be different.

8. **C** The author of Passage 1 states that *at best* the journey home will point you to your origins, "to where you started," and will let you know how your origins have "helped to shape you." In other words, the most positive outcome of your attempting to go home would be for you to *grasp how your origins have formed you.*

9. **B** The author feels trapped between Wolfe's certainty that one cannot go home again and Haley's certainty that one *can* do so, that one can find the way back to one's ancestral homeland and return to one's roots. He is torn between extremes, uncertain about just what he is looking for—his conflicting desires clearly show his *ambivalence about his journey.*
   Choice A is incorrect. The author has no desire to know what his ancestors looked like. He is not seeking to convey his resemblance to them.

Choices C and D are incorrect. Nothing in the passage supports them.

Choice E is incorrect. Though on one level the author deeply desires to trace his roots (as Haley did), on another he feels attempting to do so is a meaningless exercise. Thus, he chiefly conveys his ambivalence about his journey.

10. **A** A *paradox* is a seemingly contradictory statement that may perhaps be true in fact. Here the author was, in Africa, his ancestral homeland, but it did not feel like home to him. He clearly found his situation paradoxical.

11. **E** Africa held or *possessed* symbolic significance for the author of this passage.

     Remember: when answering a vocabulary-in-context question, try substituting each answer choice in the original sentence for the word in quotes.

12. **D** Though the author earns his living as an arts administrator, he thinks of himself as a poet, a creative artist. When he says he needed time for his own work, he is referring to his *creating poetry*.

13. **C** The author essentially looks down on his administrative work. Though it is time-consuming, leaving him with little time to compose poetry, it is not a taxing or *demanding* job.

14. **B** The author describes a scene in which he, a Japanese-American child watching old World War II movies, playacted being an American G.I. shooting down Japanese soldiers. Rather than siding with the Japanese soldiers whom he physically resembled, he took the part of their opponents. This episode serves to show how much he *identified himself as an American*.

     Choice A is incorrect. The author had no particular hatred for Japan or the Japanese. He merely felt they did not have much to do with his life.

     Choice C is incorrect. Though he has mentioned the fakery of Japanese films, he does not describe the American-made war movies in order to show that they are better than Japanese films.

     Choice D is incorrect. Nothing in the passage supports it.

     Choice E is incorrect. Childhood experiences playing soldiers would be unlikely to motivate anyone to travel to Japan.

15. **D** Bali is in the South Pacific. The Bahamas are in the Caribbean. The primary thing these islands have in common is that they are classic *exotic destinations* for vacationers.

16. **E** Like the author of Passage 1, the author of Passage 2 feels *marked ambivalence* about his prospective journey. He is happy to have won the fellowship, but unhappy at the prospect of having to spend a year in a country he finds relatively unappealing.

17. **D** In the final lines of Passage 2, the author creates a picture of his imagination as a swimmer, "unconsciously swimming the Pacific" toward Japan, going against the tide of his family's earlier movement from Japan to America. This picture is *an extended metaphor* or image.

18. **A** In both passages, the authors are concerned about their racial or *ethnic identity*. The author of Passage 1 is seeking to discover "how much of being black" comes from his African origins. The author of Passage 2 has to a degree denied his ethnic identity ("Much of my life I had insisted on my Americanness, had shunned most connections with Japan and felt proud I knew no Japanese") and yet has celebrated his Japanese heritage in his verse.
Choice B is incorrect. The authors are not seeking to establish their independence as individuals. They are seeking to discover the nature of their ties to their ancestral homelands.
Choice C is incorrect. While the authors may wish to learn more about their ancestors, they do not worship them.
Choice D is incorrect. There is nothing in either passage to support it.
Choice E is incorrect. While Passage 1 mentions Haley's attempts to trace his roots, its author has no such attempts in mind. Passage 2's author never mentions genealogical research.

19. **C** Use the process of elimination to arrive at the correct answer to this question.
The author of Passage 2 insists that Japan "didn't have much to do with" his present life. This parallels the statement in Passage 1 that Africa held "only a symbolic significance" to the author. Therefore, Choice A is incorrect.
The author of Passage 2 asserts that he "had insisted on" his Americanness and "felt proud" of knowing no Japanese. Like the author of Passage 1, who "did not feel African," the Japanese-American author of Passage 2 did not feel Japanese. Therefore, Choice B is incorrect.
The author of Passage 2 states that his "reasons for going [to Japan] were not very clear." He hardly knew why he was going there. This parallels the comment in Passage 1 that its author

"hardly knew what" he was looking for in Africa. Therefore, Choice D is incorrect.

The image of "memories hidden in [one's] genes" awakening in Passage 1 has its counterpart in Mura's image of how his poetic imagination had been returning to his ancestral past, "unconsciously swimming the Pacific." Therefore, Choice E is incorrect.

Only Choice C is left. It is the correct answer. Passage 1's author is so torn between Africa and America that he comes to feel like a "waif without a home." There is nothing corresponding to this idea in Passage 2. Throughout Passage 2, its author insists on his Americanness, identifies with the GI's in World War II movies. He clearly feels America is his home.

Section 9 Mathematical Reasoning

1. **B** $3x = 36 \Rightarrow x = 12 \Rightarrow \dfrac{x}{3} = \mathbf{4}$.

2. **C** If $\dfrac{7}{11} a = \dfrac{7}{11} b$, then $a = b$, and $\dfrac{a}{b} = \mathbf{1}$.

3. **C** Set up a proportion:

$$\frac{2.2 \text{ pounds}}{1 \text{ kilogram}} = \frac{120 \text{ pounds}}{x \text{ kilograms}} . \text{ Then}$$

$$2.2x = 120 \Rightarrow x = \frac{120}{2.2} = 54.54....$$

Therefore, the **3** students weighing more than 120 pounds are the 3 who weigh more than 54.54 kilograms.

**Quickly multiply by 2.2: $56 \times 2.2 = 123.2$, so 56, 57, and 61 kilograms are all more than 120 pounds. The other two weights are less.

4. **D** Since the value of a share doubled every year, each year it was worth *half* as much as the following year. In 1990 a share was worth $80, so in 1989 it was worth half as much, or $40; in 1988 it was worth $20; and in **1987** it was worth $10.

Use TACTIC 10: backsolve, starting with C, 1986. If a share was worth $10 in 1986, then it was worth $20 in 1987, $40 in 1988, $80 in 1989. That's a year too soon. Start a year later—1987**.

5. **B** If a is the average of 10 and some other number, x, then

$$a = \frac{10 + x}{2} \Rightarrow 2a = 10 + x \Rightarrow x = \mathbf{2a - 10}.$$

**Use TACTIC 11. Pick a number for a, say 5. Since 5 is the average of 10 and 0, check the five choices to see which one equals 0 when $a = 5$. Only B: $2(5) - 10 = 0$.

6. **B** The percent increase in a quantity is

$\dfrac{\text{actual increase}}{\text{original}} \times 100\%$ (FACT 26). For *each* year calculate

the actual increase and divide. For example, in 1990 the increase was \$100 (from \$150 to \$250), so the percent increase was

$\dfrac{100}{150} \times 100\% = 66.66\%$. In **1991** the increase was \$200 and the

percent increase was $\dfrac{200}{250} \times 100\% = 80\%$. Check the other

choices; this is the greatest.

7. **C** The interior of the star is a hexagon, a six-sided polygon. The sum of the six angles in a hexagon is $(6 - 2)180 = 4(180) = \mathbf{720}$.

Use TACTIC 2: trust the diagram. Since each of the six angles clearly measures more than 100° but less than 150°, the total is more than 600 but less than 900. Only **720 is in that range.

8. **B** If each side of the square is π, then its perimeter is 4π. Since the circumference of the circle is equal to the perimeter of the square, $C = 4\pi$. But $C = 2\pi r$, and so $2\pi r = 4\pi \Rightarrow r = \mathbf{2}$.

9. **E** Just calculate the first 5 terms: $a_1 = 1$;

$$a_2 = 1^2 + 1 = 2; \ a_3 = 2^2 + 1 = 5;$$
$$a_4 = 5^2 + 1 = 26; \ a_5 = 26^2 + 1 = \mathbf{677}.$$

10. **E** The perimeter, P, of $\triangle BCD = BC + CD + BD$. Since $BC + CD = 7$ (it is one-half the perimeter of rectangle $ABCD$), $P = 7 + BD$. But BD cannot be determined, since it depends on the lengths of sides $\overline{BC}$ and $\overline{CD}$. Both rectangles in the figure have perimeters that are 14, but the values of BD are different. The perimeter of $\triangle BCD$ **cannot be determined from the information given.**

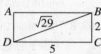

11. **D** If a represents Jordan's average after five tests, then he has earned a total of $5a$ points. A grade of 70 on the sixth test will lower his average 4 points to $a - 4$. Therefore

$$a - 4 = \frac{5a + 70}{6} \Rightarrow 6(a - 4) = 5a + 70 \Rightarrow 6a - 24 = 5a + 70 \Rightarrow$$

$$6a = 5a + 94 \Rightarrow a = \mathbf{94}.$$

**Use TACTIC 10: backsolve, starting with choice C, 90. If Jordan's five-test average is 90, he has 450 points and a 70 on the sixth test will give him a total of 520 points, and an average of $520 \div 6 = 86.666$. The 70 lowered his average 3.3333 points, which is not enough. Eliminate A, B, and C. Try D, 94. It works.

12. **E** $g(-10) = f(3(-10)) = f(-30) = (-30)^2 - 3(-30) = 900 - (-90) = 900 + 90 = 990$

**$g(x) = f(3x) = (3x)^2 - 3(3x) = 9x^2 - 9x.$

Then $g(-10) = 9(-10)^2 - 9(-10) = 900 + 90 = \mathbf{990}.$

13. **A**

$$\frac{12a^2b^{-\frac{1}{2}}c^6}{4a^{-2}b^{\frac{1}{2}}c^2} = 3a^{2-(-2)}b^{-\frac{1}{2}-\frac{1}{2}}c^{6-2} = 3a^4b^{-1}c^4 = \frac{3a^4c^4}{b}.$$

14. **B** The graph of $y = f(x - 2)$ is obtained by shifting the graph of $y = f(x)$ 2 units to the right. Therefore the x-intercept $(-3, 0)$ shifts 2 units to $(-1, 0)$; the **only** x-coordinate is **–1**.

15. **E** Store 2 sold 30 DVDs at $50, 40 DVDs at $80, and 20 DVDs at $120.

   Store 2: $(30 \times \$50) + (40 \times \$80) + (20 \times \$120) = \$7100$.

   Store 1 sold 10 DVDs at $80, 20 DVDs at $100, and 20 DVDs at $150.

   Store 1: $(10 \times \$80) + (20 \times \$100) + (20 \times \$150) = \$5800$.

   Finally, $\$7100 - \$5800 = \mathbf{\$1300}$.

16. **C** According to the triangle inequality (FACT 48), the sum of the lengths of two sides of a triangle must be greater than the length of the third side. There is only one way to pick a number, *a*, from *A* and a number, *b*, from *B* so that their sum is greater than 7: $a = 3$ and $b = 5$. There are three ways to choose *a* and *b* so that their sum is greater than 6: $a = 2$ and $b = 5$; $a = 3$ and $b = 4$; and $a = 3$ and $b = 5$. Therefore, in all there are **4** ways to pick the lengths of the three sides.

Section 10 Writing Skills

1. **D** Wordiness. Choice D makes the writer's point simply and concisely.

2. **D** Error in subject-verb agreement. Remember: the subject's grammatical number is not changed by the addition of a phrase that begins with *along with, together with,* or a similar expression. The subject, *princess,* is singular. The verb should be singular as well. Only Choice D corrects the error without introducing fresh errors.

3. **B** Lack of parallelism. Choice B tightens the original loose sentence, neatly linking its similar elements (*the smallest* and *the most truculent*) with the connective *yet* to produce a balanced sentence.

4. **C** Lack of parallelism. Choice C balances the past tense verb *took* with a similar verb in the past tense (*incorporated*), linking them with the connective *and*.

5. **C** Misplaced modifier. Who are away on leave? Not the rooms, but the students!

6. **D** Error in logical comparison. Compare students with students, not students with a time period ("the middle of the twentieth century").

7. **E** Error in usage. A comedy duo by definition consists of two comedians.

8. **C** Error in modification. Ask yourself who was writing the review. Was it the production? No, the production was *being* reviewed: the reviewer was the paper's theater critic. Only Choice C rewrites the sentence so that the phrase *Writing a review of opening night* correctly modifies *critic.*

9. **C** Dangling modifier. Who was afraid of meeting strangers? Obviously, Elizabeth Barrett. Choice C rearranges the sentence to eliminate the dangling modifier. (While choice E also rearranges the sentence so that the opening phrase modifies Barrett, it introduces a comma splice.)

10. **D** Wordiness. Choice D eliminates the unnecessary words *for* and *they.*

11. **D** The suggested revision tightens this ineffective compound sentence in two ways: first, it eliminates the connective *and;* second, it repeats *a landscape* to emphasize its importance.

12. **D** Error in logical comparison. Compare numbers with numbers, not numbers with minivans.

13. **C** Double negative. Change *could hardly do nothing* to *could hardly do anything.*

14. **C** Error in logical comparison. Compare cities with cities, not cities with mayors.

NOTES

NOTES

NOTES

NOTES

NOTES